D1071689

"The Chiefs Now in This City"

"The Chiefs Now in This City"

INDIANS AND THE URBAN FRONTIER IN
EARLY AMERICA

Colin G. Calloway

OXFORD
UNIVERSITY PRESS

OXFORD
UNIVERSITY PRESS

Oxford University Press is a department of the University of Oxford. It furthers
the University's objective of excellence in research, scholarship, and education
by publishing worldwide. Oxford is a registered trade mark of Oxford University
Press in the UK and certain other countries.

Published in the United States of America by Oxford University Press
198 Madison Avenue, New York, NY 10016, United States of America.

© Oxford University Press 2021

All rights reserved. No part of this publication may be reproduced, stored in
a retrieval system, or transmitted, in any form or by any means, without the
prior permission in writing of Oxford University Press, or as expressly permitted
by law, by license, or under terms agreed with the appropriate reproduction
rights organization. Inquiries concerning reproduction outside the scope of the
above should be sent to the Rights Department, Oxford University Press, at the
address above.

You must not circulate this work in any other form
and you must impose this same condition on any acquirer.

CIP data is on file at the Library of Congress
ISBN 978–0–19–754765–6

DOI: 10.1093/oso/9780197547656.001.0001

1 3 5 7 9 8 6 4 2

Printed by Sheridan Books, Inc., United States of America

To Marcia, Graeme, and Meg

CONTENTS

LIST OF FIGURES AND PLATES

PREFACE AND ACKNOWLEDGMENTS

I N THE COURSE OF RESEARCHING and writing two previous books—*Pen and Ink Witchcraft: Treaties and Treaty Making
in American Indian History* (2013) and *The Indian World of George
Washington: The First President, the First Americans, and the Birth of a
Nation* (2018)—I became aware of a story I was not telling, and
not even really seeing. Tribal leaders regularly traveled to early
American cities, primarily on diplomatic business. Sometimes they
went alone, more often they went in groups, and occasionally they
brought a crowd. Cumulatively over the course of the seventeenth
and eighteenth centuries, hundreds of Indian people spent hundreds of days in cities. What did they do when they weren't doing
business, and what did they make of it all? The answers lie in the
shadows of more fulsome descriptions of the negotiations they
engaged in and the agreements they made, and piecing together
glimpses of their other experiences has involved extensive needle-
in-the-haystack research in government records, individuals'
journals and correspondence, and the surprisingly large number
of newspapers of early America.

For her assistance in surveying newspapers, I am grateful to
Sabena Allen (Tlingit), who worked with me on the project as a
Presidential Scholar when she was an undergraduate at Dartmouth
College. For assistance in retrieving and delivering multiple sources,
I am grateful, as always, to my colleagues in Dartmouth's Baker-Berry
Library. For a congenial environment conducive to productivity,
I am again thankful to my friends and colleagues in Native American
Studies. Two anonymous readers who read parts of the manuscript
in its raw, early stages offered generous advice and constructive
suggestions. I am also grateful to Nathaniel Holly for sharing his dis-
sertation with me as I finalized the manuscript, and to Mary Bilder

for sharing an unpublished essay. At Oxford University Press, my editor, Timothy Bent, demonstrated sustained support, gave the manuscript thorough and thoughtful attention, and offered keen insights, and Amy Whitmer guided it expertly through production. Everyone involved in turning the manuscript into a book reinforced my conviction that when I publish with Oxford, I can take the highest standards for granted.

CHIEFS AND CITIES: A NOTE ON TERMINOLOGY

Colonial officials, observers, and the press routinely referred to tribal delegates as Indians and as "the chiefs now in this city." In a book that has much to do with colonial perceptions and representations, I follow the sources in using *Indians* or *Indian people*, although I sometimes employ the terms *Native* and *Indigenous* as well.

Both *chief* and *city* are rather imprecise, generic terms that can have different definitions and connotations. Native American societies had many kinds of leaders who performed different roles in different circumstances—in war, peace, trade, council, ceremony, diplomacy, and the mediation of disputes within and between communities—but Europeans, and later the United States, applied the term *chief* loosely, with little understanding of how power was acquired and exercised. Although some individuals in this book are distinguished as sachems, sagamores, micos, war chiefs, civil chiefs, or spiritual leaders, for the most part, as in the colonial sources, *chief* is used as a term of convenience that embraces a variety of Indigenous leadership roles. Similarly, in dealing with colonial leadership, I have used the title *governor* throughout rather than make repeated distinctions between governor, lieutenant governor, and deputy governor.

Like *chief*, *city* (and *town*) can have various meanings, depending on time, place, perception, and purpose. Urban historians debate about what exactly constitutes a city. At one level a city is a large town, but cities were much smaller in the seventeenth and eighteenth centuries than today, and in North America than in Europe and Asia, and official designations vary between, say, the United States and England, where for a long time city status was associated with having a cathedral. Expecting towns and cities to have institutions, stones, and structures, European colonists saw none in Native America. The cluster of communities at Kaskaskia at one point housed 20,000 inhabitants, a population no colonial city matched until the second half of the eighteenth century, but the French called it "le grand village." Today, we often use *city* and *town* interchangeably. We may live on the outskirts of a city and go "downtown" to work or spend an evening "out on the town." I follow the same practice.

The Chickasaw and Choctaw Indian Chiefs now in this City, will be present . . . this evening at the New Theatre.
—*Gazette of the United States,* July 3, 1795

"The Chiefs Now in This City"

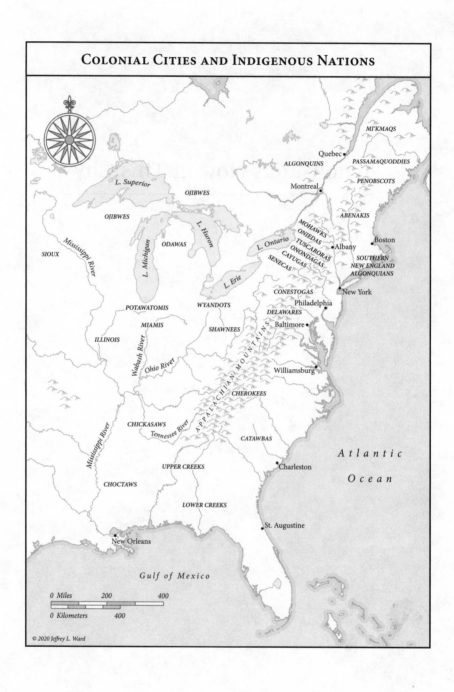

COLONIAL CITIES AND INDIGENOUS NATIONS

MI'KMAQS

Quebec
ALGONQUINS
PASSAMAQUODDIES

Montreal
PENOBSCOTS

L. Superior

OJIBWES
ABENAKIS

OJIBWES

MOHAWKS
ONIEDAS
Boston

L. Huron
ODAWAS
TUSCARORAS
Albany

SIOUX
L. Ontario
ONONDAGAS

Mississippi River
CAYUGAS
SOUTHERN
NEW ENGLAND
ALGONQUIANS

L. Michigan
SENECAS

L. Erie

CONESTOGAS
New York

POTAWATOMIS
WYANDOTS
Philadelphia

DELAWARES

MIAMIS
Baltimore

ILLINOIS
SHAWNEES

Wabash River

Ohio River

APPALACHIAN MOUNTAINS
Williamsburg

CHEROKEES

CHICKASAWS
Tennessee River
CATAWBAS

Mississippi River

UPPER CREEKS
Charleston
Atlantic

CHOCTAWS
Ocean

LOWER CREEKS

St. Augustine

New Orleans

Gulf of Mexico

0 Miles   200   400

0 Kilometers   400

© 2020 Jeffrey L. Ward

Introduction: Native Americans' Urban Frontiers

I N THE FALL OF 1784, François Marbois, secretary to the French legation to the newly independent United States, traveled to the country of the Oneida Indians, one of the Six Nations of the Iroquois league in upstate New York. He wanted to see the Indigenous peoples of the country firsthand and believed that time was short, "for the advance of European population is extremely rapid in this continent, and since these nations live chiefly by hunting and fishing, they cannot remain in the neighborhood of cultivated regions. They go farther away, and soon it will be necessary to look for them beyond the Mississippi or even in the ice-covered regions around Hudson Bay." Ignoring the fact that Iroquois women had cultivated immense fields of corn, beans, and squash for centuries—and that American troops had destroyed forty Iroquois towns, 160,000 bushels of corn, and countless orchards in Iroquois country just five years before—Marbois saw Oneida country as a wilderness. Traveling with his wife by horseback along Indian paths, he reflected on the transformations that civilization would surely bring to the landscape before him:

> In a century, and perhaps sooner, agriculture and commerce will give life to this savage desert. This rock will furnish stones to the city which will be built on the banks of that stream. There will be a bridge here and a quay there. Instead of this marsh there will be a public fountain; elegantly dressed

ladies will stroll in the very place where I walk carefully for fear of rattlesnakes: it will be a public park, adorned with statues and fountains. A few ancient trees will be exhibited as the precious remains of the forest which to-day covers the mountain. I see already the square where the college, the academy, the house for the legislature, and the other public buildings will be placed. Do not take this for a dream, for beginning with Philadelphia there are twenty cities on this continent which, a hundred years ago, had no more existence than this one which I have just built.[1]

Marbois's vision is replicated in both popular and academic retellings of American history. In the colonial era, establishing urban spaces was seen as a way to cultivate civic communities and virtues, which in turn helped to justify the dispossession of and subjugation of Native people who, living in a state of nature, were implicitly non-civil. Clearing forests, building houses, and constructing cities promoted and accelerated the process of civilization. Panoramic views of early American cities displayed busy harbors, brick houses, grand public buildings, and church steeples on the skyline. The architecture, order, and refinement of life there signaled progress beyond a state of barbarism. City views often placed Indian figures in the foreground—witnesses to the flourishing urban settlement but apart from it (Figure 0.1).[2]

Figure 0.1 John Smibert, *View of Boston*, 1738. Oil on canvas. Photo: Granger.
Edinburgh-born John Smibert (1688–1751) arrived in Boston in 1729 and made a living there as a portrait painter. His panoramic view of the city places the Indian figures conventionally in the foreground.

As Americans pushed west in the late eighteenth and nineteenth centuries, the communities they built brought schools, churches, government, and social mores. In the thinking of many Americans the urban frontier marked the line between civilization and savagery.[3] Indians occasionally returned to attack and burn towns that had been built on their lands, but in general, they receded to disappearance, driven away by the decline of game, the pressure of population, war, and disease. Looking back on such developments early in the twentieth century, Boston residents staged a theatrical performance entitled *From Cave Life to City Life: The Pageant of the Perfect City* in which the Indians "slowly retire before the advancing city and withdraw to their distant forests in the west."[4] Indians and cities, it seems, could not coexist; "one must necessarily be eclipsed by the other," historian Coll Thrush noted in his book *Native Seattle*.[5] Cities represented progress and modernity; Indians represented an unchanging and primitive past.

Even as late as the mid-twentieth century the United States government's policy of relocation operated on the assumption that moving Indian people from rural reservations to major cities would so completely immerse them in mainstream American life that they would effectively cease to be Indians. Since then Indian people have migrated in such numbers that today most of the people who identify as Native American on the United States census are urban dwellers. Scholars have produced an extensive literature on Native American movement to and life in modern American cities and pay increasing attention to Indigenous urban studies.[6] Nevertheless, reservation Indians still attract far more attention than urban Indians, and a pervasive notion persists that Native people who live in cities are somehow less Native.[7]

With a few exceptions, and less so in Mesoamerica and South America than in North America, Native American presence and participation in the life of early American towns and cities have been slighted.[8] In fact, towns and cities dotted the landscape of America long before Europeans arrived, and they became part of the colonial world in which Indians operated after Europeans arrived. Despite the assumptions of their retreat from urban areas, Indian people frequently moved toward rather than away from them, as they responded to new centers of power, adapted to new pressures, and took advantage of new economic opportunities. When Indian people went to town it was usually not to inflict violence; more often, it was to make, preserve, or restore peace, to trade, or to find work. Sometimes it was purely tourism. Delegations of tribal leaders walked the streets of

Albany, Boston, Charleston, Philadelphia, Williamsburg, Montreal, Quebec, New York, New Orleans, and Santa Fe. In Williamsburg, Virginia, before the Revolution, Thomas Jefferson recalled, Indians "were in the habit of coming often, and in great numbers, to the seat of our government," and Jefferson, for his part, "was very much with them."[9] Writing to his uncle from New Orleans in 1780, Spanish governor Bernardo de Gálvez said his time was taken up by "the multitude of Indians who come to this city."[10] Indian visitors to cities often stayed for weeks and even months, during which time they joined in urban life. Walk around Colonial Williamsburg or the historic Old City in Philadelphia, where people could travel on foot from any part of town to any other part, and it is not difficult to appreciate how visible Indian delegations would have been when they were there.[11] On occasion, delegates from different tribes bumped into one another on city streets.

This book's purpose is simply to show how often delegations of Indian people traveled to cities in early America and to consider what they might have experienced while they were in and about town. It pays less attention to the treaties that Indian delegates negotiated and signed when they were there.[12] Hundreds of books and essays focus on encounters between Indians and Europeans, but those encounters typically occur on the edges of Indian country. American history likewise normally views frontier towns as perched on the western territories of the colonies or the new nation. But for Indian people facing east from the interior of the continent, the urban frontier lay in places such as Charleston, Philadelphia, and New York. As handfuls of European colonists with a precarious toehold on the North American continent constituted a "frontier" when they touched the edges of a vast Indigenous world, so Indian visitors to early American cities created their own frontier, one stretching along the edges of a vast Atlantic world. Colonial settlers came to see a frontier "anywhere Indians were," as historian Patrick Spero puts it.[13] One might argue that Indians saw a frontier as anywhere colonists were.

Like other frontiers, the Indians' urban frontier was porous and permeable, a zone of cultural interaction rather than a hard line, and it contained intellectual spaces structured by convention and protocol as well as physical spaces that generated both cooperation and conflict.[14] Whether for formal or informal reasons, Indian people sometimes visited early American cities in large numbers and stayed for weeks. During that time, they talked, ate, drank, smoked, traded, sometimes shared ceremonies and festivities, and generally rubbed shoulders with the residents, colonial dignitaries, and curious onlookers who came to watch the public spectacle and political theater. On those occasions colonial towns became hubs of the kind of cross-cultural encounters that occurred across America.[15] Indian visitors also found other Indian people living and working in cities, just as Europeans met European traders, hunters, agents, missionaries, and captives in Indian villages. Frontier zones included both the foreign and the familiar.

Early American cities, then, were points of convergence and connection that drew people and resources from far and wide, brought Natives and newcomers together in shared spaces and relationships, and linked Indigenous and colonial networks and lives.[16] Atlantic seaport cities in particular were seats of government and nodes of trade and communication, imperial places tied both to the maritime world and to the hinterland, and centers for the circulation of goods, ideas, and culture.[17] Indian people who traveled to Boston, New York, New Orleans, Philadelphia, and Charleston found themselves in places that, to them, were simultaneously American frontiers and Atlantic ports. When Europeans went to Indian towns to trade or to live, they connected to social, economic, political, kinship, and even ritual networks that fanned out across Indian country far beyond their gazes. Sometimes they created their own networks.[18] Indians who were in port cities, even for a short time, touched networks that spread across the Atlantic and beyond. Sometimes they too created their own networks. For example, in 1773 the Delaware chief White Eyes or Koquethagechton traveled from the Ohio Valley to New Orleans, where he traded 1,500 deerskins, 300 beaver pelts, and other furs to a Louisiana merchant house. He then sailed to Philadelphia with £200 in hard currency credit and bought a batch of European imports, which he shipped west to the Ohio Valley.[19] Well known in Philadelphia, White Eyes spent much of the winter of 1775–76 there and addressed the Continental Congress there in April 1776.

The travels of Indian people like White Eyes who shuttled back and forth between colonial cities in North America have generally received much less attention than those who traveled to cities on the other side of the Atlantic. They had been doing that, voluntarily or involuntarily, since Columbus hauled Native people from the Caribbean back to Spain as slaves, and many writers have traced their voyages and explored Indigenous participation in transnational networks. Pocahontas is the most famous Indian visitor to

England, but her Powhatan delegation in 1616 followed a string of earlier transatlantic travelers: three captured Mi'kmaqs presented to the king in 1502; Manteo and Wanchese under Sir Walter Raleigh's sponsorship from Roanoke in the 1580s; four Inuits (all of whom died) in 1576–77; three Virginia Indians in the 1580s; five Wabanakis kidnapped on the coast of Maine in 1605; and an Indian abducted from Martha's Vineyard in 1611. Squanto, a Patuxet from the coast of Massachusetts, crossed and recrossed the Atlantic a few years later, as did a Nipmuc Indian named John Wompas in the 1670s.[20]

In the eighteenth century, a number of Indian delegates visited European capitals, where imperial powers competed for their allegiance. Among the emissaries to London were the four "Mohawk Kings" or "Indian kings" who were invited there in 1710 at a time of conflict with the French in Canada in an effort to bolster Britain's alliance with the Iroquois. (The Iroquois were then known as the Five Nations: the Mohawks, Oneidas, Onondagas, Cayugas, and Senecas; they became the Six Nations when the Tuscaroras joined a dozen years later.) One of the emissaries was actually a Mohican and none of them were kings, but they were treated as visiting royalty. In addition to an audience with Queen Anne, they met with representatives of the Church of England, attended the theater and the opera, saw the sights, and had their portraits painted (which hung in Kensington Palace until Queen Elizabeth II donated them to the Portrait Gallery of Canada in 1977). In 1713 a young "Yamasee Prince" traveled from Charleston to London, where he spent almost two years being educated to become a missionary for the Society for the Propagation of the Gospel, was baptized, and met King George I.[21] The French also courted Indian allies. In 1725, a delegation of five Illinois and Missouri chiefs from the western prairies accompanied French explorer Étienne de Veniard, Sieur de Bourgmont, to Paris, along with a Missouri woman, who may have been Bourgmont's mistress or daughter, and a Comanche slave. They attended the theaters and street fairs of Paris and visited the court of Louis XV.[22]

Delegations of Creeks, Cherokees, and Mohegans followed in the 1730s. In 1734 the Yamacraw chief Tomochichi traveled to London with General James Oglethorpe to meet the trustees of Georgia and King George II; he was accompanied by his wife, Senaukey, and his nephew. Like earlier visitors to London, they toured the city and went to the theater. They also visited Kensington and Lambeth Palaces. They evidently were impressed, but not too impressed. According to one nobleman he met, Tomochichi "observed we knew many things his Country men did not, but doubted if we were happier, Since we live worse than they, and they more innocently."[23]

Multiple delegations traveled to London in the 1760s. The Mashpee Wampanoags on Cape Cod sent their schoolteacher Reuben Cognehew to plead their case for greater self-government from Massachusetts in 1760. Lieutenant Henry Timberlake accompanied three Cherokee chiefs there in 1762. In addition to the usual attractions—Westminster Abbey, St. Paul's Cathedral, the Tower of London—the three young men apparently attracted "groupies" and inspired ribald verse (printed and sold for 6d. a copy) about "*Wives, Widows and Matrons* and pert little *Misses* . . . pressing and squeezing for *Cherokee Kisses*," their "soft Female Hand, the best Weapon I wean is, To strip down the Bark of a *Cherokee P——s.*" Timberlake returned with another group of Cherokees three years later.[24] Stockbridge Indians made the voyage in 1766. The Mohegan preacher Samson Occom traveled through England and Scotland in 1766–68, delivering sermons and raising money for the Reverend Eleazar Wheelock to establish the future Dartmouth College. Occom met King George III and the archbishops of Canterbury and York, and he too toured Westminster Abbey and the Tower of London. Two Narragansett brothers, John and Tobias Shattock, went in 1768; Tobias died of smallpox in Edinburgh. The Mohawk chief Joseph Brant or Thayendanegea visited London in 1776 and again in 1784. He met the king and queen and a number of lords and ladies, and he accompanied the Prince of Wales on jaunts through the city's nightlife, frequenting places Brant thought "very queer for a prince to go to."[25] He obviously did not know the royal family very well.

Like early explorers and colonists in America, Indians who crossed the Atlantic discovered new lands, new people, and new ways of life. In the streets, pubs, palaces, and churches of Britain they pioneered new frontiers and, as with visitors from other parts of the empire, their experiences made Britain as much of a "contact zone" as the colonies themselves.[26] Indians were curiosities and sometimes celebrities. The press covered their visits, often in considerable detail, although newspapers often were more interested in what the visitors revealed about British society than in the Indians themselves.[27]

The Indian people who traveled to North American capitals made shorter journeys, went more often, and traveled in larger numbers. Relatively familiar sights on the streets of Philadelphia or Charleston, they did not generate the same level of media attention as did "exotic" visitors to London or Paris. Nor have they received as much attention as Indian delegations to Washington, DC, in the nineteenth and twentieth centuries.[28] Nevertheless, in traveling to early American cities they were making their own voyages of discovery.[29] They made these centers of colonial trade and power in North America part of their wider geography as they confronted new challenges and charted new courses.[30]

Little is known about how delegates were selected, who self-selected, who volunteered and why, or who just tagged along for the ride. Colonists assumed that those who did the talking were chiefs. However, as Cary Miller observes in her study of Anishinaabe leadership, "when *chief* became the general term that Europeans used for any individual in any tribe or culture group who exercised influence, it masked the rich variety of leadership structures developed by the original peoples of North America."[31] Many delegates were indeed chiefs; others may or may not have been; some were not. The Oneida chief Shickellamy, for example, served as a "half king" representing the Six Nations in the Susquehanna Valley in the 1730s and '40s and frequently traveled to Philadelphia from his town at Shamokin (now Sunbury) on the Susquehanna River. However, he was not a hereditary chief and there is no evidence that he was accorded the status of a head warrior. Shickellamy was valued for his eloquence and his diplomatic abilities. He was, said Governor Patrick Gordon, "a Person of Consequence."[32] Likewise, the Onondaga orator Canasatego often appeared in Philadelphia as the speaker for the Six Nations, but it is not clear to what extent he acted for the league council or on his own authority. Treaties list him as an Onondaga chief, but as he did not carry any of the fourteen known hereditary sachem titles, it is unlikely that he was a league chief. It is possible that the British wanted to endow him with an authority he may not have had.[33]

   Some delegates lacked the status to serve as effective spokesmen for their people. Others may have been mouthpieces for leaders who stayed home, or they were selected for their oratorical skills rather than any actual leadership role. In 1751 when the Cherokee "emperor"—as the English called him—fell ill on the way to Charleston and had to return home, he nominated another member of the delegation, Outacite or Mankiller of Hiwassee, "to be the Mouth of the Nation." The spokesman for a dozen Cherokees who traveled to Philadelphia in June 1758 acknowledged, "I am not a Chief Man myself, I am deputed by the Chiefs of my Nation to travel this Way." Two Shawnee deputies at Lancaster in 1762, said: "Our Chief men are not here, but we are sent by the Chief men to speak for them, & what we say comes from their Hearts."[34]

In some cases, and perhaps in Canasatego's case, the experience of traveling to colonial capitals gave individuals a new source of influence at home. Some may have hoped that accompanying a delegation would enhance their status. The Oneida Peter Oneyaha or Beech Tree, a Turtle clan hereditary sachem who had visited Boston thirteen years before, explained to the New York commissioners of Indian affairs in 1790 that "when the sage Chiefs go out upon Business some of the young warriors always attend them, to take care of them, as well as to learn the Manner in which public Business is to be transacted."[35] In other words, they went for the experience.

Colonial governments struggled with the decentralized and diffuse political structures of Native societies and usually expected Indigenous leaders to exercise more authority than they actually did. Contrary to European practices, none exercised absolute or even far-ranging power. Typically, they led by building consensus rather than issuing commands, and they lacked the means to enforce their will. "All the authority of their chief is in his tongue's end; for he is powerful only in so far as he is eloquent," wrote the Jesuit missionary Paul Le Jeune in the 1630s. English colonists agreed. They "move by the Breath of their People," wrote William Penn. In "a perfect Republican Government" where no one had the power to compel, "the Arts of Persuasion alone must prevail," added Cadwallader Colden, a future governor of New York, in the 1720s. Their powers were "rather persuasive than coercive," echoed an English traveler in the 1770s.[36] Native leaders sometimes had a hereditary claim to leadership, but generally people followed them because of their charisma and reputation, because of kinship ties and obligations, because of their access to spiritual power, and because they exemplified the virtues and values of the community.

New forms of leadership and new kinds of leaders emerged in response to colonialism. Escalating warfare strained social and political structures. European policies and influences both consolidated and fragmented power in ways that undermined traditional patterns of leadership. Typically, older civil or village chiefs, often called sachems in Algonquian and Iroquoian societies, guided their community in daily affairs and in reaching consensus on issues of importance; younger war chiefs exercised temporary authority while away fighting but relinquished it when they returned to the village. As war and trade increasingly dominated life, however, European traders and officials who supplied the guns and other goods Indian leaders needed to command a following could direct the flow to those leaders they favored. European allies bolstered war chiefs with weapons and uniforms, and war chiefs exerted increasing influence in tribal councils where issues of war became paramount. Europeans began to "appoint" chiefs and hang medals around their necks to designate their status.[37] Delegates who traveled to colonial capitals negotiated treaties and carried out many traditional leadership responsibilities, but they too were called upon to perform new—and sometimes performative—roles in a new urban environment. People whom colonists recognized as "chiefs in the city" therefore often fulfilled particular roles, with particular skills.

Some were well fitted to play the part of "chief in the city." The eastern Delaware chief Teedyuscung evidently had what it took. Conrad Weiser, a Pennsylvania German interpreter and intercultural diplomat with extensive experience, said that although Teedyuscung "is a Drunkard and a very Irregular man, yet he is a man that can think well."[38] Teedyuscung could not read or write but he spoke English, and command of the appropriate foreign language was a valuable attribute. The Mohican chief Hendrick Aupaumut, educated in the mission village of Stockbridge in western Massachusetts, was a regular visitor to Philadelphia in the 1790s and undertook four trips to the Ohio country as an intermediary between the United States and the western Indian nations. Timothy Pickering, secretary of state under George Washington and John Adams, said Aupaumut was "intelligent and spoke the English language familiarly and with such a degree of correctness as to be easily & distinctly understood and he wrote a legible hand."[39] Joseph Brant had been educated at Eleazar Wheelock's Charity School in Connecticut and could read and write in English. Brant's ties to Sir William Johnson, the British superintendent of Indian affairs, and visits to England gave him connections in important circles and experience dealing with colonial officials. Allan Maclean, the British commander at Fort Niagara after the Revolution, said Brant was "better educated & Much More intelligent than any other Indian." British ambassador Robert Liston thought him "determined," "able," and "artful." New York governor George Clinton described him to George Washington as "a Man of very considerable information, influence and enterprise" whose friendship was "worthy of cultivation at some Expense."[40] Other leaders who traveled to the city were products of intermarriage with Europeans, such as Alexander McGillivray, the son of a Scottish trader and a French-Creek woman of the Wind Clan, who was educated in Charleston and attained a prominent position among his mother's Creek people.

Familiarity with Anglo-American culture naturally gave such Native visitors an advantage in negotiating the cultural and political landscapes of colonial cities. Others had to cultivate their role—or be cultivated. The Seneca war chief Cornplanter or Kayenthwahkeh (sometimes called Obeal or Captain Abeel after his father, an Albany trader named John Abeel) fought against the Americans during the Revolutionary War, but he ceded tribal land at the Treaty of Fort Stanwix in 1784 and in 1786 traveled to Philadelphia and then to the capital, New York City, where he addressed Congress. The Ohio Land Company in 1788 granted him a tract of land in recognition of his service to the United States and "the Friendship he has manifested to the Proprietors of Land purchased by the Ohio Company."[41] A rival of Joseph Brant, Cornplanter sought to position himself as the key player in Iroquois–U.S. relations.[42]

Europeans' preoccupation with issues of war and trade— traditionally areas of male responsibility—caused them to underestimate, ignore, or dismiss the leadership roles exercised by Indian women, who generally played a more prominent role than women in colonial society. In imposing their gendered systems of authority, Europeans undermined divisions of responsibility that helped ensure balance in many Indian societies, just as they undermined generational divisions of responsibility by courting younger war chiefs and bypassing older civil chiefs.[43] Not surprisingly, documents written by European males make little mention of female chiefs in the city. One woman, however, is visible in the written records and received special treatment. Elisabeth or Isabelle Montour (1667–c.1752), generally called Madame Montour, told Witham Marshe, whom she met in her old age at the Treaty of Lancaster in 1744, that she had been born in Canada to a French father, had been captured by the Iroquois when she was about ten, and had lived with them so long that she was "almost an Indian." She married an Oneida and had several children, one of whom, Andrew Montour, became a noted interpreter. She herself served as an interpreter, speaking French and Iroquoian languages and picking up English from traders and visits to Philadelphia when she accompanied male delegates to renew treaties of friendship. According to Marshe, she was held "in great esteem with the best sort of white people, and by them always treated with abundance and civility; and whenever she went to Philadelphia (which formerly she did pretty often), the ladies of that city always invited her to their homes, entertained her well, and made her several presents."[44] Catherine Phelps, an English Quaker traveling through the American colonies in the 1750s, attended a meeting in

Philadelphia between visiting Indians and Quakers. "Several of their women sat in this conference," she noted. They did not say much, but "I was informed that they admit their most respected women into their councils."[45] It evidently took a woman to record the presence of women, but the decline in female participation continued during the course of the eighteenth century. Mohawk clan mother Molly Brant—Joseph's sister and, by then, Sir William Johnson's widow—upbraided Indian emissaries sent by the United States in 1792: "If these Indians were upon good business, they would certainly follow the customs of all nations," she said. "They would have some women with them, but now they have none."[46]

Some delegates who traveled to the city were old enemies who had adopted new strategies in the wake of defeat. Both the Miami war chief Little Turtle and Blue Jacket of the Shawnees fought against American expansion, made their peace with the United States, and then took their people along paths of accommodation. Credited with leading the Northwest Indian confederacy to victory over the American army in 1791 and then leading it to make peace in 1795, Little Turtle traveled east several times. James Wilkinson provided him with a letter of recommendation to Washington at Pittsburgh, December 26, 1797: "Should this Letter be presented to you, it will be from the Hands of the Miamis Chief the Little Turtle, who in balancing a visit to the Town of Boston, or Mount Vernon, has decided in favor of your Seat." Little Turtle possessed, Wilkinson observed, "ideas more correct, and a mind more capacious in this Chief, than any of his race."[47] Little Turtle actually met John Adams, who was president by the time he arrived in Philadelphia.

Sometimes colonists did not inquire too closely into the status of those they designated as "chiefs," especially where land sales were concerned. Complaints that some with no authority or "a few of our wrong headed young men"—as Joseph Brant called them—had sold land were common. Brant told the governor of New York in 1789: "We endeavoured to explain to you that you have not treated with the Chiefs, nor with Persons authorized by them to dispose of our Country, but we are now sorry to find you do not wish to be convinced of an Error, which you took no previous steps to avoid."[48]

After traveling days and sometimes weeks to get there, Indian delegates often had to wait around in the city. There was a lot of downtime before and between meetings with colonial officials.[49] Many of the Indians who traveled to Albany to meet with colonial governors in 1754 were there for nearly two weeks while everyone waited for the Mohawk chief Hendrick and a delegation from Canajoharie to show up.[50] The Cherokee chief Attakullakulla, known to the English as Little Carpenter, was a frequent visitor to Charleston and often brought an entourage; roughly seventy warriors and several women accompanied him for more than two weeks of talks with Governor William Lyttelton early in 1757 and had plenty of time to spend in town.[51] Alexander McGillivray and Creek delegates who signed the Treaty of New York in the summer of 1790 spent more than a month in the city. That fall, Seneca delegates Cornplanter, Half Town, Big Tree, New Arrow, and Guyasuta traveled to Philadelphia. They first met with the Pennsylvania Executive Council, then addressed a series of speeches to President Washington regarding their treatment by the United States and the lands they had lost since the Revolution. It took Washington almost a month to reply as he waited for secretary of war Henry Knox to gather information and brief him on Indian affairs in upstate New York. In the end, the Senecas wound up spending almost six months in Philadelphia.[52]

What did Indian delegates do during the days, weeks, and sometimes months they were in cities? What did they make of the urban

Figure 0.2 Fanciful depiction of George Washington leading a group of Indians in generic Plains garb along neatly paved streets during the Treaty of New York with the Creeks. *Harper's New Monthly Magazine*, 99 (Oct. 1899), 745.

environment in which they found themselves and the townsfolk they encountered in noisy streets, in busy markets, and on bustling wharves? What were their reactions? (Figure 0.2)

Cultural contact involves mutual acts of discovery, and reconstructing the historical experiences of Indigenous peoples means exploring plural understandings of the past.[53] Many historians have pored over the writings of colonial travelers for deeper understandings of Native American society and culture, yet few have looked to Native American travelers for alternative understandings of early American society and culture. An extensive literature examines the imperial gaze, but Indigenous eyes are as important as imperial eyes in understanding contact. The voices and views of people marginalized by power, race, class, gender, region, or even just number should not be limited to casting light only on their own lives. Was the cultural gulf Indian visitors looked across then greater than the temporal gulf we look back across now? Can we assume that we automatically understand eighteenth-century Americans better than did Indian people who met them in the same world at the same time?

The challenges of reconstructing Native American history from records compiled by non-Indians are particularly acute in trying to reconstruct the lived experiences, reactions, and attitudes of Indian visitors to early American cities. Educated individuals such as Joseph Brant, Hendrick Aupaumut, and Alexander McGillivray were, as we've seen, literate in English (and Brant's handwriting was more legible than that of many of his colleagues in the British Indian department), but few Native delegates recorded their impressions on paper.[54] Official records document the speeches they made in formal councils and treaty negotiations. They say little about what the visitors did during their downtime, however, when they were not "on-stage." A myriad of individual interactions occurred off the record. Financial records and other federal archival materials that might have offered the best means of documenting Indian delegations in the early Republic were lost when fire engulfed the War Department in 1800 and have had to be reassembled.[55]

Commentaries in the press and other publications that purported to report Indian comments and opinions about what they saw in the cities sometimes included more invention than accuracy. In the spring and summer of 1795, newspapers carried the story of a Creek chief named Tomo Cheeki who had traveled to Philadelphia five years earlier as part of the delegation that made a treaty with the federal government and who reputedly stood out for "the gravity of his deportment." While the other Indians were shooting arrows at halfpennies set on a post for the boys in the city, "he employed himself in noting down observations on the buildings of the place, the character of the inhabitants, the politicks of the white men, and such other particulars as occurred from a situation, to him, so new and strange." While the other delegates "were carousing in taverns and dramshops," he would spend his time walking in the fields and woods on the outskirts of the city, smoking his pipe or fishing. He "seemed generally absorbed in thought, now and then noted down his remarks in his own language, [and] expressed great delight at the manners of civilized society." After the delegation departed, the landlord of the house where Tomo Cheeki had stayed found a large bundle of papers behind in an old hamper in a corner of his room, which he took to be the notes and comments the chief had written down while he was in the city. The manuscripts lay forgotten until a former Indian captive was found to translate them into English. Published "for the amusement and information of the curious," they were serialized in the *Jersey Chronicle* and reprinted in other newspapers. Tomo Cheeki's first impressions of Philadelphia; his disgust at the whites' crowded dwellings, superfluous wants, assaults on nature, and treatment of the Indians; and his sage reflections on the comparisons of so-called civilized and savage societies offered a telling Indigenous critique of city life.[56]

Or so it seemed. Although it might be tempting to take an Indian visitor's criticisms of city life at face value, Tomo Cheeki was in fact a fictitious character, the creation of poet, essayist, and editor Philip Freneau.[57] The whole story was made up. A Yamacraw Creek named Tomochichi had established amicable relations with Governor Oglethorpe of Georgia and led a delegation to England—in 1734. Alexander McGillivray's delegation of more than two dozen Creek chiefs stopped in Philadelphia on their way north to negotiate the Treaty of New York in 1790, but no one by the name of Tomo Cheeki signed the treaty.[58] There is no doubt that Indian visitors to the cities of early America took note of what they saw and, as they had in London, often served as mirrors, providing implicit and explicit commentary on the virtues and vices of society. Nonetheless, we have to look beyond Tomo Cheeki to find evidence and examples of what they thought and said. A tradition of ventriloquism—in which sage or ostensibly naive Indigenous speakers or Asian princes, real or imagined, delivered incisive criticisms and satirical comments on so-called civilized society but actually functioned as a mouthpiece for an author's own critiques of the hypocrisy, mendacity, immorality, and brutality of European society—was well established by the eighteenth century.[59]

Natives' responses can sometimes be more reliably discerned from their behavior than from words ascribed to them. Even when their words and reactions were not totally fabricated, they were often filtered by non-Native observers and news reporters who may have been expressing what they thought the Indians should have been thinking. Benjamin Franklin provided anecdotes, examples, and words from Indians, whose comments on white society were as much Franklin's as their own. "Our laborious manner of life compared with theirs, they esteem slavish and base; and the learning on which we value ourselves, they regard as frivolous and useless," he wrote.[60]

Nevertheless, tainted records are better than no records at all and not without value as historical sources. Native opinions presented by non-Natives are not necessarily fiction. Newspapers, journals, minutes of treaty negotiations, expenses entered in account books, and observations by non-Native visitors who happened to be in town around the same time as Indian delegates and saw the same things they saw all afford glimpses into what Native people did, witnessed, and perhaps even thought. Native Americans did not keep diaries and journals of their trips (an exception being Hendrick Aupaumut, who wrote a journal of his diplomatic mission to the West that was published in 1826), but European and American travelers who did described many of the same things the Indians would have seen. The many newspapers of early America printed reports and rumors of Indian wars, raids, and threats.[61] They also paid attention when Indian delegations arrived in town. Sometimes newspapers and correspondents mentioned or indicated Native reactions to the urban environments in which they found themselves; sometimes what Indian people actually said made its way into the press.

Throughout their time in town Indian visitors were subject to observation and comments. (After Samson Occom returned from England he told Wheelock he had felt like "a Gazing Stock, Yea Even a Laughing Stock, in Strange Countries.")[62] They also, of course, observed and commented on what they saw, and non-Indians knew it—even if they rarely knew what the Indians had to say. "Savages we call them, because their manners differ from ours, which we think the perfection of civility," wrote Benjamin Franklin; "they think the same of theirs."[63] Robert Hunter, the twenty-year-old son of a London merchant, kept a diary of his travels from Quebec to the Carolinas in the mid-1780s. He seems to have been primarily interested in recording observations on the opposite sex, although he also described the Indian people he met, and recognized that it was a two-way exchange of views: "I observed one fellow laughing and making his remarks upon everybody and everything that passed. I have no doubt but that he thought our manners and customs as curious as we think his."[64] Such curiosity and comment could only have increased when Indian people had more opportunity to reverse the gaze and more occasion to observe the behavior of white people in their crowded and noisy urban settings. Temporarily immersed in Euro-American culture, chiefs now in the city saw "civilization" up close and personal.

Native peoples who traveled to early modern European cities were generally impressed by the size of the populations, the architecture, and technology. Still, they noted multiple shortcomings among people whose personal hygiene left much to be desired, who scrambled to accumulate wealth while others starved, and who avowed but did not practice Christian values.[65] Native people who visited early American cities had many similar responses. Delegates who went there for their own Iroquois, Cherokee, or Delaware reasons obviously interpreted what they saw and experienced by drawing on Iroquois, Cherokee, or Delaware philosophies, language systems, social values, and worldviews, not on Euro-American equivalents. Teedyuscung and Joseph Brant may have spoken English when they were in the city, but presumably they thought in Lenape and Mohawk. Without the ties of kinship, cycles of ceremony, and ethics of reciprocity that maintained balance and social well-being in Indigenous communities, Indian visitors may have seen more dystopia than order and civility in urban life. Yet their individual responses were surely as varied as individual responses among non-Indian visitors. Different people took note of different things, focused on particular aspects, and had personal as well as cultural reactions.

Indian diplomats also, diplomatically, often kept their private thoughts to themselves and made their reactions hard to read. Shickellamy, it was said, had mastered the art of concealing his feelings.[66] But most observers understood that Native "stoicism" was affected or imputed. At a tavern in Pittsburgh in 1797 English traveler Francis Baily encountered a young Indian on his way home whom Baily remembered seeing a year before when the Indian had just arrived in Philadelphia: "He talked English very well, but was very shy when any one spoke to him, as all the Indians are, though upon better acquaintance he would be facetious, and sometimes would be ridiculously antic."[67] Even after traveling to London and back in 1762, the Cherokee chief Ostenaco gave little away during a two-hour conversation with Governor Lyttelton of South Carolina, who thought him "astonishingly reserved and silent upon everything he has seen."[68] Though some Indian travelers may have been understandably reticent in their dealings with Europeans—Ostenaco's guarded conversation may have had more to do with distrust of the governor after the Cherokee War than with natural reserve—others were careful to present themselves as impassive observers.

Following Indian people through the streets of early American cities requires searching through the records to find moments when people came to town and came together to do things other than commit violence. Those interactions complicate standard narratives of unremitting conflict, confound enduring stereotypes of savagery, and remind us that Indian people dealt with non-Indians in multiple ways and in multiple places. Indian leaders who incorporated urban landscapes into their geography and included urban visits in their repertoire of strategies in dealing with colonial powers broke down binaries, the "either-or" categories that so often assign Native Americans to static positions as "warlike" or "friendly," committed to resistance or accommodation. During the course of the eighteenth century Indians learned to navigate the streets and social mores of towns and cities as they learned to navigate the challenges and conditions of colonialism itself. In doing so they disturbed assumptions that Indians remained separate from cities and could do nothing but retire "before the advancing city and withdraw to their distant forests in the west."[69]

CHAPTER 1

The Towns and Cities
of Early America

SUPERINTENDENT OF INDIAN AFFAIRS SIR William
Johnson described Peter Kalm as "an Injinious Botanist from
Sweden" and in 1750 provided an Indian escort to accompany
him from the Mohawk Valley to Niagara Falls. Kalm was a keen observer, but there was much he failed to see. He assumed, like many
others, that North American cities were a European invention: "The
Indians have always been as ignorant of architecture and manual
labor as of science and writing. In vain does one seek for well-built
towns and houses, artificially built fortifications, high towers and pillars, and such like among them, which the Old World can show from
the most ancient times. Their dwelling places are wretched huts of
bark, exposed on all sides to wind and rain."[1] From the inception of
English colonization, city building was associated with establishing
political and social order.[2] The absence of cities and their attendant
architecture, political spaces, and social structures, therefore, im-
plied disorder.

Kalm was wrong. The Indigenous peoples of North America
created and inhabited ordered environments. They generally built
with wood rather than stone, but they developed various and often
highly sophisticated forms of architecture that were suited to particular environments and different seasons, provided space for ritual
and religion as well as family life, and accommodated shifting social,
political, and economic purposes.[3]

For most of the continent's history, America's towns and cities were Indigenous. Archaeologists studying pre-Columbian towns and cities differ in the emphases they place on physical size, population (and population density), social and political structure, function, and other factors; "urban," as one says, "is in the eye of the beholder."[4] Even so, many Indigenous cities were impressive to European eyes and by European standards. When Hernán Cortés invaded Mexico in 1519–23, Bernal Díaz del Castillo, one of his Spanish soldiers, recalled they were "amazed" to see "so many cities and villages built in the water and other great towns on dry land." The capital of the Aztec Empire, Tenochtitlán, on the site of present-day Mexico City, was laid out on a semi-grid pattern, with plazas, temples, and pyramids, a system of causeways and canals, and aqueducts bringing fresh water to the city. Its streets and markets bustled with activity, and with between 200,000 and 250,000 inhabitants, Tenochtitlán was larger than any European city at the time.[5] While Christians were erecting Gothic cathedrals in twelfth- and thirteenth-century Europe, Indian people in the Mississippi Basin were constructing temple mounds around open plazas, creating ritual spaces, and demonstrating the power of their chiefdoms through building. A thousand years ago, a Native American metropolis existed on the banks of the Mississippi River at the site of modern-day East St. Louis. Cahokia (as it was later named after the tribe living in the area) was a planned city with scores of packed-earth pyramid mounds, plazas, and more than 10,000 inhabitants; perhaps another 20,000 lived in outlying towns and farming settlements. Trade networks fanned out from Cahokia across the interior of the continent.[6] Spanish invaders in the sixteenth century beheld the impressive mound architecture of these ancient civilizations throughout the Mississippi Valley and the Southeast. Americans who came across earthwork remains in the Ohio Valley in the late eighteenth and nineteenth centuries speculated about who could have built them—surely not Indians, they thought.[7]

When Frenchman Jacques Cartier visited the Iroquoian town of Hochelaga (modern Montreal) in 1536, he found fifty bark longhouses, all protected by an eighteen-foot-high log palisade (Figure 1.1). Huge cornfields surrounded the town. More than one thousand men, women, and children came out to meet the newcomers, and threw so many loaves of cornbread into the French boats "that it seemed to rain bread."[8] When Spaniards pushed north into New Mexico, they called the Indian peoples living in the Rio Grande Valley "Pueblos" because they lived in towns (*pueblos*). They heard of

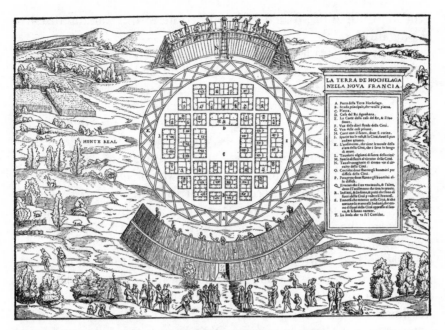

Figure 1.1 Woodcut engraving of Hochelaga, depicting its longhouses and palisades from above. Published in Venice by Ramusio, based on account of Jacques Cartier. World History Archive/Alamy Stock Photo.

large towns among the Hasinai and other Indigenous confederacies farther north, on the southern prairies.[9] Archaeologists now believe they may have located the site of the "lost city" of Etzanoa at the junction of the Arkansas and Walnut Rivers in Kansas. Etzanoa was the "Great Settlement" of the Quiviras or Wichitas, which Spanish conquistador Juan de Oñate described in 1601 as comprising some 1,200 round houses thatched with bundles of prairie grass and surrounded by fields of corn, beans, and calabashes.[10] Le Grand Village du Kaskaskia, as the French called the main settlement of the Illinois confederacy, had perhaps 8,000 people. Jesuit Claude Allouez in 1677 found the population had swelled with the influx of people from other tribes, so he could not get an accurate tally. He counted 351 lodges. Located at the head of the Illinois Valley, on the edges of the eastern woodlands and the western tall grass prairies, Kaskaskia was just the largest in a string of villages in the area that continued to attract and incorporate other peoples. For a few years in the early 1680s, according to the historian Robert Morrissey, this village cluster constituted "the largest population center on the continent north of Mexico—20,000 people within walking distance of one another."[11]

Irish-born trader James Adair, who lived among the south-eastern Indians from the 1730s to the 1760s, said that Choctaw towns in the lower Mississippi Valley were "populous" and "extensive"; in most the lodges were scattered, but those closest to the Creeks in the east and Chickasaws to the north were "compactly settled" for defense. In the lower Choctaw towns Adair found "thick settlement."[12] The Creek confederacy of 15,000–20,000 ethnically and linguistically diverse people lived in more than fifty towns or *talwas,* and satellite towns, *talofas,* stretching across northern Florida, western Georgia, northern Alabama, and eastern Mississippi, and divided into two geographical divisions, Upper and Lower Creeks. "The Creek world," writes historian Joshua Piker, "was a world of towns." *Talwas,* organized around a square and a sacred fire, were the focus of Creek life and also functioned as political and diplomatic centers. The *micos* or chiefs with whom colonial powers dealt were generally town headmen. The trading path that ran from Charleston via Augusta entered Upper Creek country at Okfuskee on the Tallapoosa River, one of the largest and most important towns, with a population of 1,500 in 1763, slightly fewer people than inhabited Williamsburg at the time. Creek life revolved so much around towns that Creek people assumed Europeans organized their lives in similar ways; indeed, they sometimes referred to colonies as "towns."[13]

Some Indian towns were more important for what happened there than for how many people lived there, and they exerted an influence out of proportion to their size. Like Creeks, Cherokee people inhabited a world of towns and dealt with colonial powers as towns. Although Cherokee towns declined in number in the eighteenth century as war and disease took a heavy toll, and relationships between communities changed under the impact of colonialism, Chota, the capital of the Overhill Cherokees in the Little Tennessee and Tellico Valleys, grew to prominence in midcentury. Lieutenant Henry Timberlake, a Virginian who also accompanied the Cherokee delegation to England that year, credited Chota with 175 warriors in 1762, although his data may not have reflected recent losses occasioned by war and disease. British Indian superintendent John Stuart said it had 100 warriors in 1764. Their figures suggest a population of somewhere between 400 and 700 (although that number grew on occasions when Cherokee delegates from other towns assembled at the townhouse, which Timberlake said was large enough to hold 500 people). Nevertheless, on the map of Cherokee country he sketched in 1762 Timberlake described Chota as "the Metropolis." Located at the terminus of a trade route from Charleston and Savannah, it was well situated in the deerskin trade that was crucial both to Cherokees and to South Carolinians, and it emerged as the political and diplomatic center in Cherokee dealings with the colonists. Chota was also a ceremonial center, a "beloved town," where no blood was shed, and where emissaries came and went in peace.[14]

Like the Cherokees, the Iroquois suffered catastrophic losses from war and disease in the seventeenth and eighteenth centuries. By 1763, the British estimated, the Six Nations could muster 2,230 warriors, suggesting a total population of almost 9,000 people, though Sir William Johnson said they were "vastly inferior in Number to what they were 50 Years ago." Nevertheless, the Iroquois remained a potent force. The Senecas, at the western door of the league, were the most numerous, with perhaps 4,000 people in about twenty villages. Onondaga, near present-day Syracuse, New York, was estimated to have only "150 men" in 1763, indicating a total population of 600–750, but it was the "central council fire" and political heart of the Iroquois league. Delegates met there to debate and reach consensus on league business, and the wampum belts woven from marine shells that recorded diplomatic dealings with colonial and other Indigenous powers were kept there. Onondaga's influence was felt from Canada to the Carolinas and from the Ohio Valley to Paris and London.[15]

Indian towns in the interior of the continent also exerted far-reaching influence. Miamitown, located on the six-mile Maumee–Wabash portage in what is now northeastern Indiana, was a center of population, trade, and diplomacy. Jacques-Charles de Sabrevois, the first Frenchman to travel the various tributaries of the Ohio River and send a detailed overview of the region to his home government, described Miamitown in 1718 as one of the largest towns in the region, with about 4,000 men and an "abundance of women," suggesting a total population, counting children and old people, of 16,000 to 20,000.[16]

Farther west, the Mandans, Hidatsas, and Arikaras operated a trade rendezvous at their villages on the banks of the upper Missouri River, exchanging corn, beans, and squash grown by their women, and manufactured goods and guns supplied by traders from Canada, for horses, buffalo robes, and meat brought by hunters from the Great Plains. Epidemics of smallpox and the attacks of westward-moving Sioux depleted the upper Missouri tribes during the late eighteenth century, and by the time Lewis and Clark wintered there in 1804–5, the Mandans were a shadow of their former power and population, reduced to about 4,500 people inhabiting a couple of villages. Yet these "villages" were still bigger than St. Louis or even Washington, DC, at the time.[17]

Although Indian populations almost everywhere fell under the impact of European diseases and colonial disruptions, many Indian towns were as large as most non-Indian towns in North America. Diseases that raced along trade routes and devastated population centers contributed to the Europeans' mistaken impression that Indians did not live in towns. In fact, dense concentrations of population were most vulnerable to crowd-killing epidemics that originated in Old World cities and spread into the interior of the continent along networks used for slave trading, fur trading, horse trading, and other activities.[18]

The growth, and growing prosperity, of colonial port cities throughout the eighteenth century brought increasing numbers and varieties of goods from the rest of the British Empire and around the Atlantic. So many ships arrived in Philadelphia each year, said a would-be German immigrant who stepped off one of those ships in 1750, that it was "possible to get all the things one can get in Europe in Pennsylvania."[19] European goods made their way to Indian towns as well. The agricultural productivity of Indigenous women throughout the eastern woodlands made their towns prosperous, with food for trade as well as consumption. The participation of Indian men as hunters, and women as processors of pelts, in the fur and deerskin trades brought manufactured goods from British mills into Indian villages in substantial quantities—various types of fabric, including woolens, linens, cottons, and silks; scissors, needles, and awls with which to manufacture clothing; glass beads and trade silver with which to decorate clothing; metal utensils, steel tools and weapons, guns, looking glasses, combs, kitchenware, and tableware. Indigenous as well as colonial communities were experiencing a consumer revolution.[20] Frontier militia expeditions were often motivated, at least in part, by the prospect of plunder to be found in Indian towns where the inhabitants enjoyed a material standard of living equal to, and in some cases superior to, that of their colonial neighbors. American troops who invaded Iroquois country during the Revolution burned towns that were not unlike those inhabited by frontier settlers. Time and again, officers' journals described substantial communities, vast fields of corn, beans, squash, pumpkins, potatoes, and watermelons, and orchards of apple, peach, plum, and cherry trees. Many houses were constructed of hewn logs framed together, with doors, glass windows, and wooden floors; some were painted. Chenussio or Genesee Castle, the largest of the Seneca towns, contained 128 solidly constructed houses nestled in the bow of the river, with cornfields too numerous to count.[21] After the war, the Oneidas petitioned Congress to compensate them for losses they had suffered as allies of the United States. In addition to framed houses with chimneys, farm equipment, wagons, and livestock, they lost kitchen utensils, clothing, teacups and saucers, punch bowls, looking glasses, jewelry, and other items.[22] Indian delegates in American cities saw many of the same manufactured goods that they had in their own towns.

Over the course of the seventeenth and eighteenth centuries, a string of port cities developed along the Atlantic coast, points of contact between the trade networks of the Atlantic, the American interior, and the Caribbean islands.[23] European towns were late additions to the urban landscape of North America, and many of them were established at locations where Indian communities had previously existed, sometimes on their very ruins. The French built Quebec and Montreal where the Iroquoian Stadaconna and Hochelaga, respectively, had been, and Montreal grew alongside several Indian towns on the island. English colonists in seventeenth-century western Massachusetts built Springfield, Northampton, Deerfield, and Northfield in the Connecticut Valley on sites where Agawam, Nonotuck, Pocumtuck, and Squakheag had existed for hundreds of years.[24] Cities such as Philadelphia and Charleston grew because they looked west as well as east, their trade networks reached across Indian country as well as across the Atlantic Ocean, and people and goods passed through them on their way to and from the interior. Many other colonial communities depended on connections to Indian country for their existence, growth, and prosperity.

North American cities generally were tiny by modern, Old World, or South American standards. Historian Gary Nash calls them "overgrown villages" compared to the great urban centers of Europe, the Middle East, and China. Most North Americans, Native and non-Native, lived in what we might call face-to-face communities. According to the first United States census, done in 1790, less than 5 percent of the population lived in an urban center (today it's about 75 percent). Colonial armies sometimes contained more people than colonial capitals did.[25] The cities of colonial America and the early Republic were not the industrial monsters of Britain that Thomas Jefferson feared, and they bore little resemblance to the urban giants that would mushroom in the United States in the nineteenth century.[26]

Nevertheless, cities were growing, often at a dramatic rate, as immigration and the populations in their hinterlands grew. Unlike most Indian towns, colonial towns and cities revolved around business and commerce rather than kinship and community. Seaports even developed a distinctive mercantile landscape, with different zones allocated to different economic functions—wharves and warehouses on the waterfront; commercial and financial institutions further inland; then retailers, taverns, lodgings, and offices; then townhouses, law courts, and principal churches—and residential specialization and marginalization along class and ethnic lines.[27] Urban economic growth was uneven, following cycles of boom and slump, often tied to cycles of war and peace. In 1664, when the English took over control of New Netherland, the city of New York had about 1,500 residents, but it continued to function as the commercial hub of the province, and its population rose as the city's economic ties with England, the West Indies, and other American Atlantic ports grew. At the start of the eighteenth century, New York's governor, the Earl of Bellomont, described New York City to the Lords of Trade as "the growingest town in America."[28]

Established by Puritan colonists in 1630, Boston grew rapidly in the seventeenth century. By 1690 it was the largest city on the North American mainland and the center of the Puritan Atlantic, with 6,000 inhabitants. As its economy shifted from trading wampum and furs to trading slaves and sugar in the West Indies, Boston effectively became a slave society, even though most of the slaves lived and labored elsewhere.[29] New York's population at the time was about 4,500, and Philadelphia's about 2,200. By the middle of the eighteenth century, all three cities had populations between 13,000 and 16,000. Boston and New York edged a few thousand higher by 1763. Lord Adam Gordon, a British army officer who toured the colonies, exaggerated Boston's population at 23,000 in 1764, but said it had 2,100 houses, and many homes that were more spacious than in Philadelphia and New York.[30] Philadelphia replaced New York as "the growingest city" in the eighteenth century. Its population increased more than five-fold between 1750 and 1800. A German who arrived in Philadelphia on an immigrant ship carrying 500 passengers in 1750 said twenty to twenty-four ships arrived each fall he was there: "Within the space of four years the city was invaded by more than 25,000 souls."[31] Philadelphia's population reached almost 24,000 in 1763, making it the largest city north of Mexico; by 1775, it had 40,000.[32]

As American cities grew in population, commercial prosperity, social amenities, and civic development, they regarded themselves as exemplars of civil society.[33] They also experienced growing pains and problems that strained town government. Expansion and commercial development brought unprecedented levels of private and public building and generated new styles of architecture, but also generated changes in how people organized work, time, and capital. Cities were on the cutting edge of social, economic, and political change. They dismantled many traditional arrangements and communal values, restructured social groups, redistributed wealth, fostered the development of classes and class consciousness, and changed manners and morals. The French historian Fernand Braudel likened towns to electric transformers that "accelerate the rhythm of exchange and constantly recharge human life" but also increase tensions.[34]

Visitors to early American cities tended to focus on the most conspicuous signs of growth and prosperity, order and "civilization"—street layout, public buildings, ships in the harbor. Indian visitors saw those things, as well as busy workshops and printing houses, specialized craft shops and stores, and bustling seafronts. Port cities on the edge of an increasingly mobile Atlantic world often housed transient populations, people living there temporarily before they moved inland—or sailed back across the ocean. Indian visitors encountered many different nationalities, religious sects, and customs.

They also no doubt noted stark divisions between rich and poor, merchants and shopkeepers, artisans and laborers, free and unfree labor, between genders, and between black and white.[35] They would have crossed paths with elite ladies and gentlemen, laborers, slaves, servants, sailors, and—even though they might not have understood what they did or recognized them for what they were—with pawnbrokers, con artists, forgers, dancing masters, hawkers, hucksters, and thieves. There were women working in the service economy as cooks, cleaners, washerwomen, and seamstresses; female traders who used credit and family relationships to make a place for themselves in the city's informal lower-echelon economy of secondhand goods; women who ran shops, taverns, and "disorderly houses"; and sex workers along the waterfront.[36] Atlantic trade produced wealthy merchant families who dressed in the latest fashions, lived in modern townhouses, and ate at elegant tables using imported china, silver, and glassware.[37] That same Atlantic trade rendered seaports vulnerable to imported epidemic diseases and economic volatility. Poverty would have been especially visible in times of postwar depression. Indian and non-Indian visitors saw hospitals, prisons, asylums, almshouses, taverns, and brothels.

The new cities emerging in North America were a new world for most people, Native and non-Native alike. Nevertheless, the urban world was often a shared world, and sometimes Indians were even present at the creation. A Neponset sachem named Chickataubut and a group of Algonquian people came to Boston in 1631 with corn and ate meals with the colonists.[38] On February 1, 1733, about an hour after James Oglethorpe and other colonists who were selecting the site for Georgia's first settlement climbed the bluff near where Savannah would eventually be located, Tomochichi and a group of Yamacraw Creeks came to welcome them with ritual dancing and chanting, stroking them with fans of white feathers as a token of peace. Tomochichi and the Yamacraws ceded the land for the town-site. Delegations of Yamacraws, Creeks, Choctaws, and other Indians regularly came to Savannah during Georgia's early decades as the town grew into a prosperous seaport.[39]

Other cities had similar Indigenous presences. Quebec was the French gateway to the continent and attracted flotillas of Indian canoes from as far away as the upper Great Lakes. The French priest and traveler Pierre de Charlevoix, who was there in the early 1720s, said the city had "no more than seven thousand souls" (which was probably too high), and although there were many churches, he thought the cathedral "would make but an indifferent parish church in one of the smallest towns in France."[40] Peter Kalm, who was there in 1749, said most of the merchants lived in the lower city, where the houses were built very close together and the streets narrow, rough, "and almost always wet." People of quality lived in the upper city.[41] The growth of its population, which had reached 4,750 by 1744, slowed after the British captured the city in 1759. Not counting British soldiers, about 3,500 people lived in Quebec in 1763.[42]

In 1666, the year of the colony's first census, the island of Montreal had only about 650 French colonists, the town itself scarcely more than 150 residents and thirty houses. Over the next forty years the French and Indian population grew dramatically, and by 1700 some 3,000 French and 3,000 Indians inhabited the island. Montreal was the largest town but had fewer inhabitants than the combined population of the Native towns around it. When 1,300 Indian people from almost forty different nations descended on Montreal for the Great Peace held there in the summer of 1701, they doubled the size of the town. They remained for nearly three weeks as the French, the

Iroquois, and the Great Lakes tribes negotiated the terms of treaty. Most of them made the long journey to Montreal not to participate directly in the treaty negotiations but to trade at the place that had been the scene of huge trade fairs in the late seventeenth century. When the gates of the town were opened, many Indians spent their days visiting the shops of French merchants and transformed the city into a bustling market, exchanging their furs for powder, balls, vermilion, kettles, iron and copper pots, various items of hardware, and French-style clothing, including hats trimmed with fake gold lace.[43]

Half a century later, Montreal consisted of about 400 houses, along with public buildings, five chapels or churches, and a hospital. Two streets ran the length of the town, with nine or ten cross streets.[44] Its role as a trade center declined. Indian trader John Long said Montreal "has nothing remarkable in it at present. It was formerly famous for a great fair, which lasted near three months, and was resorted to by the Indians, who came from the distance of many hundreds of miles to barter their peltry for English goods." Long said the nearby Mohawk community of Kahnawake had a population of about 800 people inhabiting 200 houses, mostly stone-built; although the houses had "a mean and dirty appearance," Kahnawake was "considered as the most respectable of all the Indian villages, and the people are in a great degree civilized and industrious." Another report said Kahnawake had "a thousand souls" in 1750, and its population fluctuated between 1,000 and 1,500 in the second half of the century.[45] Indians continued to go to Montreal in large numbers to sell game and other things at the end of the hunting season.[46]

Unlike many other colonial cities that were situated on or near the Atlantic coast, Albany lay inland, 160 miles north of New York City. It could take as long as a week to get there traveling up the Hudson River. Indian affairs and the Indian trade made Albany what it was. Local Indians from the Mohawk and Hudson Valleys went there regularly to trade, as did other members of the Six Nations and more distant nations. The town retained its Dutch character, customs, and language long after the British took over and established a fort there. In the eighteenth century, Albany was actually two towns in one: a Dutch community who maintained their language, customs, and architecture, attended a Dutch Reformed church, and were active in the fur trade and other commercial pursuits; and a British garrison community with an Anglican church. The British occupied and administered Albany as an outpost of empire, which meant dealing with Indians; the Dutch continued their commerce, which meant trading with Indians.[47]

Albany still numbered only about 2,000 inhabitants (about the size of a large Iroquois town) in the middle of the eighteenth century. Two long streets running parallel to the river intersected with a third that led up to a fort on the hill, and a broad street running between the two churches served as a market (Figure 1.2). The Dutch townspeople had a reputation for money-grubbing and living frugally in cramped houses with the doors and windows shut. Many of the residents made wampum for the Indians who came to town to trade furs and smuggled goods from Canada. Visitors complained that the streets were "very dirty because the people leave their cattle in them during the summer nights." Sir William Johnson's brother, Warren, was in Albany in 1760–61 and described it as "a Nasty dirty Town"; its streets were "the Dirtiest I ever Saw, & worse than Edinburgh in Scotland for little Houses."[48] Iroquois people who came to Albany likely found such lodgings claustrophobic and unhealthy compared

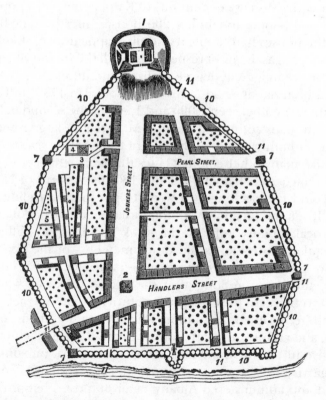

Figure 1.2 Plan of Albany, 1695. From William Barnes, *The Settlement and Early History of Albany*, 1864. North is to the right. Wikimedia Commons.

to their own multifamily longhouses, which allowed for much greater ventilation in summer months.

Albany regularly hosted large gatherings of Indians. Even after the fur trade declined in the late seventeenth century, it remained the site for Anglo-Iroquois diplomacy. Indian conferences were usually held at the fort until the 1670s, and thereafter more often in the courthouse. The most important meetings were formal full-dress councils between the governor and his retinue and delegations of Iroquois, which became annual occurrences after 1690, although most conferences were smaller affairs involving the magistrates and one or more Indians who might come at any time of year.[49] Albany was the designated "council fire" or meeting place for the Iroquois in dealings with New York and also with neighboring colonies. Governor Benjamin Fletcher told visiting Iroquois in 1693: "You know Albany hath always been the antient place of treating[;] when the Shawanno⁵ came to New Yorke to make peace I would not hear them speak until they went to Albany."[50] In 1737 Iroquois sachems declined an invitation to travel to Williamsburg and meet with the governor of Virginia, pointing out that "Albany is the Antient and fixt Place for all People to treat with them." The governor was welcome to come in person or send his deputies to meet them there, they said, in a not-so-subtle display of diplomatic one-upmanship.[51]

Peter Kalm noted that the governor of New York often conferred with the Iroquois at Albany, especially at times of conflict with the French.[52] More than 450 Indians attended a conference held there in 1745; between 150 and 200 gathered for the Albany Congress of 1754.[53] Albany lost its preeminent place in Iroquois diplomacy after Sir William Johnson made his home—first Fort Johnson and then Johnson Hall, at present-day Johnstown, New York—the go-to venue for meetings. But Iroquois delegates were frequently in Albany again as General Philip Schuyler and other colonial officials sought their alliance or neutrality when the Revolution broke out in 1775. Those delegates would have seen "about 400 Houses chiefly built after the Old low Dutch Fashion," with two Dutch and one English churches, a decaying fort on the hill, and a large and handsome house at each end of the town, one belonging to Schuyler and the other to the Van Rensselaer family.[54]

After the English takeover, local Indians continued to trade food and firewood to the residents of what is now New York City. Minisink Indians occasionally hunted as far away as the Spanish frontiers but, said one sachem, they always brought their pelts to New York: "This place being the old place & the first Citty here, they doe not Runn about to other places but alwayes Come here, to make their Covenant & speake of great things."[55] New York had a brief but significant resurgence as the center of Indian diplomacy when it became the first capital of the United States: "A new and great council fire is kindled at our beloved city of New York," American treaty commissioners informed the Indian nations in September 1789.[56]

No city received more Indian delegations than Philadelphia in the eighteenth century, however. William Penn, the first governor of Pennsylvania, established a reputation for just dealing with Indians and, Governor George Thomas reminded Canasatego, Shickellamy, and other chiefs in 1742, "made a League of friendship with you by which We became One People." Playing on his name, the Iroquois called Penn "Onas," meaning "quill" (and they applied the name to all subsequent governors). Shawnee and Susquehannock chiefs traveled to Philadelphia to bid Penn farewell in October 1701 before his departure for England, and Indian delegates made repeated visits to Philadelphia to renew and strengthen the friendship. Philadelphia was "the Place where all Indians should go, who have Business to transact with this Government," said the colony's Indian commissioners.[57] Governor William Denny told the eastern Delaware chief Teedyuscung it was the place "where the Principal Council Fire is always burning," and he urged the Ohio Indians to come to Philadelphia, "your first Old Council Fire."[58] Tribal delegations traveled to Philadelphia so often in the eighteenth century that its citizens hardly thought it unusual to see Indians walking the streets. Ironically, Philadelphia was also the place where the colonial government offered bounties on Indian scalps.[59]

Situated on a neck of land between the Delaware and Schuylkill Rivers, Philadelphia was a boom town and a bustling port. It traded grain, provisions, lumber, tobacco, livestock, meat, and wool from the interior to other colonies, especially the Caribbean islands. It imported hardware, clothing, and other manufactured goods from London and Bristol, and developed a flourishing wine trade with Lisbon and Madeira. Hundreds of ships docked at its wharves every year—about 1,800, more "than any Part of America," wrote Warren Johnson. Philadelphia shipped out nearly one-quarter of the young nation's exports. Merchants' homes reflected their wealth, and the city's public architecture reflected its importance. Johnson said about 100 new houses were built each year.[60] The city's merchants met and discussed business at the London Coffee House, located at the corner of Front and Market Streets, adjacent to the twice-weekly market. Whereas Boston was a city of winding narrow streets, Philadelphia was laid out on a rectangular grid plan, with paved streets lined with brick or flagstone sidewalks, and symmetrical spaces (Figure 1.3). The Assembly appropriated funds "for the better regulating the Nightly Watch within the City of Philadelphia, and for enlightening the Streets, Lanes, Aliles of the said City."[61]

Visitors noted approvingly Philadelphia's rectangular plan, the water pumps on the streets, its churches and fine public buildings, and the bustling market held on Wednesday and Saturday—"the best of its bigness in the known World," according to some foreign visitors. Peter Kalm thought it was easy to see "why this city should rise so suddenly from nothing to such grandeur and perfection . . . Its fine appearance, good regulations, agreeable location, natural advantages, trade, riches, and power are by no means inferior to those of any, even of the most, ancient towns in Europe." Lord Adam Gordon rated "the great and Noble City of Philadelphia . . . one of the wonders of the world." William Mylne, a Scotsman, and Josiah Quincy Jr., a New Englander, both rated it the best laid-out city they had seen.[62]

After the Revolution, Philadelphia was the biggest urban center in the United States and Pennsylvania was the most prosperous state. With red brick houses lining wide streets, "magnificent" public buildings, and ostentatious displays of wealth in clothing, furniture, and other goods, it continued to impress American and foreign visitors alike. The exiled Venezuelan revolutionary Francisco de Miranda and Élie Médéric Louis Moreau de Saint-Méry, who emigrated to the United States after the French Revolution, both thought it the most beautiful city in the country, while Italian traveler Luigi Castiglioni and Frenchman Jacques Pierre Brissot de Warville both called it "the metropolis of the United States."[63] From 1790 to

Figure 1.3 The East Prospect of the City of Philadelphia, in the Province of Pennsylvania, 1755, published 1761. Yale University Art Gallery.

1800 Philadelphia was the capital of the new nation and its intellectual and cultural center. It had a hospital, medical college, subscrip-
tion library, scientific and intellectual society, bank, and government
mint.[64] In 1683 William Penn had estimated there were eighty houses
in his new city. Indian delegates to Philadelphia in 1750 entered a
city of about 2,100 houses; forty years later they entered one with perhaps 9,000 houses, more than 400 shops and stores, and 176 taverns,
beer gardens, and coffeehouses.[65]

Philadelphia was not only the largest city in British North
America by the time of the Revolution but also the most ethnically
diverse. It drew most of its growing population from immigration,
and its population diversified as its seaborne trade expanded. In
addition to German-speaking immigrants, thousands of Scots-Irish
Presbyterians escaping rising rents, low wages, and high food costs
in the north of Ireland disembarked in Philadelphia. Ships that
carried food and flaxseed from Pennsylvania to Ireland filled up
with emigrants as well as linen for the return trip whenever hard
times struck, and whenever the linen industry tanked. Fewer than
10,000 people emigrated from Ulster to North America between
1680 and 1719; about 20,000 went in the 1720s, and perhaps as many
as 50,000 between 1730 and the start of the French and Indian War.
Most entered through Philadelphia and other Delaware River ports,
and many were indentured servants, bound by contract to work for
colonial masters for a period of years to pay off the cost of their passage. Thousands fanned out beyond Philadelphia, taking up lands
and displacing the Indian inhabitants.[66] Dr. Alexander Hamilton, a
Scottish physician who himself had emigrated to Maryland and who
visited Philadelphia in 1744, dined in a tavern, seated at a large ob-
long table "with a very mixed company" of twenty-five people that included Scots, English, Dutch, Germans, and Irish; Roman Catholics,
Anglicans, Presbyterians, Quakers, Newlight men, Methodists,
Seventh-day Adventists, Moravians, Anabaptists, and a Jew.[67] "The
town is now filled with inhabitants of many nations, who in regard to
their country, religion and trade are very different from each other,"
observed Peter Kalm a few years later.[68] Many African Americans
migrated to the city after Pennsylvania abolished slavery in 1780, and
free and enslaved African Americans constituted nearly 20 percent
of the population in 1790.[69] In addition to rubbing shoulders with
Quakers, indentured servants from Britain, Scots, Scots-Irish, Welsh,
German farmers, African slaves, and sailors from around the world
who were in port between voyages, Indian delegates in the 1790s
met refugees from the revolutions in France and Saint-Domingue

(present-day Haiti).[70] The center of Philadelphia was the most densely populated spot in North America. Most of the residents lived within four blocks of the waterfront, an area of one square mile.[71]

Images of an orderly Quaker community do not reflect the full reality of Philadelphia in the second half of the eighteenth century. Whereas its center boasted impressive civic works and an orderly urban existence, poorer outlying neighborhoods presented a very different picture. The laboring poor lived in squalid conditions, with inadequate food, clothing, and housing, struggled to make a living on skimpy wages, and faced the recurrent threat of destitution when periodic economic slumps produced wage cuts or unemployment. Women and children worked to supplement family incomes and help make ends meet, and many laborers adopted a transient lifestyle.[72] New market forces and changing economic conditions generated class divisions, social unrest, and changes in gender relations and sexual behavior.[73] Indian delegates to Philadelphia during the decade of national and international upheaval when it was the capital of the United States would have seen women taking increasingly active and public roles in the social, political, and cultural life of the city.[74]

Virginia, the largest British colony, had nearly 350,000 people in 1763, but the capital, Williamsburg, had no more than 2,000 residents, black and white. The largest urban center in Virginia was actually Norfolk, another port at the intersection of key trade networks. Norfolk thrived exporting timber, tar, and tobacco to Europe and provisions to the Caribbean, and it was the sixth-largest city in mainland British America by the second half of the eighteenth century. Like Baltimore, it had a population of more than 6,000 by 1776.[75] Annapolis, the capital of Maryland, was even smaller than Williamsburg. Andrew Burnaby, an English vicar, saw it in 1759 and reported, "None of the streets are paved, and the few public buildings here are not worth mentioning."[76]

The largest city in the southern colonies and the wealthiest in all the North American colonies was Charleston or Charles Town, the seat of government in South Carolina. Founded in 1670, it quickly became both an Atlantic seaport and the major center for trade with the southern Indian country. With a good harbor, seaborne trade with Europe and the West Indies, and a "circle" of trade with neighboring Indian nations, Charleston was "the Metropolis" of South Carolina, said the English naturalist and writer John Lawson, who began his travels from the town in 1700 accompanied by five other Englishmen, three Indian men, and one woman, the wife of their

Indian guide.[77] Focusing on Charleston exclusively as a port in the British Atlantic world ignores the inland Indian world that prompted and sustained the city: Charleston thrived because of trading paths to the hinterland as well as sea lanes across the Atlantic.[78] The deerskin trade with the Indians of the Southeast, especially the Yamasees, Creeks, and Cherokees, was key to its prosperity. The Cherokee Path ran between Charleston and Keowee, the principal Lower Cherokee town, and on to the Middle and Overhill Cherokee towns. A "white path" of peace, friendship, and trade linked Charleston to Upper Creek towns such as Okfuskee. Indian porters came and went as traders' pack trains delivered thousands of deerskins to Charleston's warehouses. Charleston exported to England an average of about 54,000 pounds of deerskins each year between 1699 and 1715, more than 355,000 pounds annually by 1758–59, and a total of more than 5 million pounds between 1739 and 1761. Those deerskins were hunted by Indian men, processed by Indian women, and transported by Indian porters or "burdeners" carrying packs weighing between 150 and 180 pounds, who then returned to their own towns with wares from Charleston.[79] Creek, Cherokee, and Catawba delegations also regularly traveled to Charleston. "This Town is of an old Standing and our Friendship is of an old Date," the Creek headman Malatchi reminded the governor in 1753, "and the Indians have frequently come down here."[80] A deerskin map, thought to have been drawn by a Catawba headman in 1721, when Catawbas, Creeks, and Cherokees were in the city to meet the new governor, shows Charleston on the left-hand side, with an inverted sailing ship in the harbor in the bottom corner, distinguished by its squares and street plan from the Indian nations represented by circles that are connected to Charleston by trading paths (Figure 1.4).[81]

Yet not all Indians who came to Charleston traveled along white paths. Indian traders transported Indian slaves from deep in the interior to be sold at auction in Charleston or shipped to sugar plantations in the West Indies. African and Indian slavery were key to the city's growth and prosperity. Governor Nathaniel Johnson and the South Carolina Council reported to the Board of Trade in 1708 that the population of the colony stood at 9,580, of whom 4,100 were African slaves and 1,400 were Indian slaves. Ships at Charleston's wharves unloaded slaves from Africa as well as from Barbados and Jamaica, and Charleston traded with Boston, Rhode Island, Pennsylvania, New York, and Virginia, "to which places we export Indian slaves, light deer skins drest, some tanned leather, pitch, tarr and a small quantity of rice."[82]

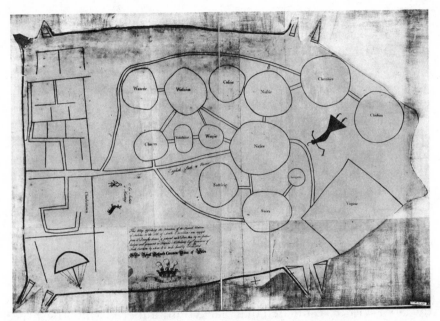

Figure 1.4 Catawba deerskin map, c.1721
"This map describing the scituation [sic] of the several nations of Indians to the NW of South
Carolina was coppyed [sic] from a draught drawn & painted on a deer skin by an Indian
Cacique and presented to Francis Nicholson Esqr. Governor of South Carolina by whom
it is most humbly dedicated to his Royal Highness George, Prince of Wales." Library of
Congress, Geography and Map Division.

John Lawson described Charleston as a town with "regular and
fair streets" and "great Additions of beautiful, large Brick-buildings,
besides a strong Fort." The inhabitants had grown wealthy through
trade, which supplied them with everything they needed for "genteel Living."[83] Governor James Glen in 1751 reported that many of
the houses cost £1,000 to £1,200 and the owners went to considerable expense in furnishing them: "Plate begins to shine upon their
side boards, and in proportion as they thrive they delight to have
good things from England."[84] Lord Adam Gordon estimated there
were about 1,500 houses, which "increase annually in a very surprising manner." Another visitor in 1765 counted 1,000 inhabited
houses and eight churches.[85] Although Charleston's streets were
broad and well laid out, they were not paved until 1800: sand
was more suitable for drainage and cleaning.[86] And, as in other
seaports, Charleston's dock area was notorious for dirt, stench, and
danger; rowdy sailors rendered the docks unsafe for decent women
even in daylight.[87]

Charleston was the major port of the South for shipping out rice, indigo, and Indian slaves bound for the Caribbean, and for shipping in African slaves. The Yamasee War in 1715, when Yamasees, Catawbas, and other Native peoples attacked English merchants across the Southeast, disrupted the deerskin trade and effectively ended the Indian slave trade, but from the 1730s to the 1820s Charleston experienced a golden age based on three low-country crops—rice, indigo, and Sea Island cotton—and, of course, slavery.[88] Josiah Quincy Jr., who was there in the 1770s, said "the general topics of conversation, when cards, the bottle, and occurrences of the day don't intervene, are of negroes, and the price of indigo and rice."[89] Charleston's population increased 400 percent in half a century. It had only about 8,000 inhabitants in 1763, but by the time of the Revolution it was the fourth-largest city in mainland British America and one of the forty largest in the English-speaking world.[90] Much of the increase was due to the import of African slaves. In Charleston as throughout the colony, "great multitudes" of black slaves performed the labor. Visitors estimated that blacks outnumbered whites by three or four to one.[91] Whatever the actual numbers, Indian people who went to Charleston saw more black faces than white ones.

In New Orleans, Indians met French, Spanish, and African people and their Creole descendants. Founded in 1718 in an area of Indigenous travel and trade linking the Mississippi Valley, the Gulf, and the Caribbean, New Orleans was the southwestern portal of France's North American empire, as Quebec was its northeastern portal, and like Quebec it commanded a key strategic location. Many Mississippian towns that served as trading and ceremonial centers had been abandoned by the time the French arrived, although the "Grand Village" of the Natchez still existed as a political, religious, and economic center for some 5,000 people in the area—a population that New Orleans did not begin to reach until the end of the French period. New Orleans was a planned city. The French engineer Adrien de Pauger had laid out the settlement in a classic eighteenth-century grid pattern, with a central square, church, and walls, but most of the buildings initially were simple wooden structures. New Orleans grew into a multiethnic community with a reputation as a lawless and disorderly place where French, Indians, Africans, poor freemen, soldiers, sailors of multiple nations, pirates, and smugglers mingled. Situated in an Indian world inhabited by the powerful Choctaws and multiple smaller tribes the French called *petites nations,* it was also a center for Indian diplomacy and trade that occupied a significant place in Indigenous networks of travel and exchange.[92]

Beyond these port cities, colonial towns were much smaller. St. Augustine in Florida, founded in the 1560s, was the oldest European town in North America, but 200 years later it was still small and confined by the water, swamps, and Indians around it. Roughly 3,000 Spaniards inhabited Florida by 1763, and most lived in or near St. Augustine, in the shadow of the fortress of San Marcos. Lord Adam Gordon said St. Augustine "has several good houses in it, the Streets are not ill laid out, but too narrow (a Spanish Mode)."[93]

Pittsburgh did not grow into an industrial and urban giant until the nineteenth century. The French made Fort Duquesne the hub of their Indian relations in the Ohio Valley and of their operations during the so-called French and Indian War, but the fort needed Indians more than Indians needed the fort, and it fell to the British in 1758 after the Indians withdrew their support. The British built Fort Pitt on the ruins of Fort Duquesne and it too became a focal point of Indian trade and diplomacy, but the community that grew up outside its walls never reached more than a few hundred people before the end of the century. When 1,136 Indian men, women, and children turned up for a treaty conference in August 1760, and when 1,100 Indians and their families arrived for a conference in the spring of 1768, their encampments would have dwarfed the embryonic settlement and turned Pittsburgh temporarily into an Indian town.[94] An English visitor in the 1780s wrote that Pittsburgh "increases very rapidly & bids fair to be very soon the Emporium, of the Western World." Yet the census of 1790 listed only 376 inhabitants, although the population passed 1,500 in 1800.[95]

Antoine de la Motte, Sieur de Cadillac, envisioned Detroit, which he founded in 1701, as the Paris of the West, the center of a grand empire built on Indian trade. He imagined creating a community where French colonists would live alongside Native peoples, whom he invited to settle on the outskirts of his fort. Located on the water corridor connecting Lake Erie with Lakes Huron and Michigan, it lay close to the Maumee-Wabash river system and the Indigenous populations of Ohio, Michigan, and Indiana. It contained a garrison and a resident population of colonists, but, like most French outposts in the West, it depended for its defense on Indian allies outside its palisades rather than on the manpower within. The population soon comprised French, Hurons, Odawas, Potawatomis, Ojibwes, Miamis, and the offspring of their unions, as well as Indian slaves. By the mid-1700s Fort Detroit had a population of between 200 (in the winter) and 400 (in the summer), with another 500 people of French back-ground living outside the fort, and villages of Odawa and Huron people nearby. Merchants trading furs, guns, ammunition, blankets, and brandy established Detroit as the center of an exchange network that stretched from Montreal to the Mississippi and a pivotal location in competing and overlapping European and Native worlds where people met for political negotiation and the rituals of diplomacy. By the middle of the eighteenth century, Detroit had grown from a fur trade outpost to an inland seaport, connected to Atlantic commerce and transnational merchandise.[96]

The British took possession of Detroit in 1760, but it remained essentially a French community and a fortified village. In 1763, there were some seventy or eighty houses within the fort, arranged in regular streets. Outside the fort, the larger community was laid out in a pattern similar to that of French settlements along the St. Lawrence: individual cabins along the river, with "longlot" plots of farmland stretching back from the riverbanks. French Canadian cottages dotted both sides of the river for about ten miles.[97] There were several Indian communities in the vicinity. Across the river a community of Hurons or Wyandots, according to British records, had 250 men, more than 1,000 people in all. There was a Potawatomi village on the western shore, about a mile below the fort, and an Odawa village a couple of miles up from the Wyandot village. The Ojibwes, Odawas, and Potawatomis, loosely joined in the Three Fires confederacy, represented one of the heaviest concentrations of pop-ulation in the Great Lakes; the British counted 720 warriors in the Detroit region in 1763. The settlers lived on good terms with the Indians, and many of the population were métis, people of mixed an-cestry.[98] By 1765 the population was more than 900. In 1770, Detroit had a population of 2,000 colonists and 2,500 Indians. As an inland seaport of the British empire, its economy and infrastructure con-tinued to grow.[99] After holding Detroit for a dozen years in contra-vention of the terms of the Peace of Paris that ended the Revolution, Britain transferred it to the United States in 1796.

The French established settlements alongside Indian commu-nities in Louisiana and the Illinois country, as well as in the Great Lakes basin. The Laclède/Chouteau family founded St. Louis in 1764 at the junction of the Ohio, Missouri, and Illinois Rivers, where mounds remained of the great Indian city that had flourished at Cahokia hundreds of years before. Several hundred Missouri men, women, and children turned up as Auguste Chouteau and his men were beginning construction, and they declared their intention to settle around the trading post. They even lent a hand building it. With a population in the hundreds rather than the thousands, colonial St. Louis was "a muddy, village-sized enclave in the middle of Indian country," but, historian Jay Gitlin cautions, it "was not a sleepy and isolated frontier town." Drawing trade from the powerful Osages and other Indian nations of the lower Missouri who gravitated to the post, and plugging those nations into the Atlantic trade system, St. Louis, like Cahokia, became a trade center in the heart of the continent, a crossroads where people from different cultures met and exchanged goods.[100] Under the Spanish regime, St. Louis was the site for annual distributions of presents to the Osages, Sioux, Iowas, Kansas, Pawnees, Omahas, Sauks, Foxes, Otos, Octoctatas, Missouris, and Kaskaskias.[101]

In the Southwest, small Spanish colonial settlements were dwarfed by neighboring Indigenous population and power. Founded in 1610, within a few years of Jamestown and Quebec, Santa Fe was a remote northern outpost, separated from the power bases of Spain's American empire, which lay many miles and many months to the south. In 1680, the Pueblo peoples of the Rio Grande Valley had besieged the town and expelled the Spaniards from New Mexico for a dozen years. Spain retook New Mexico in the 1690s and made Sante Fe the administrative capital, but the edicts of its governors carried little weight among Apaches and Comanches, who exercised real power over much of the Southwest. Comanches came to Santa Fe as one hub in the long-distance trade network based on horses and buffalos they operated on the southern plains. Plains Indians traveled to Santa Fe and San Antonio to trade for horses. Spanish Indian policy prohibited selling guns to Indians, but French and British firearms spread through intertribal trade networks in such numbers that by the 1770s southern Plains Indians were traveling to San Antonio to *sell* guns to Spanish citizens.[102]

Coastal cities and colonial towns farther inland existed on the peripheries of a vast continent that still in the eighteenth century was predominantly Native American. And, for all the growth of the urban centers in the north, as late as 1790, the three largest urban centers in North America were Havana in Cuba, Puebla in Mexico, and Mexico City.[103]

CHAPTER 2

Coming to Town

INDIAN PEOPLE TRAVELED A LOT, and they traveled far and wide, following forest paths and canoeing waterways that carried them from one communication network to another.[1] Keeping a path clear and white was a metaphor for maintaining good relationships between people, which was also a practical necessity for people who traveled to establish and renew bonds of peace, friendship, and exchange between clans, villages, and nations.[2] Clearing paths to colonial capitals extended networks of travel and communication to include other people and powers in those relationships of peace, friendship, and exchange. Indigenous diplomats regularly shuttled between Indian villages and colonial capitals, and sometimes between one colonial capital and another as they negotiated with—or played off—one power after another. Indian messengers carrying wampum belts brought news, information, and—occasionally—warnings to town.[3] Colonial governments dispatched runners with wampum belts to invite Indian delegates to town, and they followed Native protocols in ritually clearing the path to ease their journey. In 1732, for instance, Thomas Penn assured the Iroquois that he wanted "an open Road between Philadelphia and the Towns of the Six Nations" and would do all he could to keep it clear and straight. In 1757 Pennsylvania governor William Denny opened the way for western Indians to come and talk peace by sending them "a Large White Belt, with the Figure of a Man at Each End, and Streaks of Black, representing the Road from the Ohio to Philadelphia."[4]

Like other travelers, Indians passed through cities on their way to other destinations.[5] Sometimes they embarked from port cities on life-changing ocean voyages. Indian captives were held in Boston after the Pequot War in 1637 and King Philip's War in 1675–76 before being shipped to the Caribbean as slaves, and Indian slaves from across the Southeast passed through Charleston en route to the same fate in the late seventeenth and early eighteenth centuries. The four "Indian kings" who arrived in Boston prior to embarking on their transatlantic voyage to London in 1710 stayed for several months (and ran up substantial bills in food, lodging, and drink while they were there). They returned to Boston on their way home.[6] The Illinois, Missouri, Oto, and Osage Indians who traveled to Paris in 1725 went first to New Orleans to board ship. After their defeat by the French, hundreds of Natchez captives were transported through New Orleans and shipped to the Caribbean colony of Saint-Domingue in 1731.[7] Returning transatlantic travelers also passed through port cities. Ostenaco and the two other Cherokees who traveled to London in 1762 docked at Charleston on their way home and spent time there with the governor and council of South Carolina.[8] Joseph Brant sailed to England from Quebec in November 1775; when he returned in July 1776, he disembarked at Staten Island, across the bay from New York. By then, the colonies had declared their independence and the city was in rebel hands.[9]

Most Indians who came to town, however, stayed to talk, to trade, to resolve disputes, and, increasingly, to make treaties ceding land. Sometimes they came just to visit. Sassoonan or Allumapees, a Lenape or Delaware chief at Shamokin, was a regular visitor to Philadelphia in the early eighteenth century. Pennsylvanian officials favored Sassoonan as their go-to chief, ascribing to him an authority no Delaware possessed, and he played the role, making himself useful, exaggerating his influence, and bringing home gifts and goods that enhanced his status.[10] Delawares were frequently in Philadelphia in the 1730s to discuss land disputes. The Pennsylvania proprietors, John and Thomas Penn, were pushing to clear Indian title to the upper Delaware Valley, and secured their goal in 1737 when four Delaware chiefs—Nutimus, Manakihikon, Tishcohan, and Lapowinsa (see Plates 1 and 2)—went to Philadelphia and confirmed the notorious "Walking Purchase" deed that resulted in the loss of more than a million acres.[11] However, when Sassoonan arrived with a party of twenty-five men, women, and children in August 1736, he told city officials they had "not come on any particular Business, or to treat about any thing of Importance, but only to pay a friendly visit to their Brethren, whose Welfare they think themselves obliged to enquire after, as they and the Indians are one People."[12] A Kansa chief known as Coeur Qui Brule likewise wrote to the lieutenant governor of Louisiana in 1800 saying that he had wanted to see St. Louis for a long time ("depuis longtemps je désire voir la ville").[13]

Regular visitors to Quebec, New York, Philadelphia, or Charleston followed familiar paths or water routes. Indian people from the Susquehanna Valley, for example, took a branch of the Susquehanna up the Conestoga to its source, trekked three or four miles overland to the source of French Creek, and then descended the Schuylkill into Philadelphia.[14] Others traveled less often and covered greater distances. In 1695 an Ojibwe chief named Zhingobins (Little Balsam Fir) and a Mdewakanton Dakota (eastern Sioux) chief named Tiyoskate (Plays in the Lodge) with a fleet of a dozen canoes journeyed almost 1,000 miles from the western Great Lakes to Montreal to offer trade and alliance to the French governor, Louis de Buade, Comte de Frontenac. Hundreds of French-allied Indians converged on Montreal that summer. Spreading out a beaver robe and laying on it twenty-two arrows, representing the villages of his tribe, Tiyoskate asked for a path to be opened so that his people could receive iron weapons in trade from the French.[15] Sioux delegates repeated the journey for the Great Peace held at Montreal in the summer of 1701. Other delegations followed. In 1742, the Marquis de Beauharnois, governor of New France, invited all western nations to a council in Montreal. Two Mdewakanton chiefs, Sacred Born and Leaf Shooter, made the two-month voyage from the Upper Mississippi, traveling, they said, "from halfway across the world" to negotiate an alliance. They met with the governor and were hosted in the homes of Montreal's elite. By the middle of the century, Sioux visits to Montreal had become almost a regular event.[16] At the beginning of the American Revolution, in 1776, the Mdewakanton chief Wabasha, or Red Leaf, who had visited the governor of New France in Montreal almost thirty years earlier, traveled again all the way from the upper Mississippi Valley to Quebec City, this time to reaffirm the Dakota alliance with King George III. British officials welcomed him as a man of "uncommon abilities" and "a prince of an Indian" with a formidable warrior force behind him. Governor Guy Carleton hosted him at a state dinner, and Wabasha was taken aboard a fifty-gun man-of-war, HMS *Isis,* and given an eight-gun salute.[17]

Cherokee delegates from Chota traveled an estimated 500 miles to Charleston, and Attakullakulla described his journey to Williamsburg in 1751 as long and tedious: "We have traveled through Bushes and Bryers to see our friends in Virginia," he said.[18] Chickasaws traveled hundreds of miles from the lower Mississippi Valley to Charleston to "renew their Friendship."[19] Eleven Choctaws arrived in the fall of 1760 after "a long Journey, it being four Moons since we left our Nation," as they told their colonial hosts. On the way they stopped for two months in Creek country and then went to Savannah and conferred with the governor of Georgia.[20] A Choctaw chief named Franchimastabé led a delegation to Mobile to make a treaty with Spain in 1784. Another Choctaw chief, Taboca, with a delegation that included ten women, journeyed more than two months to Hopewell, North Carolina, to attend a treaty with the United States in the winter of 1786. They apparently spent a month in Charleston, where local newspapers advertised for "Any Person who can speak the Chactaw, or Chickesaw language, so as to serve as Interpreter to the Chactaw Indians now in Charlestown." Taboca, who described himself as the "Great Traveller" and "a headman in my nation, to receive and give out talks," went on to visit Philadelphia in June 1787, when the Constitutional Convention was meeting. He met Benjamin Franklin, George Washington, and Henry Knox. The Spanish governor Manuel Gayoso de Lemos noted in a dispatch that Washington treated Taboca "with great civility," opened his house to him, and made him "welcome at the most private times." Taboca returned home by boat down the Ohio and the Mississippi.[21] Other delegates traveled similar distances. It was 800 miles from the closest Miami town in the Ohio country to Philadelphia.[22] Delegates from the Wabash and Illinois tribes covered some 1,600 miles traveling to Philadelphia and back in 1792–93. Their leader, the Kaskaskia chief Jean Baptiste DuCoigne, had made the trip east before, visiting Virginia governor Thomas Jefferson during the Revolution.

The Choctaws who made the trek to Hopewell saw their journey as a spiritual voyage, hedged about by ritual, as well as a physical and political trip.[23] The written records tell little about Indian travels that occurred "offstage," as it were, and less about how Indian people understood and experienced that travel, but it is clear that they often imbued their journeys along white paths of peace to colonial cities with a profound spiritual meaning. Emissaries on diplomatic business did not take just any route, or even necessarily the most direct and most traveled paths. As Conrad Weiser noted, they followed "the usual Road that ambassadors travel."[24] They offered tobacco and other gifts at particular sites along the way and observed protocols to access or appease spirits that existed "in everything, in stones, rivers, trees, mountains, roads, &c."[25] Passing through the territories of other Indian nations required proper care and attention to protocol; so too, presumably, did leaving familiar forest paths and embarking on roads that led them past fields and fences. On the final stages of the journey to town, the ritual stopping points were inns and taverns rather than rocks or waterfalls, the sacred sites were marked by churches, and Euro-American norms of travel conduct prevailed.[26]

Like Europeans who ventured into Indian country, Indians who traveled to cities often did so warily. Hostile populations, both Indian and white, might render their journeys perilous, especially in times of war. After the Oneida chief Shickellamy died in 1748, his son John (Tachnechdorus) served as the Iroquois representative in the Susquehanna Valley dealing with Pennsylvania. But the French and Indian War in the mid-1750s shattered earlier patterns of coexistence; now war parties ravaged the frontier and the Pennsylvania government offered bounties on the scalps of Indian men, women, and children. Traveling between the Susquehanna and Philadelphia, John Shickellamy was cursed and insulted by "fearful ignorant people" who told him, "to his face, that they had a good mind to Scalp him."[27] As peacemaking efforts gathered traction a few years later, officials issued passports requiring military and civil officers to offer assistance to Indian delegates and ensure their safe passage to and from Philadelphia.[28] William Denny ordered an escort for Teedyuscung, "as this will be the most respectful to the Chief, and the most likely to keep both the Country People and the Indians from committing any Irruptions on one another."[29] Animosities toward Indians during the Revolution were so charged that Governor Patrick Henry of Virginia had to order militia companies to protect Cherokee delegates on their way to Williamsburg from "a Design of assassinating those Chiefs," and several groups of backcountry settlers planned to murder a Delaware delegation on its way to Philadelphia in 1779.[30] And in the midst of war with the western tribes in 1792, the United States government assigned officers to help get Iroquois delegates safely through the Susquehanna Valley settlements.[31] As if escalating interethnic hostilities did not pose danger enough, travelers on the roads near Philadelphia also faced the threat of highway robbers.[32]

Like all travelers, Indians had to contend with bad weather, bad luck, swollen rivers, and, as they got closer to town, bad roads with deep ruts.[33] And there was always a possibility of accidents. The Seneca chief Cornplanter "left his two wives & a number of Children in Care of the Commanding officer" at Fort Pitt and traveled to

Philadelphia to visit Congress in 1786.[34] In April he traveled by coach from Philadelphia to New York. Unfortunately, the coach overturned. The silver gorget he was wearing gashed his forehead, leaving his left eye permanently disfigured and costing him his sight in that eye.[35]

Sometimes other Indians added to the peril. Iroquois war parties regularly threatened western Indians traveling to Montreal to trade in the seventeenth century. Creek warriors attacked Piominko and other Chickasaw chiefs on their way to see President Washington in New York in September 1789, and Piominko narrowly escaped. The Chickasaws reached Richmond, Virginia, in mid-October, but the length of the journey, bad weather, and the lateness of the season forced them to abandon plans to continue to New York; they met with Governor Beverley Randolph and the Virginia Assembly instead.[36]

During the early years of the Republic, the federal government regularly assisted Indian delegations by making travel arrangements, providing water transportation and horses, and furnishing certificates, supplies, and escorts for the journey. It also paid daily stipends, covered the costs of their laundry and "entertainment" in the city, and in some cases bought them seats on the stagecoach between Philadelphia and New York.[37]

Whether before or after the Revolution, city authorities went out of their way to ensure that delegates received a warm welcome when they arrived. Although colonial images pictured Indians slinking quietly away from burgeoning cities, Indians who came on state visits were often welcomed and greeted with fanfare. In 1721, for instance, Sir William Keith, the governor of Pennsylvania, invited the Iroquois to come to Philadelphia "to Visit our Families and Children born there, where we can provide better for you and make you more welcome, for People always receive their Friends best at their own Houses." As peacemaking efforts with the Delawares got under way in 1757 during the French and Indian War, Governor Denny insisted that Teedyuscung come to Philadelphia, "where he will find a hearty Reception from me and the good People of this Province."[38] Sometimes military escorts met delegates as they approached town, and Indians entered to salutes of musket or cannon fire and warm words from civic dignitaries. Governor James Hamilton welcomed Cayuga messengers to Philadelphia in early spring 1762 by metaphorically wiping away "the Ice and Snow which have hurt and bruised your Legs and Feet in so long a Journey."[39]

Indian people were familiar with such ceremonies of welcome in their own diplomatic protocols. Iroquois communities ritually

greeted visiting emissaries "at the woods' edge" and escorted them
to the site of negotiations, symbolically clearing their eyes, ears,
hearts, and minds with words and wampum strings to create a
healthy environment for open and harmonious exchange. Indian
delegates performed their own rituals when they entered alien
urban environments. In fall 1721 a Chickasaw chief and a group
of Cherokees arrived in Williamsburg with a proposal for opening
trade with Virginia. When the Indians were brought into the council
chamber, it was recorded, "they entered singing, according to their
Custom; And the Great Man of the Chickasaws carrying in his hand
a Calamett of Peace, first presented a parcel of Deer Skins, which
he spread upon the Shoulders of the Governor and divers of the
Council." He was making the council chamber a Chickasaw ritual
space before he began his speech. Twenty-one years later, in the
council chamber at Charleston, Chickasaw delegates saluted the governor "after the manner of their Country . . . by laying the Wings of
Eagles over his Shoulders."[40]

When the "Indian kings" passed through the streets of London
in 1710 they swept up "in impromptu festivals" people walking
through the city. The English poet, playwright, and politician Joseph
Addison recalled, "I often mix'd with the Rabble and followed them
a whole Day together, being wonderfully struck with the Sight of everything that is new or uncommon."[41] Indian visitors were much more
common on the streets of Philadelphia or Charleston than in Paris
or London in the eighteenth century, but they still attracted curiosity and crowds. City newspapers regularly informed their readers
when Indian delegations were arriving or passing through on their
way to do business elsewhere. Dr. Alexander Hamilton found himself in Boston in 1744 at the same time an Iroquois delegation led by
the Mohawk chief Hendrick—"a bold, intrepid fellow"—was there
for a conference with delegates from the New England tribes. "We
were called to the windows in the auction room by a noise in the
street which was occasioned by a parade of Indian chiefs marching
up the street. . . . The fellows all had laced hats, and some of them
laced matchcoats and ruffled shirts, and a multitude of plebs of their
own complexion followed them."[42] In June that year, the Onondaga
chief Canasatego and 252 Iroquois people arrived in Lancaster,
Pennsylvania, some sixty miles west of Philadelphia, for a treaty
conference with commissioners from Maryland, Pennsylvania, and
Virginia. By the 1760s Lancaster was a busy trading hub, and by
the 1780s it merited description as "the largest inland Town in the
United States."[43] In 1744, however, it was just fifteen years old and

still a small frontier town. Nevertheless, a crowd of people turned out, curious onlookers from the locality, eager to witness the big event. They followed the Indian cavalcade to the courthouse, where the commissioners were dining, and Canasatego sang a song in his native language, calling on the assembled parties to renew previous treaties and make a new one.[44]

The scenes in Boston near the end of the century were not unlike those in London near the beginning. "When the Indian Chiefs lately paid us a visit," a writer for the Boston *Mercury* reported in May 1793, "all ranks of people were seized with a notion of gazing at them, though the sight of an Indian can be no novelty in this country. Observing an uncommon gathering in the street, people running out of houses and shops without hats, I eagerly enquired the cause (supposing there was a fire or some terrible calamity) when behold two Indians were taking a walk. In this manner they were harassed daily, till I believe the poor fellows were heartily glad to take their departure."[45] In Philadelphia, gangs of boys dogged the heels of Indian delegates through the streets and seem to have been a recurrent nuisance, firing toy arrows and playing with marbles on the pavement. During the visit of an Iroquois delegation in spring 1792, one concerned citizen complained in the press about "the unmannerly behavior of the boys towards the Indian Chiefs now in this city."[46]

It cannot have been easy for Indian people to make their way through throngs of curious onlookers, no matter how warm the welcome. After all, city dwellers read and heard reports of Indian raids on the frontiers, some citizens who had lost loved ones no doubt harbored hatreds, and old fears and cries for vengeance might rise up at any time. Indian delegates arriving in the city may have experienced an ordeal not unlike that of white captives who had to run a gauntlet between rows of people brandishing sticks when they arrived in Indian communities.[47]

Voluntary visitors to Indian communities received much better treatment, however. When Father Jacques Marquette and his companions arrived among the Illinois Indians in 1673, "all these people, who had never seen any Frenchmen among them, could not cease looking at us," he wrote; but "all this was done noiselessly, and with marks of great respect for us." As the Frenchmen were escorted through a town of 300 houses after a feast, "an orator continually harangued to oblige all the people to come to see us without annoying us."[48] In their own towns, said Benjamin Franklin, curious Indians observed newcomers from a discreet distance; in contrast, "when any of them come into our towns, our people are apt to croud round them, gaze upon them, and incommode them where they desire to be private; this they esteem great rudeness, and the effect of the want of instruction in the rules of civility and good manners."[49] After years of missionary work among the Indians of Pennsylvania and Ohio during the Revolution and the early years of the Republic, Moravian John Heckewelder said that Indians "sometimes amuse themselves by passing in review those customs of the white people which appear to them most striking. They observe, amongst other things, that when whites meet together, many of them, and sometimes all, speak at the same time, and they wonder how they can thus hear and understand each other." Not only did white people talk loudly, Indians said, but "when Indians come among them, they crowd quite close up to us, stare at us, and almost tread upon our heels to get nearer. We, on the contrary, though perhaps not less curious than they are, to see a new people or a new object, keep at a reasonable distance, and yet see what we wish to see."[50]

First-time Indian visitors surely experienced a degree of culture shock during their first days in town. Europeans built different kinds of buildings with new styles of architecture around different structures of space, and with different concepts of land use. Often laid out in grid form, and characterized by squares instead of circles, cities were visible manifestations of an alien culture and way of life for Indian people. In addition to adjusting to the physical urban landscape, Indians entered a new sensory environment. They heard and smelled the city as well as saw it. The hubbub of crowded streets would have bombarded their senses with a cacophony of noises: iron-rimmed cartwheels rattling on cobblestones, market traders hawking their wares, mechanical clanking from mills, church bells tolling. Although we cannot assume that Native Americans responded to sights, sounds, and smells in the same ways that colonial Americans did (or that seventeenth- and eighteenth-century people responded to them as we would),[51] they surely would have turned up their noses at the noxious smells that emanated from tanneries, tallow chandlers, privies, and sewers, and at the odors generated by large numbers of humans and animals in confined spaces.

The Mohegan preacher Samson Occom, in London in 1766 raising money for the future Dartmouth College, left a famous account of his first Sunday evening in the city, where he "Saw Such Confusion as I never Dreamt of—there was Some at Churches Singing & Preaching, in the Streets some Cursing, Swaring & Damning one another, others was hollowing, Whestling, talking gigling, & Laughing, & Coaches and footmen passing and repassing, Crossing and Cross-Crossing, and the poor Begars Praying, Crying, and Beging upon their knees."[52] Indian people in American cities presumably experienced less assault on their senses than did Occom amid the chaos and cacophony of the imperial capital, but consider John Adams's entry in his diary in March 1759:

> Who can study in Boston Streets? I am unable to observe the various Objects, that I meet, with sufficient Precision. My Eyes are so diverted with Chimney Sweeps, Carriers of Wood, Merchants, Ladies, Priests, Carts, Horses, Oxen, Coaches, Market men and Women, Soldiers, Sailors, and my Ears with the Rattle Gabble of them all that I cant think long enough in the Street upon any one Thing to start and pursue a Thought. I cant raise my mind above this mob Croud of Men, Women, Beasts and Carriages, to think steadily. My Attention is sollicited every moment by some new object of sight, or some new sound. A Coach, Cart, a Lady or a Priest, may at any Time, by breaking a Couplet, disconcert a whole Page of excellent Thoughts.[53]

It is safe to assume that people from Norridgewock, Buffalo Creek, or Chota who arrived in Boston, Philadelphia, or Charleston would have experienced at least as much sensory overload when they encountered the city as Adams did after traveling a dozen miles or so from Braintree, Massachusetts.

City talk would also have taken them aback. William Penn said that Indians "speake little, but fervently & with Elegancy."[54] Mi'kmaq people in Nova Scotia ostensibly told the French missionary Chrestien Le Clercq in the 1670s that "Indians never interrupt the one who is speaking, and they condemn, with reason, those dialogues and those indiscreet and irregular conversations where each one of the company wishes to give his ideas without having the patience to listen to those of the others." For this reason, the missionary added, "they compare us to ducks and geese, which cry out, say they, and which talk all together like the French."[55] Even John Adams, who was not known for holding his own tongue, noted that New Yorkers "talk very loud, very fast and altogether."[56] A Scottish visitor in the 1790s said that the Indians he met "never speak in a hasty or rapid manner, but in a soft, musical, and harmonious voice."[57] In addition to the noise and loud talk, Indian people must have been taken aback by the profanity; as Warren Johnson observed, "There is noe Oath in the Indian Language."[58]

Yet Indians who came to busy cities may have been less surprised than some other visitors by the babel of languages they heard. Native America was crowded by multiple language families and hundreds of languages long before Europeans arrived and added their languages to the mix. By the time of the Revolution, for instance, Indians in upstate New York were accustomed to hearing not only Mohawk, Oneida, Onondaga, Cayuga, Seneca, and Tuscarora spoken, but also English, French, High Dutch, and Low Dutch.[59] What language city residents spoke may have troubled Indian visitors less than *how* they spoke. Indians may have been discomfited by loud and aggressive talk, but they were not always ignorant of its content. Although French, Dutch, and English interpreters translated multiple Indian languages during the Albany Congress in 1754, Thomas Pownall, a future governor of New Jersey and Massachusetts who was there as an observer, reported, "Many of the Indians know English. Many almost all the Albany people speak Indian." The Mohawk chief Hendrick said: "There are some of our People who have large open Ears and talk a little broken English and Dutch, so that they sometimes hear what is said by the Christian Settlers near them."[60] Various reports in the 1750s noted that the Delawares "all speake English more or less" or "mostly all Spake English."[61] William Denny reported to the Pennsylvania proprietors that "almost all the Delawares speak English, and Teedyuscung We know does." Teedyuscung's fluency caused consternation because he and other Delaware leaders "went frequently to People's Houses, and might converse with whom they please," which was not what Denny wanted when Quakers were working, in the words of trader and agent George Croghan, "to Sett up Teedyuscung Against ye Governor."[62] Although Teedyuscung understood English, he insisted on having an interpreter at treaty conferences to translate his words for the English and their words for him, and he took the unprecedented step of demanding his own clerk, saying he "would by no means be led by the Nose." He got his request. His clerk was Charles Thomson, who published *An Enquiry into the Causes of the Alienation of the Delaware and Shawnee Indians from the British Interest* in 1759 and signed the Declaration of Independence in 1776.[63]

When western Indians went to Montreal in 1694–95, the French were preparing to invade Iroquois country and the visitors "saw every thing had a marvelous aspect for the war that had been so loudly preached in their villages."[64] Colonial governments on both sides of the Atlantic saw visits by Indian delegations as opportunities to impress Indigenous leaders with the power and progress on display in their cities, and colonial officials arranged tours and demonstrations to that end.

The European convention of firing cannon to honor and impress visitors as they arrived and departed was well established in America by 1700, and Indian people frequently welcomed visitors to their villages with rounds of gunfire. Still, it could prove alarming. Gunfire from ships anchored at Philadelphia that summer not only frightened local women and children but also prompted three Senecas, who were there negotiating with the government, to make a hasty departure, thinking the gunfire a sign of hostility toward them. The governor explained that firing guns when friends were coming aboard was an English custom, and he arranged for the Senecas to go on board the vessel, which they did, according to the Provincial Council minutes, to their "great satisfaction."[65] The four "Indian kings" were impressed by British power even before they set sail for England. While they waited for their ship in Boston, they watched English regiments display their firepower, saw cannon fire from the castle, and sat in a small dinghy surrounded by five battleships that fired volleys from their decks. Each chief was given an army uniform trimmed with gold and silver lace.[66] Cherokee delegates in Charleston in 1721 were taken on board HMS *Flamborough*, which they evidently talked about at length when they got home.[67]

In the fall of 1723, Boston welcomed a delegation from the Six Nations, Mohicans, and Scaghticooks. After a conference with Governor William Dummer and the General Assembly, the Indians were treated to a display of new technology—a gun that, although loaded just once, fired eleven times in two minutes. They were then presented with an ox, which they killed with arrows, "dress'd according to their own Custom," and cooked in a kettle over a fire on Boston Common. The governor and "several of our principal Gentlemen favour'd them with their presence," the *Boston Gazette* reported; there was music and dancing, and several thousand spectators turned out "to behold and hear their barbarous Singing and Dancing."[68]

Rival colonies tried to outdo each other in the hospitality and generosity they showed their Indigenous guests. When South Carolina failed to deliver the trade it had promised, Cherokees turned to Virginia, and Williamsburg gave them appropriate attention. In August 1751, Attakullakulla led a delegation to Williamsburg as an "Embassador from the Emperor of Chota to negotiate a Treaty of Peace and Commerce with this Government," reported the *Virginia Gazette*. The president of the Virginia Council assured the Cherokees that "everything will be provided for you, while you continue here, to render the Place agreeable to you." Council member John Blair

noted in his diary that he made arrangements with the owner of the
Raleigh Tavern to have the Indians "accommodated" at the Apollo
Room while they waited for the president of the council, and that
the Indians "marched in good order with beat of drum through
the town, and made a handsome appearance in their new clothes."
There was almost an ugly incident when a party of Nottaways also
showed up and the Cherokees squared off for a fight, but several
gentlemen intervened and got the two groups to meet in the marketplace, "each Party singing the Song of Peace. After many of their
accustomed Ceremonies, they joined Hands and smoked the Pipe
of Peace together." Such a large crowd gathered to watch that the
Indians had to relocate to the courthouse to settle their differences.
The Cherokees spent the next evening at Blair's house and left
"much delighted with ye musick of Spinnet."[69]

The so-called emperor himself, Amouskossitte, came in the
fall of the following year "with his Empress and their Son the young
Prince, attended by several of his Warriors and great Men and their
Ladies." They were received at the Governor's Palace "with all the
Marks of Civility and Friendship" and attended the theater. The
city was "illuminated" to celebrate King George II's birthday on
November 9, and Amouskossitte and his wife and son attended "a
ball, and a very elegant entertainment at the Palace," where there
was "a brilliant appearance of ladies and gentlemen," followed by
a fireworks display.[70] Cherokee chiefs received the red-carpet treatment again in Williamsburg during the French and Indian War, when
Virginia needed them as military allies rather than just trade part-
ners. On his arrival in 1756, Ostenaco and his wife rode down Duke
of Gloucester Street in Governor Robert Dinwiddie's coach between
lines of militia forming an honor guard and were invited to dinner
at the College of William and Mary. Governor Francis Fauquier, who
took office in 1758, said Ostenaco was "much caressed and courted"
by his predecessor.[71]

Colonial officials saw to the Indians' needs and comforts, but
the visits were expensive and governments also took care not to
be too extravagant. The sums expended varied according to who
was visiting, why, and when. A young Conestoga chief, Tagotolessa,
whom the English called "Civility," came to Philadelphia with an interpreter named Harry to deliver a message in June 1713, and the
council "Ordered that care be taken of them whilst in Town, and that
the Treasurer (Civility being now one of the Chiefs of their nation)
provide for him a good Stroud, a Shirt, a hatt, and a pair of Stockins
& a match coat for Harry, with some small tokens for his children,

with some Rum, Tobacco & bread." There were more gifts for Civility when he was in Philadelphia two years later.[72] Civility's fortunes declined over time, however. He postponed a visit to Philadelphia in 1728 because the death of his only child "putts all other thoughtts out of my mind That I do nothing butt Crye Every Day, and Cannot bear to Come Into the Sightt of my friends."[73] Conestogas continued to visit Philadelphia in these years, but Civility lost his influence as Shickellamy increased his.[74] When Civility accompanied a group of Oneidas and half a dozen Onondagas to Philadelphia in September 1734, the council was unsure what would be the appropriate gift to give the Indians in return for their present of skins and wampum: "It was observed," read the official report, "that they had come hither without any Authority from the Six Nations; had nothing of Importance to deliver, and were only to be regarded as Privat Persons, and therefore, to discourage others from visits of this kind, it might not be amiss to give them no more than just the value of what they had presented." The council settled on £20 worth of gifts.[75] Civility's stock continued to diminish. Two years later, Iroquois delegates in Philadelphia told colonial officials that Civility had no power to sell land and if he did so "the Indians will utterly disown him."[76]

British colonial officials were less inclined to pinch pennies when Indian delegates came to town at times of escalating tensions with the French. In such circumstances, hosting and entertaining Indians was cheap at the price and, Governor George Thomas told commissioners from Virginia and Maryland in 1744, "will not put you to so much Expence in Twenty Years as the carrying on a War against them will do in One."[77] With war against France looming and the Anglo-Iroquois alliance on the verge of fracturing, Hendrick and the Mohawks who attended the Albany Congress in the summer of 1754 "were handsomely entertained at the Court House." Six months later, in January 1755, Hendrick and a party of Mohawks traveled to Philadelphia at the governor's invitation. Members of the governor's council, which had been tight-fisted when Civility came to town twenty years earlier, met them on their way and asked them to pause and give the city time to plan for their arrival. The Mohawks entered along Second Street with the town militia drawn up on both sides of the street, and a crowd of people followed "with Acclimations of Huzza for King Henry [Hendrick]." The delegates stayed for ten days and "were elegantly entertained by the Mayor." Hendrick was feted as a celebrity and had his portrait painted (see Plate 3). He was killed at the Battle of Lake George that September.[78]

The Seneca Guyasuta, who had fought *against* the English, merited no bean counting either. William Johnson described him as "a great Chief of much Capacity and vast Influence among all the Nations." In the fall of 1772 "the House agreed to allow £25 to be given by his honor as a present to Keyashuta, the Seneca Indian Chief, now in town on a visit to the Government."[79]

Teedyuscung visited Philadelphia so many times in the 1750s that the colonial capital was as much a part of his orbit as were the Indian towns in the Susquehanna and Wyoming Valleys, and more so than the western Delaware towns in the Ohio country. Teedyuscung proclaimed himself "king" of the Delawares, which he was not, and expected royal treatment when he came to town. Timothy Horsfield, a justice of the peace at Bethlehem, tried in vain to discourage Teedyuscung from going to Philadelphia in October 1757, "being senceable he will not only be a troublesome Guest but bring Charge on the Province."[80] But the war with France was going badly and the following July, as Teedyuscung and fifty Indians approached Philadelphia for negotiations that would eventually lead to peace with the Ohio tribes, the governor sent Conrad Weiser and provincial secretary Richard Peters to meet the delegates at Germantown and escort them to town. City officials conducted ceremonies of welcome and condolence with wampum strings. For his part, Teedyuscung brought a teenage captive named Sarah Decker and handed her over to the governor as a gesture of peace.[81]

Indian delegates brought gifts as well as received gifts—such exchanges were, as noted, an essential lubricant of diplomacy—and were not above exploiting and escalating the practice. The custom of presenting colonial governors with beaver pelts apparently tempted these governors to try to outdo one another and be lavish in *their* gifts to Indians. Iroquois delegates at a council in Albany in August 1700 received so many gifts that they sold some of them to town residents in exchange for beaver skins—an interesting reversal of fur trade exchange roles on the streets of Albany—and then added the pelts to the presents they gave the governor.[82] Bringing and giving gifts also conveyed messages. In the summer of 1730 Chikagou, who had been to Paris five years before, led a delegation of Illinois Indians to New Orleans. To show their allegiance to the French, they prayed and demonstrated their knowledge of Christianity and brought presents of calumet pipes; to show their wealth and power, they brought gifts of buffalo skins and Comanche slaves.[83]

Indian men were often accompanied by their wives ("who we always want with us," said Kahnawake Mohawk delegates in 1735[84]) and children; hence delegations could number several hundred people. Delegates usually traveled to treaty conferences in the summer to coincide with their seasonal hunting and planting cycle, and many women and children tagged along to take advantage of the food and gifts provided by their hosts and to go shopping. Their arrival gave a boost to the urban economy, as tailors, silversmiths, gunsmiths, and blacksmiths sold their wares and also repaired kettles, hoes, knives, and guns that visiting Indians brought to be mended.[85] Little is recorded about what Indian women did while they were in town, but they would not have been idle. In addition to cooking and caring for children and weaving and selling baskets, they were kept busy weaving the wampum belts that were essential for conducting negotiations and for recording the agreements that were made. At the Treaty of Easton in 1756, for example, after a messenger arrived with 5,000 white wampum beads, Indian women made "a Belt of a fathom long & sixteen Beads wide," with the figure of a man, representing the governor of Pennsylvania, in the center and five figures on either side, representing the ten Indian nations present.[86] Indian women in the cities presumably had more interaction than their men with the African American, Native American, and Euro-American women, free and unfree, married and single, whom they encountered as consumers, producers, traders, washerwomen, and service providers in the streets, shops, marketplaces, and alleys.[87]

Colonial authorities sometimes tried to limit the number of Indian visits and the number of visitors. They particularly discouraged Indians from coming to town uninvited and without prior notice, as Civility had done, which left them scrambling to make appropriate arrangements for welcoming, accommodating, and provisioning their unexpected guests. More Iroquois arrived in Philadelphia in the fall of 1736 than had been there for many years, and they remained in the city at a substantial cost to the government, which voted to furnish them £200 worth of gifts.[88] George Thomas invited fifty Iroquois chiefs to Philadelphia in June 1742, "but the Wants of these people were so pressing that they very much exceeded that Number, in Hopes of obtaining Relief from us." By the time Shawnees, Delawares, Conoys, and Conestogas joined, the total number reached about 250, which strained the city's resources of both lodging and funding. The numbers may have been swelled by famine in Indian country.[89] Surprised at the large numbers of Indians coming to visit that spring, James Hamilton told the Cayuga delegation in April 1762: "Instead of such a large number of young men, Women, & Children, who occasion a heavy charge on these occasions, We should think it would be as well to appoint a proper number of your principal Men."[90] The government of South Carolina in 1736 instructed its agents among the Creeks and Cherokees to invite as few chiefs as possible to Charleston and give ample notice of their coming. Governor James Glen told Cherokee delegates in November 1751 that he had sent for a few headmen "but many more came than I expected." South Carolina passed legislation in 1762 to regulate the Cherokee trade in part because "the coming down of the Cherokee Indians to Charles Town on frivolous Occasions, hath been attended with great Expence to the Province," and it hoped to curb the traffic.[91]

What European colonists regarded as surprise visits for frivolous purposes sometimes were anything but that. For Europeans, written treaties were enough to cement friendship and alliance. Indian people, however, viewed them as pacts that needed to be regularly renewed and refreshed by in-person meetings and the exchange of gifts, which entailed traveling time and again to the cities where the alliances had been made. What colonial officials regarded as uninvited visits were often culturally mandated diplomatic necessities.

Discouraging Indians from visiting town could prove a tricky business. In the summer of 1749 about 260 men, women, and children from eleven different tribes (the Six Nations, Delawares, Shawnees, Mohicans, Nanticokes, and Tutelos) headed to Philadelphia. Conrad Weiser told Canasetego he should not go to town "with Such a great number of people that had no Business there at all" other than to get drunk and run up expenses, and warned there would not be enough food for them. Canasatego took umbrage. Iroquois delegates had always brought people with them when they came to Philadelphia "and never have been reprimanded for it after this manner," he fumed; "perhaps it is because you got all our lands that you wanted from us and you don't like to see us any more. . . . We therefore will return to our own Country and give over going to Philadelphia. [A]nd We Will not trouble our Brethren in philad[elph]ia nor you again." Realizing he had overstepped the mark, Weiser promptly backtracked; his sentiments were his own, he assured Canasatego, not those of their brothers in Philadelphia. The Indians continued on their way and arrived in Philadelphia on August 13. Together with the other Indians in the city, press reports estimated there were "probably four to five hundred Indians at one time." The area around the State House was "extremely crowded." A difficult twelve days of negotiations followed. When the Indians left town on the twenty-fifth many of them were drunk and there were more difficulties. Thomas Penn regretted that his subordinates had tried to discourage the visit. "I do not wonder at their improper behavior after being so ill treated, and fear it will be long remembered," he wrote Richard Peters; "I am satisfied they never were so slighted since my Father Setled the Country, and desire great care may be taken that they shall not be so for the future."[92]

Indians also learned to leverage English generosity by exploiting English fears that their French rivals were outspending them. "The French are more politick than You," the Oneida chief Scarouady informed the governor and council in Philadelphia in March 1755, on the eve of the French and Indian War. "If they invite the Indians to Quebec city they all return with laced Cloathes on, and boast of the generous Treatment of the French Governor." The English, by contrast, were tight-fisted with those "goods that your City is full of." A Delaware the English called Shamokin Daniel made the point more bluntly to missionary Frederick Post at the height of the war: "See here, you fools, what the French have given me. I was in *Philadelphia*, and never received a farthing."[93] The English got the message.

Indian diplomatic visits followed much the same pattern in the early Republic. When Taboca and the Choctaw and Chickasaw delegates were in Philadelphia in June 1787, the state advanced them $100, gave them silver gorgets, and paid their expenses during their stay in the city.[94] No Indian delegation's travel and arrival were better documented or more celebrated than the state visit by Alexander McGillivray and the Creeks to New York in 1790, where they negotiated the first treaty made by the United States after the adoption of the Constitution. The Creek confederacy was a formidable Indigenous power in the contest for hegemony in the American South. Colonial powers courted and cultivated the Creeks, and the Creeks courted and cultivated colonial allies.

The delegation to New York was just one of many embassies the Creeks made in the eighteenth century as they maneuvered their way through shifting landscapes of imperial competition. In May 1732, for example, some sixty-five Creek headmen and their followers headed to Charleston "to pay their Respects to the Governor" and to renew earlier treaties (made in 1717 and 1721) with the Carolina government. News accounts noted "there never was so many Head Men of the Creek Nations together, in Town before." The governor ordered the Troop of Horse and two companies of soldiers to escort the Creeks to the council chamber, where they were received "in the Form, usual on the like Occasions." (Creeks were accustomed to council houses in their own towns; this council chamber, according to one later visitor, was "about 40 feet square, decorated with many heavy pillars and much carvings, rather superb than elegant.")[95] Some ladies had gathered in the room adjoining to the council chamber to watch the welcome ceremony; according to the *South Carolina Gazette,* one of the delegates stepped forward to "take the Ladies by the Hand, according to the Indian Custom," but then "made a sort of Retreat and expressed himself so particularly as to say That *he was sensible it was not made to touch such Things as these*"—evidence, suggested the paper, of "the Awe that Beauty strikes, even upon Savages." The governor ordered "proper Lodgings and Entertainment to be provided for them, where they will be permitted to refresh themselves for a few Days." A Charleston merchant paid for the chiefs to be taken on board *The Fox,* a frigate, and treated to a fifteen-gun salute. Newspapers reported they were "well pleas'd with the Presents and Entertainment they have received."[96] Five years later the *South Carolina Gazette* covered another group of Creeks in Charleston who, on a Saturday afternoon in July 1737, "were invited by several Indian Traders to a Diversion in a Sloop upon the River with Musick, and in the Evening handsomely treated at Capt. Pinckney's." (William Pinckney later served as commissioner of the Indian trade.)[97] They may even have attended a play; Charleston's first theater had opened two years earlier.[98]

Creek delegates, especially from Okfuskee, continued to visit Charleston, although Savannah took on a larger role in Creek relations as Georgia grew.[99] In early summer 1735, for example, a delegation of almost fifty Creeks from the Chattahoochee River, at the request of the British in Georgia, traveled 300 miles to Savannah. The colonists welcomed them with a military parade, a salute of forty-seven cannon, and gifts. Two Creeks then stepped forward and for two days related a story about the origins and identity of their people.[100]

During the French and Indian War, colonial governments neglected Creek visitors at their peril. When Henry Ellis arrived in Savanah in February 1757 to take up his position as lieutenant governor of Georgia, he was alarmed to find that twenty-nine Creeks "had been many days in town without being taken any notice of" by his predecessor. Two years into the French and Indian War, with things going badly for the British, Ellis pointed out, was "a time that could not justify such a neglect." He immediately ordered provisions for the visitors, treated them as honored guests, and held audiences with them. He sent them on their way with gifts and promised that Georgia would pay 20 shillings for every enemy scalp and 40 shillings for every prisoner they brought in. "Thoroughly convinced of the importance of standing well with these people I shall exert every means and employ every art that contribute to that end," he informed the Board of Trade in London.[101]

Ellis's timely intervention evidently worked: 150 Creeks from twenty-one towns traveled to Savannah in the fall of 1757 to strengthen their friendship with Georgia. They received the royal treatment. Captain Jonathan Bryan and "the Principal Inhabitants of the Town on Horseback" met them about a mile outside of town, welcomed them in the governor's name, and escorted them to Savannah, where they formed "two Lines through which the Indians marched" into town, regaled by salutes of cannon. Ellis gave a welcome speech at the council house, assured them he would make it his personal business to see they were supplied "with everything the Plantations afforded," and told them he had had a large house built to shelter them. He also offered to repair their guns and saddles at government expense while they were in town. Wolf King, a chief from the town of Mucklassee, replied that he and his fellow Creeks had made many trips to meet English governors "but never had more Satisfaction than we feel on this Occasion." Ellis then "invited the Head Men to dine with him at his own House where they were entertained in the kindest and most friendly manner to their entire Satisfaction." Over four days and nights before formal talks got under way, Ellis hosted the Creek leaders at his home, occasions for displays of hospitality and for private conversations.[102]

In February 1758 Wolf King and a delegation of Upper Creeks arrived in Charleston. Governor Lyttelton of South Carolina intended they should "sup out of the same Dish and eat at the same Table with him." The Creek delegates were immediately escorted by the Charleston Troop of Horse to the council chamber, where they were received by a company of grenadiers and had an audience with the governor. Lyttelton ordered that they be given presents to demonstrate the king's generosity and be shown "every thing worth their Observation in this Place." He had fine clothes made for all the headmen so that "they would appear in Red like Warriours"; he had them taken on board one of the king's warships so that "they might see the firing of the Guns"; and he showed them British soldiers so "they would observe how able and powerful the Great King was to protect all his Children White and Red and to Chastise his Enemies." A party of Cherokees was also in town; it was vital to create a good impression on both nations to counter French "artifices and Insinuations."[103]

Creek emissaries continued to be active on the eve of the Revolution. A party led by Emistisigoe received the usual military escort when it arrived in Savannah in 1773.[104] And they did not restrict their travels to English cities. Between February 1775 and March 1776, a dozen Creek delegations boarded Spanish fishing vessels and sailed to Havana, Cuba, then a bustling, crowded port city of about 40,000 people, to make a commercial alliance with Spain.[105]

After the Revolution, Alexander McGillivray continued to court Spanish officials.[106] Although he claimed to speak for the entire Creek nation, McGillivray lived very differently than most Creeks. He had studied Greek, Latin, English history, and literature; he accumulated personal wealth and property, owned slaves, managed a large plantation, and participated in the Atlantic market economy. He was frail and chronically ill, afflicted with rheumatism, migraine headaches, alcoholism, and syphilis. Nonetheless, Spain, Britain, and the United States all recognized his abilities, political savvy, and connections.[107] McGillivray played the field as rival powers vied for control in the South, and he realized the Spaniards posed less of a threat to Creek lands than did the new United States. He exploited Spanish fears of an American invasion and American fears of a war with Spain. He traveled to Pensacola and signed a treaty on June 1, 1784, in which Spain promised to protect Creek lands and provide trade and appointed McGillivray as commissary for the Creeks at a monthly salary of 50 pesos, about $600 per year. He emerged from the treaty as the key intermediary between the Creek and Spanish nations.[108] He also served as a secret partner in the loyalist Scottish mercantile firm Panton, Leslie, and Company, which Spain permitted to continue doing business, and he grew wealthy as the company extended its operations from Florida to the Mississippi.[109]

As Georgia settlers encroached on Creek land, President George Washington endeavored to stave off an Indian war that might embroil his young nation in conflict with Spain. He was also mindful that the United States had a puny army and had better cultivate the friendship of an Indigenous power that could muster 5,000 warriors.[110] After some unsuccessful diplomatic efforts in Creek country, Washington invited McGillivray to bring a delegation to New York City. Inviting the Creeks to the nation's capital was consistent with Henry Knox's position that "independent nations and tribes of Indians ought to be considered as foreign nations, not as the subjects of any particular state." McGillivray accepted the invitation, although he was under no illusions about Washington's motives.[111]

Washington's emissary, Colonel Marinus Willett, originally planned to bring the delegation to New York by ship, but the Creeks claimed to be afraid of water. (The delegates to Havana evidently had conquered their fears.) Instead, the group set off over land in June 1790. McGillivray rode at the head of the procession on horseback or with Willett in a carriage, and twenty-six chiefs and warriors followed in three wagons.[112] Washington asked the governors of Virginia, Maryland, and Pennsylvania to furnish the Creeks "with whatever might be deemed a proper respect" to keep them in good humor, and received assurances that the Creeks would receive "every proper attention."[113] In town after town, prominent citizens and civic leaders gave the travelers warm welcomes and crowds turned out to see them. On July 6, the Creeks arrived in Richmond, Virginia, where entertainment was provided at the theater, to which "the Judges of the Court of Appeals, the gentlemen of the bar and heads of the Executive Departments" were also invited. On the eighth, McGillivray and Willett dined at the academy with the governor, council, judges, lawyers, "and other persons of distinction." No sooner did they arrive in Fredericksburg the next day, said Willett, than "we were hurried to the theatre" and, despite the disruption of their travel schedule, "could not avoid remaining at that place all day." A public dinner for the chiefs followed.[114]

They reached Philadelphia on Saturday evening, July 1. Church bells rang, artillery fired a salute, and a company of light infantry escorted them to their lodgings at the Indian Queen Hotel, located at the southeast corner of Fourth and Market Streets. Although Philadelphia had had plenty of Indian delegations before, this was "the largest body of Indians, that has appeared in this metropolis for many years," noted the *Pennsylvania Gazette*, and a large crowd assembled. The president and supreme executive in council issued a formal welcome to the city, and "the chiefs were received by our citizens with every mark of attention."[115] On Monday they were "shewn a great many curiosities in and about Philadelphia," received a formal visit from a committee of the Society of Friends, and had a public dinner, followed by the theater at night.[116] No wonder McGillivray, who had fallen violently ill, found the trip "tedious & fatiguing."[117]

Traveling by sloop to New York the next day, the Creeks landed at Murray's Wharf on the afternoon of July 21. According to the first U.S. census that year, 33,130 people lived in New York. Many of them turned out to see the Creeks, who disembarked to church bells, cheering crowds, and a salvo of cannon. Preceded and followed by a line of troops, members of New York's Tammany Society, wearing the

dress of their order—or what they imagined to be Indian regalia—
and carrying bows, arrows, and tomahawks, escorted the Creeks up
Wall Street (Figure 2.1). A band played, the chiefs sang a song, and
spectators crowded the streets and windows. The procession stopped
at Federal Hall, where the members of Congress were assembled on
the balcony, then carried on to Washington's house, and finally to the
City Tavern on Broadway, where the Creeks were to be lodged during
their stay, and where secretary of war Henry Knox and Governor
Clinton of New York hosted them at dinner; "an elegant entertainment finished the day." The Indians' "behavior indicated strong
marks of their approbation of the reception which they met with
in this city," reported the press. It was the biggest celebration since
Washington's inauguration, and "not the least irregularity or accident happened."[118] Like previous Creek delegations in Charleston,
the Creeks in New York were treated to "an entertainment" held on
board ship, which Washington, Knox, and "a very respectable company of officers and citizens" attended.[119]

A VIEW OF THE FEDERAL HALL OF THE CITY OF NEW YORK,
as appeared in the year 1797, with the Adjacent buildings thereto.
Drawn expressly for D.T. Valentine's Manual.

Figure 2.1 John Joseph Holland, A View of Broad Street, Wall Street, and Federal
Hall, New York, 1789, as they would have appeared when the Creek delegation passed by.
New York Public Library Digital Collections.

Building on British and colonial precedents, Americans in the early Republic frequently took to the streets in acts of popular protest, orchestrated celebrations of birthdays and victories, public displays of national unity, and increasingly political demonstrations.[120] Nevertheless, the spontaneous outpouring of enthusiasm for Indian visitors was remarkable. Indian delegates always attracted curiosity, but the mass turnouts that greeted their arrival in American cities suggest that even as the United States built a nation on the dispossession and disappearance of Indians, Indians themselves had considerable crowd-pulling power.

The 1790s were busy years for Indian delegations traveling to the seat of the new government as well as to rival capitals. Indicative of the tumultuous situation in the South, while McGillivray and his delegation were in New York negotiating with Washington, William Augustus Bowles and a delegation of eight Creeks and Cherokees were in Quebec meeting with Lord Dorchester. Bowles, a former loyalist from Maryland, masqueraded as the self-styled director general of the Creek nation. As McGillivray's delegation sailed out of New York, Bowles's delegation sailed for London, where they stayed for five months. Although the Indian delegates dined with the Spanish ambassador in London, Bowles lobbied in vain to gather British support for a scheme to wrest West Florida from Spanish control. (After a series of misadventures, Bowles was incarcerated in a Spanish dungeon in Havana, where he died in 1805.)[121] In the international contest between Spain and the United States for control of the lower Mississippi, Choctaws, Chickasaws, and Cherokees traveled to New Orleans so often and in such numbers that colonists living along the Gulf Coast complained about the damage caused to their crops and livestock by passing delegations.[122]

As we've seen, Indian people had always traveled to Philadelphia to trade, but Moreau de Saint-Méry, who was in there in the 1790s, said that when Indians came to town it was "always for some political reason."[123] The United States was at war with the Northwest confederacy of tribes that was fighting to stop American expansion at the Ohio River, and Indian diplomats shuttled in and out of the capital as the government tried to secure or preserve their friendship and enlist their assistance as allies or intermediaries. The United States could ill afford to have the Senecas, the westernmost and largest of the Six Nations, join the confederacy. Recognizing that the murder of two Seneca chiefs at Pine Creek in northern Pennsylvania threatened to do just that, the Pennsylvania Council invited Cornplanter and other

Senecas to Philadelphia. Cornplanter, Half Town, Big Tree, New Arrow, and Guyasuta arrived in town in October 1790. The government asked the Reverend Samuel Kirkland to go to Philadelphia to meet with the delegation. Kirkland was torn. He had other plans for the winter—translating hymns and psalms and making preparations to move his family closer to Oneida in the spring—but Cornplanter (whom he called "Abiel") was "a particular friend." Kirkland went, leaving on December 2 and arriving in Philadelphia on December 20. Cornplanter welcomed him and explained the purposes of their visit, which included—music to Kirkland's ears—obtaining assistance in agriculture and "the arts of civilized life." It was the first of many conversations.

> I spent about three weeks with the deputation of Senekas in the city of Philadelphia. Nor do I now regret my journey. I think I never enjoyed more agreeable society with any Indian than Abiel has afforded me. He seems raised up by Providence for the good of his nation. He is a person who exhibits uncommon genius, possesses a very strong & distinguishing mind, & will bear the most application of any Indian I was every acquainted with. When the business he came upon did not require his immediate attention, he would be incessantly engaged in conversation upon the Subject of divine Revelation.

Cornplanter would not let his companions sit down to a meal without having Kirkland bless the food, and he was so concerned with the spiritual needs of his people that he "pined" and lost weight while "his companions enjoyed the luxuries & fattened upon them." Kirkland thought him exceptional in his sobriety; Cornplanter told him he had never been drunk in his life. Kirkland returned to Stockbridge on January 12, 1791.[124] The Seneca chiefs remained in Philadelphia until March as their negotiations with the president dragged on. Governor Mifflin worried about the escalating costs but, he reminded the Assembly, it was worth it if it helped assuage their resentment over the murder of their chiefs at Pine Creek.[125]

The pace of Indian diplomacy picked up after the Northwest confederacy smashed General Arthur St. Clair's army on November 4, 1791, the first major defeat of the American army.[126] So many delegations came to Philadelphia in the next few years that government officials were sometimes caught off guard. On December 28, 1791, a Cherokee delegation disembarked in Philadelphia after sailing from Charleston: Nenetootah or Bloody Fellow, Chutloh or King Fisher, Nontuaka or the Northward, Teesteke or the Disturber, Kuthagusta or the Prince, and a woman named Jean or Jane Dougherty. Accompanying them were two interpreters, James

Carey, who had been captured as a boy and raised as a Cherokee, and Schucwegee or George Miller, a young Cherokee who for many years had been a prisoner with the whites.[127] They came to request an increase in annual payments for the lands they had relinquished at the Treaty of Holston in July with William Blount, governor of the Southwest Territory. The secretary of war, Henry Knox, was "surprised with the visit."[128]

In an effort to buy time while it rebuilt its armed forces and to exploit divisions in the Indian confederacy, the United States tried to initiate peace talks with the western tribes and secure the aid or at least the neutrality of other tribes.[129] It commissioned Kirkland to bring a delegation to the capital. Kirkland, accompanied by Oneidas Skenandoah, Good Peter, Peter Otsiquette, and Jacob Reed as well as by the Stockbridge Mohican Captain Hendrick Aupaumut, traveled to the western reaches of Iroquois country to invite chiefs from the Onondagas, Cayugas, and Senecas. So many wanted "to see the Great Council of the 13 fires, & to get a peep at the great American Chief" that Kirkland brought nearly fifty people. Red Jacket, Farmer's Brother, Big Tree, and many other chiefs accompanied the missionary down the Susquehanna Valley. Again, officials were caught by surprise. Henry Knox had ordered Timothy Pickering, whom President Washington had appointed as commissioner to the Iroquois, to invite the chiefs "to repair to this city with all convenient speed." Pickering had issued the invitation, but he knew nothing about the delegation coming until Knox crossed the street one day and told him the Indians were on their way.[130]

They arrived in Philadelphia on March 13, 1792. Landing at the Market Street wharf, they were saluted by a discharge of cannon, welcomed by the governor of the state, and escorted by a detachment of light infantry to Oeller's Hotel, which had opened for business in 1791 on the south side of Chestnut Street, near the State House.[131] Papers beyond Philadelphia picked up the story of their welcome. "The bells were kept ringing all the evening," reported the *Middlesex Gazette* in Connecticut and *Spooner's Vermont Journal.* "This is the first time we have heard of joy bells at the approach of savages."[132] So soon after St. Clair's defeat, there was real interest in the Indians' visit. The Philadelphia press printed a full list of the names and places of residence of the "Sachems and Head Warriors of the Five Nations" who were in town.[133] At the same time, a publisher on the corner of Chestnut and Second Streets was selling the printed minutes of a multitribal council, held in the wake of their victory over St. Clair, hot from the presses.[134]

President Washington also invited Joseph Brant to Philadelphia in 1792 in the hope of securing his assistance in dealing with the western confederacy and "to impress him with the equitable intentions of this government towards *all* the Nations of his colour."[135] What Brant referred to as "this jaunt to the American seat of Government" was no small matter. The government assigned $400 for the journey and sent Dr. Deodat Allen to accompany Brant, who also traveled with a servant and, for part of the way, his son, Isaac. It took almost a month to travel from Brant's home on the Grand River in Upper Canada (now Ontario), cross the Iroquois homeland in upstate New York, pass furtively through the Mohawk Valley (where American settlers had bitter memories of "monster Brant" from the Revolution) to Albany, and head down the Hudson River to New York City, where he called on an acquaintance, the merchant Richard Varick. Brant had enjoyed shopping in London, and he went shopping in New York, ordering a blue cashmere coat and overalls for himself at a tailor. He then proceeded to Philadelphia, where he arrived on June 20 and received the grand reception he had been promised.[136]

There were Senecas in Philadelphia again in February 1793— Farmer's Brother, the Young King, China Breast Plate, the Infant, John, and Solomon. The War Department ordered Quartermaster General Samuel Hodgdon to deliver seven new rifles to be given to them, as well as to Red Jacket, who was absent. If the Indians preferred that the guns be packed up for transportation, Hodgdon was to take care of it.[137] Then, after negotiating the Treaty of Vincennes in 1793 to separate the tribes of the Wabash region from the Northwest confederacy, Brigadier General Rufus Putnam brought a delegation led by the Kaskaskia Jean Baptiste DuCoigne. The government also invited more southern Indians to the capital.[138] In June 1794, twenty-one Cherokee chiefs and head warriors arrived aboard the brig *Fame* and "were conducted from the place of landing to the accommodations provided for them by the Governor of this State."[139] The Cherokees had barely left before a Chickasaw delegation arrived; in fact, the Chickasaws inquired about them.

In gratitude for Chickasaw assistance during St. Clair's campaign, when Piominko had brought a company of scouts but could not prevent the American army from being surprised and slaughtered, Washington invited Piominko "and three other great chiefs, to repair to Philadelphia," where they would be "kindly received, well treated, and return to their country enriched with presents." Piominko went with more than a dozen chiefs, as well as warriors and boys. When they reached Winchester, Virginia, the townspeople gave them a royal welcome and a military escort (which was very different from the treatment they received at some other points on their journey). The soldiers in the escort "and a large concourse of respectable citizens fraternized with them" at a local tavern. The Chickasaws resumed their journey, the press reported, with "countenances expressive of the heart felt satisfaction they experienced from the marked friendship and attachment evinced towards them by the citizens of Winchester."[140]

They arrived at Philadelphia on July 7 and met with Washington at his official residence on Market Street at noon on July 11. The president told them Henry Knox would furnish them with goods for themselves, their families, and their nation, and that if they wanted to see New York he would make arrangements for their accommodation there. He then smoked the peace-pipe, and ate and drank with them before he retired.[141] Ten days later, the Chickasaws met again with Knox, who gave Piominko peace medals for the delegation and a document that delineated Chickasaw territorial boundaries.[142]

Another delegation of three Chickasaws and three Choctaws arrived in Philadelphia in early July 1795.[143] Six months later, Timothy Pickering, who was now secretary of state, complained to William Blount that half a dozen Choctaws and Chickasaws had turned up at Philadelphia without an interpreter or guide, "and we cannot tell the object of their journey except that they might expect to be cloathed and receive presents." The government gave each one clothes, an ax, and a rifle, and furnished them with a wagon and a guide to begin their return journey to Knoxville. Pickering urged Blount to do what he could to discourage "such irregular and unauthorized visits."[144]

At the Treaty of Greenville in 1795, a year after General Anthony Wayne defeated the Northwest confederacy at the Battle of Fallen Timbers in August 1794, the Shawnee war chief Blue Jacket, speaking on a string of blue wampum, asked if two chiefs from each tribal nation could pay Washington a visit "and take him by the hands: for our younger brothers have a strong desire to see that great man, and to enjoy the pleasure of conversing with him." The Shawnees had been engaged in almost continual war against the Americans and no Shawnee chief had yet visited the nation's capital. In the fall of 1796, a multitribal delegation embarked from Detroit for Philadelphia. As a war chief and member of the Pekowi division, Blue Jacket now deferred to Painted or Red Pole, a civil chief of the Mekoche division, which had responsibility for healing and diplomacy. Nevertheless, he understood that meeting Washington in Philadelphia could help maintain his own leadership status as the Shawnees entered a new era of dealings with the United States. Before the Indians set out, an army officer who had fought against him observed that "Blue Jacket is used to good company and is always treated with more attention than other Indians."[145] Blue Jacket and Little Turtle were rivals: each claimed credit for having defeated St. Clair's army. Little Turtle refused to travel in Blue Jacket's company and did not make the journey.[146] After weeks of grueling progress across the mountains and passing through "shabby towns with flea-bitten taverns," the western chiefs reached Philadelphia in November. They met Washington, expressed their allegiance to the United States, and asked that the Greenville treaty line, which had been run too far to the west, be modified to follow the Great Miami River down to the Ohio.[147] They left Philadelphia with good words and commissions from Washington but no alterations in the boundary.

Delegates kept coming during Philadelphia's final years as the nation's capital. Joseph Brant and Cornplanter went again in the winter of 1797; this time they traveled together. Brant met Robert Liston, George Hammond's replacement as British minister to the United States, attended a dinner hosted by New York senator and future vice president Aaron Burr, and sat for another portrait, this time by Charles Willson Peale (see Plate 12). But he did not keep the appointment the new secretary of war, James McHenry, made for him with Washington.[148] Little Turtle made his appearance in January 1798 with a delegation of Miamis and Wyandots; he was the celebrity in the group.[149] Two Kahnawake chiefs traveled 500 miles on foot in the dead of winter bringing a black wampum belt to warn of a multitribal movement brewing in the north.[150] In November, five Odawa, Potawatomi, and Ojibwe chiefs went to do "general business" with the government in Philadelphia, stopping in New York City on their way.[151] The Chickasaw chief Ugulyacube, or Wolf's Friend, in Philadelphia in January 1799, wanted an audience with President John Adams and expected an annual stipend from the government. Secretary McHenry advised the president against it.[152]

By 1800, when the federal government moved to Washington, tribal delegations—and concern about the expenses they involved—were a fixed feature of U.S. Indian policy. Government officials now increasingly viewed them as supplicants, but tribal nations had racked up years of experience traveling to cities to refresh their alliances, conduct their foreign policies, and assert their sovereignty on colonial ground.

CHAPTER 3

The Other Indians in Town

INDIAN DELEGATES MAKING THEIR WAY to colonial and early Republic cities would likely have met Indian people working as farmhands, living on the outskirts of town, and returning from town. When they arrived, they would have seen, and been seen by, other Indian people who were already there. Tribal delegates stayed for a time, attracted attention, and returned home. Other Indian people attracted much less attention, frequented cities more regularly, and in some cases lived and worked there.

Many of America's cities began life as multiethnic communities, trading centers where Indians and Europeans mixed, mingled, and married, and where Indian people were often a common sight and constant presence. As we've seen, rather than retreating from cities, Indian people often gravitated toward them for diplomacy and, as they did with colonial forts, incorporated them into their economic strategies and cycles as well.[1] Even in California, Indians adjusting to the disruption of their traditional economies began to look for work in the pueblo of Los Angeles almost as soon as it was founded in 1781.[2] Indian peoples did not migrate as laborers to the cities of North America in the numbers as Indigenous peoples did to silver mining cities such as Zacatecas in northern Mexico or Potosí in Peru, which, at 13,000 feet above sea level, grew into one of the biggest cities in the Western world, with a combined Spanish and Indigenous population of 100,000 by the beginning of the seventeenth century.[3] Nevertheless, the urban frontier in North America attracted as well as repelled.

Boundaries between colonial communities and Indian country were porous: people came and went; raided and traded; ate, drank, and smoked together; slept together. Indian people came to town to sell baskets, brooms, pottery, pelts, and food, to purchase goods, and to get their guns mended. In the wake of land loss and the disruption of their traditional economies, itinerant basket- and broom-makers maintained a precarious livelihood with a mobile economy that involved regular stops in towns and cities to market their wares.[4] Other Indian people lived and worked there as slaves, domestic servants, laborers, craftsmen, and prostitutes. Indian sailors and soldiers spent time between voyages and campaigns. Many Indian people merged unnoticed into the poor neighborhoods and lower echelons of society, creating their own webs of interaction and spheres of activity in the urban environment; some maintained connections with their home communities. Survival in the cities demanded different forms of adaptation and persistence than were needed to deal with Europeans in Indian country.[5]

The laws that colonies passed regarding and regulating Indian people varied by time and place and in war and peace, but collectively they convey a sense of how much Indians were part of colonial society and shared urban spaces, living and working in close quarters, sometimes even intimacy, alongside colonists—although not on equal terms. In addition to making laws to prepare for defense against Indian attack and to pay bounties on the scalps of enemy Indians, colonies passed laws to regulate trade with Indians, regulate purchases of Indian land, regulate wampum, pay bounties to Indians for killing wolves, encourage the use of Indians in whaling, prohibit selling guns to Indians or repairing guns for Indians, curb sales of alcohol, and prohibit selling boats and horses to Indians. Laws imposed taxes on owners of Indian servants, protected Indian servants, and required payment of wages to Indian laborers; they restricted Indians' movements, set curfews on when Indians could be out and about, and punished runaway Indian servants; they prohibited citizens from entertaining Indian servants or slaves in their home, and punished citizens for giving Indians lodging overnight. Such legislation often applied to any Indian, mulatto, or black servant or slave. Laws also governed freed Indian slaves and servants. There were laws to prevent Indians from working on the Sabbath and to exclude them from coming into town on the Sabbath except for religious instruction; a Massachusetts law passed in 1644 specified that "neither shall they come att any English house upon any other day in the weeke, but first shall knock at the dore, and after leave given, to come in." There were laws to prohibit intermarriage; to include, exclude, or exempt Indians from militia service; to promote Christianity among Indians; to establish courts and judges in cases involving Indians; to prevent Indians from being sued for debt; and to punish idleness and stealing by Indians. Penalties often required Indians to pay off their fines by working for colonists.[6]

In 1656, New Amsterdam citizens—there were about 1,500 of them at the time—had to be prohibited by law from giving Indians lodging overnight, clear evidence that they were doing so.[7] Indian trade was so important to New Amsterdam and Albany that Dutch authorities passed laws restricting itinerant traders and entrepreneurial colonists from going into Indian country to do business, to ensure that the Indians would bring their trade to the town marketplace.[8] Iroquois hunters preferred to take their pelts to Albany because they got better prices than if they sold them to traders operating in Iroquois country.[9] Indians came to town regularly and in large numbers. In August 1665, for example, there were 400 Mohawks and Oneidas in Albany, with a group of Onondagas expected shortly.[10] Indians from "the far nations" in the Great Lakes country also journeyed to Albany. According to one report, Odawas "and the Indians who wear pipes thro' their noses" traded at Albany from the time it was settled.[11] Miami Indians were traveling to Albany to trade by the early eighteenth century and, according to Governor William Burnet in 1721, the far nations "flocked" to Albany.[12]

Indian people mingled with Dutch inhabitants on Albany's streets. Such close relationships in peacetime sometimes produced problems in times of conflict. One Dutch account blamed traders and colonists for cultivating familiarity that bred contempt and led to deteriorating relations prior to the "New Netherland War" or Governor Kieft's War in 1643–45: "For, not satisfied with merely taking them into their houses in the customary manner, they attracted them by extraordinary attention, such as admitting them to Table, laying napkins before them, presenting Wine to them and more of that kind of thing."[13] Local Mohawks and Mohicans evidently developed a taste for Dutch baked goods. Townsfolk responded by baking for the Native American market, and prices rose. In 1649, in response to numerous complaints, the authorities in New Netherland issued an edict regulating the sale of bread to Indians. Because wampum was the common currency of the colony, Indians who possessed it in large quantities had greater spending power than colonists and were buying fine white bread; the majority of the non-Indian inhabitants were wampum-poor and could afford only coarse brown bread. The ordinance, renewed periodically over the next decade, declared that "no Bakers shall be at liberty to bake or sell to the Natives or Christians any fine bolted or white Bread, or Cakes for presents." At times, Dutch authorities worried as much about "contraband cookies" as they did about illegal sales of guns and alcohol![14]

When Captain Jonathan Bull of Connecticut arrived in Albany in 1683 with two Indian servants, they promptly ran away to the nearby Native community at Schaghticoke. The court at Albany could do no more than recommend that the runaways be returned; Bull "was not allowed to take them away by force," the court minutes stated, "because all Indians here are free."[15] Practice was somewhat different, of course. There were unfree Indian workers in Albany, as in other cities. In 1763, for example, a young Indian woman named Margaret, in return for food and lodging, bound herself as a servant to one Abraham Wendell of Albany, along with any children she might have "during All the Days of their Natural Life." Three years later, Wendell signed the indenture over to Sir William Johnson.[16]

Albany's magnetism drew Indians to other communities closer to Indian country. Iroquois people canoeing the Mohawk River on their way to and from Albany often stopped off at Schenectady. Sometimes they outstayed their welcome, "doing nothing" or drinking, according to one complaint. In 1697 Schenectady's population, black and white, was only 297; the arrival of dozens, or sometimes even hundreds, of Indian people passing to and from Albany during the summer trading months would have been significant. There was some Native presence year-round as well, and Indians regularly visited Dutch homes. Like neighboring Albany, Schenectady was a community where whites and Indians not only traded but sometimes lived in the same houses, slept in the same rooms, and ate at the same table.[17] During the infamous French and Indian attack on Schenectady in 1690, the raiders killed some sixty inhabitants but spared about thirty Mohawks who were sleeping there.[18] Dr. Alexander Hamilton said Schenectady in 1744 was nearly as large as Albany and consisted mainly of brick houses, but described it as still "a trading village, the people carrying on a traffic with the Indians."[19] Even the governor of South Carolina knew that Schenectady was "the Embarkadier for the Indian Trade to Oswego. The Indians come mostly in light Birch Canoes from their several Countries, and leaves their Canoes at Schenectady."[20]

Iroquois people traveled to Albany from the north as well as the west. Mohawks from Kahnawake maintained an active smuggling business operating across the imperial border and came to Albany to buy goods for French merchants in Montreal. Cadwallader Colden told Benjamin Franklin in 1753 that the last time he was in Albany "there was at least 200 of them stout young fellows at one time in the Town." Even the Mohawk chief Hendrick complained that Indians from Canada engaged in smuggling and "for that Purpose are Constantly at Albany."[21] Mohawks and other Iroquois people included Albany in their seasonal round of economic activities. A Polish traveler in the late 1790s described how they took up residence "in small and remote taverns" on the outskirts of the city, made brooms, shovels, and other items to sell in the market, and then bought woolen blankets, guns, and ammunition before returning to their villages for the winter.[22] Albany was accustomed to Indian people walking its streets even when there were no delegates in town.

In New France, Montagnais and Algonquin people likewise frequented Quebec. French plans for bringing Christianity and civilization to Native peoples involved encouraging them to settle near the city. As in New Spain, religious orders in New France took Indigenous children into their convents and established schools with rudimentary room and board where they received instruction in Christianity, language, reading, and writing.[23] In 1633 Father Paul LeJeune, superior of the Jesuit missions, established a school for Indian children from neighboring tribes, and Huron families were encouraged to live near the French so that the seminaries would, as LeJeune put it, "be filled with little Huron girls." Numbers were small, but by the end of the decade there were seminaries for Montagnais, Algonquin, and Huron boys and girls in Quebec.[24] Algonquin and Montagnais people also went to the Hôtel-Dieu, the first hospital in North America, which opened at Sillery in 1637 and then moved to Quebec. A handful of nuns ministered to "all sick persons, both French and Savage," and were often overwhelmed in times of epidemic. The nuns tended to old and ill Native people, taught the children, prayed with them, and in some cases induced them to accept baptism and convert to Christianity.[25]

At the end of the seventeenth century, a time of recurrent conflict between France and England and their respective Indian allies, Mohawk families sometimes traveled from New York to visit relatives who had settled on the St. Lawrence. According to a French chronicler, they were "left at perfect liberty, and walk daily in the streets of Montreal with as much confidence as if the Peace were perfectly ratified."[26] Montreal continued to grow as a center of trade, Christianity, and smuggling for multiple tribes. The several thousand Indian people who lived nearby and the hundreds more who camped nearby during trading season meant that a significant proportion of Montreal's population was Indian. Many French colonists living in Montreal actually interacted with Indians more than did colonists living closer to Indian country because Indian people visited the city more often than French settlements in the countryside. The French originally had built a palisade around Montreal as a defense against Iroquois attacks, and a devastating Mohawk raid on Lachine at the upper end of the island in 1690 endured in French memories, but in the first half of the eighteenth century the wall functioned mainly to control traffic into and out of the city. Soldiers at the city gates inspected goods, checked papers, and questioned anyone they thought did not belong. But, as historian Brett Rushforth notes, "the soldiers knew that Indians did belong in the city, so they rarely interfered with their passage into and out of town." Indian people from near and far walked the streets: "Mohawk women came to Montreal to visit French chapels, Nipissing men brought deer meat to the market square, Oneida families visited their French friends, enslaved Apache girls carried water to the garden."[27]

Free Indians who came to Montreal met enslaved Indians there. Indigenous slaves from beyond the Mississippi were collectively called "Panis" by the French, although only some were actually Pawnees. They worked as laborers at the docks, in mills and warehouses, and as weavers and shopkeepers, though most were urban domestics who worked in French homes, shopped in the markets, and ran errands. In 1709, 13 or 14 percent of Montreal households had at least one Indian slave.[28] Dining at the home of a prominent family in Montreal in 1742, the Mdwekanton Sioux chiefs Sacred Born and Leaf Shooter were shocked and disgusted to find themselves being served by two recently baptized Sioux children held as slaves. French Indian allies had delivered dozens of Sioux women and children to Montreal the previous year to be sold as slaves. The children "started to cry when they saw us," the chiefs told Governor Beauharnois, and they asked him to release the children. Anxious for peace and alliance with the Sioux, the governor agreed to return the slaves, although there is no evidence that the children accompanied the chiefs back home.[29]

Indians were in and about town in seventeenth-century New England as well. They frequented Boston for trade and diplomacy and they lived and worked there. The sachem Chickatabout made repeated visits, trading and building relationships, before he died in the smallpox epidemic of 1633.[30] After the Pequot War of 1636–37, many Indian captives were sold to Boston citizens and added to the city's supply of unfree labor. Governor John Winthrop added at least five Pequot captives to his Boston household, alongside his other Indian servants. Indian servants were such a common sight in Boston that several Indian captives escaped by dressing "in the garb of servants."[31] Boston in 1644 appointed one blacksmith to repair the guns of "those sachims which have submitted themselves to our government," and in 1648, on the request of the Puritan missionary John Eliot, granted merchant William Phillips a monopoly on selling wine to Indians.[32] Indian people came to town so often and in such numbers that colonial authorities sometimes passed laws to *prevent* them from coming to town. The Connecticut preacher and historian Benjamin Trumbull said that Indians "lived promiscuously with the English in all parts of the country, they were generally as well acquainted with their dwellings, fields, and places of worship, as themselves." Consequently, when King Philip's War broke out in 1675, severing patterns of coexistence between Indians and colonists, the Indians had the advantage in setting ambushes.[33]

Fifty Mohegan Indians entered Boston in late July 1675, to affirm allegiance with the English, but Boston prohibited Indians from the city in times of war in 1675 and 1689. Connecticut prohibited Indians from living within a quarter mile of colonial settlements and from walking into them at night.[34] Still, Indians were taken to Boston as prisoners of war during King Philip's War. When the Narragansett sachem Canonchet went to Boston in the fall of 1675 to try to forestall conflict between his people and the English, he would have seen Christian Indians held as prisoners. Indians from neighboring "praying towns" were incarcerated on Deer Island in Boston Harbor, where they suffered starvation and exposure in the winter of 1675–76, searing the island into the "memoryscape" of New England Indian people.[35]

A Nipmuc leader named Wuttasacomponom, known to the English as Captain Tom, was a Christian convert and preacher at the praying town of Hassanamesit and had tried to keep the war away from his town, but under pressure from his warriors he joined the Indian resistance. Captured with his family, Wuttasacomponom was taken to Boston for trial and hanged. John Eliot said he died with his hands raised in prayer. His public execution served as a clear warning of the fate that awaited praying Indians who "revolted."[36] In September 1676, as the war was winding down, New Hampshire merchant Major Richard Waldron seized almost 400 Indian people at Dover by subterfuge, staging a mock fight, and shipped some 200 to Boston, where they were sold into slavery in the Caribbean. Many Indian prisoners who were found, or assumed to be, guilty of hostilities died on the gallows on Boston Common. As many as forty-five were hanged or shot there in August and September 1676 alone.[37]

As they had after the Pequot War, the English shipped many Indian captives out of Boston Harbor to a short life as slaves on Caribbean sugar plantations. Others who came in and gave themselves up were assigned as laborers in neighboring towns and their children handed "unto such of the English as may use them well" until they were twenty-four or twenty-five. John, sachem of the Nipmuc town of Pakachoag, brought thirty-two children to Boston in 1676. In some cases, their parents were dead; in others, the parents consented. The General Court assigned the boys and girls to work as servants in households in and around the city; they were to be instructed in English and Christianity, and punished if they tried to run away.[38] Uprooted from their home communities and without networks of support, many orphans bound out as indentured servants experienced isolation, exploitation, dependence, and poverty.[39]

Abenaki chiefs were held prisoner in Boston in 1698.[40] Abenaki prisoners were taken to Boston again during Dummer's War, 1722–25, actually a series of conflicts between New England colonists and Wabanaki peoples. The Indian delegates who were in the city in September 1723, where they were treated to a firearms demonstration and an ox roast on Boston Common, may have seen or heard of Indian prisoners being sold by Captain John Lovewell's company of volunteer militia, who brought scalps as well as prisoners to Boston to collect the bounties. In January 1725, for example, they brought a scalp and a teenage boy they had taken north of Lake Winnipesaukee the previous month, "for which good Service, and for their further Encouragement," they were paid "Fifty Pounds over and above One Hundred and Fifty Pounds allow'd them by Law."[41] In September 1726, a fishing vessel brought three Indian men, one Indian woman, and two infants to Boston as prisoners.[42]

In addition to Indian slaves and servants from New England, Boston acquired them from the Carolinas and Spanish Florida via Charleston, which shipped them to New York and New England as well as to the West Indies. They became part of Boston's unfree labor force, its underground economy, and its underlife, mingling and intermarrying with other marginalized people.[43] Court records reveal the continuing presence of Indian people in the city. The Inferior Court of Boston recorded in 1683 that Jonathan Avery was "licensed to continue practice of physic and surgery to Indians."[44] In February 1691 the same court sentenced Sarah Jones to fifteen lashes for "lascivious carriage with an Indian"; Degoe, the Indian in the case, received the same punishment.[45] The court sentenced Indian people for drunkenness, sexual and physical assault, burglary, theft, and receiving stolen goods, and Indian servants for stealing and running away from their master or mistress. Sometimes punishment involved shipment to "the plantations," meaning Caribbean slavery. Sam, an Indian convicted of burglary, was branded on the forehead with the letter *B*.[46] Courts also sentenced Indians, and their families, to servitude for lawbreaking and debt.

Indian delegations to Boston would have been aware of both Indian slavery and Indian servitude there. In July 1728, newspapers advertised a young Indian woman to be sold in Boston by one John Brewster "at the End of Cross-Street."[47] Newspapers also carried notices of Indian slaves and servants who had run away from their masters, including "Spanish Indians," probably imported from Florida or the Southwest.[48] The *Boston News-Letter* in September 1728 carried one such notice:

> Ran away from the Gray-hound in Roxbury, on the Lord's Day the 15th Instant, A lusty Indian Woman, Named Bersheba Larrens, she had on a Red flower'd Callico Jacket & Peticoat, a quilted Peticoat. Whosoever shall take up the said Runaway and her Convey to Roxbury, shall have 20 Shillings reward & necessary Charges paid.[49]

What Bersheba's situation was at the Gray-hound and what prompted her to run away when she did are not known.

The devastation of King Philip's War was supposed to have driven Indians out of the region, but Sarah Kemble Knight, traveling from Boston to New Haven in the fall of 1704, saw Indians "every where in the Towns I passed."[50] Most Indian people in Boston gravitated there in the wake of social and economic disruptions in their own communities, often joining relatives who already lived there. Most entered the ranks of the urban poor and lived alongside African Americans. The city in 1746 reported that "great Damage arises to the Inhabitants of the Town of Boston by negro's and Indians keeping Hogs" and took measures to control their pig-keeping activities and to limit the spaces in town where Native Americans and African Americans could gather.[51] At least as many Indians lived in Boston in 1764 as lived in the Indian town of Natick, and thirty years later a missionary named Gideon Hawley complained that many young Wampanoag women from Mashpee went "to Boston for months together . . . to the injury of their morals." An Indigenous community developed in the city as Native sailors, domestics, and travelers merged into its back streets and alleys. Crispus Attucks, a sailor or dockworker of African American and Native American descent, possibly from Natick, became famous as a martyr after his death in the Boston Massacre.[52]

Indian people who immersed themselves in the lower echelons of urban life became invisible to outsiders. An Italian visitor to Boston shortly after the Revolution said that Indians "live at a great distance and very rarely come to the city, so that there are many inhabitants who have never seen any of them."[53] A few years later, a French traveler crossed the Atlantic on the same ship as Peter Otsiquette or Ojekheta, a young Oneida whom the Marquis de Lafayette had adopted when he was a teenager and taken to France. After several years abroad, where he received an education, learned French and English, and became accustomed to moving in polite society, Otsiquette returned home in the summer of 1788. He caused as much surprise in Boston as he had in Paris, said the traveler, "for Indians are never seen there."[54]

They were not seen but they were there, often in plain sight. Native American people generally existed on the margins of New England town life, living and laboring among colonists but remaining invisible in most records. Although they did not usually show up on town voting and tax lists or birth certificates, they did appear in other records as officials in the late eighteenth century tried to deter undesirable people from taking up residence and seeking poor relief by a process known as "warning out" those who did not belong in town. The majority of Native people identified in these records were women—often their husbands had gone to sea—but even as officials recorded their presence, they contributed to their apparent absence by increasingly designating them as black or mulatto.[55] A Boston city clerk named Robert Love warned out two Indian women in 1765: Pennelape Whinkake, who came to the city from Newport, Rhode Island, and Deborah Jennins, who came from Ebintown. Both lodged with a Robert McCurday, who had a tavern in Boston's South End, where they may have worked as servants or prostitutes.[56]

Like their non-Indian neighbors, Indian people adapted to an increasingly urban and industrial environment. Some migrants may have developed new identities as they rebuilt their lives in the city. Others maintained ties with their home communities and sometimes traveled back and forth, working seasonally.[57] A mobile Indian labor force developed as people moved from job to job, city to city, and home community to urban slum. Press reports of a murder in Connecticut afford a glimpse into the mobile networks that connected Indian people in different towns. An Indian named Toby and his wife celebrated Christmas 1794 in a tavern in East Hartford with an Indian from Providence who was visiting them. The next day, Toby found the visitor and his wife in an amorous embrace. Grabbing a pitchfork, he killed the man and wounded his wife so badly "that there is little prospect of her recovery." Toby was committed to jail in Middletown.[58]

Patterns of mobility that included cities continued in nineteenth-century New England. Many young women left home to find work in textile mills in Lowell and Worcester, Massachusetts, or in Manchester, New Hampshire; many men moved to Boston or New York for work in heavier industry. In Worcester and other central Massachusetts communities, Nipmucs and other Native people, often intermixed with African Americans, went about their business, working as plumbers, chair caners, barbers, shoemakers, servants, day laborers, mill operatives, railroad engineers, and even specialty bakers.[59]

Two Shawnees showed up in Philadelphia one day in 1704. They had been sent ahead to ascertain what quantities of goods were available and at what prices before more Shawnees came to trade.[60] Nineteenth-century histories of Philadelphia reported that from a very early period it was common for groups of Indian men, women, and children to visit the city, "not for any public business, but merely to buy and sell and look on." On such occasions "they went abroad much in the streets." The women made baskets from ash strips and sold them to visitors. Parties of Indians usually stayed for two or three weeks and lodged around the State House yard. Old people recalled that Indians came so frequently to the city to trade and see the sights that their visits "excited no surprise."[61] Gottlieb Mittelberger, a German immigrant who lived in Pennsylvania in the early 1750s, said it was not uncommon to see Indians. "Every fall they come to Philadelphia in huge numbers, bringing with them various kinds of baskets which they can weave neatly and beautifully, different kinds of hides, as well as precious furs."[62] On the afternoon of May 1, 1762, a well-to-do young Quaker woman named Hannah Callender Sansom noted in her diary, without further comment, that she "walked over to the State house to see some orderly Indians."[63] As in New England, by the end of the eighteenth century, indigent Indian women appeared in Pennsylvania town records as officials tried to manage and limit increasing demands on poor relief.[64]

In addition to traveling to Charleston on diplomatic missions, Indians went there to trade deerskins, to arrange or patch up trade relations, and to complain about the activities of traders in Indian country who peddled alcohol and gave short measures. Indian women accompanied trading groups and also went by themselves. Trader James Adair said the baskets Cherokee women wove were "highly esteemed" for utility, beauty, and variety and brought a good price in Charleston. So many Cherokee women peddled baskets and other items on the streets of Charleston and Savannah that by the 1730s the British authorities established a pass system to limit their number.[65]

As the center of the southeastern Indian slave trade, Charleston in its early years was a busy place for trading Indians as well as for trading with Indians. Cherokees were both participants and victims. In one of the earliest Cherokee delegations to Charleston, twenty chiefs in 1693 asked the governor to provide protection against Indian slave raiders and restore some Cherokees who had been taken captive. Unfortunately, the captives had already been sold "off country," probably to the West Indies. In August 1713 Cherokees complained to the Board of Indian Commissioners that two of their women were kept as slaves near Charleston. In February 1717, "four Indian Women with their two Children, . . . were sold together for seventy-five Pounds." That June Cherokee burdeners delivered more than 900 deerskins to Charleston along with twenty-one Indian slaves. And in November 160 Cherokee burdeners brought 160 packs of skins and three Indian slave boys. The burdeners were paid in cloth for their labor and travel and provided with a daily supply of corn for their sustenance while in Charleston; the boys were sold the next Saturday "for ready Money; according to the usual Manner."[66]

On one occasion, rather than being sold as a captive, a woman sold a captive. In the fall of 1716, a Cherokee named Peggy, along with two Cherokee men, her son, and a prominent Charleston trader who appears to have been her husband, traveled some 200 miles to Charleston to exchange a French prisoner whom her brother had bought and given to her. She wanted reimbursement of the purchase price, which included a gun and various other items, and gifts in recognition of her friendship and services. After three weeks during which her husband used his influence with the right people, the Assembly duly granted Peggy "a Present of a Suit of Calicoe Cloaths, for herself, and a Suit of Stuff and a Hat, for her Son," as well as providing lodging and paying for "Diet and Entertainment" during the four weeks the Cherokees spent in Charleston. Peggy's story was unusual, but mobile Cherokee women clearly considered Charleston as within their orbit, whether they were selling baskets or Frenchmen![67]

In addition to its numerous Indian slaves, Charleston, like Boston, held Indian people as prisoners in times of conflict. In a major breach of trust and alliance, six Shawnees on their way to raid Catawbas were imprisoned in 1753, ostensibly for murdering white men. Attakullakulla and other Cherokees in town at the time witnessed the interrogations and warned the governor that it was a bad move.[68] Charleston also held prisoners before and during the Cherokee War in 1759–61. Cherokee women who had frequented Charleston for decades were now, as prisoners of war, subject to abuse. Governor William Bull worried about lodging the female prisoners in the Charleston barracks, fearing they might be "insulted" by the "sailors who are now very numerous in Town."[69]

Indian people were present and participated in the life of St. Louis and New Orleans from their beginnings, and throughout their history. Indians from both sides of the Mississippi traded at St. Louis, and sometimes they traded Indian slaves. In 1770, in a town with a total population of about 500 residents, thirty-seven colonists held eight Indian men, eighteen women, and forty-three children in bondage.[70]

Alibamons, Biloxis, Chaouachas, Chitimachas, Houmas, Pascagolas, and Tunicas from the Gulf Coast as well as Choctaws from upriver gravitated to New Orleans in the early eighteenth century, as did members of more distant tribes (Figure 3.1). Sometimes Indians moved their villages closer to the city. They provided services as guides, pack horsemen, boat crews, auxiliaries for military campaigns, and slave catchers; they traded goods, and especially produced food for the growing urban population by farming, hunting, and fishing. Every year New Orleans exported tens of thousands of deerskins harvested by Indian hunters. New Orleans was a seaport where, in the words of one French observer around 1750, "the inhabitants, sailors, Indians, and slaves run around freely inside as well as beyond the town."[71] The colonial populace lived alongside and traded with the Indians who inhabited the region. With labor and women in short supply, they also held some of these people as slaves in Mobile and New Orleans. Indian men, women, and children worked as slaves and servants in households and in shops. Authorities tried to control Indians as they did slaves.[72] After Governor Alejandro O'Reilly issued a proclamation extending Spanish law to Louisiana in 1769, however, Indian slaves working on plantations also went to New Orleans to file suits for their freedom.[73]

Indian delegates frequented New Orleans to renew or renegotiate alliances as Britain, France, and Spain tussled for influence among the tribes in the mid-eighteenth century; consequently, formal displays of reciprocal alliance, in historian Dan Usner's words, "were as much a part of the city's calendar as were Easter, Christmas, and the king's birthday."[74] Even after New Orleans declined as a center of Indian diplomacy, and despite the tribes' falling populations and diminishing political influence and economic status, the city continued to thrive as a center of Indian trade. Adapting to changing circumstances, land loss, economic disruption, and new opportunities, Indian people came to the city to peddle herbs, roots, game, prepared food, and baskets in the markets, to work for cash, and to perform as "Indians" in public spaces. After the city's first public

Figure 3.1 Alexandre de Batz, "Desseins de Sauvages de Plusieurs Nations, New Orleans, 1735"

Indian people from near and far traveled to New Orleans for trade and diplomacy. Artist, architect, and engineer Alexandre de Batz (1685–1759) drew this group of men, women, and children "of several nations" on the levee in New Orleans, where they have brought buffalo ribs, buffalo tallow, and bear oil to sell. De Batz's notations identify a Renard (Fox or Mesquakie) female slave at bottom left, Illinois Indians from the upper Mississippi, an Atakapa man from the Gulf coast holding a calumet pipe at far right, and an enslaved African boy. Courtesy of Peabody Museum of Archaeology and Ethnology, Harvard University.

food market was instituted in 1784, Indians naturally participated in what became known as the "French Market." Choctaw, Chitimacha, and Houma people selling their wares remained a notable aspect of New Orleans street life throughout the nineteenth century.[75]

Certain places became seasonal campgrounds for Indians visiting New Orleans. On a Sunday afternoon stroll outside the town gate in 1799, Pennsylvanian Fortescue Cuming saw some fifty Indians in a temporary encampment near a brickworks. Although he emphasized their indolence and intoxication, he also noted that the women were weaving baskets, mats, and other items for sale in the city. Indians often interacted with slaves and working-class whites in back-of-town areas. The first recorded game of lacrosse took place in New Orleans in June 1764 when a delegation of Biloxi and other Indians from the Gulf Coast got together near the city to play and attracted numerous spectators. In the nineteenth century lacrosse became a popular spectator sport, with crowds gathering at the grounds to watch Indian, white, black, and mixed teams compete.[76]

Indians frequented other urban areas as well. Marietta, Ohio, the Ohio Company's model frontier town in the Northwest Territory, attracted Indian visitors in its early days. When Rufus Putnam, one of the founders of the Ohio Company, established Marietta in 1788, Hopocan, also known as Captain Pipe, and twenty other Delawares attended a banquet, Putnam's first meal in the town. Missionary John Heckewelder said the Indians were welcomed to Marietta with pipes, drums, and three cannon shots. Delawares attended Marietta's first July 4 celebration. Putnam said neighboring Delawares and Wyandots showed up "almost every day."[77] Isaac Weld, an Irishman traveling in North America in the 1790s, said that the streets of Detroit were "generally crowded with Indians of one tribe or another." They went there regularly to trade, but in spring 1796 they were "very numerous in this Town" because land speculators had invited them there to sell land.[78] Elizabeth Simcoe, wife of the first lieutenant governor of Upper Canada, did not like the Mississauga Indians, whom she described as lazy, dirty, and drunken, and she particularly did not like seeing them on the streets of Kingston. "These uncivilized People saunter up & down the Town all the day, with the apparent Nonchalance, want of occupation & indifference that seems to possess [London's] Bond street Beaux," she wrote in her diary in 1792.[79]

In addition to seeing Indian slaves and servants, Indian delegates on occasion saw Indian students, and sometimes they left Indian students there. The Jesuits ran a boarding school for Huron boys near Quebec, while Ursuline nuns housed and educated Indian girls in both Quebec and New Orleans. Christian Indians attended grammar schools in Cambridge and Roxbury outside Boston in the 1650s and '60s, and a handful attended Harvard. The Brafferton Institution at the College of William and Mary was founded as a seminary for Indian youth, and although the numbers fluctuated, delegates to Williamsburg could have seen as many as two dozen Indian students during the school's heyday from 1710 to 1722.[80] If they did, they were not necessarily impressed. At the Treaty of Lancaster in 1744, the Onondaga spokesman Canasatego famously declined Virginia's offer to educate young Iroquois, saying, "We love our Children too well to send them so great a Way," and, at least in Benjamin Franklin's retelling of the event, provided a scathing critique of English education that rendered Indian students "totally good for nothing."[81]

Indigenous communities recognized that they needed to have young people educated in the ways of the colonizers. Jonathan Cayenquiloquoa left two sons, and Andrew Montour three children, to be educated in Philadelphia in 1756.[82] Unfortunately, many students likely agreed with Canasatego. Governor Dinwiddie told Cherokee chiefs that some of their young men who were sent to the college in Williamsburg in the spring of 1756 "did not like Confinement," "could not be reconciled to their Books," and within a couple of months "went away of their own accord, without leave." In other words, they dropped out and took off for home.[83] A Seneca chief named Kisheta sent his son to Philadelphia so that "the little boy" could learn English and become an interpreter, but the Indians took him back home in 1762 and he apparently never used his new skills as an interpreter.[84] Delaware chiefs who visited Congress and George Washington in 1779 left three boys who enrolled in the College of New Jersey (the future Princeton). U.S. Indian agent George Morgan secured quarters for them and Congress funded them. Things did not go well, however. The oldest, Thomas Killbuck, was homesick and became addicted, it was said, to "Liquor & to Lying." His younger half-brother, John Killbuck, got one of Morgan's maids pregnant. A congressional committee in 1785 reported that the young men had not been attentive to their studies for some time, and when Thomas and John asked permission to go home to Ohio, Congress granted it. John's new wife and child went with him. The third boy, George Morgan White Eyes, did better. He was seven or eight years old when he started school. He won a prize at his grammar school commencement and described his time at the college as his "happiest moments." He lived for a time at Morgan's home in Princeton, but when Morgan had to travel west on business, he sent White Eyes to live in New York, where he evidently neglected his studies. White Eyes wrote to President Washington complaining of being dependent on charity, of insufficient support, and of "cruel Usage." He said he would rather have been left in the wilds of his native country than "experience the heart breaking Sensations I now feel." He subsequently sold what belongings he had, moved to Ohio, and rejoined his Delaware people.[85] Washington said the kind of education given "to those young Indians who have been sent to our Colleges" was not "productive of any good to their nations" and was even, "perhaps, productive of evil." In his opinion, introducing agriculture and civilization in Indian communities was far more effective than placing Indian students in college.[86]

Alexander McGillivray took two young relatives, his nephew David Tate, who was ten or twelve, and a teenager called David Francis, to New York in the summer of 1790. When the delegation returned home after the treaty was signed, the young men stayed behind. McGillivray said that Henry Knox took his nephew "under his charge in order to give him a cultivated education."[87] Another Creek delegation left two more boys, Alexander Durant, a son of McGillivray's sister, and James Bailey, and Cherokees left a boy named Thomas Wilson in Philadelphia in 1796 to be educated by Quaker families.[88]

When Cornplanter was in Philadelphia in 1791 he asked Washington to take care of nine Seneca boys and give them an education. He hoped such an arrangement would strengthen his people's ties to the United States and improve their chances of survival within the new Republic. Washington declined, offering to send a schoolmaster to Seneca country instead, so Cornplanter asked the Quakers to take two boys, including his own son, Henry O'Bail or Abeel. The Quakers agreed.[89] With sponsorship from Timothy Pickering, Henry spent three years in school, first at a Quaker school in Philadelphia, then at an academy for higher learning in New York, and finally at Dr. Hunter's School in Woodbury, New Jersey. But when it became "evident that he could derive no advantage by continuing here," Pickering "made no objection to his going home."[90]

The Quakers continued the practice of taking in young Indians to live and learn with them, at the request of their parents and with the approval and sometimes the financial support of the federal government. In 1795 Philadelphia Quakers established the "Indian Committee" to undertake missionary projects and guide the Indians' transition to "civilized life." Their first mission was to the Oneidas but, lacking resources and individuals willing to live in Indian communities, they began placing Indian girls with families in the Philadelphia area. By the late 1790s Quakers had at least nine young Indians living and receiving an education in and around the city: Thomas Wilson, James Bailey, and Alexander Durant; and half a dozen girls, four Stockbridge Mohicans and the others Tuscarora. One of the Stockbridge girls was Hendrick Aupaumut's daughter, Margery. The girls were homesick and Margery returned home in May 1798, although the other Stockbridges stuck it out until 1801. In January 1799 the War Department reimbursed Henry Drinker for his expenses lodging, boarding, and educating Wilson. Two years later, it reimbursed him for paying passage to Savannah for Bailey and Durant to go home.[91]

Urban environments could provide refuge in times of war. Mohawks and Oneidas sought safety in Albany when the French invaded Iroquois country in 1696.[92] Indian refugees flooded into St. Augustine after English and Indian raids destroyed the Spanish missions in Florida in 1704. They joined the Spanish and Indian communities already there. In 1736 as many as 1,350 Indians lived in half a dozen towns around St. Augustine and the city had an Indian church.[93] In January 1755, the same month that Hendrick and a delegation of Mohawks were in Philadelphia, a dozen Cherokees arrived. They had been taken prisoner by "French Indians" two years before and were making their way home after having escaped from Canada. On their way to Philadelphia they stayed two nights at the house of Quaker merchant Isaac Norris "and behaved themselves very orderly." In the city, they were given lodgings in the State House. Conscious of the Cherokees' potential role as allies in the emerging conflict with France, the government provided them with clothing for their journey home.[94]

However, cities, and the Indian people living in or close to them, were not immune from the repercussions of war and the hatreds it generated. At the beginning of 1763, according to John Heckewelder, Indians living on the north branch of the Susquehanna River "traveled as usual through the settlements of the white people without fear." By the end of the year, Samuel Foulke, a member of the Pennsylvania Assembly, wrote in his journal, Indian hating "Spread like a Contagion into the Interior parts of ye province & Even ye City it self."[95]

Colonial settlers on the western frontier of Pennsylvania endured the brunt of devastating raids by the Shawnees, Delawares, and other tribes during the French and Indian War. The British victory in 1763 that should have brought peace to the frontier instead brought renewed warfare after the British cut back on gifts and supplies to Indian people, sent garrisons to occupy posts in Indian country, and broke promises to safeguard Indian lands. A Delaware prophet named Neolin preached a message of spiritual and cultural revitalization grounded in resistance to the British, and a multitribal coalition of warriors led by the Odawa war chief Pontiac and the Seneca Guyasuta wrought havoc, attacking British forts and back-country settlements. Reeling from Indian raids and frustrated by the Quaker Assembly, which they felt had done little or nothing to protect them, Pennsylvanian backcountry settlers accused local Indians of complicity in the war.

With fears and tensions growing, about 150 Delaware men, women, and children from the Moravian mission villages near Bethlehem arrived in Philadelphia in November 1763 seeking refuge. "A great mob gathered around them," wrote Heckewelder, "deriding, reviling, and charging them with all the outrages committed by the enemy," and "threatening to kill them on the spot." The Indians kept silent, relying on the providence of God, the missionary said. The Munsee Delaware spiritual leader Papounan or Papunhang brought twenty-one or twenty-two people from Wyalusing. The government housed them first in barracks and then, to remove them from incipient violence on the streets of the city, moved them south of the city to Province Island in the Delaware River, where they were housed in the quarantine station used for sailors and immigrants.[96]

Then, on December 14, a group of Scots-Irish vigilantes calling themselves the Paxton Boys murdered and scalped half a dozen Indians at Conestoga Town. The Conestoga Indians wore English clothes, went by English names, lived in cabins, peddled baskets and brooms among their colonial neighbors, and lived under the protection of the governor and Assembly. Two weeks later—two days after Christmas—the Paxton Boys rode into Lancaster in broad daylight and broke into the workhouse, where the city magistrates had given refuge to fourteen other Conestogas. The Conestoga men, women, and children sat in a circle and prayed; the Paxton Boys shot them, scalped them, and hacked them to pieces.[97]

The authorities tried to remove the Moravian Indian refugees from Philadelphia, to get them out of harm's way, and place them under Sir William Johnson's protection in New York. Accompanied by their missionaries, the Indians loaded their old people, the blind, the sick, and the children with their baggage in four wagons and made their way out of the city. "The crowds of people were very large, so that we could hardly force our way through," said one missionary, and again the Indians were "cursed and reviled in a dreadful manner." Seventy Highland soldiers, survivors of brutal campaigns in the West Indies and the hard-fought Battle of Bushy Run the previous summer, joined them outside the city as an escort. At first some of the soldiers "acted quite wild and particularly harassed our young women." The soldiers came to respect their charges, but Governor Cadwallader Colden and the New York Council refused passage to the Pennsylvania Indians and most were returned to Philadelphia, where yet again a crowd followed them back through the streets. The Indians lived fearfully in the city barracks amid reports and alarms that the Paxton Boys were coming to kill them.[98]

In February 1764, about 250 Pennsylvania settlers and militia marched on Philadelphia. They declared they were coming to kill the Christian Indians and the Quaker Israel Pemberton, and they demanded that the legislature raise more troops to defend the frontiers. Benjamin Franklin hastily organized residents to protect the city and averted the crisis by negotiating with the rebels at Germantown. A war of words and pamphlets followed. The Paxton Boys remained adamant that there was no such thing as "friendly Indians." At the height of the crisis, soldiers were posted to guard the Moravian Indians in their barracks, four cannon were loaded with grapeshot, and as many as 200 citizens turned out to defend them against the rebels, with even Quakers taking up arms. The governor himself spent a night in the barracks with them. "Our poor people long for a place where they can live halfway safe again," one missionary said.[99]

The Moravian Indians remained confined in the Philadelphia city barracks for fourteen months. After the crisis passed, crowds of Philadelphians regularly came to see the Indians, especially to watch their church services and hear them singing. They came in such numbers that the guards had to restrict their access so that the Indians were not overrun. The Indians made baskets, wooden spoons, moccasins, toy bows and arrows, and other craft goods to sell to the visitors so that they could buy bread. Meanwhile, members of their congregation died of dysentery, smallpox, and other illnesses. The survivors sought solace in the Bible and prayer, "since the words which the Brethren say to us from the Savior are our comfort, particularly in our current sad and difficult circumstances, when almost all people hate us and want to kill us." Finally, in April 1765 the missionaries and their Christian converts moved to the Wyalusing

Valley, some 160 miles northeast of Philadelphia, to get far away from future threats.[100]

After almost a decade of war against Indians, many colonists now hated and killed Indians simply because they were Indians. Cities could be places of coexistence and refuge for Indian people, but cities, even the City of Brotherly Love, could also be places of fear and racial violence.

Whether Indian people traveled regularly or relocated permanently to early American cities, whether they were slave or free, and whether they sought work or refuge there, they had to adjust to new and alien environments. Native people on the streets, in the markets, and coming in from outlying settlements found new ways to make a living and to survive as Indians over time, making cities, in Dan Usner's words, a "laboratory of Indian adaptation" and "a useful way station in a new pattern of adjustment and survival."[101] Indian diplomats meeting in formal negotiations in cities often created Indigenous space by their use of ritual, language, and custom. Indians already in the cities also made urban space Indigenous space. Outside the council chamber and beyond the treaty grounds, there were places where Indian people lived and worked, rebuilt their lives and communities, developed their own networks, maintained their own values, and created their own urban homelands.[102] When towns-people gathered to gawk at tribal delegations, how many faces in the crowd belonged to Native people, swept up in the throng or anxious to see other Indians enter their city?

CHAPTER 4

Taking Their Lives
in Their Hands

I N JANUARY 1732, THE PENNSYLVANIA Assembly was
adjourned because there was smallpox in Philadelphia.[1] Later
that year, hearing that Shawnees from Allegheny country had
visited the French in Montreal, the government of Pennsylvania
sent a message, accompanied by a large wampum belt and some
rum, inviting their chiefs to Philadelphia. Two Shawnee chiefs,
Opakethwa, the speaker, and Opakeita, accompanied by two young
men, Quassenungh and Kataweykeita, arrived on September 28 to
meet with the council. After several days in the city, Quassenungh
came down with smallpox, although there were no reported cases in
the city at the time. Opakethwa stayed in town to take care of him.
Quassenungh seemed to recover, but then Opakethwa caught the
disease, died, and "was next day handsomely buried." Later, as recorded in the minutes of the Provincial Council, Quassenungh "was
seized with Violent Pains, and languished till the 16th of January;
he then dyed, and was likewise the next day buried in a handsome
manner." The government covered the Shawnees' expenses while
they were in town, as well as nursing costs, medical bills, and funeral expenses—a total of £43 14s. 5d. In addition, it paid for a small
present to Kataweykeita, "who came hither to visit Quassenungh a
little before his Death, & was the Bearer of the Messages from this
Government touching his and Opakethwas Death." The government
also sent two yards of black cloth and a handkerchief with a message

informing Quassenungh's father, an old chief named Kakowatchy, of the death of his son.[2] The deaths of Opakethwa and Quassanungh discouraged subsequent Shawnee visits to Philadelphia. Shawnees who were invited in 1737 said they were too "much affected with Grief to think we should go to the place where two of our Brothers had died." They made the trip two years later, in the summer of 1739, and brought "a little Deer's hair to put on their Graves."[3]

Cities were unhealthy places, and Indian delegates often tried to avoid them during times of disease. Tiyoskate, the Dakota chief who traveled a thousand miles to Montreal in 1695, never returned home: He fell ill in the city and died a month later.[4] Disease cast a pall over the Great Peace of Montreal in the summer of 1701. Kondiaronk, the elderly spokesman for the Hurons of Michilimackinac, said "there had been much rumor that disease was great in Montreal." Some Native emissaries fell ill on their way to the city; others turned back. Kondiaronk himself developed a violent fever and died on August 2, two days before the peace was signed. To demonstrate esteem for the deceased chief at a critical moment in the peace process, the governor of New France, Louis-Hector de Callière, ordered a full funeral that combined Native ritual and European ceremony. An escort of sixty French soldiers led the funeral procession, followed by sixteen Huron warriors, their faces blackened in mourning; then came the town's clergy and six war chiefs carrying the flower-covered coffin. Kondiaronk's brother and children, other Hurons and Odawas, the governor, and more officers brought up the rear. Kondiaronk was buried with military honors in Montreal's Notre Dame church, which was hung with black drapery. The peace was ratified the next day. Other Huron and Miami chiefs died of the deadly "cold," but many refused treatment at the hospital, "imagining they would be poisoned there."[5]

Indian delegates who survived the hazards of travel risked their lives when they entered crowded and unhealthy urban environments, especially port cities, where ships brought diseases from the Caribbean and more distant regions. A conference with a delegation of four Penobscots and Norridgewocks in Boston was interrupted in January 1728 for the funeral of Weneremet, one of the emissaries. After the funeral the governor in council offered condolences and informed the other three Indians "that a Present of a Mourning Ring would be made to the Sachem of Norridgewock and also a Ring and some Cloathing and Provisions to the Widow." The Indians expressed thanks "for the great care that had been taken of him and for his decent and respectful interment."[6]

It's not clear what Weneremet died of, though Boston offered plenty of possibilities. Smallpox struck the city in 1666 and in 1677–78. Another outbreak in 1720–21 affected almost 6,000 people, at least half the population, and more than 840, almost one in twelve, succumbed. Smallpox returned in 1730 and, despite the protections offered by inoculation, infected 4,000 people and killed 500. In 1751–52 smallpox struck Boston again, brought by a ship from London. More than 7,660 people contracted the disease (2,109 of them caught it through inoculation); 569 died. More than 1,800 inhabitants fled the city. Smallpox returned in 1764, 1776, 1778, and 1792, although increasing reliance on inoculation, or variolation—a process that involved infecting the patient with live smallpox matter—helped reduce mortality rates. Scarlet fever in 1735–36 affected 4,000 people in Boston, but with a relatively low mortality rate, killing more than 100. As Boston recovered from smallpox in 1765, it suffered an outbreak of diphtheria.[7]

Disease in their own villages sometimes prevented delegations from traveling to colonial towns. More than 450 Iroquois people arrived in Albany for a treaty conference in the fall of 1745. None of them were Senecas, noted the record of the proceedings, "it being . . . a Time of great Sickness and Mortality among them, which prevented their Coming."[8] Disease threatened to derail negotiations at Albany four years later, when, Conrad Weiser said, "so many accidents happened which are looked upon by the Indians as bad omens." Soon after they arrived they came down with smallpox "and the other distemper Called the long feaver," which together carried off more than 200 Albany residents and made "sad work" among the Indians; "most of them fell Sick before they Came home and a great many died."[9]

Mid-eighteenth-century Philadelphia was a hazardous place.[10] It was especially dangerous for new arrivals entering an unfamiliar disease environment, where they would be exposed to measles, whooping cough, diphtheria, various vaguely defined fevers, and, of course, the dreaded smallpox. Tanning yards dumped animal carcasses and other waste into Duck Creek, a stream that meandered from the Delaware River through the heart of the city and into a swamp. Putrifying carcasses, garbage, and excrement turned the creek into sludge. Its stench assailed the nostrils; it polluted drinking water, causing dysentery, and it attracted mosquitos that carried yellow fever (a viral infection that attacks the liver, giving its victims a yellow pallor). In poorer neighborhoods residents emptied refuse and excrement into gutters and alleys, and dogs, pigs, and rodents rooted through the garbage.[11] Smallpox was a recurrent scourge. In 1731 it "proved Mortall to many." In 1736 it carried off Benjamin Franklin's four-year-old son. It returned in 1750–51, 1756, and 1759, and struck several times between 1765 and 1775. An outbreak of diphtheria killed children in Philadelphia in the winter of 1763. Scarlet fever killed children in 1764 and again in 1769. Typhus (a common shipboard disease), typhoid fever, consumption, and dysentery were recurrent.[12] Provincial secretary Richard Peters reported in September 1741 that "a Malignant fever has been lurking more or less in Town the greatest part of this Summer," although it did not rage with the violence of the yellow fever outbreak six years before. "There is reason to think by this & other Fevers always shewing themselves first in some or others the houses about the Dock that this quantity of Filth & Mudd breeds or at least very much contributes to the malignancy of the Distempers," Peters said.[13] An epidemic broke out in the summer of 1754 after "sickly Vessels" unloaded "distemper'd Persons and their infected goods." Efforts to contain it proved ineffective, and Governor Robert Hunter Morris urged more stringent legislation to prevent ships and their passengers from bringing infectious diseases to the city.[14]

Twenty Oneidas died in Philadelphia in 1749. The next year Oneida chiefs said they lost so many men every time they traveled to Philadelphia that it seemed "the evil Spirits that Dwell among the White People are against us and kill us." They declined an invitation to visit Virginia because they could only assume that traveling deeper into the colonial settlements would be even more dangerous.[15]

Indians were particularly wary of Charleston, especially in the summer, when the air was "very unhealthy." Many delegates braved the dangers. Creeks and Cherokees went to Charleston in July 1721, although Cherokee chiefs said that when they had last visited, sickness in the city had proved "very fatal" to many of their people. Plenty of Cherokees traveled to Charleston for a treaty that November, and ninety-nine Creeks went in June 1753. Nevertheless, despite Governor Glen's assurances that Charleston was healthy in the fall when "the Heats are over, and even the Musqitoes are gone," Indians remained fearful of the city, hampering British diplomatic efforts at the beginning of the French and Indian War. Connecorte of Chota, whom the English called Old Hop because of his lameness, declined Glen's invitation in 1755 to send a delegation because he had "from Time to Time . . . sent down the best of his Warriors to Charles Town, and that by Reason of Sickness they contracted there, or on their Journey homewards, they had lost their Lives and their Bones did yet lye on the Path." (Glen agreed to meet them halfway, at the Saluda River; 500 Cherokees assembled for a conference there.) When Glen's successor, Governor Lyttelton, arrived to take up his post in 1756, he invited Attakullakulla and Connecorte "to come see him at Charles Town and have a good Talk together," but they put him off until the fall because "we have often lost People by going down in the Heat of Summer." Creeks told Lyttelton the next year that "we are afraid to come to Charles Town for Fear of Sickness." Cherokee warriors repeated the refrain in 1758: "Wee lost a great many of our People by Sickness going down in the Summer."[16]

They had good reason to be concerned. Charleston was the deadliest city in mainland America. Hot weather and swamps spawned mosquitos and malaria, which added to infectious diseases such as smallpox and yellow fever to produce staggering mortality rates, even among elite classes. In just eight years, between 1738 and 1746, merchant Thomas Lamboll buried two wives and four children, all aged three years or younger. Five of the deaths occurred in the lethal months between April and November.[17] In its early years, Charleston suffered from what was called "country fever" every summer, and outbreaks of yellow fever in 1699, 1703, and 1706. Smallpox struck in 1698. In 1738, despite efforts to prevent the disease from spreading by outlawing the risky practice of inoculation, smallpox infected 2,100 people, almost half the population, and then spread with devastating results to the Cherokees. When Colonel Henry Bouquet's Royal American Regiment arrived with a few cases of smallpox in June 1757, the people of Charleston were "so frightened at the mere name of that disease" that Bouquet worried they would refuse him entry. They were right to be afraid. In 1760, more than half the city's population of 8,000 contracted the disease and more than 9 percent of the population died.[18] A British naval officer described Charleston in verse in 1769:

> Black and white all mix'd together
> Inconstant, strange, unhealthful weather
> Burning heat and chilling cold
> Dangerous both to young and old
> Boisterous winds and heavy rains
> Fevers and rheumatic pains
> Agues plenty without doubt
> Sores, boils, the prickling heat and gout
> Musquitos on the skin make blotches
> Centipedes and large cock-roaches.[19]

Indian delegations had to weigh the chances of infection and survival when smallpox was around, taking into account the virulence of the disease and their own immunity (if they had already had the disease) or lack of it. Colonial authorities usually warned Indian delegates when there was disease in town. One hundred Iroquois people traveling to Philadelphia in September 1736 were detained on the outskirts of the city because many residents had been sick "& now the small pox are there." Since the Indians had come to respond to a treaty held in public in Philadelphia, protocol required them to give their answer in the same place, but they were advised to spend no more time there than was absolutely necessary. The Iroquois were assured that "the Distemper is as yet but young, & just begun in the place; that it is only in the heart or near the middle of the town." They were offered lodging on the outskirts, "where if they take care they may for a few days be in but very little or no danger." They decided to risk it and carried on to Philadelphia the next day.[20]

In March 1756, the Oneida chief Scarouady, his Mohawk brother-in-law Contochqua (whom the English called Moses the Song), Conrad Weiser's adoptive Mohawk brother Jonathan Cayenquiloquoa, and more than twenty men, women, and children arrived in Philadelphia, accompanied by interpreter Andrew Montour and escorted by British Indian agent Daniel Claus. Unfortunately, according to Richard Peters, "fatigue and fresh Fish of which the Indians are fond threw them into pleuritick Disorders, and they had like to have all dyed, but with the favor of Providence only one dyed." Moses the Song fell violently sick with food poisoning on Sunday, March 28 and died on Monday morning. He was buried with military honors in the Christ Church graveyard. The governor's council, commissioners, militia officers, and prominent Philadelphia citizens attended the funeral.[21] Sir William Johnson met with the Iroquois delegates when they returned from Philadelphia and performed a condolence ceremony for the death of "our worthy friend Moses."[22]

The Seneca chief Kanuksusy, or Newcastle, wrestled with whether or not to go to Philadelphia when smallpox was there. He had been going to the city for ten years. He first visited in 1747 with a delegation of ten Indians from the Ohio country who asked the Pennsylvania government for weapons to help them fight the French. George Washington met him in 1753 and gave him the name Fairfax, after Lord Fairfax of Virginia. Kanuksusy was one of a handful of Indians who accompanied General Edward Braddock's disastrous campaign against Fort Duquesne in 1755, after which Robert Hunter Morris gave him a new name, Newcastle. He acted as an intermediary between the government of Pennsylvania and the neighboring tribes, and was reckoned a true friend to the English.[23] In the spring of 1756, on a mission to the Indians of the Susquehanna River for Morris, Newcastle left his daughter (or niece) Canadahawaby at a trading post on the Susquehanna and asked that she be taken to Philadelphia so that he could meet her there when he returned. Morris ordered Captain Thomas McKee to escort the girl but "not suffer her to come into ye City . . . if she has not had ye Small Pox, as it is now in Town . . . ; if she has had ye Small Pox, you may bring her to Mrs. Boyl's in Chestnut Street." McKee escorted her to Thomas Penn's country home at Springetsbury Manor on the outskirts of the city, but two Indians took her into Philadelphia; this angered Morris, who had her sent to Richard Peters's house until Newcastle returned.[24]

During a council in Philadelphia in July 1756, Pennsylvania officials warned Newcastle, Teedyuscung, and the other Indians that there was smallpox there "and that it was of a bad sort." They offered to lodge them at Springetsbury Manor, "where they might Escape the Infection and be well Entertained."[25] The Indian delegates managed to avoid the disease during the summer but not in the fall. On November 3, Conrad Weiser told Teedyuscung that the governor and council invited the Indian delegates to come to Philadelphia, "where you could be entertained better, and everything might be done with more Solemnity," but if they preferred, the Pennsylvanian officials would come to them. "I must tell you (in order to deal fair with you) that the Small Pox are in Philadelphia, but not very bad, and you perhaps are not afraid of them, as of late you had them among yourselves."[26] The conference was held at Easton, but Weiser was wrong about the danger in Philadelphia. Newcastle, his nephew, and several other Indians contracted smallpox and died. Newcastle's dying request was that "I must be buried with my friends, the Quakers, when I am dead." He was laid to rest according to his wishes, in the Quaker cemetery, just three days after Weiser had tried to reassure Teedyuscung that the smallpox was not bad. A huge funeral cortege followed the casket through the streets of Philadelphia. Richard Peters said it was a particularly bad outbreak: "Many Children, and Others have dyed of the foul disease." When it "got among" the Indians, the Quakers cared for them, a physician attended to them, and the government did everything in its power to help, to no avail. Governor William Denny asked William Johnson to hold condolence ceremonies for Newcastle.[27]

Treaty conferences that were supposed to be held in Philadelphia sometimes were moved inland to a safer environment at Lancaster. A treaty in April 1757 was disrupted when Indian delegates heading to Philadelphia came down with smallpox. Teedyuscung had promised to come, and Denny wanted to avoid "the Inconveniences to the

Government" that would occur if the conference were held anywhere but in the city. Although trader and agent George Croghan did his best to convince the Indians, they remained afraid of Philadelphia, "as many of the Indians dyed there in the Fall and Winter." Many of them were already ill with smallpox. They delegated three men to travel on to Philadelphia but held their conference at Lancaster, saying they were anxious to get home in time for planting.[28] In the spring of 1762 Governor James Hamilton was due to meet with the western Delaware chiefs Shingas and Tamaqua (the Beaver) in Philadelphia. Instead, he sent them word and a wampum belt to tell them he had "kindled the Council Fire at Lancaster" because there were "some Remains of the Small Pox" in the city and it might spread in the warm weather.[29] Indians, of course, were not the only people to steer clear of infected cities. "The smallpox is in town," Thomas Jefferson added in a postscript to his friend (and future governor) John Page in 1763, "so you may scratch out that sentence of my letter wherein I mentioned coming to Williamsburgh so soon."[30]

Smallpox remained a threat during the American Revolution. It affected armies in the East and reached pandemic proportions in the West, where thousands of Indian people died. The dozen Delaware chiefs who traveled to Philadelphia in the spring of 1779 to meet with the Continental Congress camped on the common to avoid catching smallpox.[31] After American troops burned their villages in 1779, 300 Cherokee refugees arrived in British-held Savannah in March 1780 but, finding the disease there, quickly moved on to "shun the smallpox."[32]

Not all delegates' illnesses were due to epidemics, and not all were fatal. In spring 1766 a Tuscarora sachem named Diagawekee became ill after traveling from the Susquehanna to visit Governor William Tryon in Brunswick, North Carolina. He had the mumps. Tryon had a doctor look after him and supplied him "with everything he wanted." Diagawekee recovered in about a week. "He dined Twice at my Table, which was as often as his Health would permit," Tryon informed Sir William Johnson, adding with a note of surprise that he "found him not only Humanized but really Civilized." "In Testimony of his Regard for the Care I had taken of Him in his Illness," Diagawekee gave Tryon his name, which "is to remain to all future Governors of North Carolina." Since he did so at Tryon's request, it is difficult to know if Diagawekee's gift was heartfelt.[33]

A well-traveled Oneida chief named Da-ya-gough-de-re-sesh or Saghughsuniunt, known to the English as Thomas King, ended his travels in Charleston. King had visited other colonial cities—he spoke at a meeting in Philadelphia in 1759 and went to Boston in 1763.

William Johnson described him as "a forward fellow fond of giv^g himself consequence," though also "a Man of very good Address & Abilities" whom he often employed as an envoy. In 1770 he sent King with a multitribal delegation to negotiate a peace between the northern and southern tribes. King traveled from Iroquois country to the Shawnees and then to the Creeks and Cherokees, although Johnson complained that he spent too much time socializing ("reveling," he said) in Indian villages along the way. King reached Charleston in late August 1771 and spent a dozen days there. After thirteen months on the road, he was anxious to get home. Johnson maintained that Indians did not like traveling in sailing vessels, as it made them seasick; King, however, wanted to return by sea "and expressed a Strong Inclination to see the great City of Philadelphia." Governor William Bull arranged passage for him. King did not live to see Philadelphia. He came down with a violent fever and despite the attention of two physicians died on the night of September 5. Bull ordered "a decent funeral according to the English manner, as I knew not how to do him funeral honour according to the Custom of his Country, for we are intirely at a loss for an Interpreter of his Language." Johnson dispatched a messenger carrying a wampum belt to inform the various Indian nations of King's death, and a condolence ceremony was held the next month during a conference in Philadelphia.[34] The rest of King's party boarded ship for Philadelphia. "Anawacks the next in authority to Thomas King" died at sea, and a third delegate was so affected with lameness that he was unable to go with the others to see Sir William. Deprived of the three elder chiefs, Johnson had to rely on the younger men to give him an account of the embassy.[35]

Sometimes Indian delegates were unwell even before they arrived in town. Alexander McGillivray was ill for several days after reaching New York in the summer of 1790. Abigail Adams, who met him, described McGillivray as "grave and solid, intelligent and much of a Gentleman, but in very bad Health."[36] Although eighteenth-century New York, like other port cities, suffered recurrent bouts of smallpox and other diseases, observers attributed McGillivray's chronic ill health to loose living.

One of the Indians in Samuel Kirkland's delegation to Philadelphia in the spring of 1792 was twenty-six-year-old Peter Otsiquette. On March 19, after less than a week in Philadelphia, "the young chief," as he was dubbed in the press, died suddenly, ostensibly of pleurisy. Anxious not to let his death derail negotiations before they started, the government arranged a very public funeral on the afternoon of March 21. The body was carried through the streets from Oeller's Hotel to the cemetery of the Second Presbyterian Church in

Mulberry Street, accompanied by a solemn dirge. Soldiers with arms reversed and drums muffled preceded the coffin; six chiefs followed, with the other Indians, clergy, secretary of war Henry Knox, army officers, and prominent citizens behind. Press reports estimated that 10,000 people attended the funeral.[37] "No quorum present this afternoon," Jacob Hiltzheimer, a German immigrant and city official, noted in his diary, "owing to so many of the members attending the Indian funeral from the Hotel on Chestnut Street to the Presbyterian ground on Arch Street."[38] A young Quaker woman, Elizabeth Drinker, also noted the funeral in her diary and said Otsiquette was buried "with great parade." It was the size of the funeral that attracted her attention, not the death itself. Drinker's diary is an almost daily record of deaths and funerals, childhood illnesses, sickness among friends, family, and neighbors, and fears of epidemic disease; "a sight daily to be seen, burials, tis strange it makes so little impression on the living," she reflected.[39] On March 26, together with Kirkland and their interpreter, some of the chiefs attended divine service at St. Paul's Church. After the service the minister expressed condolences to the Indians for the loss of "the young Prince, your brother." "We mingle our tears with yours, and mourn with you on the sorrowful occasion," he said. He then asked the congregation to remain seated in their pews while Kirkland and the chiefs filed out in "perfect order."[40]

Otsiquette was not the only delegate to die in the city that spring. "I partake of your sorrow on account that it has pleased the Great Sprit to take from you two of your number by death, since your residence in this city," George Washington told the Iroquois delegation in late April. "I have ordered that your tears should be wiped away according to your custom, and that presents should be sent to the relations of the deceased." Then, perhaps recalling his own dark days after the deaths of his half-brother Lawrence and his daughter-in-law Patsy Custis, he added, "Our lives are all in the hands of our Maker, and we must part with them whenever he shall demand them; and the survivors *must submit* to events they cannot prevent."[41] The Iroquois found it hard to be consoled; "we looked upon your present as drowned in tears," they told Timothy Pickering.[42]

According to newspaper reports, Karontowanen (also called Keondowanie, Kalonowea, or Big Tree), "head warrior from Genesyo," died at his lodgings in April after being ill no more than twenty hours and was buried in the Quaker cemetery.[43] Either the newspapers mistook the identity of the dead chief or two men had the same name, for three months later Big Tree was on his way to Allegheny with Cornplanter.[44] According to the prominent Iroquoian scholar William N. Fenton, Big Tree's Seneca name was Seriohana or

Serihowaneh.[45] This Big Tree died by his own hand, apparently taking hemlock in a traditional method of suicide and then stabbing himself. American sources attributed his suicide to profound grief at the death of his friend General Richard Butler in the rout of St. Clair's army in 1791 and increasing melancholia over his failure to take three lives in vengeance, as he had pledged. Anthony Wayne, commanding the American army, reported to Henry Knox on January 1794, "We have to lament the unfortunate death of Capt Big Tree a Seneka War Chief, who put a period to his own existence on the 23rd Instant about 3. OClock PM." The United States had lost "a true and faithful friend." Wayne sent a speech of condolence and gifts to the Senecas.[46]

A delegation from the Wabash and Illinois tribes suffered particularly heavy losses in Philadelphia. In May 1792, Washington sent General Rufus Putnam, along with Mohican emissary Hendrick Aupaumut, Moravian missionary John Heckewelder, and William Wells, a former Miami captive and son-in-law of Little Turtle, as interpreter, to Vincennes to make a treaty and detach tribes on the lower Wabash from the Northwest confederacy, which had destroyed the American army seven months before.[47] At the end of the negotiations, Putnam told the Indians that President Washington wanted to meet some of them, "take them by the hand, and smoke the pipe of peace with them, at his council fire—there to brighten the chain of friendship, and personally convince you of the goodness of his heart." If each tribe would send one or two delegates, Putnam would cover all expenses and provide safe conduct and accommodation on both legs of the journey.[48]

Sixteen men and three women representing the Kaskaskias, Piankashaws, Peorias, Potawatomis, Kickapoos, Mascoutens, Weas, and other tribes accompanied Heckewelder by land to the falls of the Ohio, by water to Pittsburgh, and then on to Philadelphia by land. They carried a wampum belt of peace to present to Washington and asked him to protect their lands from American encroachments. Jean Baptiste DuCoigne, who led the Kaskaskia delegates (Figure 4.1), was the son of a Kaskaskia mother and French Canadian father who had been captured by the Cherokees and later employed as an interpreter by the British. DuCoigne had assisted George Rogers Clark as an emissary to the Wabash tribes during the Revolution and had visited Thomas Jefferson at Monticello in 1781, just days before Colonel Banastre Tarleton's raid drove the then governor of Virginia from his home. Although the Kaskaskias had suffered massive population losses during the previous century, their friendship was important with the fight against the British still raging. Jefferson had described DuCoigne to the Marquis de Lafayette as someone "whose

Figure 4.1 "Indian of the Nation of the Kaskaskia." Engraving based on a drawing by General Victor Collot, 1796. The individual is sometimes identified as Jean Baptiste DuCoigne. Everett Collection Historical/Alamy Stock Photo.

rank, services, disposition, and proposal are such as required attention from us and great respect." He told DuCoigne, "We, like you, are Americans, born in the same land, and having the same interests," gave him a bronze medal, and smoked the pipe with him. DuCoigne named his infant son, who accompanied him, Louis Jefferson, and gave the governor several painted buffalo skins, which Jefferson studied and promised to "always keep them hanging on the walls in remembrance of you and your nation." The Kaskaskias traditionally had practiced hereditary chieftainship, with the role passing from father to son, and DuCoigne's relationship to chiefs was through his mother, but other factors came into play. "He is the best Speaker; and therefore we have chosen him to speak our Sentiments," the Indians explained at the Treaty of Vincennes. DuCoigne was eager to renew his acquaintance with secretary of state Jefferson soon after the delegation arrived in late December 1792.[49]

The embassy was a disaster. At least eight members of the delegation died. One, who had been suffering from pleurisy—which causes an inflation of the tissue separating the lungs from the chest wall—died on the way. Then, in the first month in the city, seven died of smallpox. The tragedy was amplified by the fact that, as one newspaper reported, "two of them took it the natural way—the other five had been inoculated." On February 4, six chiefs and two women dined with Washington (who had lifelong immunity to smallpox, having had it as a young man). DuCoigne handed the president a black pipe to smoke in remembrance of "our chiefs who have come here and died in your bed. It is the calumet of the dead. Take it and smoke it in remembrance of them." He added, "The half of my heart, father, is black. I brought the Piorias to you, half of them are dead. I fear they will say it was my fault."[50] A white pipe was then passed and smoked to clear the air for peace talks to proceed. A Kickapoo chief named Shawas, or the Little Doe, carried the pipe around to be smoked, although he told Washington, "I am still very ill and unable to speak." An Ouiatenon or Wea woman, identified only as "the wife of the Souldier," spoke for a chief known as Great or Grand Joseph, who had died. "If he had lived, you would have heard a good man, and good words flowing from his mouth," she told the president. "He was my uncle, and it has fallen to me to speak for him." Three Legs, a Piankashaw, said he was "not a Village-chief, but only a chief of war," yet now he had to speak "for a young chief whom I have lost here."[51]

The president sent representatives to attend the funerals. Knox wrote a note to Tobias Lear, Washington's secretary, on Sunday morning, January 6, 1793: "Will you and the other gentlemen of the family find it convenient to attend the funeral of the Indian chief at ½ past 12 o'clock this day from Oeller's Hotel."[52] The eight chiefs were buried in St. Peter's Episcopal Church, at Third and Pine Streets. Church records reveal their names (also recorded on a historical marker in the church yard) and the dates and cause of death (smallpox) but not the precise location of their burials:

Jan. 06 La Gese, a chief of the Potowatamies on the Illinois River, age 36
08 Apautapea, a Penkeshow War Chief, age 25
09 Bigigh Weautono, War Chief of the Wabash Nation, age 52
09 Barkskin, of the Penkeshow Nation, age 26

10 Grand Joseph, Great Chief of the Veattonno [Ouiatenon] Nation, age 63
13 Wapeteet, Chief of the Payugheya Nation, age 60
17 Toma, War Chief of the Pawaunia Nation, age 62
April 06   Little Elk, an Indian Chief.[53]

The rest of the delegates remained in Philadelphia until May. As they departed for home, Washington reminded them to reflect on the power they had seen and consider what Indian enemies of the United States might expect if they did not listen to offers of peace. He gave each chief a medal to wear as a symbol of loyalty and provided a letter of protection to help ensure a safe journey. The white wampum belts and peace pipes the Indians had given him were deposited, ironically, in the War Office.[54] Nine days after his dinner with the Indians, and while they were still in the city, Washington submitted the Treaty of Vincennes to the Senate for ratification. The fourth article of the treaty guaranteed the Indians "all the lands to which they have a just claim" and recognized their right to sell or not as they wished. Concerned that this did not grant the United States pre-emptive right to the tribes' lands, the Senate postponed discussion of the treaty until the next session of Congress. The Indian delegates apparently were not informed. "Most of the principal Chiefs of the Wabash Indians who visited this City having died with the smallpox, it would have been improper & nugatory to have attempted with the remainder any explanation of the fourth article of the treaty," Knox told Washington.[55] In January 1794 the Senate refused to ratify the treaty. The delegates from the Wabash had died for nothing.

The surviving members returned home, missing the epidemic of yellow fever that hit the city in the summer of 1793. Although smallpox was the deadliest disease in Philadelphia before the Revolution, yellow fever was a recurrent visitor and caused massive destruction of human life. Its first symptoms resembled a common cold, but it could kill a healthy adult in less than ten days. Doctors had no reliable cure for yellow fever (and apparently still don't) nor any way to stop an outbreak because they did not know its cause. Both the virus and its host species, the *Aedes aegypti* mosquito, originated in West Africa and spread through the slave trade, finding a new home in Caribbean port towns, the traffic hubs of the Atlantic world. *Aedes aegypti* breeds in tiny pools of water and so could thrive in urban spaces and in the water supplies of eighteenth-century ships. Yellow fever hit Philadelphia and Charleston in 1699, killed 570 people in New York in 1702, and "carried off an abundance of People" in Charleston in 1706. Seven major outbreaks of yellow fever struck Charleston in the next sixty years; New York and Philadelphia each suffered four. Then the frequency and ferocity of outbreaks abated.[56] However, as the United States expanded its overseas trade and developed a thriving commerce with the West Indies, ships fanning out from the Caribbean carried the disease to ports in Europe and North America. The influx of French and British soldiers and sailors to the West Indies aggravated the situation. In 1793 yellow fever returned to Philadelphia, probably brought by mosquitos transported with refugees from the revolution in Saint-Domingue.[57]

Like smallpox survivors, people who survived a bout of yellow fever acquired immunity for life, so it produced relatively few fatalities in environments where the population was stable. But it found sources of previously unexposed victims in the bustling new ports of the United States. Unlike smallpox, yellow fever targeted healthy young adults, rather than children or the elderly. Unlike smallpox, yellow fever did not spread into the interior because *Aedes aegypti* had a short flight range, so outbreaks occurred and remained near the waterfront. It spread along the coastal cities over the next few years, reaching as far north as Boston and Portsmouth, New Hampshire. New York, Philadelphia, Baltimore, and Charleston suffered repeated outbreaks. The only protection lay in flight to the countryside, which brought economic, social, and political disruption and distress. "A malignant fever has been generated in the filth of Water street" in Philadelphia, Jefferson wrote James Madison on September 1, 1793; "every body, who can, is flying from the city, and the panic of the country people is likely to add famine to disease."[58] Piominko and four other Chickasaws on their way to see President Washington reached Abingdon, Virginia, but turned back after William Blount warned them of the epidemic. Blount thought it for the best: "By this determination," he wrote Knox, "the United States are relieved from a heavy expence, which certainly must have attended the journey, and the President and yourself from the trouble of what appeared to me an unnecessary visit."[59] Yellow fever hit Philadelphia again in 1794, 1797, and 1798 (when it killed the aforementioned Jacob Hiltzheimer), and outbreaks continued for a dozen years.[60]

It might be thought that Indian visitors to Philadelphia in the second half of the eighteenth century had access to the best medical care in North America. The first general hospital for the poor in the British colonies was established in Philadelphia in 1752, the first medical school was established at the University of Pennsylvania in 1765, and eminent Philadelphia physicians such as Dr. Benjamin Rush had received the best medical training available, in Rush's case at the University of Edinburgh. Unfortunately, with the exception of inoculation, which gained increasing credit for saving lives,

extending eighteenth-century health care to visiting Indians usually did them few favors. The state of medical knowledge, the lack
of understanding of infection, the emphasis on purging, vomiting,
and bleeding as go-to remedies, and the imprecision with which
medicines were administered were as likely to kill as cure a patient.
Warren Johnson said the hospital in Philadelphia in 1760 was "very
bad" and "their Bedlam is in the Hospital."[61]

Based on their own notions of civility, Europeans frequently
complained that Indians lacked both civility and cleanliness, but Native
people had their own codes of what constituted civil behavior, and by
many accounts Indigenous standards of cleanliness surpassed those
of Europeans.[62] The Jesuit Paul Le Jeune reported that Natives were
appalled to see Europeans blow their nose into a square of white linen
and then put the handkerchief and mucus into their pocket.[63] The Earl
of Bellomont, as governor of New York, complained that his conference
with Five Nations delegates in Albany in 1700 was "the greatest fatigue
I ever underwent in my whole life. I was shut up in a close chamber
with 50 sachems, who besides the stink of bear's grease with which they
plentifully dawb'd themselves, were continually smoking tobacco or
drinking drams of rum."[64] The sachems' feelings about being cooped
up with the earl and his entourage are not recorded. Indian peoples
regularly practiced ritual bathing, but it would be more than a hundred
years before Americans started bathing regularly for health and cleanliness; before then, according to one source, "most Americans passed
through life without bathing more than once a year."[65] Unwashed
people crowded into confined spaces with minimal sanitation meant
that eighteenth-century cities offered plenty to repulse any visitor.

Before germ theory identified particular agents as the cause
of diseases, people explained epidemics by theories of miasmas and
contagion. Diseases emanated from foul-smelling miasmas created
by piles of refuse and fermented vegetable or animal material and
spread from person to person.[66] Benjamin Rush spoke of "Diseases
from the influence of Devils—They Reign in the Air . . . The devil
has the power of death—of course of diseases."[67] Governor Thomas
Mifflin's recommendations following the yellow fever outbreak of
1797, which killed 1,250 people in Philadelphia and its suburbs and
would have killed more had not inhabitants evacuated, revealed the
continuing problems. Mifflin urged the State Assembly to establish
a board of health, make better provisions for quarantining people
and cargoes, and establish a public hospital on the common for
inhabitants infected with contagious diseases. Between July 1 and the
end of October, ships from the Mediterranean, the coast of Africa, the
West Indies, and points south of Florida were to undergo quarantine.

But the only way to protect the public health from domestic sources of contagion, according to Mifflin, was to pay "attention to the cleanliness of the city, its avenues, and vacant lots" and ensure clean water supplies.[68]

Putting oneself in the hands of European doctors could prove as hazardous as coming to disease-ridden towns in the first place. In the seventeenth century, Indian people who resorted to the Hôtel-Dieu in Quebec in times of sickness were likely to be purged and bled, although some went to ask for medicine.[69] Different cultural views caused Indian people to look askance at European practices and treatments they saw in the cities. In 1749, the governor of South Carolina invited a delegation of Chickasaws to Charleston. On their way, the Chickasaws were struck with smallpox. Then, on the "very day we arrived," said trader James Adair, who accompanied them, one of the king's surgeons amputated a soldier's wounded arm. When Adair told them about it the Indians were horrified at "such a barbarous amputation." They felt "such butchery would not only disfigure, but disable the poor man the rest of his life." It would have been more humane to cut off his head; better "to die once, than to be always dying," they said.[70]

It is not surprising then, that Indian people preferred their Native healers and remedies when possible. These healers, many of them women, possessed a rich knowledge of the healing properties of plants and where to find them. Like other forms of life, plants possessed power, and healers performed rituals and ceremonies to render their herbal remedies effective.[71] When Jacques Cartier and his French crew got sick at the Indian town of Hochelaga in the winter of 1535–36, the Indians cured them of what turned out to be scurvy.[72] Naturalist John Lawson acknowledged the skill of Indian physicians and the efficacy of their herbal medicines. "An *Indian* hath been often found to heal an *English*-man of a Malady," he wrote, "which the ablest of our *English* Pretenders in *America*, after repeated Applications, have deserted the Patient as incurable; God having furnish'd every Country with specific Remedies for their peculiar Diseases."[73] John Heckewelder, who lived with Indian people and had himself benefited from their cures, thought Indian physicians were "perhaps more free from fanciful theories than those of any nation on earth." Instead, "their science is entirely founded on observation, experience and the well tried efficacy of remedies. There are physicians of both sexes, who take considerable pains to acquire a correct knowledge of the properties and medical virtues of plants, roots and barks, for the benefit of their fellow-men. They are very careful to have at all times a full assortment of their medicines at hand, which they gather and collect at the proper seasons."[74] In the late eighteenth century, Quaker families in Chester County, Pennsylvania, suffering from sickness turned with success to Hannah Freeman, a local Delaware woman well known for her knowledge of and skill with herbal medicines.[75]

Indian people also drew on their own beliefs, medicines, and rituals when confronted by deadly new diseases.[76] Nevertheless, cures introduced from the Old World proved most effective in dealing with diseases introduced from the Old World. In 1798 Little Turtle traveled to Philadelphia with William Wells in another vain attempt to get the president to change the western boundary established by the Treaty of Greenville. At Pittsburgh, which was still a frontier town although it was making the first steps toward becoming a commercial and manufacturing center, they stayed at the Black Bear Inn. Outside, Indians and whites frequented the taverns and brothels, pigs and dogs rummaged in garbage, and "to the odors of privies, pigsties, stables, slaughterhouses, and scum-covered ponds was added the pervasive smell of coal smoke, the local fuel of choice, which was plentiful in nearby hills and streams."[77] Little Turtle fell ill on the road to Philadelphia and arrived in December in bad health. Secretary of war James McHenry sent him to Benjamin Rush on Walnut Street, who inoculated him against smallpox by variolation. He was the first American Indian to receive federal inoculation, and he stayed at Rush's home for several weeks while he recovered. He was also treated for gout and rheumatism at the government's expense.[78] By the time he met President John Adams, Little Turtle had recovered from smallpox "and what is worse, a severe fit of the Gout," the president informed James Wilkinson. "We shall endeavour to make him happy here and contented after his return."[79] Rush introduced his son James to Little Turtle, who gave the young man the name White Loon. "It was the name of his Sister's Son whom he had adopted."[80]

Despite advancements in medical knowledge and practice, cities remained perilous places for Indian visitors.[81] After Edward Jenner developed vaccination against smallpox using cowpox, when Little Turtle returned to the new capital in 1801, Jefferson urged him to be vaccinated and sent him home with live vaccine and instructions on how to administer it to his people.[82] Nevertheless, Indian delegates in the nineteenth and twentieth century continued to risk their health and their lives when they traveled to Washington, DC.[83] Compared with the thousands of deaths from recurrent epidemic diseases in Indian country, relatively few Indian people died and were buried in eastern cities. Yet in churchyards in Charleston, Philadelphia, and Washington, to borrow an image from the English war poet Rupert Brooke, there is some corner that is forever Indian.

Smearman, Helen E

95950

Friday, February 18, 2022

31183205128652   The Chinese in America :

Picturing Chiefs in the City

IN THE NINETEENTH CENTURY, THE United States government regularly and routinely made portraits of Indian delegates in Washington. Thomas L. McKenney, commissioner of Indian affairs from 1816 to 1830, hired artist Charles Bird King to paint portraits of Indian visitors to the capital. Over the course of eight years, King produced more than 100 portraits at a cost of at least $3,000. Defending himself against charges of extravagance, McKenney argued that the portraits were more than a record of the visits and of an interesting people; they were also an important attribute of policy because painting a portrait conveyed respect. "They see this mark of respect to their people, and they respect it," he said. The first known photographs of Indians in Washington were taken in 1857, after which capturing images of visiting delegates, individually or as a group, became standard. Commercial photographers cashed in on public interest in seeing "wild-looking" Indians, and some studios had closets full of "Indian clothing" in case the delegates were not appropriately attired when they turned up for their sittings. The photographs served as records of the delegations but also, often, as representations of "Indianness" at a time when the prevailing assumption was that the people being photographed belonged to a "vanishing race." Hundreds of photographs were taken.[1]

Things were different in the eighteenth century. There was far more interest in depicting Indians in Britain—where, as we've seen, they were an exotic curiosity and tended to be portrayed as visiting dignitaries—than in the American colonies. The portrait of Pocahontas in 1616 showed her dressed as a lady at court; the "four Indian kings" donned red cloaks in their portraits by John Verelst, as did Cherokees in images painted in the 1760s. The mezzotints made after Verelst's paintings of the four Indians were officially distributed to colonial council chambers, and when Governor Francis Nicholson returned to America from England in 1711 he brought copies of the pictures for each of the Five Nations of the Iroquois "& gave each Nation a sett & 4 in Frames to be hung up in the Onnondage Castle the center of the 5 nations where they always meet."[2]

Painting a portrait was expensive and time-consuming, and so it was generally reserved for people of wealth and position. The few portrait painters working in America in the first half of the eighteenth century were found primarily in and around Boston, New York, and Philadelphia. Portraits conveyed power, prosperity, and refinement, distinguishing elite colonists not only from the lower classes but also from Native Americans, who usually did not employ or enjoy the luxuries of portraiture.[3] It was unusual, if not remarkable, to paint Indian subjects. Nevertheless, Indian delegates provided an opportunity, and were deemed sufficiently significant, for artists to create portraits of individuals rather than idealized or demonized representations of Indianness.

At a meeting at Pennsbury in 1735, Pennsylvania proprietor John Penn paid the Swedish-born artist Gustavus Hesselius (1682–1755) £16 to execute portraits of two Lenape or Delaware chiefs, Tishcohan and Lapowinsa. Owning a portrait could be a mark of status as much as sitting for a portrait was, and having a portrait painted of a foreign delegate with whom one was negotiating was a mark of respect in Europe. Penn was likely flattering the chiefs as he tried to secure their agreement to the notorious Walking Purchase deed, which they gave in Philadelphia two years later. Hesselius was the leading artist in the mid-Atlantic colonies in the first half of the eighteenth century, and it was said that he "generally does Justice to the men, especially their blemishes, which he never fails showing in the fullest light." His portraits of Tishcohan (Plate 1) and Lapowinsa (Plate 2) are perhaps the first faithful and objective portraits of individual Indian people.[4]

Plate 1 Tishcohan. Oil on canvas. Historical Society of Pennsylvania Philadelphia History Museum, Historical Society of Pennsylvania Collection, Gift of Granville Penn. De Agostini Picture Library/Bridgeman Images.

Plate 2 Lapowinsa. Oil on canvas. Historical Society of Pennsylvania Philadelphia History Museum, Historical Society of Pennsylvania Collection, Gift of Granville Penn. Courtesy of Historical Society of Pennsylvania Collection/Bridgeman Images.

Plate 3 "The Brave old Hendrick the great Sachem or Chief of the Mohawk Indians."
Library of Congress, Prints and Photographs Division.

Theyanoguin, known as Hendrick, had his portrait painted by the Welsh-born painter William Williams when the Mohawk chief was in Philadelphia in 1755, although the original appears to have been lost. This hand-tinted engraving (Plate 3) is widely considered the most accurate likeness. It depicts Hendrick's facial markings and white hair and shows him as he might have appeared in his diplomatic role at conferences in Albany, Boston, and Philadelphia, holding a wampum string and wearing a ruffled shirt, frock coat, and three-cornered hat. Copies of the engraving were sold in London after Hendrick's death at the Battle of Lake George later that year.[5]

According to the artist John Trumbull, who had just completed a life-size portrait of George Washington, after the president dined with the principal Creek chiefs who were in New York in the summer of 1790, he took his dinner guests into the room where the portrait was standing. "When the door was thrown open, they started at seeing another 'Great Father' standing in the room" and approached the portrait with wonder and astonishment. Trumbull wanted to make portraits of the Creek chiefs, who he thought "possessed a dignity of manner, form, countenance and expression, worthy of Roman senators," but said he found it impracticable after their experience with Washington's portrait; "they had received the impression, that there must be magic in art which could render a smooth surface so like to a real man." Unable to get them to sit for him, he resorted instead to "obtaining drawings of several by stealth" (Plates 4–7).[6]

It is doubtful that the chiefs were as open-mouthed as Trumbull described or as naïve as he assumed. Well-traveled chiefs would have seen portraits before. As he prepared to set sail for London in 1762, the Cherokee chief Ostenaco dined at the College of William and Mary, hosted by a professor (and future president of the college), the Reverend James Horrocks. When Horrocks showed his guests a portrait of King George III, Ostenaco's reaction was hardly one of awestruck wonder. He studied the portrait carefully and then said that he had been wanting to see the king for a long time: "This is his resemblance, but I am determined to see him myself."[7] He did so when he was in London—and had his own portrait painted while he was there.[8] The Creeks had certainly seen portraits before as their journey from Georgia was punctuated by official receptions and state dinners along the way and during the weeks they had spent in New York. Alexander McGillivray would not have been overawed by a portrait. The astonished Creeks may just have been playing along.

Plate 22.   Page 153.

*Tuskatche Mico, or the
Birdtail King of the Cusitahs.
N. York July 1790 — J. T.*

Daggett, Hinman & Co. Sc.

Plate 4 Tuskatche Mico, also called the Bird Tail King or White Tail King of the Cusitahs.
The Miriam and Ira D. Wallach Division of Art, Prints and Photographs: Print Collection,
New York Public Library.

Plate 5 Hysac, or the Woman's Man. Courtesy of Fordham University Library, Bronx, NY.

Plate 20. Page 165.

Stimafutchki, or Good-Humour of the Coosades, Creeks. New York July 1790 I.T.

Plate 6 Stimafutchi, or "Good Humor" of the Koasati. Yale University Art Gallery.

Plate 7 Hopothle Mico, or Talassee King. Yale University Art Gallery.

Like the Creeks in New York, the Iroquois delegates in Philadelphia in 1792 were deemed worthy subjects of portraiture. They too probably would have seen portraits before: visitors to Johnson Hall saw prints of paintings by Titian, Poussin, and Watteau lining the halls, and Sir William himself had had his portrait painted.[9] John Trumbull painted miniatures of the Oneida chief Good Peter, a Seneca named the Infant, and a chief identified only as the Young Sachem (Plates 8–10). According to the list of delegates printed in the *General Advertiser,* Good Peter, who was seventy-five at the time, was "a man of the first character for probity and good sense." The Infant, also known as Hauaugaikhon and Post Biter, was from Genesee and at 6 feet 4½ inches was "the tallest man of the Five Nations." The "young sachem" may have been an Indian called the Young King or a young Governor Blacksnake.[10]

Plate 8 Good Peter. Yale University Art Gallery.

Plate 9 The Infant. Yale University Art Gallery.

The Young Sachem.
A Chief of the Six Nations
Painted 1792
1832-42

Plate 10 The Young Sachem. Yale University Art Gallery.

Plate 11 Cornplanter. New-York Historical Society.

The Seneca chief Cornplanter was a regular visitor to Philadelphia in the late 1780s and 1790s. F. Bartoli, a recently arrived London-trained artist, painted his portrait in New York City in 1796 (Plate 11), depicting the war-chief-turned-delegate "dressed in garments whose classical overtones are modified by fanciful Indian accessories."[11]

Joseph Brant posed for at least thirty-nine portraits during his lifetime, and did so on both sides of the Atlantic. He purchased and brought home one of the portraits (by Francis Riguad) done in London in 1786. As one scholar of Brant's portraiture notes, "The expectations of an Indian chief's self-representation were reinforced not only through frontier negotiations but also in urban spaces seemingly far from the world of trade and treaties." Brant understood the power of performed identity and by a mix of Anglo-Indian clothing and symbols manipulated "contemporary visual codes of identity to present himself as both a modern gentleman and Native diplomat."[12] Brant sat for this portrait by Charles Willson Peale, the first American artist to paint him, in Philadelphia in 1797 (Plate 12).[13]

Plate 12 Joseph Brant/Thayendanegea (1742-1807) by Charles Willson Peale, from life, 1797. Courtesy of Independence National Historical Park.

In other portraits, notably the famous one painted by Gilbert Stuart in 1786, Brant looks troubled, even anguished. In Peale's portrait, the fifty-four-year-old Brant looks calm and confident, as befits someone who came to the nation's capital and declined to meet the most powerful man in America, George Washington.

CHAPTER 5

Lodging, Dining, and Drinking

" WHEN A MAN IS TRAVELLING he must eat and Drink," Teedyuscung reminded Governor William Denny during a council at Philadelphia in March 1758.[1] The governor needed little reminding. The previous August, as Teedyuscung made his way from the Treaty of Easton to Indian country and then returned two weeks later on his way to Philadelphia with a peace belt, he had stopped at the Crown Tavern in Bethlehem for several days at government expense, which included meals for himself, his wife and children, and several other companions, but mostly beer, wine, rum, and cider.[2] When Indians came on official business, they lived in or close to town, they expected food and lodging to be provided for them while away from home, and they spent a lot of time eating and drinking. "We desire you will give us something to eat, for this is always the Custom when We meet the Governor at a Council Fire," Seneca George told a Pennsylvania official.[3]

Sometimes delegations camped on the outskirts of the city, especially when they came in large numbers. The 1,300 Indian people who spent nearly three weeks negotiating and trading in Montreal in the summer of 1701 constructed lodges outside the palisaded walls, creating a temporary, multiethnic Indigenous community alongside the French.[4] Indians came to Albany so often and in such numbers—in June 1677, for example, about 200 Mohawk warriors were encamped around it—that making arrangements for their lodging was a recurrent concern for the authorities. Indians who came to trade or attend treaty conferences camped on the hill outside the palisades. Local ordinances in the 1670s and '80s required them to leave town when the bell rang at eight in the evening and spend the night in lodgings constructed for them at public expense outside the gates. The ordinances prohibited Albany residents from visiting the Indian lodgings and, except for "some old sachems" whose accommodation required special approval, they were "expressly forbidden to lodge any Indians with their packs in their houses in the evening, after the ringing of the bell, . . . or to allow them to camp on their lots, they being required to lodge in the Indian houses." Fines of wampum were imposed "for each Indian or pack which shall be found in such place." In 1716 and again in 1723 the Albany Assembly passed laws and provided funding to build two wooden houses or sheds, seventy feet long by fifteen feet wide, on the hill behind the fort, to accommodate Indians who came to trade. The sheds not only provided shelter but also, being public space, helped to protect the Indians from being cheated out of their furs when traders took them "privately into their houses" and plied them with liquor.[5] Indians on diplomatic business lodged at the site as well. After dinner one night during the Albany Congress in 1754, Thomas Pownall walked "up the hill on the Back of the Town to View the Indians."[6]

The 250 or so Iroquois people who arrived in Lancaster for the treaty in 1744 were escorted "to some vacant lots in the back part of the town." Utilizing poles and boards that had been placed there for the purpose, they built a small village of wigwams and cabins, where they lived for the duration of the negotiations. During the next two weeks of the summer, Indians and colonists frequently ate, drank, and smoked together. Maryland's treaty secretary, Witham Marshe, went with some companions to the Iroquois camp to watch their dances, and he visited some families in their wigwams. Marshe thought Indians "will not, on any occasion whatsoever, dwell, or even stay, in houses built by white people."[7] He was wrong. Indians frequently lodged in colonial houses, sometimes even in people's homes, during treaty councils and at other times. Nevertheless, temporary accommodations in purpose-built lodgings on the edge of town assuaged citizens' fears and got Indians off the streets at night.

Smaller groups more often lodged in town. When Penobscot chiefs Loron and Ahanquit arrived in Boston in July 1725, the governor appointed two officers to take care of them and get them "good Lodgings and refreshments."[8] The costs of refreshments could mount quite high. A bill for entertaining Mohawk delegates in Boston in July 1731 included 28 gallons of Madeira wine, a barrel of small beer, three casks of cider, half a dozen of Bristol beer, brandy, rum, lime juice, nutmegs, mustard, vinegar, pipes and tobacco, 55 pounds of roast beef, 48 pounds of mutton, 28 pounds of bacon, legs of pork, loaves of bread, 29 pounds of Cheshire cheese, sugar, a dozen glasses and punch bowls, pitchers, and mugs. A bill for food and lodging for twenty-two "French Indians" (Kahnawake Mohawks) for nineteen days in Boston in July 1735 came to £78 7s. 6d., in addition to room and board for Joseph Kellogg, a former captive, who accompanied the delegation as interpreter. It included two dinners and suppers with the "Eastern Indians"; wine, rum, beer, and cider; tobacco; laundry; and doctor's bills for "nursing and attendance for sundry of them with External applications for six days." And there were expenses for losses and damage: "4 Gross of London Pipes broke and carried away"; "breaking and carrying away 14 mugs and cups and 6 Glasses," "breaking two Tables Sundry Chairs and Sundry Knives," and broken windows. The damage to the house and furniture amounted to at least £4. Five Pennacooks who stayed for a week that summer cost 4s. a day, with additional expenses for rum, cider, and tobacco pipes and for breaking three glasses and two mugs.[9] "I hope you are kindly Entertained and have all things necessary for your Comfort," Governor Jonathan Belcher told Loron, Arexis, and two other Penobscot chiefs who arrived in Boston in August 1740. They said they did.[10]

Fifteen Iroquois chiefs and their 100 followers who went to Philadelphia in September 1736 told Conrad Weiser that, as there were so many of them, they would leave it entirely up to him "whether he can find houss-room for us in that town." Living outdoors was not a problem, they said; they were used to it (and they may have preferred it to stuffy Philadelphia houses if the weather was warm that September). James Logan, president of the Pennsylvania Council and acting administrator after the death of Governor Gordon that year, hosted the Iroquois for three days and three nights at Stenton, the president's suburban home, rather than have them arrive in Philadelphia in the midst of an election. Weiser expended £15 on wagons, fresh beef, and some alcohol for the travelers. He finally brought them into the city on the last day of the month.[11]

Another large party of Iroquois, led by the Onondaga Canasatego, arrived at Stenton at the end of June 1742 and then carried on to Philadelphia, joined on the way by a party of Conestogas and Nanticokes from the lower Susquehanna, who brought the total to more than 220 people. The government treated the delegates to a "handsome Dinner" at the proprietor's house. Toasts were drunk to the king, the proprietors, and the Six Nations. At one point the conversation flagged, the records noted, but "after another Glass of Wine, *the Indians* returned to the Discourse."[12] Even so, at the end of the conference, Canasatego, a man with a prodigious capacity for alcohol, complained, "We have been stinted in the Article of Rum in Town. We desire that you open the Rum Bottle and give it to Us in greater Abundance on the Road." He also apologized for the mess they'd made:

> When we first came to your Houses we found them clean and in Order; but we have staid so long as to Dirty them, which is to be imputed to our different Way of living from the White People, and therefore as we cannot but have been disagreeable to you on this account, We present You with some Skins to make your Houses clean, and put them into the same Condition they were in when we came amongst You.

Governor George Thomas replied, explaining the challenges of finding lodging:

> We wish there had been more Room and better Houses provided for your Entertainment, but not Expecting so many of you, we did the best we could. 'Tis true there are a great Many Houses in Town, but as the property of other people, who have their own ffamilies to take Care of, it is difficult to procure Lodgings for a large Number of people, especially if they come unexpectedly.

Thomas ordered wagons to carry goods and supplies for their journey home. The council, which had already set aside £100 to defray Weiser's expenses in conducting the Indians to and from Philadelphia, added more money to purchase twenty gallons of rum "to Comfort them upon the Road."[13]

Indian people who went to Philadelphia to sell baskets and trade usually camped in the State House yard. City annals in the nineteenth century recorded that "such of the Indians as came to the city on public service were always provided for in the east wing of the State-house, up-stairs, and at the same time, their necessary support there was provided for by the government."[14] In March 1775, a Scottish visitor watched as members of a delegation of thirty Tuscarora, Nanticoke, and Conoy men, women, and children from the upper Susquehanna, who were in town "on a friendly visit to this Government," shot arrows at a halfpenny placed on top of a post in front of the State House. The government provided the delegation with clothing, ammunition, and other necessities out of "humanity, as well as good policy."[15] During the Revolution, the Board of War ordered that the old library in the west wing of the State House be prepared for a dozen or so Delawares expected in Philadelphia in May 1779, but the Pennsylvania Council thought it would not be appropriate to lodge the Indians there. The lower room of the west wing had always been the secretary's office, and the secretary refused to give it up except, he wrote, "in some case of real necessity."[16]

Finding lodgings in town was not easy. Sometimes Indians stayed in individuals' homes. Creek and Cherokee delegates in Charleston in January 1726 were given separate lodgings: the Cherokees at the watch house, the Creeks at the house of agent Captain Tobias Fitch. (Keeping them separate mattered: there was almost a violent clash in 1752 when a party of Cherokees who had recently "been lodged at a House a little within Charles Town" returned to find a party of Creeks camped there.)[17] Thomas Jefferson recalled that the Cherokee chief Ostenaco "was always the guest of my father, on his journeys to and from Williamsburg."[18]

On his frequent visits to Philadelphia, apparently, Teedyuscung "always regarded himself as at home" with the family of Quaker Isaac Norris, "where he was always welcomed."[19] Smaller groups and prominent chiefs sometimes stayed at the three-story, brick-built Indian Queen, one of the best inns in the city and the preferred lodging for British officers. Located on Fourth Street between Market and Chestnut Streets, the Indian Queen at the time of the Revolution was described by one traveler as having "five large rooms on the first floor, to entertain companies, two large kitchens, cellars under the whole, 16 lodging rooms on the second and third stories, besides four large garret rooms for servants; four rooms in the house can be made into two, which will entertain from 80–100 gentlemen." The inn also had stables, carriage sheds, granaries, and laundry facilities. The exiled and well-traveled Venezuelan patriot Francisco de Miranda rated the Indian Queen "the best I have known." The Indian King hotel, a converted mansion, had eighteen rooms and stables for up to a hundred horses. The fashionable City Tavern (Figure 5.1), constructed in 1773 on Second Street between Walnut and Chestnut, was the largest. Patrons entered by a flight of stone stairs to the first-floor bar and meeting rooms. The City Tavern contained two coffee rooms for business and conversation and an adjacent long room that provided space for banquets, balls, and other gatherings. An English visitor who lodged there in the 1780s said the tavern was "reckoned one of the best on the Continent."[20]

Cornplanter and the Six Nations chiefs who arrived in Philadelphia in the fall of 1790 stayed longer and proved more expensive than anticipated. Their visit was "a very unlucky Circumstance,"

Figure 5.1 City Tavern, at left, in William Birch's engraving, "Bank of Pennsylvania, South Second Street, Philadelphia," *Birch's Views of Philadelphia*, Published by W. Birch, 1800, Plate 27. Sarin Images/GRANGER

one merchant and contractor pointed out to Governor Mifflin, "as the Assembly has made no provision for them."[21] Then Big Tree injured his leg, which a doctor treated but which prevented him from traveling home. Rather than return home with the rest of the Seneca delegates, Cornplanter and Half Town requested permission to stay in Philadelphia until the legislature assembled or President Washington arrived. The council gave orders to find them suitable lodgings in private homes, but owing to "some difficulties occurring," it was agreed they should stay at the home of one William Hassel until the president arrived. Hassel was allowed £50 toward expenses for lodging them.[22] Cornplanter requested a substantial loan to buy supplies for the Indians, but the council declined. It would provide "every thing which can be considered as essential to their comfortable residence in the city, and to their safe and happy return to their families," but no more.[23]

Six Nations delegates who traveled to Philadelphia in March 1792 were quite particular about their lodging. The Reverend

Samuel Kirkland wrote Henry Knox that the Senecas from Buffalo Creek, the delegates from Genesee, the Onondagas, and the Oneidas and Tuscaroras would each require "one large lodging room with a fireplace," as well as a large room where the chiefs could meet in council. Kirkland and Peter Otsiquette (also called French Peter) each wanted a room for himself.[24] The delegates stayed at Oeller's Hotel, which had opened just the year before and was now the largest and most luxurious hotel in the city. It became "the place to drink, dine, game, and be seen," and the preferred accommodation for Indian delegations.[25] They would have found themselves in what Moreau de Saint-Méry described as "the most beautiful and comfortable inn in the United States."[26] Henry Wansey, an English traveler in the summer of 1794, recommended Oeller's as "the most agreeable lodgings in Philadelphia," except when Congress was in session, "for then it is always full." The hotel's "mammoth" sixty-foot-square assembly room contained "a handsome music gallery at one end, papered after the French taste, with the Pantheon figures in compartments, imitating the same style as lately introduced in the most elegant house in London."[27] The twenty or so Cherokee delegates who were in town when Wansey arrived were not so fortunate; they all lodged "in a kind of barn, at the west end of High-street, not far from the new mansion building for the President."[28] Oeller's Hotel burned down in 1799. After the nation's capital moved to Washington the next year, certain hotels in that city too specialized in, and even competed for, the business of providing lodging for Indian delegates.[29]

Delegates no doubt appreciated the comforts of hotels, but that did not mean they preferred them to their own, more open dwellings at home, especially in the stifling heat of summer in Philadelphia or Charleston. Nor were they necessarily strangers to such comforts. The Shawnee chief Blue Jacket visited Philadelphia in 1796. At home, he and his French-Shawnee wife slept in a four-poster curtained bed.[30]

When Indians camped in large numbers on the outskirts, food and other provisions would be delivered to them, but individuals and smaller groups were invited to dinners, formal and informal, in town.[31]

Formal dinners entailed more than just sharing a meal. They could be occasions to flatter and exert influence. Anxious to secure Lapowinsa's agreement to the "Walking Purchase" deed when he was in Philadelphia in May 1735, Thomas Penn took him for a lavish

dinner and loaded him with gifts.[32] Dinners were also a form of political theater, establishing relationships between hosts and guests;
they were an opportunity for the host to demonstrate hospitality,
display wealth, and assert status through food and wine, seating
arrangements and manners, and the meanings attached to all those
things. Indian people, of course, attached their own meanings to
such things. Iroquois delegates at a dinner at the Treaty of Lancaster
in 1744 attracted derisive comment because they were, as Witham
Marshe noted, "not accustomed to eat in the same manner as the
English, or other polite nations do." The rituals of the dinner table
included not only knowing how to handle a fork and sip from a
wineglass but also when to speak and what constituted appropriate
dinner conversation.[33] That left plenty of opportunities for cultural
misunderstanding and faux pas. At a state banquet in Philadelphia
in 1757, Teedyuscung—not known for his tact at the best of times—
inquired after the health of Governor Denny's wife. He may have
picked up on the rumors that were circulating about a troubled
marriage. Unfortunately, Mrs. Denny was having an affair and about
to elope with her lover, if she had not already done so.[34]

Indian guests would have found many familiar foods when
they sat down to eat. Cuisine in cities such as Charleston that linked
the coast and the interior included wild game, fish, and plants
that Indigenous people had hunted, harvested, and gathered for
centuries.[35] In some cases, Indian delegates would have dined on
food provided, and even brought to market, by Indian people.
Nevertheless, the dinners they attended were often elaborate affairs
with extensive menus. Invited to dinner at the home of one wealthy
Philadelphia merchant, Alexander McGillivray and the Creeks were
served turtle, fowl, pork, flummery (a kind of pudding), jellies,
sweetmeats, trifles, whipped syllabub (a frothy drink), and floating
island (a dessert), as well as peaches, pears, other fruits, raisins, and
almonds.[36]

When the Creek delegation reached New York, Henry Knox
and leading citizens and government officials dined with them at
the City Tavern on Broadway.[37] McGillivray lodged at Knox's home—
perhaps so the secretary of war could keep a close eye on him—while
the rest of the delegation roomed at New York's Indian Queen Hotel
and outside the city at the Richmond Hill estate and mansion, in a
more rural part of Manhattan near Greenwich Village. Writing to
her sister, Abigail Adams said her "Neighbours the Creek savages"
were lodged nearby. "They are fond of visiting us as we entertain
them kindly, and they behave with much civility." They were the first

Indians Abigail had seen and she thought them "very fine looking Men." After dinner one of them gave her an Indian name, although she did not understand its meaning.[38] At one "grand dinner" for the Creeks the government invited four or five Kahnawake Mohawks who were in town on their own business, as well as a South Pacific Islander.[39] The Creek delegates also attended at least one of President Washington's levees or receptions—they were there when John Routledge Jr. presented Washington with the key to the Bastille that Lafayette had sent him.[40] The government spared no expense in hosting the Creeks: It expended more than $20,500 in making the Treaty of New York.[41]

Tribal delegates often found themselves dining in homes where furniture, clocks, cutlery, china, tea, sugar, and cloth were not only items of comfort but also luxury items displayed as markers of status. The display of prestige goods and fashions was becoming the measure of social standing in town and country alike but was most concentrated and visible in the cities.[42] A French visitor to Philadelphia in 1791 described it as a "mania for luxury."[43]

The dinner guests were not necessarily out of their element when confronted with china teacups, silver cutlery, and wineglasses. The Swedish naturalist Peter Kalm observed Iroquois women drinking tea, and superintendent of Indian affairs Sir William Johnson included teapots, tea, and sugar among the gifts he presented to the families of chiefs. At his home in the Mohawk Valley, Johnson and his Mohawk partner Molly Brant served guests—most of whom were Indians—punch and Madeira wine in "the most fashionable Glasses," and tea in "large China Breakfast Cups & Saucers," with sugar and milk to taste. As evidenced by the inventory of Sir William's property when he died, Indians who visited Johnson Hall saw walnut, mahogany, cherry, and marble-top tables, backgammon tables, and card tables; mirrors and framed pictures, four-poster feather beds, curtains, and carpets; china tea services, sugar dishes, tea and table spoons, "French forks," punch bowls, glasses and decanters, linen tablecloths and napkins, and even a parrot in a cage. A Moravian store that opened in Bethlehem in 1753 offered its Indian and non-Indian customers a full range of foods, clothing, tools, and utensils, including teapots, guitars, violins, snuff, candlesticks, coffeepots, tea, chocolate, coffee, brown sugar, wine, silk, and hair powder.[44] By the time of the Revolution, Oneida people ate with spoons from pewter plates at meals illuminated by candlelight, sipped out of teacups filled from teapots, and served beverages from punch bowls.[45]

Tribal leaders from northwest Ohio who traveled to Philadelphia in the late 1790s were accustomed to visiting Detroit, where local merchants shipped an array of utilitarian and luxury merchandise from across the Atlantic, including dining ware, dinner and tea services, tea, coffee, and sugar. The Irish traveler Isaac Weld said the shops in Detroit were well supplied, "and you may buy fine cloth, linen, &c. and every article of wearing apparel, as good in their kind, and nearly in as reasonable terms, as you can purchase them at New York or Philadelphia." The stores of the British Indian department in Detroit also housed an impressive stock of merchandise.[46]

Washington invited twenty-two of the visiting Iroquois chiefs (as well as Kirkland and the interpreter) for dinner on Monday, April 22, 1792. "It is," the secretary of war added, "the President's desire that the most respectable of the chiefs be invited."[47] Unlike the delegates dining at the Treaty of Lancaster almost fifty years earlier, many of the dinner guests Washington had in mind would have eaten in style before. Washington and his cabinet wined and dined Joseph Brant during his visit to Philadelphia in 1792, but Brant was not overly impressed by Philadelphia or by dinners with Washington. He had dined with aristocracy and royalty in London. A guest at Brant's home on the Grand River in Canada that same year said the Mohawk chief was "well acquainted with European manners" and lived in an elegantly furnished mansion. "Tea was on the table when we came in, served up in the handsomest China plate." Two black servants, "one in scarlet, the other in colored clothes, with silver buckles in their shoes, and ruffles, and every other part of their apparel in proportion," served dinner and a selection of port and Madeira wines. After a night of dancing, the guests retired to comfortable beds and slept on fine Irish linen under English blankets.[48] Although motivated by political rather than culinary considerations, Brant felt that dinner with Washington was something he could skip during his next visit to Philadelphia in 1797. Henrietta Liston, wife of the British ambassador Robert Liston, said that Brant visited them often when he was in town in 1792.[49] He dined with Liston again on this visit and attended a dinner hosted by Aaron Burr, but pointedly did not keep his appointment with the president.[50]

Washington did not lack for Indigenous dinner guests, however. At his three-story presidential mansion on Fifth Street, he dined with Hendrick Aupaumut and Iroquois delegates on February 11, 1793. On December 5, 1795, he dined with visiting Cherokees. On November 28, 1796, he invited Blue Jacket and the delegation of western tribal leaders to dine with him at four o'clock in the afternoon. It was the start of a busy week. On December 3, 1796, John Adams, who attended dinner with the Chickamauga chief Kunoskeskie, also called John Watts, and a large number of Cherokee chiefs and their wives, wrote Abigail that the president had dined with "four Setts of Indians on four several Days." Blue Jacket was no doubt impressed, but he was not likely overawed. A white woman who had been held captive by the Shawnees said she always liked to visit Blue Jacket's home, where the family ate with silver cutlery and always offered her tea.[51]

Indians also dined privately with officials and agents. In February 1756, during a conference in Philadelphia, Conrad Weiser invited Tachnechdorus (John Shickellamy) and his wife to breakfast for what he called "a private Interview."[52] Delegates dined with private citizens and with foreign visitors as well. Cornplanter, Guyasuta, Half Town, Big Tree, and New Arrow had many invitations to dinner while they were in Philadelphia between fall 1790 and spring 1791. Jacob Hiltzheimer recorded in his diary that after church on Sunday, October 24, he went to dinner at General Thomas Mifflin's, where the Senecas were among the twenty or so guests.[53] On March 27, Hiltzheimer returned home in the afternoon to find "Cornplanter's son, Jack, and other Indians at my house, who called to see me."[54] Cornplanter also ate supper and conversed with French traveler Ferdinand Bayard while he was in Philadelphia.[55] In June 1794 the minister to the French Republic hosted a dinner for "the Indian chiefs now in this city," a delegation of Cherokees and Chickasaws.[56]

Indians had been dining with Philadelphia Quakers for years. Delawares at a meeting at Fort Pitt in 1765 said they were "the first nation that met the Quakers when they first came to Philadelphia," and Quakers often invited Delaware and other Indian delegates to their homes or visited them at their lodgings, to the consternation of colonial officials who worried about parallel negotiations. In the spring of 1756, for example, Six Nations chiefs, along with Conrad Weiser, Andrew Montour, and Daniel Claus, dined at Israel Pemberton's house with a few other Friends. After dinner "a free conversation occurred on public affairs." Hannah Callender Sansom noted in her diary in January 1758 that she went to visit her friend Polly Pemberton and found Teedyuscung at the Pemberton house. His presence there merited no further comment.[57] At a time when Quakers were working with Teedyuscung to secure justice for the Delawares with regard to land frauds and also to further their own political agenda and undermine the proprietary government, Teedyuscung was a regular visitor in Quaker homes. William Johnson, who resented the Quakers' interference in Indian affairs, complained that Teedyuscung was "constantly nurs'd and Enrtertain'd at Pemberton's." During the Paxton protests in 1763 Israel Pemberton became a target for anti-Quaker propagandists who claimed that Indians were "invited from House to House, to riots at Feasts," and that Pemberton "kept his House and Stable open for these Wretches and their Horses."[58] The Cherokee delegates who arrived in Philadelphia in December 1791 also met with members of the Quaker Friendly Association that winter.[59]

On such occasions, exoticism often gave way to familiarity, as illustrated by the entries in Elizabeth Drinker's diary. On April 5, 1792, twenty people joined the Drinker family for dinner, including thirteen Indians and two interpreters. "They dined in ye back parlor and had a talk after dinner in the back garden; went away about 5 o'clock."[60] Hendrick Aupaumut became something of a regular at the Drinker home when he was in Philadelphia. On April 15, 1798, he joined a group of guests for dinner there after meeting. The next day, he called while the family was eating dinner. He had bruised the middle finger of his left hand a week or ten days before when the sash of a window fell on it, and his whole hand was badly swollen. As he was soon going to be making the long journey home, Elizabeth gave him a silk handkerchief to use as a sling. Hendrick dropped in again two days later. The family had already eaten, but they "laid a cloth on the tea table for him, [and] he dined heartily." This time Elizabeth "gave him fine rags to dress his finger." Hendrick talked of leaving the next day, though he "breakfasted here" on the eighteenth and did not finally bid the Drinker family farewell until the nineteenth. He took his thirteen-year-old daughter, Margery, home with him. Margery was one of six Indian girls who had come to live with Quaker families near Philadelphia in November 1797. She had been living on a farm in Chester County but was very homesick for her own country.[61]

Even old enemies came for dinner. Little Turtle and his warriors had routed the American army in 1791. Yet when he and William Wells were in Philadelphia in 1798 they may have been invited to dine at the opulent mansion on Third Street of Anne (known as Nancy) Bingham, the wife of Senator William Bingham; called "the queen of Federalist society," she hosted elaborate balls, dinners, and salons in imitation of those she had attended when she had lived in Paris.[62] Learning that Little Turtle was in Baltimore in 1801, retired secretary of war James McHenry, who had befriended him when he was in office, invited him home for dinner at Christmas.[63] Just a few years later, Sir Augustus John Foster was at a dinner party in Washington that included a group of Indian delegates from the West. They behaved without "the slightest impropriety," and the British diplomat suggested "their manners were perhaps more gentlemanlike" than those of most of the other guests, a comment that probably revealed more about his opinion of Americans than about the dining etiquette of Indians.[64]

Alcohol often flowed freely when Indians came to town. People in colonial and early national America consumed prodigious amounts of alcohol—according to one estimate, annual per capita consumption of hard liquor alone, mostly rum, and not counting beer, cider, and wine, was almost four gallons a head.[65] Taverns proliferated as cities grew. Only two years after the founding of Pennsylvania, William Penn complained about the disorders caused by having too many taverns in Philadelphia. By 1744 there were more than 100 licensed public houses in the city; eighteenth-century Philadelphia had more public houses per capita than Paris or Rotterdam. Some had names like the King of the Mohawks. Boston at midcentury had about 150 taverns, New York about 200—one for every 115 inhabitants. The increasing availability and decreasing price of rum, either from the West Indies or distilled in America from molasses, generated new drinking habits and more public drunkenness. Dr. Benjamin Rush in 1784 published *An Inquiry into the Effects of Spirituous Liquors,* an essay that was reprinted many times in Philadelphia newspapers as some people feared that Americans were becoming a nation of drunkards.[66]

Like British pubs in the twentieth century, taverns in early America were centers of community life where people gathered to socialize, discuss politics, and transact business as well as to drink. Taverns that catered to the social elite grew up away from the waterfront as port cities increased in size and prosperity. At their best, urban taverns were public spaces where the patrons—white males—demonstrated civility. Depending on location and circumstance, however, they also could become scenes of vice and disorder. In Philadelphia, the Indian Queen and Indian King taverns were relatively grand, but laborers, sailors, sex workers, and underclasses frequented taverns closer to the waterfront, some of which were little more than holes in the wall. The area north of Arch Street between the Delaware River and Third Street earned the name "Hell Town." Sometimes elite males frequented these places to sample the diversions they offered. Taverns occasionally held bearbaiting, cockfighting, dogfighting, and other public entertainments and attractions. The Indians who were in Philadelphia at the time may have seen the camel exhibited at the Indian King tavern in 1740, or the leopard exhibited there in 1744.[67]

Indian people had encountered alcohol long before they went to town. Injected into Indian country from the days of earliest contact, alcohol promoted trade and destabilized communities. Indian people often got drunk, often complained about the amount and easy availability of alcohol, and often requested assistance from colonial authorities in stopping or at least regulating the rum trade.[68] Sassoonan and his Delaware companions evidently went on a bender when they were in Philadelphia on business in June 1715, causing a nuisance in the taverns and streets. Governor Charles Gookin told them he had thought they would have taken better care of themselves; otherwise he would have prevented them from buying liquor. Sassoonan asked the government to stop rum from being traded in the Indians' villages, but all it did was tell the Indians themselves to stave in the casks.[69] In Philadelphia in 1731, Sassoonan informed the council that many horseloads of rum passed by his door, "& it all comes from Philadelphia." He asked Governor Patrick Gordon to keep the rum in Philadelphia and keep rum traders away from Indian towns; if any Indians wanted it, they should go to Philadelphia for it, he said, though he subsequently modified his position.[70] Angry that traders brought too much rum into their villages, Shawnee chiefs tried staving in the casks but, as they told British agents in 1771, "it is You that make the Liquor, and to you we must look to Stop it. . . . [W]e all know well that it is in your great Men's Power to Stop it, and make us happy, if they thought it worth their Trouble."[71]

In general, colonial authorities did not think it worth their trouble. Their efforts to curtail and regulate the alcohol trade were too few, too limited, and too easily evaded. Liquor was traded wherever colonists and Indians met—at trading posts, in Indian villages, and in towns and cities. Virtually every major settlement had liquor purveyors, and all the major cities participated in the liquor trade. The prominent Philadelphia trading company of Bayton, Wharton, and Morgan shipped enormous quantities of alcohol to frontier posts for distribution into Indian country.[72]

Colonial and city authorities did make efforts to curb Indian drinking in town and tried to ban Indians—as well as blacks, women, and servants—from taverns, although with limited success.[73] One New Netherland official complained to Director General Peter Stuyvesant in 1660 about the number of drunken Indians he saw, and reported having heard "that they sit drinking publicly in some taverns."[74] When the Dutch traveler Jasper Danckaerts visited New York City in 1679 he pictured the residents busy fleecing Indians who came to town to trade. "Whenever they see an Indian enter the house, whom they know has any money, they immediately set about getting hold of him, giving him rum to drink, whereby he is soon caught and becomes half a fool," and easily cheated. Selling alcohol to Indians was illegal, Danckaerts said, "yet everyone does it."[75] New York City initially allowed Indian and black people into taverns, but in 1680 lawmakers prohibited serving Native Americans and African American slaves.[76] A year later, however, a Minisink sachem complained that when his people came to New York to trade beaver for winter clothing, "finding Rumm in every house," they squandered their pelts, succumbed to drinking binges, and suffered sixty deaths in just three years.[77] In September 1687, Albany mayor Peter Schuyler said that Indians were hanging around Schenectady "drinking continually."[78]

At the Great Peace of Montreal in 1701, the governor and the intendant issued a ban on selling alcohol during the conference, which many of the visiting chiefs appreciated.[79] Pierre de Charlevoix reported Indians drunk in the streets of Montreal in the 1720s. Inebriated Indians were arrested but rarely prosecuted, however; the authorities were more interested in going after the suppliers of alcohol than in attempting to prosecute Indian consumers, who resisted the imposition of French jurisdiction.[80] Restrictions remained loose after the British took over Montreal; Indians and colonists sometimes drank together in taverns, as shown in a sketch by John André, the officer and spy who was executed for his role in Benedict Arnold's infamous plot (Figure 5.2).

There were plenty of other opportunities for visiting Indians to drink to excess in town. Indeed, they could not help but encounter alcohol. Indian people who lived there found their own tavern spaces in backrooms and back alleys.[81] Laws excluding Indians, along with slaves and apprentices, from Philadelphia taverns were difficult to enforce when Indian delegates lodged at inns such as the Indian Queen.[82] And colonists often sold liquor from their homes. Some delegates who became inebriated in Philadelphia in the spring of 1693 asked the governor to "pardon it and not putt them in the stocks, for they knew no better, and the Christians did sell them the Liquor."[83] James Logan complained in 1736 about seeing Indians on the streets of Philadelphia "much disordered by Liquor, which 'tis believed they have been furnished with from some of the low Tippling Houses in this City." Time and again officials issued

Figure 5.2 Quebec Tavern Scene, 1775, by John André. William L. Clements Library, University of Michigan.

proclamations prohibiting alcohol sales during treaty negotiations, but tavern keepers and private retailers, "solely intent on their own private Lucre," continued to peddle rum and other strong liquor to Indians, "to the great Disturbance, Offence and Danger of the Inhabitants, and manifest Prejudice and Hindrance of the Business to be transacted at such Treaties."[84]

Officials tried to prevent or at least limit such behavior. In August 1755, with Indians "come to Town, heated wth their Journy and in Liquor," Governor Morris placed constables at the State House yard, where the Indians were lodged, with orders "that they permit none of ye Towns people to come to them."[85] Nevertheless, Indian residents and visitors seem to have had little trouble getting enough drink to get drunk.[86] The Oneida chief Scarouady was in Philadelphia for a conference in April 1756 but was "in Liquor two Days, and was incapable of being conferred with."[87] Teedyuscung had a reputation as a hard drinker—it was said he could "drink three Quarts or a Gallon of Rum a Day without being drunk"—and evidently did not let up when he was in town. His wife, who took the name Elisabeth when she was baptized in 1750, preferred to lodge at the Crown Tavern in Bethlehem when he was doing business in Philadelphia; she was reluctant to join him there, she said, "because of his debauched way of living." Teedyuscung did not get drunk easily, but during a conference at Easton in July 1757, he "and his wild Company were perpetually Drunk, very much on the Gascoon [a colloquial term for braggart] and at a time very abusive to the Inhabitants, for they all spoke English more or less." In December 1759, after a few days in Philadelphia, Teedyuscung turned up drunk for the start of the formal conference at the State House.[88] But even Teedyuscung "earnestly desired that a Stop might be put to the sending such excessive Quantities of Rum Into the Indian Country, and that at Treaties especially particular care might be taken to prevent Indians getting it."[89]

What happened in Philadelphia happened in other cities. When the Creek chief Acorn Whistler was in Charleston in the spring of 1752 he was, he said, "about the Town drinking" and got drunk.[90] Creek and Cherokee visitors would have found easy access to public houses and other sources of liquor in midcentury Charleston, a city with licensed taverns clustered around the waterfront—there were about 100 licensed taverns for its 4,000 residents—and illegal establishments also selling drink.[91]

In fact, colonial governments sometimes encouraged tavern keepers to provide hospitality to visiting Indian delegations and reimbursed them for doing so.[92] Although Albany tried to restrict sales of alcohol and the city fathers issued a proclamation in 1689 that banned inhabitants from selling or giving strong liquor or beer to Indians "upon any pretence whatsoever," it exempted alcohol given as part of the ritual of diplomacy; if the city fathers saw fit, they could "give any small quality of Rum to any Sachims who come here about Publick Businesse."[93] The governor issued a proclamation prohibiting the sale of liquor to Indians during the Albany Congress of 1754, but in a city where four inns, two taverns, five dramshops, three liquor retailers, one mead house, forty-seven merchants, and ten Indian traders provided multiple sources of alcohol, citizens regularly circumvented such prohibitions. According to one report, traders sold the Indians so much rum that they lay "dead drunk, in the Face of Day, at their Doors."[94]

Whether or not colonists deliberately employed alcohol during negotiations to defraud Indian delegates, negotiations often occurred in an environment where alcohol flowed. Treaty conferences regularly involved drinking rounds of toasts. Although Penobscot and Norridgewock delegates in the 1730s and '40s voiced concerns about the rum trade in their country, their negotiations in Boston frequently began, ended, and were punctuated with rounds of toasts—to the king's health, to the governor, to the tribes, to the delegates' families, and so on.[95] The formalities at the Treaty of Lancaster opened on June 22, 1744, with Governor George Thomas and the commissioners from Maryland and Virginia welcoming the Iroquois and drinking to their health with wine and punch. Canasatego and other chiefs returned the compliment, drinking in turn to the health of the governors of Pennsylvania, Virginia, and Maryland. On Saturday, June 30, according to the official record of the treaty negotiations, "the three Governments entertained *the Indians,* and all the Gentlemen in Town, with a handsome Dinner." Witham Marshe's unofficial journal provided more details: twenty-four chiefs of the Six Nations dined with the treaty commissioners at the courthouse, along with "a great many gentlemen of the three colonies" and "a large number of the inhabitants of Lancaster likewise present to see the Indians dine." There was much drinking of toasts. The governor drank to the Indians' health, and the Indians drank to the governor's. The governor and commissioners then drank to the king's health, which the Indians did "in bumpers of Madeira wine," although they were surprised by the English custom of giving several huzzas on drinking the king's health. After the multiple rounds of toasts, the commissioners produced a deed for the Indians to sign, "releasing all their Claim and Title to certain Lands lying in the Province of Maryland."[96]

Meetings between treaty commissioners and Indian delegates sometimes took place in taverns. In Albany colonial commissioners in 1775 met the Indians in both the Dutch church and at Cartwright's Tavern. For two weeks in February 1789 Iroquois men and women met with the New York commissioners, and conducted the opening rituals of condolence and presentation of wampum, in Isaac Denniston's tavern, also known as the King's Arms, on the corner of Green and Beaver Streets. The meeting ended with a land cession. The records do not state whether or not alcohol was consumed, or whether local patrons watched the proceedings as they drank their ale.[97] A French traveler recalled that during his visit to the United States in 1791 "the chiefs of the Cherokees, delegates to Congress to obtain a treaty of alliance, were living in New York City in a state of continuous drunkenness," with the American government covering their bar bills in full expectation of receiving full compensation in the articles of the treaty they would make.[98]

Despite the pleas of Indian leaders and the efforts of colonial officials, alcohol consumption when Indian delegates came to town was considerable. Alcohol consumption fueled negative images about Indians among observers. It also fueled negative images of colonists among Indian people, who heard officials complain about their drinking but saw them do nothing to curtail the flow of alcohol. Colonists knew, and some worried, about the devastating effects alcohol had in Indian communities. Nonetheless, they worried more about the prospect of intoxicated Indians on their streets. For their part, chiefs in the city were usually less concerned about their own drinking when in town than about the many unscrupulous traders who carried large quantities of rum to Indian villages and sold it to the inhabitants "to their great Loss and Damage."[99]

The hospitality accorded Indian delegations was an essential lubricant of diplomacy, but it was not always freely given. People in government complained about the expense, and people outside government complained about what struck them as a cynical practice of bribing Indians with indulgence. A correspondent in Philadelphia during the visit of nearly fifty Iroquois in spring 1792 wrote: "I saw a dozen of them this morning in a stage wagon with a couple of waiters attending them, and they appeared to be highly pleased. The Cornplanter's son was on horse back! and was laced off from head to feet. He resembled a knight of the renowned order of LA MANCHA." This was certainly the best way to fight Indians, opined the correspondent: $10,000 spent "corrupting them" was more effective than half a million dollars spent on the military. If the chiefs and principal men could be induced to visit Philadelphia once a year, "I shall think a most important point is gained."[100] The costs of Little Turtle's visit in 1798 accumulated. Captain Donald Grant Mitchell of the Corps of Artillerists and Engineers ran up more than $740 in expenses for Wells, Little Turtle, and himself, "traveling from Pittsburgh to Philadelphia, and residing there, and from Philadelphia to Detroit, and returning to Pittsburgh."[101] Nevertheless, the federal government operated for years to come on the assumption that it was cheaper to lodge, feed, and entertain Indian delegates than it was to fight Indian warriors.

Such grudging hospitality and calculated generosity ran counter to values and practices in Indian communities, where hospitality and generosity were a way of life. Iroquois visitors to Philadelphia in 1736 explained that among their own people "there is never any Victuals sold, the Indians give to each other freely what they can spare, but if they come among our People, they can have none without paying; they admire we should take Money on this Score."[102] John Heckewelder said Indians "are hospitable to all, without exception, and will always share with each other and often with the stranger, even to their last morsel." They showed hospitality to a stranger "partly on account of his being at a distance from his family and friends, and partly because he has honored them with his visit, and ought to leave them with a good impression on his mind."[103] Traveling through Cherokee country in 1797, Louis Philippe, the future king of France, observed, "Hospitality is the rule among all Indians. All their guests make free with anything in sight, and they imagine that matters are the same with us, so that without actually stealing, they help themselves to whatever is loose," which caused problems with property-minded colonists, of course.[104]

"I know the kindness with which you treat the strangers that visit your country," the governor of Pennsylvania told the Iroquois delegates in Philadelphia in the spring of 1792, rather defensively, "and it is my sincere wish, that, when you return to your families, you may be able to assure them, that the virtues of friendship and hospitality are also practised by the citizens of Pennsylvania."[105] When it came to generosity and hospitality, evidently, Native Americans, not American city dwellers, set the standard for civility.

CHAPTER 6

The Things They Saw

I N 1791 TIMOTHY PICKERING INVITED a delegation from the Six Nations to visit President Washington and discuss plans for introducing agriculture. He had no doubt that "the dignity of the President & the splendor of his house" would "excite their reverence," but he also intended to impress them with the nation's capital itself: "The public buildings in Philadelphia—the extent & populousness of the city, the vast quantities of goods in every street, and the shipping at the wharves will so much exceed any thing they have seen before, and so far surpass their present ideas that they cannot fail to wonder and admire."[1] Such thinking had brought Indian delegations to colonial capitals for almost a hundred years and would continue to bring them to the nation's capital for the next hundred years.[2]

European and American officials expected Indian visitors to be suitably and unanimously impressed with city life, and the press often portrayed them as primitive sons of the forest baffled and amazed by the things they saw. Yet the visitors perhaps were not as impressed as officials and journalists assumed they would be. Isaac Weld related the story of a group of Iroquois delegates who were underwhelmed by what they saw in Paris, and then he added, "The Indians, whom curiosity or business leads to Philadelphia, or to any of the large towns in the States, find, in general, as little deserving of notice in the streets and houses there as these Iroquois at Paris; and there is not one of them but what would prefer his own wigwam to the most splendid habitations they see in any of these places."[3]

There were few mansions in the American colonies before the end of the seventeenth century, but in the course of the eighteenth century wealthy Americans built provincial two- and three-story versions of Georgian English houses. The houses of ordinary people changed little in their basic plans over this time, but Indian delegates who visited the homes of urban elites later in the century would have been welcomed into spaces arranged for greeting and meeting, moved through rooms that were larger, warmer, lighter (illuminated by bigger sash windows and by candles of wax and spermaceti rather than tallow), and more richly furnished, and ascended broader staircases than their forefathers had done when they visited.[4] Native people were no doubt impressed by multistory stone buildings and architecture, although French missionary Chrestien Le Clercq said that a Mi'kmaq in 1677 asked him why men who were five or six feet tall needed houses sixty to eighty feet high and pointed out that his people "have in our dwellings all the conveniences and advantages that you have in yours, such as reposing, drinking and sleeping, eating and amusing ourselves with our friends."[5]

Gottlieb Mittelberger, who arrived in Philadelphia from Germany in 1750, reported a similar reaction in his travelogue. He was impressed by Philadelphia's size, beauty, broad streets, and architecture. There were houses of up to four stories high, and the magnificent new courthouse (or City Hall) was 100 feet long by 100 feet wide. "It takes almost a whole day to walk around the city; and every year approximately three hundred new homes are built. It is thought that in time Philadelphia will become one of the world's largest cities," he noted. The Indians he met were less impressed: "When the savages come into the city of Philadelphia and see the beautiful and marvelous buildings there, they are amazed and laugh at the Europeans for expending so much care and cost on their houses, saying: 'That was quite unnecessary. After all, one could exist without such houses.'"[6]

Indian delegates were given tours that showed a city's best sides—grand buildings, displays of wealth, and demonstrations of power—but they were not simply passive tourists. Sometimes they actively sought out particular places to visit and things to see and do. Sometimes they went shopping. When they were out and about they got a "street-level perspective" on the city[7] (Figure 6.1). They could not have avoided seeing, smelling, and hearing other sides of urban life that the government was less inclined to show them: the stink of human and animal waste and refuse thrown into streets and gutters; mud on unpaved streets that humans shared with horses,

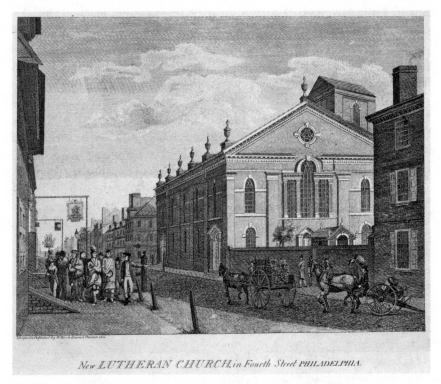

New *LUTHERAN CHURCH, in Fourth Street* PHILADELPHIA.

Figure 6.1 An Indian delegation in Philadelphia gets a tour of the city.
"New Lutheran Church, in Fourth Street Philadelphia." *The City of Philadelphia as it appeared in the Year 1800.* Plate 6. Published by W. Birch, 1800. Library Company of Philadelphia.

pigs, and goats; the din of the markets and wharves; the wretched living conditions of the working poor; problems with water supply, street maintenance, drainage, sewage and sanitation, crime and prostitution, police protection, fire prevention, traffic regulation, public health, and poor relief; disparities of race; and routine human suffering on a scale unknown in Indian communities. Visitors were impressed that elite Philadelphians kept their streets clean and in good order.[8] However, streets in the poorer neighborhoods were often filthy. Not until 1797 did the city impose fines on people who left their rubbish in the streets.[9] Thomas Condie and Richard Folwell, who wrote a history of the yellow fever outbreak in 1798, touted the elegance and cleanliness of Philadelphia but lamented the filth that people tossed into the rivers, streets, and gutters. The open sinks into which its gutters emptied "exhale the most noxious effluvia; for dead animals and every kind of nausea, are thrown into them, and there remain until they become putrified."[10] Joseph Brant was in Philadelphia in 1797, and Little Turtle was there in 1798; the stench would have hit them before they hit the streets.

Nevertheless, Indian visitors found plenty to interest and impress them. The one exception to the Iroquois indifference, real or assumed, that Isaac Weld reported was the shipping activity in the port, which "seldom fails to excite their admiration."[11] When the Iroquois who were in Philadelphia in the fall of 1736 went out to see the sights, Conrad Weiser took one group to the waterside and aboard one of the ships in the harbor.[12] Philadelphia's noisy and bustling waterfront continued to attract Indian visitors throughout the century (Figure 6.2). They watched cargoes from around the world being unloaded, stored in the warehouses along Water Street, or loaded onto wagons for transportation inland. They saw ships being built. A single ship could take a year to build and require more than a hundred workers and at least thirty craftsmen, including shipwrights, joiners, ropemakers, blockmakers, carpenters, sailmakers, riggers,

ARCH STREET FERRY, PHILADELPHIA.

Figure 6.2 "Arch Street Ferry, Philadelphia." *The City of Philadelphia as it appeared in the Year 1800.* Plate 4. Published by W. Birch, 1800. Library Company of Philadelphia.

blacksmiths, caulkers, founders, braziers, glaziers, painters, coopers, and tanners.[13]

By 1796, when the delegation of northwestern Indians led by Blue Jacket and Painted Pole or Red Pole arrived, Philadelphia had some 50,000 inhabitants and was the showcase of the nation. Like previous Indian delegations, they walked the city's cobbled streets along brick sidewalks, looked up at three-story red brick houses, and noted the whale oil lamps and public water pumps. They also walked in the new parks, where they saw and were seen by the Philadelphia gentry (Figure 6.3). The square behind the Pennsylvania State House was landscaped as a park in 1784.[14]

When they visited the High Street (also called Market Street) market, held on Wednesday and Saturday mornings between Front and Fourth Street, they would have seen stalls stocked with beef, mutton, pork, and veal; venison and other game; turkeys, geese, ducks, pheasants, quails, and wild pigeons; many kinds of fish; "marvelously large lobsters, each of whose claws is as big as a man's hand,"

Figure 6.3 Indian delegates stroll in the park behind the State House in Philadelphia. "State-House, with a View of Chestnut Street Philadelphia." *The City of Philadelphia as it appeared in the Year 1800.* Plate 21. Published by W. Birch, 1800. Wikimedia Commons. Public domain.

as Gottfried Mittelberger noted; and fruits and vegetables.[15] The market building was one story high, almost half a mile long, and a hundred feet wide, supported by brick pillars. Reverend Manasseh Cutler said many people considered the market "the greatest curiosity in the city." He was there early on the morning of July 14, 1787, as it came to life.

> By the time it was fair daylight, the marketers seemed to be all in and every thing arranged. The crowds of purchasers filled every avenue so that it was almost impossible to pass. The stalls were furnished with excellent meat, and there was every kind of vegetable and fruit which the season afforded. The crowds of people seemed like the collection at the last day, for there was of every rank and condition in life, from the highest to the lowest, male and female, of every age and every color. Several of the market women who sold fruit, I observed, had their infants in their arms and their children about them, and there seemed to be some of every nation under Heaven.

Cutler, a Congregational minister from Ipswich, Massachusetts, wondered, "What would the delicate Boston ladies think, if they were to be abroad at this hour?" Everything was "bustle and hurry," and "a buzzing murmur of voices resounded through the crowds." He made his way from one end of the market to the other, "viewing everything that was going on, and gazing at the numerous strange faces which appeared wherever I turned my eyes."[16]

Visiting delegates would not have strayed far from the center of Philadelphia before they saw other aspects of city life. They would have been aware of (even if they did not visit) bawdy houses and a growing urban culture of personal pleasure and leisure that included gambling, drinking, and casual and extramarital sexual relations. Illegitimate births were on the rise, and prostitution was pervasive.[17] William Black, the secretary to the Virginia commissioners heading to the Treaty of Lancaster in 1744, found himself, like many tribal delegates over the years, in Philadelphia with time on his hands while he waited for the treaty participants to assemble in Lancaster, and like them, he spent time out and about in the city. Black was accosted by a prostitute as he returned to his lodgings one night, although, given his predilection for and interest in the opposite sex, he may have been on the prowl.[18] French traveler Jacques Pierre Brissot de Warville said in 1788 that the sex trade in Philadelphia was "not carried on so scandalously as at Paris or London" and was "almost imperceptible," but ten years later a Brazilian visitor described it as commonplace and obvious; prostitutes crowded the streets at night promoting their trade in full public view. Sex workers did a lively business on Water Street down by the docks, but there were brothels on the main streets too, as well as in back alleys, and sexual commerce also took place in theaters, in the backrooms of taverns, and on the streets. Booksellers sold bawdy texts and homoerotic books from London and Paris.[19] Doctors advertised cures for venereal disease in Philadelphia newspapers. Moreau de Saint-Méry reputedly introduced condoms to the city. He opened a bookstore and printshop in December 1794 and carried "a complete assortment of them" during the four years he ran his shop. They sold well. "The use of this medium on the vast American continent dates from this time," he wrote.[20]

Saint-Méry found similar street scenes in New York when he was there. New York by then had a population of 40,000 free people and 2,500 slaves. It was, as he put it, "less citified" than Philadelphia but a more bustling trade center. Unlike Philadelphia's grid plan, the streets of New York ran in multiple directions. Many of them were narrow, unpaved, and lacked sidewalks, and they were "not particularly clean." It was not unusual to see all kinds of animals wandering about, especially cows and pigs. Saint-Méry complained that although people washed windowpanes and sidewalks on Saturday, "nobody bothers to remove the dead dogs, cats and rats from the streets." There were "many houses of debauchery," and he claimed to be shocked that in some parts of the city whole areas "are given over to street-walkers for the plying of their profession" and "women of every color can be found in the streets, particularly after ten o'clock at night, soliciting men and proudly flaunting their licentiousness in the most shameless manner."[21]

Whether or not they indulged personally, Indian delegates who walked out of their lodgings on an evening in Philadelphia or New York in the 1790s could not have avoided encountering commercial sex and at least glimpsing the underworld of an Atlantic port city. It appears that, as Herman Viola concluded from a review of reported, and underreported, cases of venereal disease among tribal delegations to Washington, DC, in the nineteenth century, "the Indians were able to sample all the diversions of civilized life."[22]

Tribal delegates got to see the sights. In Philadelphia after the Revolution they visited Charles Willson Peale's museum. Peale opened his museum to the public at his home at Third and Lombard Streets in 1786; in 1794, to accommodate the expansion of his collections, he moved it to the American Philosophical Society at Fifth and Chestnut Streets (and in 1802 it moved again to the

Pennsylvania State House, now Independence Hall). The museum featured paintings of the nation's founding figures and patriotic displays, as well as stuffed animals, birds, fish, insects, shells, and scientific demonstrations—it was in effect the first popular museum of natural history. Peale described his eclectic collection of "Natural Curiosities" from North America and around the globe as "a world in miniature." The Blue Jacket delegation visited the museum during their tour of the city after meeting President Washington. As the chiefs entered the museum, they found themselves face-to-face with a huge stuffed buffalo. They also saw a display of peace pipes from the Treaty of Greenville, brought back by Anthony Wayne and gifted to the museum a year before. They were not the only Indian delegates in town—or in the museum. Walking through the displays, Blue Jacket's group suddenly encountered a party of southern Indians— not only Creeks and old allies such as the Chickamauga Cherokee John Watts, but also Choctaws and Chickasaws, including Piominko and George Colbert, who had assisted the Americans in the late war against Blue Jacket's confederation. There was an awkward moment, after which the two tour groups kept to different parts of the room, as if each wanted nothing to do with the other. Then the chiefs "cautiously approached each other" and arranged a second meeting at the museum. Blue Jacket and Seneca chief Red Jacket asked secretary of war James McHenry to convene a formal peace conference on December 2.[23]

In 1797 the museum added to its collections ten life-size wax figures of Native peoples from different parts of the world, including Red Pole and Blue Jacket—"celebrated Sachems of North America," as one newspaper called them.[24] When Little Turtle visited the museum the next year, he saw a portrait of Joseph Brant and the wax replicas of Blue Jacket and Red Pole. He asked to have his own portrait painted, and McHenry arranged for Gilbert Stuart to do it. Little Turtle sat for his portrait in Stuart's studio, which was in a stone barn behind his house on Main Street in Germantown, along with an Irishman whose portrait Stuart was painting at the same time (Figure 7.7).[25] (The original portrait of Little Turtle was destroyed when the British burned Washington in the War of 1812.)

Indian visitors sometimes had the opportunity to observe scientific experiments. On one visit to Philadelphia, the Seneca chief Guyasuta had witnessed electrical experiments, which interested and impressed him so much that when he returned to the city in November 1772 after conducting business "of the greatest importance" with Sir William Johnson at Johnson Hall, his first request was to see more experiments with lightning. He also planned to attend the public lectures being given at the College of Philadelphia by Ebenezer Kinnersley, a contemporary of Franklin in electrical discoveries.[26]

The ill-fated delegates from the Wabash tribes, who suffered such losses to smallpox, were in Philadelphia at a time when an exhibition of a different kind was staged: the first hot-air balloon ascension in the United States, on January 9, 1793. Jean-Pierre Blanchard, the famous French aeronaut who had flown a balloon in Paris in 1784 and subsequently co-piloted one across the English Channel, announced that he would ascend from the yard of the Walnut Street Prison (Figure 6.4). Thomas Jefferson informed his daughter Martha Jefferson Randolph of the arrival of the Kaskaskia chief Jean Baptiste DuCoigne and Blanchard in Philadelphia in the same short letter. Some newspapers carried coverage of the ascension and notice of the Indians' presence in the city, and in some cases their deaths, on the very same page.

Figure 6.4 The first hot-air balloon ascension in America occurred while delegates from the Wabash and Illinois tribes were in Philadelphia. GRANGER.

People flocked from the surrounding countryside for the big event. Tickets sold at $5 per head for a seat within the jail yard. While Washington, Adams, Jefferson, Madison, Monroe, and other well-to-do citizens took their seats, huge crowds gathered at Potters Field, now Washington Square, across the street from the prison. Whether members of the Indian delegation were invited to attend along with government officials or whether they joined the "thousands of citizens from every part of the country, who," reported the *Weekly Register,* "stood gratified and astonished at his intrepidity," they could hardly have missed it. At 10:05 a.m. Blanchard began his ascent, waving the American and French flags. The crowd cheered, cannons fired, and the band played. After a forty-six-minute flight, during which he drank "excellent wine," Blanchard landed some fifteen miles away, near Woodbury, New Jersey.[27]

Indians who visited European cities were amazed, perhaps above all else, by the sheer numbers of people. Some said they marveled to see "as many people in the streets of Paris, as there were blades of grass on the prairies, or mosquitoes in the woods."[28] Most American cities were smaller, but by the time Little Turtle visited Philadelphia the city was larger than many in England. Its population had passed 44,000 in 1790, according to the U.S. census, and would reach 61,559 in 1800.[29] During January and February 1798 Little Turtle met nine or ten times with the French scholar Constantin-François de Chasseboeuf, Comte de Volney, who shared Jefferson's interest in American Indian origins, languages, and customs. With William Wells interpreting, Volney wrote down his observations and some of his conversations with Little Turtle.[30] On one occasion, some Quakers came to Volney's house to visit Little Turtle and suggested he stay as long as he liked in Philadelphia, "even his whole life," assuring him that he would want for nothing if he did so. Why not accept the offer? Volney asked him after the Quakers had left. According to Volney, Little Turtle thought about it for a while and then replied:

"Yes, I have pretty well accustomed myself to all I find here. The clothes are warm and good in my opinion: these houses are excellent defenses against the rain, wind, and Sun; and in them we find everything that is convenient: this market" (that of Second street was under the windows) "furnishes every thing that can be desired, so that there is no occasion to hunt for venison in the woods. Taking all things together you have the advantage over us; but here I am deaf and dumb. I do not talk your language; I can neither hear, nor make myself heard. When I walk through the streets, I see every person in his shop employed about something: one makes shoes, another hats, a third sells cloth, and every one lives by his labor. I say to myself, which of all these things can you do? Not one. I can make a bow or an arrow, catch fish, kill game, and go to war: but none of these is of any use here. To learn what is done here would require a long time, be difficult, and the success uncertain. Old age comes on: if I were to remain with the whites, I should be a piece of furniture useless to my own nation, useless to the whites, and useless to myself. What is to be done with a useless piece of furniture? I must return to my own country."[31]

It was market day, and during their conversation Little Turtle watched attentively from the window what was going on in the street below. Volney asked what was engaging his attention and what surprised him most about Philadelphia. "In observing all these people," Little Turtle replied, "two things ever astonish me: the extreme difference of the countenances, and the numerous population of the whites" who covered the country "like swarms of flies and gnats." He found their booming population "inconceivable." Meanwhile, Indigenous populations were melting away. He attributed the different demographic trajectories to American agriculture and property owning and to the Indians' dependence on hunting: "If we do not change our course, it is impossible for the race of red men to subsist." Having lived in the Miami towns in northwestern Ohio where enormous fields of corn, squash, and beans had sustained large populations and brought prosperity to the inhabitants, Little Turtle knew there was more to it than switching from hunting to agriculture, but his explanation convinced Volney "that this man has not without reason acquired in his own nation and in the United States the reputation of a person superior in understanding to most of the savages."[32]

In addition to seeing the sights and experiencing the hustle of city life when they were out and about, Native American delegates also encountered aspects of civil society that puzzled or offended them. So many people crowded together in one place yet unconnected by ties of clan and kinship reflected, indeed created, disorder and lack of community, not order and civility.

Indigenous delegates to Paris and London were repulsed by the accumulation of personal wealth and class distinctions they saw. According to the Baron de Lahontan, Indians who had been to France "were continuously teasing us with the Faults and Disorders they observ'd in our Towns, as being occasioned by Money."[33] (At least he said they were—the baron was known to invent "Indian voices" to critique his own society.) Indian people had similar reactions in eighteenth-century American cities, centers of commerce whose primary purpose was the business of making money. According to John Heckewelder, they "wonder that the white people are striving so much to get rich, and to heap up treasures in this world which they cannot carry with them to the next."[34] Such behavior ran counter to values and practices in Native communities. "Give them a fine Gun, Coat, or other thing, it may pass twenty hands, before it sticks," wrote William Penn. "Wealth circulateth like Blood, all parts partake."[35] Alexander McGillivray, Jean Baptiste DuCoigne, and Joseph Brant appear to have had little problem with the concept of accumulating personal wealth, but the communal values of Indigenous society and the capitalist values of early American society collided in urban streets and marketplaces, as they did in other times and places.

Indians also came face-to-face with concepts, standards, and practices of justice that shocked them. In their communities, public opinion, kinship networks, and clan vengeance worked to maintain order and see justice done. "They love justice and hate violence and robbery, a thing remarkable in men who have no laws or magistrates," said Jesuit missionary Pierre Biard of the Montagnais and Algonquins in the early seventeenth century. "There is no force, there are no prisons, no officers to compel obedience, or inflict punishment," Benjamin Franklin echoed, while naturalist William Bartram admired how civil government among the southeastern tribes functioned without "coercive laws, for they have no such artificial system."[36] In stark contrast, two Indians, Kaelkompte and Keketamape, appeared in irons before a Special Court of Oyer and Terminer at Fort Albany in February 1672/73, were tried before a twelve-man jury, and found guilty of murdering a soldier from the garrison. They were condemned to be hanged by the neck "until they are dead, dead, dead, and thereafter to hang in chains."[37] Indians were appalled to see children convicted of crimes; poor people imprisoned for stealing food; whipping, branding, and executions for theft; soldiers flogged for dereliction of duty; and criminals hanged by the neck. They sometimes intervened to plead for clemency.

Town jails often held Indian people. Sometimes they were there for breaching the many laws and regulations to which they were subject. Sometimes they were awaiting sentencing or punishment for more serious crimes. In 1763 an Indian prisoner, Abraham Wnupas (Wompas?), penned a letter begging for a speedy trial or release from the Albany jail, where he was being held on a murder charge.[38] Sometimes the prisoners were urban residents; sometimes they were sent from far away.[39]

What constituted justice? Europeans demanded retribution for murder but not for supposedly legitimate killings in war. Indian people often were less concerned with punishing an individual murderer than with exacting revenge on the group to which the killer belonged. In 1665, for example, five Mohawks were apprehended in Massachusetts and imprisoned in Boston. According to the chronicler Daniel Gookin, neighboring Indians "flocked into Boston, in great numbers, not only to see those Maquas, but earnestly to solicit the court not to let them escape, but to put them to death, or, at least, to deliver the Maquas to them to be put to death. For, said they, these Maquas are unto us, as wolves are to your sheep."[40] A killing could generate a cycle of revenge killings. That was why, according to the ubiquitous Seneca messenger Silver Heels, Cayugas killed four Englishmen to avenge the death of a Cayuga who was shot in Albany in 1759 for murdering a trader.[41]

However, Indigenous systems also included measures for conflict resolution, and focused on healing, repairing relationships, and restorative justice rather than retributive justice. If the killer and victim belonged to allied groups, justice could be satisfied, and recurrent retribution avoided, by "covering the dead" with gifts or by giving a life to make up for taking a life. Abenakis who killed a Stockbridge Indian in 1759 ceremonially atoned for their deed by sending the Stockbridges wampum belts and "replaced the Man who was killed with a Panis slave."[42] After one Cherokee killed another in a drunken brawl in 1774, clan vengeance was avoided when "the Relations of the Survivor paid in Matchcots, Blanketts, Guns Shot Pouches, Paint, Beads, Basketts etc. to the Amount of Seven Hundred pounds weight of Leather to the Relations of the deceased."[43]

It was a form of justice Europeans found difficult to accept.[44] "We have heard that it is a Custom amongst you, when an Indian happens to be Killed, that his Relations often demand & expect Money or Goods for satisfaction," Sir William Keith informed Conestogas in Philadelphia in 1722, following the murder of one of their people. "The Laws of our Great King will not suffer any such thing to be done amongst us," he informed them. If the murderer was convicted, he must hang. When the English did give gifts to "cover the dead Bodies," Governor Patrick Gordon explained to Sassoonan after another murder six years later, "we give them not as the Price of Blood, or to make Satisfaction for the Death of our Friends. Justice must be done according to our Law, & we give them only as a Mark of our Grief, that the relations be more easy in their Minds, that they may know we grieve with them."[45] In the spring of

1752, a dozen Cherokee chiefs were attacked by Creeks as they set out for home from Charleston. The colonial authorities demanded "that some of them must suffer Death for Nothing else would make Satisfaction to the English." The Creek headman Malatchi agreed that Acorn Whistler was the ringleader who should be executed for his alleged role in the attack, so "the Blood of the Acorn Whistler was Shed as a Satisfaction to the English for the Blood of their Friend the Cherokees Shed in Charles Town and to wash away the offence for ever."[46] Insistent on capital punishment in an Indian-on-Indian killing, the English were even more so when Indians killed whites: "For the Future," Governor Glen warned the Creeks in 1753, "Nothing will be deemed a Satisfaction for the Lives of any of our People but the Lives of them who were guilty of the Murder."[47]

After a white man murdered an Indian in 1761, Governor James Hamilton assured Teedyuscung that the perpetrator would be tried in the king's courts as if he had murdered a white man and, if found guilty, executed, "as the English Laws are deservedly very strict in matters of bloodshed." He said much the same to Indians who came to Philadelphia after the murder of a Native family in 1762.[48] In reality, Indian people knew that colonists who murdered Indians rarely went to trial, let alone to the hangman's noose. On the rare occasions when Indian-killers were sentenced to death, Indians often asked to be present to witness that the white man's justice actually was carried out.

Even where colonial law insisted on "justice," however, tribal law and Indian pressures sometimes functioned to secure peace and restore order. Native people were so numerous in and around Montreal that the French authorities knew better than to attempt to impose their jurisdiction, and they applied laws with respect for, and even in conjunction with, Indigenous perceptions of justice.[49] With the city's imbalance of French and Native population and power, Montreal's practices stood in stark contrast to the judicial treatment of Indian people in the growing towns and cities of English colonies. Yet even there, justice could not always afford to be blind to Indian power and practices. After a young Catawba was sentenced to death in Charleston for the alleged rape of a white girl in 1742, the Indians pleaded for clemency since this was his first offense and they had been unaware of the penalty. Their agent was "unwilling to Ruffle them too much by Insisting on the death of the Criminal" and presented their case, and the board recommended that the governor grant a pardon. In spring 1757, local tribes lobbied for the release of two Stockbridge Indians who sat in the Albany jail awaiting trial for the murder of a German colonist the previous fall. British fortunes in the war with France were going from bad to worse and it was no time to alienate their Mohican and Mohawk allies, so Sir William Johnson recommended the Stockbridges' release.[50] Disagreements over punishments could reflect contests over space, sovereignty, and authority as much as philosophical and moral differences.[51]

Although notorious for rituals of torture and inflicting cruelty on their enemies, Indian people sometimes found the unforgiving nature and public brutality of justice as administered by Europeans on their own citizens difficult to swallow. Hangings, whippings, brandings, and pillorying were common and public in the eighteenth century. In Philadelphia there was a whipping post and pillory at Third and Market Streets, across from the Old Stone Prison, at the head of the marketplace; shoppers could watch the punishments being carried out and hurl abuse at the offenders as part of the ritual of public humiliation. Sometimes the offenders were Indians. In Philadelphia in 1730, "G. Jones, and one Glasgow, an Indian, stood an hour in the pillory, and were whipt about the town, at the cart's tail—both for assaults with intent to ravish—the one, a girl of six years of age." Depending on the severity of the sentence, whippings could be life threatening.[52] One of the soldiers escorting the Moravian Indian refugees back to Philadelphia in January 1764 "was whipped until he was bloody" for insulting an officer, "which quite shocked our Indians," wrote one of the missionaries.[53]

Capital punishment, and hangings in particular, distressed many Indian people. In 1698 Iroquois interceded with the governor of New York in Albany asking that he pardon a soldier who had murdered a sachem and was in jail under sentence of death.[54] A Delaware named Mamataguin, sentenced to death in 1785 for murdering two white men, said he had "no objection to be tomahawked by some great man" but was "shocked to die by hanging."[55] William Johnson told the Earl of Dartmouth that Indians were "universally averse to our modes of Capital punishment."[56] Johnson's eldest son, Peter Warren Johnson, sent by his father to Philadelphia to learn business, witnessed a public hanging there in April 1774. Described by someone who saw him there as "a very sober good Lad," fifteen-year-old Peter was a Wolf clan Mohawk by his mother, Molly Brant, and had grown up in the Irish-Iroquois world of his father's household. Things were different in Philadelphia. Public executions were common: forty-four individuals were hanged in Philadelphia before 1776, and another sixty-two were executed in just twenty-four years from 1776 to 1790. At the time Peter was there, Pennsylvania executed people for at least eighteen offenses, including murder, rape, arson, robbery, burglary, sodomy, and counterfeiting. Peter attended a public hanging where five people were executed for their crimes: a sergeant for killing his wife, another man for robbery, a third for forging money, a fourth for breaking and entering, and a woman for killing her child.

Executions were protracted public rituals. If the ones Peter Johnson witnessed followed the usual practice, the condemned walked from the prison, accompanied by clergy, judges, a sheriff, and guards, through the city streets and past crowds of onlookers to one of the city's four public squares or a specially cleared area. There, ideally, the condemned individual would confess his or her crime, which served to justify the punishment and to provide a moral lesson for the hundreds of people who assembled to watch, and the execution was carried out. The execution of Moses Paul, an Indian who killed a white man and attributed his crime to the evils of drink, and the famous sermon preached by the Mohegan minister Samson Occom at the event in New Haven in 1772 fit the bill. But the execution Peter witnessed was, he wrote his father, "the Most Dismal sight I ever Saw."[57]

Indian visitors to Philadelphia would also have seen from the outside the city's prisons, poorhouses, and hospitals, and may have found difficulty in distinguishing among them. Philadelphia after the Revolution was reforming its poor relief as well as its prisons, with growing concern for the "deserving poor," although such relief was designed to reform the behavior of the poor rather than improve their conditions. The hospital for the indigent, sick, and insane was still under construction when Johann David Schoepf, a German botanist and physician, visited the city in the summer of 1783, as was the workhouse for the old, poor, and maimed.[58] Five years later, Jacques Pierre Brissot de Warville described the house of correction on the outskirts of the city as an institution where Philadelphians placed "the poor, the sick, orphans, women in travail, and persons attacked with venereal diseases" and confined "vagabonds, disorderly persons, and girls of scandalous lives." He saw there "all that misery and disease can assemble."[59]

Reverend Manasseh Cutler, in Philadelphia in July 1789 on Ohio Company business, accompanied Dr. Benjamin Rush as he did his rounds at the hospital and was impressed by the facilities. Female patients occupied the top floor, men the floor below, and the cells of "the *Maniacs*" the lower story, partly underground. These cells were about ten feet square and "as strong as a prison." Some of the inmates had beds; most had clean straw. "Some of them were extremely fierce and raving, nearly or quite naked; some singing and dancing; some in despair; some were dumb and would not open their mouths; others incessantly talking." Cutler found it "curious indeed to see in what different strains their distraction raged. This would have been a melancholy scene indeed, had it not been that there was every possible relief afforded them in the power of man."[60] Brissot de Warville agreed that the hospital for lunatics was far more humane than similar institutions in Europe, but the sight of inmates "affected me more than that of the sick. The last of human miseries, in my opinion, is confinement; and I cannot conceive how a sick person can be cured in prison, for confinement itself is a continual malady."[61] Brissot de Warville spoke from experience, having been imprisoned in the Bastille in 1784 on charges of publishing seditious or pornographic pamphlets, but his was a view that Indian visitors would have shared. (Back in France, Brissot de Warville was arrested again when the tide of the French Revolution swung against his moderate Girondin party, but he was not confined for long: He went to the guillotine in October 1793.)

The many Indian delegates who passed through the city in the early 1790s would have seen the same prisons and witnessed much the same scenes that other visitors described. The Old Stone Prison, built around 1723, consisted of a two-story building, fronting on High Street, which served as the debtors' jail, connected by a high wall to another building that fronted on Third Street for criminals, called the workhouse. A new prison, the Walnut Street Jail, built in 1773 to accommodate increasing population, stood at Sixth and Walnut Streets, at the foot of the Mall outside the State House (Figure 6.5). The prison and the prisoners were divided into large rooms: male convicts on the second story of the east wing; female convicts on the first floor of the west wing; male vagrants on the first floor of the east wing; female vagrants on the second floor of the west wing. The jail served as the state prison and suffered from serious overcrowding, which made discipline and supervision difficult and tended to increase rather than reduce criminality.[62] Apparently, passers-by needed no tour to get a sense of "its unsavory contents." Cutler was there on a warm day, so the prison windows were open.

Your ears are consulted with their Billingsgate language, or your feelings wounded with their pitiful complaints. Their long reed poles, with a little cap of cloth at the end, are constantly extended over into the Mall, in order to receive your charity, which they are incessantly begging. And if you refuse them,

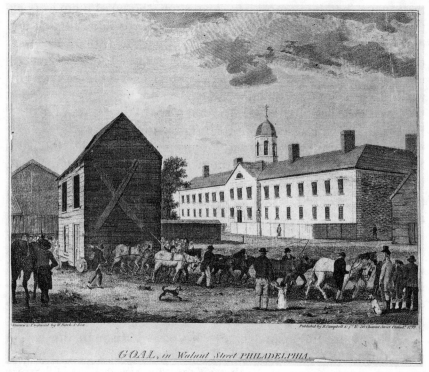

Figure 6.5 The Walnut Street Jail. *The City of Philadelphia as it appeared in the Year 1800.* Plate 24. Published by W. Birch, 1800. Library Company of Philadelphia.

they load you with the most foul and horrid imprecations. In short, whatever part of the Mall you are in, this cage of unclean birds is constantly in your view, and their doleful cries attacking your ears.

Many Western societies were replacing public executions with private punishments, and the debate over finding alternatives to the death penalty was especially acute in the United States after the Revolution.[63] The Pennsylvania legislature reformed its penal system and also refashioned the jail itself to provide more capacity for solitary confinement and monitoring of the inmates' behavior. In 1786 the legislature discontinued the public whipping post, reduced the number of capital offenses, and experimented with a program of public penal labor in the streets. Four years later it replaced public labor with imprisonment, and in 1794 it restricted capital punishment to cases of first-degree murder. Benjamin Rush took a leading role in implementing changes designed to transform individual character through imprisonment and solitary confinement, separating inmates from the public and subjecting them to a supervised life of discipline, labor, health, and morality in penitentiaries, rather than inflicting bodily violence as a spectacle in public.[64] Julian Ursyn Niemcewicz, a Polish visitor in the late 1790s, was so impressed with the prisons in Philadelphia that he thought there was not "in the world an establishment conceived with better judgment and more humanity."[65] Indian people, however, would have been appalled.

They saw many other unfree people in the cities. In addition to indentured servants and Indian slaves, they came face-to-face with African slavery. Indigenous societies took, kept, and traded captives. Some Indian people held black slaves, and some developed racist attitudes similar to those of white slaveholders. Alexander McGillivray and some other Creeks held slaves, and Jean Baptiste DuCoigne and the Kaskaskia delegation would not have been fazed by the sight of black slaves and servants in Philadelphia; the Illinois country had long been a region where Indian, French, African, and mixed-race individuals mingled and where slavery, both Indian and African, was part of the fabric of life.[66] However, the sheer scale and brutality of race slavery on display in the cities of early America disturbed many Indian people, who often said that colonists intended to reduce *them* to slavery.[67]

Indians could not have avoided seeing African slaves bought and sold in Charleston, which served as the slave market for much of the Lower South.[68] However, they did not need to travel into the Deep South to witness slavery and the slave trade firsthand. Gentlemen bought and sold human beings in the taverns and coffeehouses of northern cities. Philadelphia's London Coffee House advertised for sale "a very likely breeding Negroe woman . . . fit for any Business either in Town or Country" in 1736. Sassoonan came to the city that year, as did more than a hundred Iroquois. In 1763, the Coffee House offered for sale "a likely healthy Negroe Wench about 24 Years of age." Moravian Indians sought refuge in Philadelphia that year.[69] A Scottish visitor in New York on the eve of the Revolution wrote home that "it rather hurts a Europian eye to see so many negro slaves upon the streets."[70]

Like visitors from Europe and the North, Indians people who traveled to cities in the South would have witnessed routine violence meted out to slaves and gruesome punishments that included gibbeting, drawing and quartering, and the display of decaying corpses and body parts for public view. Cities were not only economic and political centers but also judicial centers, where justice was administered in public even for crimes committed elsewhere.

For example, the Louisiana colony's only public executioner lived in New Orleans. Indians living in or visiting New Orleans in spring 1744 would have seen or heard of the execution of a black slave who allegedly killed a soldier and was broken on the wheel in the public square and his body left on display for twenty-four hours.[71] A French traveler in Williamsburg in 1765 saw "three Negroes hanging at the gallows" for robbery. Walking through a wood on his way to dinner at the home of a Charleston planter, the French American farmer and writer J. Hector St. John de Crèvecoeur came upon a black slave suspended in a cage and left to die who begged for poison to end his torment. Crèvecoeur's host explained that the slave had killed an overseer and that "the laws of self preservation rendered such executions necessary."[72] Josiah Quincy Jr., who was appalled by slavery, acknowledged that Charlestonians were hospitable and polite but questioned "what proportion there is of true humanity, Christian charity and love."[73] Whether or not they witnessed public displays of violence, so-called savages confronted with the systemic savagery of slavery must have asked the same question.

Such questions also occurred when Indians attended city churches that reflected Christianity's grandest aspirations yet exposed its failings and hypocrisies. Teedyuscung, kept waiting by Pennsylvania officials observing the Sabbath in July 1756, complained that "the Indians knew nothing of Sunday." In fact, he knew all about the Sabbath, having been baptized six years earlier, taken the name Gideon, and lived for a time in a Moravian mission community.[74] Rather than encountering Christianity for the first time, many Indians went to church as usual on Sunday when they were in town, and they sometimes attracted almost as much attention as Indians who went to the theater, as other members of the congregation craned their necks to get a glimpse of them at prayer.

In 1730, Chikagou and Mamantouesna led a delegation of Illinois Indians to New Orleans to reaffirm their alliance with the French. Large numbers of Illinois had already converted to Catholicism. During the three weeks they were there, wrote the Jesuit missionary Mathurin Le Petit, the Illinois delegates "had no other residence but with us," and "charmed us by their piety." They heard Mass every morning, recited the rosary every evening, and even shared a Gregorian chant with Ursuline nuns, the nuns chanting the first couplets in Latin and the Indians responding in their own language. "This spectacle, which was novel, drew great crowds to the Church, and inspired a deep devotion," said Le Petit. He doubted that many French people were "so well instructed in Religion."[75]

Seeing Indians in church may have been a novelty for urban residents, but being in church was nothing new for many Indian people. Colonial travelers often noted the presence of Indians in church congregations. When Alexander Hamilton, the itinerant Scottish doctor, attended a chapel in Boston in 1744, some Indians sat in a nearby pew. What struck him as noteworthy was not the presence of Indian congregants but how bad they smelled.[76] More often, observers were impressed by the decorum and devotion of Indian congregations and by the sweet singing of Indian choirs, especially in their own churches.[77] Many Indians came from communities that had long exposure to Christianity, some had adopted elements of the Christian religion into their own belief systems, and some were active members of their own churches at home. Peter Kalm listed the various churches in Philadelphia—English, Swedish, German Lutheran, German Reformed, Presbyterian, Quaker and other meeting houses—"for God is served in various ways in this country."[78] Indians who came to town often belonged to different dominations themselves.

Mohawk people who frequented Albany, for example, adopted several versions of Christianity. Some went specifically to receive baptism for themselves or their babies, although they understood the power and purpose of baptism differently than did their ministers. In July 1690, a Mohawk named Tejonihokarawa along with two other Mohawk men, three women, and four children arrived at the Dutch Reformed Church in Albany and asked to be baptized. Tejonihokarawa took a new name, Hendrick. (Not to be confused with the later Mohawk with that name, he was one of the "four Indian Kings" who later went to London.)[79] Before they got a chapel in their own community, many Mohawk converts considered Albany a safe space where they could perform their Christianity out of sight of their non-Christian relatives.[80] Catholic Mohawks from Kahnawake who were in Albany to trade in 1700 declined the offer of ministers and churches as inducements to "come home" to the Mohawk Valley and the Church of England.[81] That same year the Five Nations requested a Protestant minister at Albany, and four years later the Anglican church began missionary work among the Mohawks.[82] The English built a chapel for the Mohawks at Fort Hunter and then a stone church with a minister.[83] The Mohawk community at Canajoharie, where Mohawk people read the prayers, raised money to help build its own church in 1770.[84]

It was hardly surprising, then, that on Sunday, June 30, 1754, during the Albany Congress, Theodore Atkinson, the leader of the New Hampshire delegation, and other onlookers attended a church service to which the Mohawks were summoned in their own language, and they found that it "was Performed with the utmost Decency," that many of the Indians "had books & responded," and that some recited psalms and prayers.[85] Or that on Sunday, August 28, 1775, when the Continental commissioners were negotiating with the Six Nations and Albany was "crowded with Indians & Soldiers," Reverend Samuel Kirkland delivered a sermon and the Oneida congregation sang anthems. The next evening, Tench Tilghman, serving as secretary for the commissioners, sat for almost an hour listening as Stockbridge Indian girls sang hymns.[86] An officer in the Continental Army who attended a service preached in the Oneida language a couple of years later said the Oneida congregation listened with such reverence and sang so beautifully that "their devout Behaviour struck me with Astonishment & made me blush with shame for myself and my own People."[87]

When McGillivray and the Creeks were in New York in 1790 the city had twenty-two churches representing thirteen denominations.[88] The Creeks were more likely impressed when they attended divine service at Christ Church in Philadelphia.[89] Founded in 1695 and rebuilt between 1727 and 1754, Christ Church, an ornate Georgian church rivaling London's most fashionable churches, had a 196-foot spire, making it the tallest building in the United States at the time the Creeks visited (Figure 6.6).[90]

Churches were also places where worshippers were on display, where they went to see and be seen.[91] Treaty commission secretary William Black, who had "an eye for the ladies" and often described the objects of his admiration in detail, was delighted to see "so fine a Collection" of "Fine Women" in one place when he attended church in Philadelphia.[92] Indian churchgoers, like most people, would have had more varied interests than Black did, but they would certainly have been observing and observed.

Their own observations were not always positive. Indians frequently pointed to the hypocrisy of so-called Christians and asserted that Native people already lived "Christian lives." Benjamin Franklin related a purported conversation between Canasatego and Conrad Weiser in which the Onondaga's actual or feigned ignorance of the Sabbath served to expose the hypocrisy of Christians. "I have been sometimes at Albany, and I have observed, that once in seven days they shut up their shops, and assemble all in the great house; tell me, what is it for? What do they do there?" Franklin had Canasatego ask. "They meet there," Weiser replied, "to hear and learn *good things*."

Figure 6.6 Christ Church, Philadelphia. Library of Congress, Photographs and Prints Division.

Canasatego allowed that that was what they *said* they did, but his experience in going to Albany to trade convinced him "that whatever they pretended . . . , the real purpose was to consult how to cheat Indians in the price of Beaver." If they went to church so often to learn how to do good, he thought, they must surely have learned before now. If a white man traveled to their community, Indians would give him food, lodging, and hospitality and ask nothing in return. "But if I go into a white man's house at Albany, and ask for victuals and drink, they say where is your money; and if I have none, they say, get out, you Indian Dog." Clearly, white people did not learn to do good by attending church.[93] This was not all Franklin's invention. The Mohawk sachem Hendrick echoed Canasetago's views and language about the citizens of Albany, who, he said, "caressed" smugglers from Kahnawake but treated other Indians like "their dogs."[94]

Indian people who judged Christians by their actions and not their words often gave missionaries a hard time. Conestogas told a Swedish missionary in 1710, "We find the Christians much more depraved, in their morals than ourselves."[95] In the Ohio country in the 1770s the speaker of the Delaware Council matched Reverend David McClure in debate and told him, "The white people, with whom we are acquainted, are worse, or more wicked than we are, and we think it better to be such as we are than such as they are." Stuck for an answer, all McClure could say was, "If you want to see christians you must go to Philadelphia"—which unfortunately didn't get around the fact that these Delawares did not want to see Christians.[96] Red Jacket's famous response to Quaker proselytizing among the Senecas in 1800—expressing astonishment "that the white people, who have the good book called the Bible among them, that tells them the mind of the Great Spirit . . . are so bad, and do so many wicked things, and that they are no better"—was part of a long-established Indigenous critique.[97]

Early American cities represented pinnacles of colonial achievement and epitomes of civilization, supposedly what distinguished settler colonists from the Indigenous inhabitants of the continent. Chiefs in the city certainly saw many things that, as Timothy Pickering anticipated, caused them "to wonder and admire." Yet admiration of buildings, streets, markets, and ships was tempered by doubt about the values, practices, and humanity of the society that constructed them. Cherokees in Charleston clearly were mystified by a society that accorded titles and status to "young, lazy, deformed white men, with big bellies, who seemed to require as much help to move them along, as over-grown old women." Cherokees only conferred titles of distinction on people who deserved them, they said.[98]

CHAPTER 7

Performance and Performers

EIGHTEENTH-CENTURY LONDONERS WHO FLOCKED, and sometimes paid, to see Indigenous visitors expected them to satisfy fantasies about wild and exotic savages and at the same time conduct themselves in a manner that befitted their status as visiting "kings." Over time, Indians who crossed the Atlantic became both emissaries and entertainers.[1] American city dwellers did not regard Indian visitors as quite so exotic or have such extreme expectations.

Nevertheless, whether Indian delegates were in formal negotiations or touring the city, they were onstage in the public sphere. Crowds did not gather to gawk at Indian people who lived and worked among them and did not flock to see local Native women who came to peddle baskets and brooms on market days. Delegates from more distant and often still-powerful tribes were a different matter. Colonial authorities took steps to keep Indian visitors entertained, but the visitors were also part of the entertainment and they knew it. They attended formal functions and informal events where, like Indians in London, they were expected to perform dual roles, demonstrating and verifying their "Indianness" and also conducting themselves as dignified ambassadors and worthy allies. Chiefs in the city sometimes played such roles, though they did so to promote their own agendas and often challenged rather than pandered to white expectations. They also performed other roles that emphasized their value as intercultural intermediaries rather than their exoticism as distant Others. City-going chiefs knew, or quickly mastered, the arts of diplomatic theater.

Negotiations between colonial officials and Indian leaders were hedged about by performances, rituals, and symbols that communicated messages about power and sovereignty. Clothing and coded gestures sometimes conveyed as much meaning as spoken words.[2] Then as now, people dressed to impress. Indian delegates' performances began with how they dressed when they were in town. At the same time, their temporary celebrity status gave them access to the right places and occasions to mingle with members of fashionable society, and ample opportunity to see urban residents dressed in their finery. Those who traveled to Paris or London saw the latest fashions firsthand. An Illinois Indian who visited Paris in 1725 told French naval officer Jean-Bernard Bossu in the 1750s that he remembered the enormous height of the women's headdresses as well as the height of their heels. Thinking of current fashions, Bosso wondered "what he would have said if he had seen the exaggerated width of their hoop skirts and the narrowness of their waists strangled by that piece of armor called a whalebone corset"[3] (Figure 7.1).

As the seaports of early America grew into commercial entrepôts, textiles from Britain and around the world arrived as fast as sail

Figure 7.1 A French officer named Du Bois was said to have fallen in love with and married a Missouri woman when she visited Paris in 1720 with Étienne de Veniard, Sieur de Bourgmont. This lunette by Ernest Leonard Blumenschein (1874-1960) in the Missouri State Capitol in Jefferson City pictures the bride coming home in elegant Parisian dress, and her people appropriately impressed. State Historical Society of Missouri.

could carry them. Wealthy urban residents proclaimed their status, identity, and gentility not only by their homes, furnishings, imported goods, and manners but also by parading their fashionable dress in assembly rooms, ballrooms, theaters, taverns, churches, parks, the streets, and other "see-and-be-seen" spaces. Clothing expressed one's position in society and reflected access to sources of power and culture. Fashions changed and were contested: the curled wigs and full coats of the late seventeenth century gave way to smaller wigs and shorter coats during the course of the eighteenth, while hooped petticoats—made first of whalebone and then cane as a way to display dresses made of sumptuous fabrics —became fashionable after the start of the eighteenth century and remained so until the end of the century. The politics of fashion shifted. American urban consumers emulated the latest British styles; then rejected the extravagance of British fashion as reflecting the debauchery and corruption of an imperial tyrant; then adopted the Parisian styles of a national ally; and then, recoiling from the excesses of the French Revolution, dressed to reflect Federalist privilege or Republican virtue.[4]

Whatever the fashion, Indian visitors would have understood that clothes revealed great disparities and inequality in eighteenth-century American society. "One can easily distinguish a rich woman from one of the common people," observed a Polish visitor to Philadelphia in the late 1790s.[5] Gentry wore well-cut coats, brocade waistcoats, lace cuffs, and rich fabric; working people wore leather aprons, open shirts, and coarse cloth. Beggars, laborers, slaves, washerwomen, butchers, blacksmiths, and others were distinguishable by their dress.[6] Indian visitors would have learned quickly that clothing denoted occupation, age, and religious denomination. Teedyuscung, no stranger himself to sartorial splendor when the occasion merited or demanded it, would have seen rather different clothing when he dined at the Pembertons' Quaker home than when he dined with members of Philadelphia's social elite.

Dressing up and dressing down conveyed messages as well as status. Quakers favored plain clothing. Benjamin Franklin famously affected the clothes of an artisan but actually wore different styles of clothing at different times and places for different occasions and purposes. George Washington mimicked British fashion as much as any colonial American, yet wore a suit of simple American homespun for his inauguration as the president of a new republic. Indian delegates in New York and Philadelphia saw public and often ostentatious displays of consumption—women in hooped skirts with huge and elaborately adorned hairstyles, men in powdered wigs and "foppish" attire. Congressman John Fell wrote in 1780 that women's dress in Philadelphia, formerly a bastion of Quaker conservatism in clothing, was "quite equal to the dress of the ladies that I have seen in the boxes in the playhouses of London" and "even along the Streets resembles in a great degree the Actresses on the Stage."[7]

Even a British visitor thought the dress of midcentury Boston citizens "Very genteel & In my Opinion both Men & Women are too Expensive in that respect."[8] John Adams, about to depart for "that nasty, dirty Town of Boston" in 1763, complained in a letter to Abigail about the "Parade, Pomp, Nonsense, Frippery, Folly, Foppery, Luxury," and other excesses that were common in the city.[9] It was not surprising, then, that some Indians, in Gottlieb Mittelberger's words, were "especially amazed about European garments and finery. Indeed, they will even go so far as to spit when they see them."[10] The elaborate displays of fashion in New York and Philadelphia would have raised Indigenous eyebrows.

But Native people themselves dressed the part long before Europeans arrived, using clothing, hairstyle, and personal ornament to express status, power, and identity.[11] As the Atlantic economy extended its reach into the interior via the fur and deerskin trades and commercial hubs like Detroit, Indian women incorporated a wide variety of new cloths, from coarse cotton and woolens to fine linens and silk, as well as manufactured shirts and blouses, buttons, beads, ribbons, and trade silver, generating a flowering of Indigenous fashion in which color, fabric, and ornamentation conveyed tribal identity, wealth, and status.[12] Some Indian people wore items of European clothing at home, and delegates to cities often donned waistcoats, coats, and hats. The Creek woman Coosaponakeesa wore a red stroud petticoat when she accompanied Tomochichi and other Yamacraws to meet and greet James Oglethorpe and the first Georgia colonists at what became the site of Savannah in 1733. Her choice of dress was intentional and announced her role as an influential woman, a trader, and a valuable intermediary in the incipient relationship between Georgia colonists and Creeks.[13] A painting of the Yamacraw delegation to London the next year shows Tomochichi's wife, Senaukey, wearing the dress of a colonial woman. Ten years later a visitor to the home of the Narragansett sachem "King George" Ninigret observed that his wife "goes in high modish dress in her silks, hoops, stays, and dresses like an English woman."[14] Native people were become increasingly accustomed to the kind of clothing they saw in the cities.

The Creek chief Emistisego said that Indians "are not known by their Dress[,] a King being scarce to be distinguished from a Common Man," and William Bartram agreed. Nevertheless, as Scottish traders increased their presence and commerce in Creek country during the eighteenth century, Creek people adopted elements of Highland dress, and Indian leaders dealing with Europeans readily adopted material markers of status.[15] Colonial Indian agents not only gave clothing to Indian families but also distinguished chiefs with gifts of the kind of clothes that designated men of status in European society. In 1759, for example, Sir William Johnson, who was notorious for extravagant spending of the government's money, gave an Onondaga named the Red Head "a Green Silk Gold laced Waistcoat" that cost £5. That was nothing compared to the ensemble given to Cherokees and Catawbas in Charleston in May 1741. The Cherokee chief Moytoy received "a Scarlet Coat and Breeches and a green Waist Coat, a Sword and Gun, a Ruffled Shirt, Hat, etc.," and the other headmen were given scarlet coats, breeches, shirts, laced hats, shoes, and guns.[16]

As in other times and places, clothing in early America functioned as a language, and mixing Indigenous and European clothing said a lot.[17] European traders and agents wore items of Native clothing to do business in Indian country. Indian leaders wore elements of Western clothing and jewelry to signal their role as cultural intermediaries and their capacity to do business with colonists, and delegates often donned their finest apparel when they traveled to Montreal, New York, or Philadelphia, perhaps putting on items of European clothing they had been given at a treaty conference or on previous visits and reserved for such occasions[18] (Figure 7.2). A chief named Teykorimat dressed like a Frenchman and carried a cane when he went to salute the governor of Quebec in 1669.[19]

At the Treaty of Montreal in the summer of 1701, a Mesquakie (Fox) leader named Miskouensa strode across the arena in front of the 2,000 or 3,000 attendees; reaching the area where the French governor and other officials were sitting, he bowed and, with an elaborate sweep of his arm, doffed a battered old wig he was wearing as he had seen Frenchmen doff their hats. The French section of the audience burst into laughter at his clumsy and comical attempt to emulate polite manners. In fact, Miskouensa may have been making fun of French manners while at the same time proclaiming his own role as a person of influence with access to French trade and with actual or potential French loyalties. In historian Gilles Havard's view, Miskouensa's theatrics were entirely intentional: He was "asserting

Grand Chef de Guerriers Iroquois

Figure 7.2 Jacques Grasset de Saint-Sauveur "Grand Chef de Guerriers Iroquois." Los Angeles County Museum of Art.

himself politically by putting on a performance, making an exhibition of himself."[20] It was not unusual for Indian people to wear European clothing in ways Europeans thought bizarre, such as wearing a coat or shirt but without breeches. The French laughed at it but, reported one Jesuit missionary, the Indians thought it tasteful "because they regard our breeches as an encumbrance, although they sometimes wear these as a bit of finery, or in fun."[21]

Dr. Alexander Hamilton met two "French Mohawks," presumably from Kahanawake, on the road outside Boston who were "dressed *à la mode Français* with laced hats, full trimmed coats, and ruffled shirts." When the Mohawk headman Theyanoguin or Hendrick attended councils and treaty conferences in Boston, Montreal, New York, and Philadelphia, he dressed the part for the occasion, the mixture of Indigenous and European clothing and styles suggesting a man who could operate across cultures. Hamilton observed a procession of Indians attending a treaty conference in Boston in which Hendrick and the other chiefs "had all laced hats, and some of them laced matchcoats and ruffled shirts" (see Plate 3).[22]

Chiefs so adorned knew what to wear when they headed to town on official business. Teedyuscung certainly did. The Delaware chief often wore an English gentleman's suit of clothes tailored in Philadelphia, although on official occasions he sometimes sported a dark brown cloth coat laced with gold, which the French had given him. He wore ruffled shirts, riding boots or buckled shoes instead of moccasins, and checkered cloth trousers and stockings with scarlet gartering rather than leggings. A "List of Necessaries to be provided for Teedyuscung" at government expense while he was on diplomatic business in 1760 included "a good suit of Cloathes, Hat, &, that he may make an Appearance answerable to the Occasion"; it was likely quite a wardrobe.[23] Teedyuscung's son, John Jacob, followed his father's example. In 1757 he spent £15 on a regimental coat, a gold laced hat and cockade, a ruffled shirt, breeches, a pair of shoes, and a cotton handkerchief, among other items.[24] When Reverend David McClure met Guyasuta on his way to Philadelphia in the summer of 1772 the Seneca chief "was dressed in a scarlet cloth turned up with lace, & a high gold laced hat, & made a martial appearance."[25] As spokesman for his people to colonial governments, Joseph Brant dressed for his audiences. Although he often wore a suit of blue broadcloth (and his wife a gown of calico or chintz), on official visits—and in his portraits—he wore a mixture of Indian and European clothing to present himself as at once a Native diplomat and a modern gentleman (see Plate 12).[26] Little Turtle on the other hand, according to the Comte de Volney, dressed "in the American fashion, a blue suit, with pantaloons, and a round hat" when in Philadelphia and reverted to Indian dress when he returned home.[27] Delegates often wore European clothing in the city and Indigenous clothing back in Indian country. Some also returned home bedecked in hats and coats that had been presented to them as gifts, signaling the role they had played.

Elite people did not dress in their finery all the time, of course. Even the wealthy owned and wore everyday clothing. However, the presence of the Creek delegation in the capital of the new nation in 1790 prompted a string of occasions when both New York citizens and Creek visitors donned their finest. Alexander McGillivray arrived in New York dressed, the press reported, in "a suit of plain scarlet," while the other chiefs wore "their national habits." Later, for a review of the uniform companies of the New York militia with

Washington, Knox, and several principal officers, the Creeks wore clothes "made in the present fashion."[28]

The formal ratification of the Treaty of New York, held at Federal Hall on August 13, 1790, was the event of the season. Anyone who was anyone wanted to be there. When Thomas Jefferson asked Henry Knox if the official representatives of France, Spain, and Holland might bring others, including ladies, Knox replied, "The ladies by all means." It must have been quite a display as Creek men wearing turbans and feathers mingled with American women wearing turbans and feathers. People flocked to Federal Hall and onlookers filled the galleries. McGillivray and the Creek delegates entered wearing American uniforms of blue, faced with red, which the government had given them. Louis Guillaume Otto, the secretary of the French Legation, was present and described "their figures painted in all sorts of colors, their strange hairstyles with feathers, their ears covered and stretched, the thousand fantastic ornaments that they had overloaded themselves with, not even omitting a huge wig, their legs half covered and the Chinese fans which they used, contrasted utterly with the ceremony's solemnity." They wore headbands or turbans and feathers, and all were "fancifully painted, and decorated with earrings, and Nose jewels." Even so, the Creeks were in danger of being outshone. Washington, usually formal and often dressed in black, wore "vestments of rich purple satin" on this occasion, and there was "a brilliant circle of Ladies, richly habited."[29]

What "richly habited" looked like can be gleaned from the accounts of other visitors to New York at the time. As now, visitors to the city in 1790 were likely to see some outlandish displays.[30] Italian traveler Luigi Castiglioni, who was there several years before the Creeks, said that some young ladies, especially of the upper class, were "excessively given to luxury and to the mad pursuit of fashions."[31] Two years before the Creek visit, Brissot de Warville wrote, "If there is a town on the American continent where the English luxury displays its follies, it is New-York. You will find here the English fashions. In the dress of the women, you will see the most brilliant silks, gauzes, hats, and borrowed hair."[32] McGillivray and the Creeks met Henry Knox's wife—and her hair. Reverend Manasseh Cutler, who had had dinner with Mrs. Knox three years before, described her as a large woman ("very gross") who "would be very agreeable, were it not for her affected singularity in dressing her hair. She seems to mimic a military style, which to me is disgusting in a female. Her hair in front is craped at least a foot high, much in the form of a churn bottom upward, and topped off with a wire skeleton in the same form covered with black gauze, which hangs in streamers down her back. Her hair behind is in a large braid, turned up, and confined with a monstrous large crooked comb."[33] No slouches themselves when it came to headgear, the Creeks left no record of their reactions to such towering coiffures. Perhaps they were at a loss for words.

Indian delegates in early American cities of course attended a variety of events where they performed a variety of roles and where their behavior was under scrutiny. Would they act like wild Indians or with "savage refinement"?[34] Historian Philip Deloria has examined the phenomenon of white people in the colonies and later the United States playing Indian for their own purposes, to satisfy their own fantasies and proclaim their own identities. Chiefs in the city also played Indian when they were onstage, sometimes literally. Sometimes they did so in conformity with non-Indian audiences' ideas of "Indianness"; sometimes they may have done so for shock value; and sometimes they performed an Indianness that confounded rather than confirmed their audiences' expectations. Intentional self-representation in the city could be a political performance that expressed Indigenous sovereignty in the very heart of colonial power.[35] In 1742, for example, Canasatego traveled to Philadelphia to conduct business at the seat of the colonial government, but with a powerful oratorical performance he established the Iroquois treaty council as the primary public forum for negotiations and established himself as the power broker between colonial government and Native communities.[36] He made that particular city space his own and dealt with colonial power on his terms.

City-going chiefs mastered performative as well as negotiating skills. In eighteenth-century England, masked balls, or masquerades, became fashionable and controversial events—opportunities for participants, with their identities concealed, to abandon inhibitions and indulge in less restrained and even "savage" behavior. At one masquerade in London, Joseph Brant deliberately and provocatively assumed the role of a painted savage brandishing a tomahawk, only to revert to that of a gentleman.[37] He was not the first Mohawk to play an audience. American colonists, concerned to establish their identity as *not* savage, eschewed wearing masks and costumes, and balls tended to be much more formal and sedate, emphasizing order and civility. The Philadelphia Dancing Assembly, formed by the city's elites in 1749, held dances every Thursday from January through May, each one starting with a minuet. In the winter of 1755, with Britain and France on the brink of war, Hendrick and a party of Mohawks traveled to Philadelphia to reaffirm their friendship. They were entertained at the State House and also showed up at the Assembly on dance night. As if to reaffirm their identity as warriors in such circumstances, according to one correspondent, they caused quite a stir when they "danced the Scalping Dance with all its Horrors, and almost terrified the Company out of their Wits." Whether or not the Mohawks were deliberately discomfiting their hosts with a display of "savage" power, the contrast between the colonists' regulated etiquette and the Indians' wild behavior could not have been more obvious. As if to emphasize the point, the correspondent added: "I must tell you they brought with them a beautiful young Lady, who in publick made the Indian Compliment, a Tender of her Person to the Governor; as gallant a Man as he is, he was quite confounded at that Time. I know not if he accepted her."[38]

Indian delegates performed expected roles and at the same time affirmed their identity when they were hosted by the Sons of St. Tammany, who dressed as Indians for the occasion. On the eve of the Revolution, Americans invented a St. Tammany, loosely based on Tamenend, the Delaware chief who purportedly signed the famous treaty with William Penn. In the early Republic such appropriation and parodying of Native practices constituted a public declaration of an emergent national identity that in turn laid claim to an aboriginal American identity, incorporated "noble" Indian traits such as courage and freedom, and distinguished Americans from Europeans; it could also be seen as a declaration that Americans had replaced, or were replacing, the Native inhabitants as rulers of the land.[39] Tammany performances bore out scholar Homi Bhaba's observation that mimicry "is at once resemblance and menace."[40]

The Tammany Society in Philadelphia invited Cornplanter and five other Seneca chiefs to their lodge or "wigwam" in April 1786. Cornplanter "accepted the invitation as an honor done to him." Society officers—who called themselves "sachems"—escorted the Senecas individually from the Indian Queen Hotel to the lodge. Cannon were fired in salute, flags displayed, and speeches exchanged, after which the militia escorted both the Tammany sachems and the real sachems back to the Indian Queen. "The whole was conducted with great harmony and good humour; and the conduct of the Chief and his nation was grand and noble," reported the press. Not so, according to a letter supposedly from Cornplanter that an opponent of the club published in a periodical—the gathering ended "in drunkenness and disorder."[41]

Beyond the possibility that both groups were simply having a good time, Tammany members and Senecas alike were conscious that, dressed in regalia, they were on public display. Whatever the Senecas thought about white people playing Indian by donning Indian dress, orating in broken English, and performing purported rituals of peace, Cornplanter and his companions had come to Philadelphia with a serious political purpose, and they used the occasion to reaffirm their own identity as a sovereign Indigenous nation by reciting the creation stories of the Iroquois League and invoking the Covenant Chain as their symbol of alliance even as they cemented and celebrated a new alliance with the federal government.[42]

A delegation of Oneidas "were pompously introduced" to "the Wigwam of St. Tammany" in New York in February 1790. The society's "grand sachem," Dr. William Pitt Smith, "harangued them with almost every talent and acquisition of eloquence, which was answered by one of the Chiefs." After "a variety of toasts from the Savages and Sachems," read a press account in the *New York Packet,* the Indians performed several dances, accompanied by a few of the members, followed by songs, more toasts, and another long talk by one of the members. The Oneidas were said to be "amazed," and they had reason to be.[43]

Six months later, on the evening of August 2, McGillivray and the Creeks received similar treatment at a Tammany event attended by the governor of New York, the mayor of the city, the secretary of war, the secretary of state, and the chief justice of the United States. Smith spoke words of peace and friendship, McGillivray reciprocated, and a "richly ornamented" calumet was passed around until "the smoke and peace of friendship was mingled from every part of the wigwam." One of the Creeks conferred an honorific name on the grand sachem. "The variety of toasts and sociability of manners which were interchanged upon this occasion, are too numerous for us to admit at present," the press reported (although some newspapers listed the seven toasts everyone drank). By the end, "the good order and decorum observed thro' the whole evening, the pleasure painted on every countenance, the novelty and brilliancy of the scene, with the union of philanthropy and joy gave inexpressible delight and satisfaction to every spectator."[44]

Cornplanter and the Seneca delegation were "introduced" to the society again in February 1793. The grand sachem made an address to them, then read an article in the *New York Journal* explaining the principles of the society, and thanked them for their efforts in making peace with the western tribes. Farmer's Brother "replied

in an animated address," thanking the society for its polite attention and expressing his "most ardent desire for peace." After the
exchange of speeches, members of the society and one of the chiefs
sang ceremonial songs.[45]

Similar performances of Indianness no doubt occurred when
individual chiefs were inducted into the St. Andrew's Society, whose
members celebrated what they regarded as shared traits linking
Scottish clans and Indian tribes. The British superintendent of Indian
affairs in the South, John Stuart, got Oconastota inducted into the
St. Andrews Society of Charleston in 1773, making the Cherokee
chief an honorary Scotsman.[46] Alexander McGillivray was inducted
into the St. Andrews Society of the State of New York the day after
he signed the Treaty of New York in 1790. At their quarterly meeting
at the City Tavern, anxious to show their respect for the Scots-Creek
chief, the members unanimously elected him an honorary member.
McGillivray "was introduced to the presiding officers in their places,
and received the compliments of the Society," went the article in the
New-York Journal. "When the business of the Society was finished, he
partook of a collation provided for the occasion, and mingled with
great affability in the festivity of the evening. An occasional song was
prepared and sung by a visiting friend, and addressed to the chief,
in terms so artless, and yet so affecting, as touched the hearts of the
members with sensations uncommonly pleasurable."[47]

Indian visits to American cities were not usually as carefully
stage-managed as that of the four "Indian kings" in London, but
nonetheless they entailed a fair amount of performance. Like the
"Indian kings," Native leaders in American cities had to become cultural chameleons, capable of straddling and negotiating the divide
that separated them from their audience.[48] Some, certainly at first,
would have felt uncomfortable; others, particularly those who stayed
a long time or made recurrent visits, grew accustomed to the experience and grew into the role. A few became specialists in the art. They
not only performed the public rituals associated with diplomacy but
also performed songs and dances in public spaces, exhibiting their
"authentic" culture for audiences of spectators.[49] In May 1777, still
reeling from devastating assaults on their towns by American troops
during the Revolution, Attakullakulla, Oconastota, and "upwards
of fourty gentlemen and ladies of the Cherokee Nation" were in
Williamsburg to negotiate peace, which meant giving up more land.
"After the talk was concluded they favored the public with a dance
on the green in front of the Palace, where a considerable number
of spectators, both male and female, were agreeably entertained."[50]

On a Monday evening in March 1792, during the visit of an Iroquois delegation to Philadelphia, "the Indian chiefs now in this city, entertained a number of the citizens with a sight of their festive dances." Their music, on these occasions," the press reported, "is chiefly vocal, accompanied with the beat of a small drum."[51]

Sometimes observers questioned the "authenticity" of ritual performance. John Quincy Adams, the future president, attended Washington's meeting with Piominko and the Chickasaw delegation in July 1794 "and assisted in smoking the pipe with them." He was skeptical that the ceremony was really of Indian origin since some of the Chickasaws "appeared to be quite unused to it, and from their manner of going through it, looked as if they were submitting to a process in compliance with *our* custom. Some of them, I thought, smiled with such an expression of countenance as denoted a sense of *novelty,* and of *frivolity* too; as if the ceremony struck them, not only as new, but also as ridiculous."[52] Chickasaws were accustomed to sending, receiving, and smoking calumet pipes as symbols of peace and reconciliation and performing the calumet ceremony at meetings with European powers, and a Chickasaw chief had brought a calumet into the council chamber in Williamsburg more than sixty years earlier (see page 48).[53] Unless amused by American missteps during the ceremony, Piominko and his fellow delegates evidently found other things that struck them as frivolous and ridiculous.

On occasion, some chiefs in the city no doubt played to their audience. In any group some individuals will curry favor with those they think may be able to do them good—the rich, the powerful, and the well-connected. Some probably performed tongue in cheek. Some may have thought the whole thing was a lark. But those who played Indian in the city usually did so for their own purposes. Demonstrating their authenticity as Indians established their cultural and political authority.[54] Like later Indigenous people who, as one scholar puts it, "performed for Imperial eyes," they then made their own points, conveyed their own messages, and advanced their own causes.[55]

At the same time, by their conduct and comportment chiefs in the city directly or implicitly challenged the European-versus-Native binary. Their eloquence, their demeanor, and their ability to handle themselves in civil society confounded colonial images of Indian people as violent, primitive, and savage, as counterimages of whites.[56] "The brave young Warrior Sconetoyah" seems to have done just that. Like Taboca and the Choctaw and Chickasaw delegates, Sconetoyah traveled to Philadelphia in June 1787, when the Constitutional

Convention was meeting. Henry Knox said he was sent "to represent the distressed situation of the Cherokees" to Congress, and the press identified him as "son to one of the principal chiefs of that nation." Accompanied by an interpreter, he created a good impression everywhere he went. During his stay in Baltimore, reported the *New York Morning Post,* "tho' an untutored son of Nature, he behaved with the propriety of a civilized Citizen, and deservedly gained the attention of many respectable Americans and Foreigners, who entertained him with the greatest hospitality." The young chief left expressing his gratitude "to the generous inhabitants and great Warriors of Baltimore." In Philadelphia, he was introduced to the former governor of North Carolina and a number of delegates to the convention. At the State House, "he had the honor of taking his Excellency General Washington by the hand." Since he arrived in Philadelphia, the press reported, "there has been every mark of friendship shewn to him, and he has frequently had the honor to dine with several members of Congress and Convention." Washington bid him a fond farewell, wishing him success with his business and safe travel home. Everyone, apparently, had a good opinion of Sconetoyah.[57]

Native visitors were not always or easily duped by their reception, seduced by good treatment, or intimidated by what they saw at the seat of power. They knew they were entering the belly of the beast and, as Pickering told Washington before the president met with one delegation, "have been so often deceived by White people, that *White Man* is among many of them, but another name for *Liar.* "[58] Individuals as artful as Teedyuscung, Canasetego, Attakullakulla, McGillivray, and Brant were under few illusions, and they surely understood how to perform their role as "chiefs in the city." They may sometimes have acted as their hosts expected and said things their hosts wanted to hear, but they knew what they were doing. Indians playing Indian played to their audiences, but sometimes they played their audiences for fools.

In London in 1710, the four "Indian kings" went to see several plays and operas, as well as a Punch and Judy show. When they famously attended an operatic performance of *Macbeth,* the audience was so intent on gawking at them that the play was interrupted until the Indians could be removed from their box seats and placed on chairs onstage where the audience could watch them as they watched the Scottish tragedy.[59] Visiting Indian delegates regularly attended the theater in American cities as well, where, as in London, their presence often attracted more attention than the plays themselves. Theater audiences clamored to watch Indians watch staged performances.[60] When Indians attended the theater they transformed the performance.

They were participating in an emerging American cultural form. Early in the eighteenth century, traveling players performed in converted barns; by the end of the century, acting companies performed in elegant theaters. Puritans in seventeenth-century New England and Quakers in eighteenth-century Philadelphia opposed plays as morally corrupting and theaters as places that attracted and encouraged vice. In 1759 the Synod of New York and Philadelphia vehemently opposed building a playhouse in Philadelphia as "a most powerful Engine of debauching the minds and corrupting the manners of youth, by encouraging Idleness, Extravagance and Immorality." In the face of Quaker opposition, the first small theater was built in Philadelphia in 1759 but lasted only one season. A second, larger theater was opened at Southwark in 1766, at the corner of South and Leithgow Streets; it was the city's main theater for the next twenty-eight years, although its location near the dockyards rendered it increasingly unfashionable.[61]

Some Cherokees got a taste of, and developed a taste for, the theater. Looking back in later life on his trip to London with the Cherokee delegation in 1730, Attakullakulla said they had gone "to see England for our own pleasure."[62] As unlikely as that seems, they did attend performances at Sadler's Wells and the Theatre Royal at Lincoln's Inn Fields.[63] The red-carpet treatment afforded to Amouskositte, "the Emperor of the Cherokee Nation," and his wife when they were in Williamsburg in November 1752 included an evening "at the Theatre, with the Play (The Tragedy of *Othello*) and a Pantomime Performance," which, according to the press, "gave them great Surprize, as did the fighting with naked Swords on the Stage, which occasioned the Empress to order some about her to go and prevent their killing one another."[64] In 1767, as a member of a ten-man Cherokee delegation on its way to negotiate a peace with the Six Nations at Johnson Hall, Attakullakulla went to the theater in New York. Attakullakulla, Oconastota, and the other delegates arrived from South Carolina by sea in December. After an audience with the commander-in-chief, General Thomas Gage, and his officers on Monday, December 14, "the CHIEFS having been informed, that there was a *Theatre* in this City, expressed a Desire of seeing a Play acted," and Gage gave orders "that proper Places shall be got for them in the House, this Evening." In the expectation of a crowd—or perhaps to boost attendance—the newspaper not only gave instructions on purchasing tickets but also provided street directions to help people arriving by carriage avoid collisions. Such a large crowd showed up that the theater was filled to overflowing and many people had to be turned away. The play was *Richard III* (which, when it was originally staged in New York in 1750, was the first recorded production of Shakespeare in America).[65] According to press reports, the Cherokees watched the play attentively but, not being "sufficiently acquainted with the Language to understand the Plot and Design, and enter into the Spirit of the Author, their Countenances and Behaviour were rather expressive of Surprize and Curiosity, than any other Passions." Some of them were "diverted at the Tricks of HARLEQUIN" in the pantomime that followed.[66] Eighteenth-century theater performances were often variety shows that lasted four or five hours, featuring a traditional play as the main event, with music, song, and dance throughout, and followed by a lighter humorous or musical piece, such as a ballad opera or pantomime. They might also include some kind of special performance, such as Indians doing Native dances or archery exhibitions.[67]

Eleven Mohawks arrived in New York at the same time as the Cherokees. The press reported that the Cherokees met three of the Mohawk chiefs by accident the day after their arrival and ceremonially smoked the calumet of peace with them. A sloop was provided to carry both the Cherokees and the Mohawks up the Hudson River. They traveled along the Mohawk River to Johnson Hall, where Sir William orchestrated a peace in March.[68] The Cherokee chiefs returned to New York on their way home. On Monday, April 4, again on General Gage's orders, *The Constant Couple*, featuring the noted actor Lewis Hallam the Younger, was staged "for the Entertainment of the Cherokee CHIEFS and WARRIORS." Later that week, on the Friday night before they sailed for home, two plays, *The Wonder* and *Harlequin Collector*, were performed "for the Entertainment of those same Cherokee Chiefs." But the Cherokees themselves performed as well. According to the advertisement for the show:

> The Cherokee Chiefs and Warriors, being desirous of making some Return for the friendly Reception and Civilities they have received in this City, have offered to entertain the Public with, the
>
> WAR DANCE
>
> Which they will exhibit on the stage, after the Pantomime. It is humbly presumed that no Part of the Audience will forget the proper Decorum so essential to all public Assemblies, particularly on this Occasion, as the Persons who have condescended to contribute to their Entertainment are of Rank and Consequence in their own Country.

By all accounts, the Cherokees stole the show.[69]

In the Revolutionary era, American patriots denounced theatrical performances as British extravagance and corruption, although Washington himself was fond of plays. Concerned citizens
in Philadelphia in November 1783 protested against plans to open a
theater in the suburbs, fearing that stage plays and other forms of theatrical entertainment would have a bad influence on young people
and encourage drunkenness and debauchery. Nevertheless, despite
economic downturns, outbreaks of yellow fever, and political opposition, the American theater grew after the Revolution as an expression
of national identity and democracy. In 1789, the Pennsylvania legislature passed a bill allowing theatrical performances in Philadelphia.
Instead of being an illicit enterprise restricted to the outskirts of the
city, the theater was now an approved form of urban entertainment,
a forum for communicating individual and republican virtues to its
audiences, and a site for reinforcing elite distinction and refinement
rather than promoting social disorder and vice.[70] Theaters also became increasingly politicized spaces where women took more active
and public roles as playwrights, actresses, and audience members.[71]

An Italian visitor to New York after the Revolution reported
that the theater was open two or three months of the year, featuring
English tragedies and comedies performed by a mediocre troupe of
actors who made a living by going from city to city.[72] Visiting Indians
offered an opportunity to boost performances and ticket sales. In
March 1786, the theater changed its show "by particular desire" "to
the Pantomime of Robinson Crusoe, for the entertainment of the
Indian Chiefs of the Oneida Nation, now in this city." The show included "a DANCE of SAVAGES; to conclude with a VAUDEVILLE
and CHORUS." Following *The Poor Soldier,* a comic opera by John
O'Keefe about Irish soldiers returning home from serving in the
British army during the Revolutionary War, the Oneida chiefs
performed a war dance for the entertainment of the audience. Since
one correspondent described *The Poor Soldier* as "a production almost devoid of *sentiment* and *novelty,*" the audience was probably glad
to see the Oneidas.[73]

An Oneida was onstage again in New York five years later. At
the first of "four new operas and dances" scheduled to begin the last
day of February 1791, "Peter the Indian, lately arrived from his own
country," read the advance program, was to dance "in the Indian
Dress." Peter may have been Peter Otsiquette, because "his performance will be intermixed with curious and striking steps, according
to the taste of the French stage dancers." He was also to "dance the

Indian War Dance in complete armour." Even on an evening when the opera had to be cancelled, "Peter the Indian still danced."[74]

Newspapers in the summer of 1790 regularly informed their readers when Alexander McGillivray and the Creek chiefs would be attending the theater.[75] In Philadelphia on July 19, Stephen Wools, the theatrical company proprietor, chose for McGillivray's benefit *Tamerlane*, "one of the best tragedies," written by the English playwright and poet laureate Nicholas Rowe. The press hoped the performance would garner Wools "ample compensation for the failure of his former night." At any rate, it was an opportunity for people to see McGillivray: "Those who have not yet seen this extraordinary character may have their curiosity gratified without tumult or difficulty."[76]

Whether or not the Creeks enjoyed the shows, thespians thought they had a new audience. According to a correspondent from Charleston, the Harmony Hall theater's little company of comedians left the city in August and set up their scenery in Augusta, Georgia, "from whence, as soon as they hear of the return of M'Gillivray and his Indian kings, it is said, they are to proceed to the Talassee towns, to act for the entertainment of the Creeks, and other nations of the interior parts, who, by such means, it is thought will much sooner become civilized than by any others hitherto adopted."[77]

On the evening of January 4, 1792, while Bloody Fellow's Cherokee delegation was in Philadelphia, "by the request of the Indian chiefs" theater-goers were entertained by "a Company of French Dancers, On the Tight Rope," followed by "The Tragedy of Douglas," singer and actress Mrs. Kenna performing the "Death Song of a Cherokee Indian Chief," and a pantomime entitled "A French Shoemaker.[78] It sounds like Bloody Fellow and his companions got more than they bargained for. While "that celebrated Indian chief and warrior," as the *Salem Gazette* described Joseph Brant, was in Philadelphia later in the year, he attended the theater in Southwark on the evening of June 25, where "his dress and dignified comportment formed the most lively contrast to the air and blandishments of the Stage."[79]

The yellow fever epidemic of 1793 and opposition from the clergy delayed plans for a new theater in Philadelphia, but one opened on the corner of Chestnut and Fourth Streets in February 1794, called the New Hall or New Theatre to distinguish it from the old one in Southwark. Cherokees who came to Philadelphia at the invitation of President Washington attended a performance there.[80] "The INDIAN CHIEFS, now in this city, will attend the Theatre this evening," the press announced on June 20.[81] The Chickasaw and

Choctaw chiefs who were in Philadelphia in July 1795 also attended the new theater.[82]

Moreau de Saint-Méry described what they would have seen when they entered. The theater's brick exterior was rather shabby and had nothing to distinguish it from an ordinary house, but inside were three tiers of fifteen boxes each, "pleasingly arranged in a semi-ellipse," with each tier holding 255 people, for a total, he miscalculated, of 755 (Figure 7.3). The boxes were "papered with red paper in extremely bad taste" and separated in the front by small columns that obstructed the view. The upper tier of boxes had elegant gilded balustrades. The seats in the pits, between the bottom row of the tiers and the orchestra, consisted of thirteen rows of benches, each holding thirty people, almost 400 in total. The orchestra held thirty musicians. The hall was painted gray with gilded scrolls and carvings, and lighted by small four-branched candelabras; the front stage was huge, lighted by oil lamps, "as in France."[83] The theater reflected class divisions and the decline of deferential politics. Audience members from the mechanic and laboring classes, who occupied the galleries, found the kind of productions staged for Federalist elites "stuffy," and were increasingly disruptive.[84]

People increasingly turned to the circus for entertainment. Saint-Méry said Philadelphia had two circuses, "where coryphees from England often exercise their talents and amuse people with

Inside View of the New Theatre, Philadelphia.

Figure 7.3 Interior view of the New Theater, Philadelphia 1794. Courtesy of the Free Library of Philadelphia, Print and Picture Collection.

equestrian exercises."[85] He was referring to Ricketts's Circus. British equestrian performer John Bill Ricketts established the first modern circus in America. After starting his theatrical career in London's Royal Circus, Ricketts came to America in 1792. He erected a wooden building—a roofless arena with 800 seats surrounding the ring—in Philadelphia at the corner of Market and Twelfth Streets and held a riding school there, where he trained horses. On April 3, 1793, he staged America's first full circus performance.[86]

Ricketts's circus was evidently an early version of Buffalo Bill's Wild West show, and he took it on the road, playing in South Carolina, Virginia, Baltimore, New England, and Canada. In New York, in 1795, Ricketts held his show in a new arena on Broadway.[87] *The New York Daily Advertiser* in March carried advertisements of what audiences could expect: "Mr. Rickets respectfully informs the Ladies and Gentlemen of New York, that on Saturday next, he will exhibit a greater variety of Equestrian Exercises, than heretofore exhibited in this city, amongst which the Indian Chiefs, lately arrived, will with Mr. Rickets, perform on horseback, drest in the character of warriors, and go through a variety of Evolutions," followed by "surprising feats of horsemanship" and Ricketts riding "a single horse in the character of an Indian Chief." Doors opened at 5:30 p.m. for the 6:30 performance.[88]

A week later, "ever anxious to gratify the Citizens of New-York," Ricketts informed them that for the Indians' final performance on Saturday evening, before they left the city on Sunday morning, he had "at considerable trouble taught the INDIAN CHIEFS to ride on TWO HORSES in full speed" and would "ride on the INDIAN CHIEF'S SHOULDERS, a sight never before seen here." It became a standard feature of his performances. He and the chiefs were also to perform two dances, which, Ricketts assured ladies who might be considering coming to the show, would be "conducted with the greatest order and decency." To cap off the evening, Ricketts would "leap from two Horses over a Gutter 12 feet high." It was, announced the paper, a feat "never performed here in America," although it was scheduled to be repeated the following Tuesday.[89]

Ricketts closed his amphitheater in New York between fall 1795 and spring 1796 because of yellow fever, but in February he held exhibitions in the Assembly Room on Cortlandt Street that featured a trained dog performing card and other tricks, followed by "an Indian dance by four Indians now in the city."[90]

Philadelphia was the circus's home base, and Ricketts erected a brand-new building at the corner of Sixth and Chestnut Streets, opposite the new theater. Ricketts's Art Pantheon and Amphitheatre was circular, ninety-seven feet in diameter, and had a conical roof that reached fifty feet in height (Figure 7.4). It was equipped with a ring for equestrian displays and a stage, actor John Durand recalled, for "burlettes [short comic operas], farces, operas, pantomimes, and ballet dancing." The circus held an audience of 1,300 people and directly challenged the theater with lowbrow entertainment for the public. Ricketts held performances three times a week.[91]

On December 30, 1795, the *Gazette of the United States* reported that the Indian delegates from the Western Territory who had traveled 1,500 miles to see the president were to visit Ricketts's Amphitheatre the next day, New Year's Eve. Ricketts, as usual, was to "ride in the character of an Indian Chief."[92] For the show on the evening of January 2, the Chestnut Street Amphitheatre promised "a greater Variety of Equestrian Exercises" than had ever been performed in the city. Among other things, "the INDIAN CHIEFS, lately arrived here, will perform on Horseback, in the character of WARRIORS. After which one will ride Two Horses in full Speed, with

Figure 7.4 Ricketts's Circus at the corner of Market and 12th streets in Philadelphia in 1797. Watercolor by David J. Kennedy, after an original painting by F.J. Dreer, Esq. (1870). The Court House is on the left, and Oeller's Hotel, where many Indian delegates to the city stayed, is on the right. Courtesy of The Historical Society of Pennsylvania, David J. Kennedy Watercolors Collection.

Mr. Ricketts on his shoulders."[93] Ricketts named one of his horses, "an elegant charger," Cornplanter (Figure 7.5).[94]

At the show on March 10, 1796, the Native performers were "Indian chiefs from Canada." Ricketts promised they would perform a war dance followed by "a friendly dance" and that he would accompany them dressed as a warrior in both. Between the parts of the performance, he would "ride on the Shoulders of the Head-Chief TEHORACWANEGEN of the Seven Nations who . . . received universal applause at New-York last winter." The evening's performances

Figure 7.5 Print representing John Bill Ricketts and his horse Cornplanter "taking a flying leap over the shoulder of Silva, a horse of his own height." (c.1795). Harvard Theater Collection, Houghton Library.

also included, back by popular demand, Ricketts's new pantomime, "The Triumph of Virtue, or Harlequin in Philadelphia," and "other novel Entertainments" too numerous to list.[95] On the evening of Tuesday, December 10, 1796, "By DESIRE of the INDIAN CHIEFS," the amphitheater staged a three-hour entertainment that included tightrope dancing, a ballet, horsemanship, pony races, and a comic pantomime. They repeated the same performance on the following Thursday and Saturday.[96] Ricketts opened another circus in New York in 1797, on Greenwich Street.

Tehoracwanegen or Tehoragwanegen was a Kahnawake Mohawk also known as Thomas Williams. He was the grandson of the famous Eunice Williams, who had been captured in the raid on Deerfield, Massachusetts, in 1704 and adopted by the Mohawks, and who lived the rest of her life at Kahnawake. During the Revolution, Tehoragwanegen fought in British-Indian raids. After the Revolution, beginning in 1789, representatives of the Seven Nations of Canada spent seven years negotiating a land claim, during which time they made multiple trips to New York, Philadelphia, and Albany. The deputies were Tehoragwanegen and Ohnaweio, alias Good Stream, from Kahnawake, and Atiatoharonwan, alias Louis Cook, and a chief named William Gray from Akwesasne. The affair was finally settled by a treaty in New York in June 1796—and Tehoragwanegen wound up with Ricketts riding on his shoulders. (Tehoragwanegen had thirteen children; one of them, Eleazar, became an Episcopal minister, wrote a biography of his father, and later in life claimed to be the rightful king of France.)[97]

In addition to using visiting talent, Ricketts actively recruited performers from Kahnawake and other communities. John Durang accompanied Ricketts and a small company on a tour to Canada in 1797–98, performing in both Montreal and Quebec. When they visited Kahnawake, "Mr. Ricketts was in an Indian's dress which he sometimes rode in." Later, in May 1798, Durang visited the Huron village of Lorette (now Wendake) near Quebec "to get an Indian for Mr. Ricketts to stand on his shoulders between two horses." He engaged one, and six more turned up.[98] While in Montreal, Durang gave a performance indicative of what audiences in Philadelphia might have seen. He "got up" what he called "an Indian characteristic dance." Dressed in clothes he had bought from an Indian and based on "dances I learned from some Chipeway and Naudeowessie [Ojibwe and Sioux] chiefs of the West," the American actor performed the Pipe Dance, the Eagle Tail Dance, and finally the War Dance, "throwing myself in different postures with firm steps

Figure 7.6 Anne Merry (née Brunton) by Francesco Bartolozzi, published by John Bell, after Richard Cosway stipple engraving, published 22 October 1785, NPG D15292 © National Portrait Gallery, London.

Figure 7.7 Little Turtle lithograph reputedly based upon a portrait by Gilbert Stuart that was destroyed when the British burned Washington, DC, in 1814. Little Turtle, 1747?–1812, 1790s Ohio History Connection.

with hatchet and knife, representing the manner they kill and scalp and take prisoners with the yells and war whoops." A British officer who was present told him "that I excel'd as their native dances were more simple."[99]

When Little Turtle and William Wells were in Philadelphia in 1798, they visited both the theater and the circus. They stayed at the Cross Keys Tavern at Fourth and Chestnut Streets. One evening they walked two blocks to see a performance of *Romeo and Juliet* at the New Theatre. The Miami war chief credited with the destruction of St. Clair's army watched the popular English actress Anne Brunton Merry play Juliet (Figures 7.6 and 7.7). On January 10, 1798, the theater announced that "this evening, by particular desire, and for the entertainment of Little Turtle, the Indian chief," it would stage "COLUMBUS; or a WORLD DISCOVERED."[100] Before they left the city, on February 22 Little Turtle and Wells were guests along with the Philadelphia elite at the Washington Ball held in Ricketts's Circus. Watching from a box in the balcony and wearing an American officer's uniform "with enormous epaulets," Little Turtle appeared to other audience members to be "very content with the entertainment."[101]

Ricketts was still performing on December 14, 1799, when an advertisement announced that in the evening he would once again ride on the shoulders of an "Indian riding on two Horses at full speed." This time the Indian was a member of a Cherokee delegation, Ricketts "having taken the trouble to teach him since the arrival of the party in this City, all of whom will attend the performance and give the war-whoop."[102] It was one of the final performances: the circus burned down that month in a fire that also destroyed Oeller's Hotel.

Plains Indian performers in the Wild West shows of the late nineteenth and early twentieth centuries created an image of Indians as natural and skilled horsemen.[103] More than a century of movies and television perpetuated the image until it came to represent all Indian people in all periods and places. But eighteenth-century theater audiences did not have that stereotype. Indian people in the eastern woodlands, and most of those who visited eastern cities, were accustomed to travel by foot and canoe as much as on horseback. It is difficult to know what theater-goers expected when they attended such equestrian entertainments, or what Indian guests—and guest-performers—made of it. *Claypoole's American Daily Advertiser* reported on January 19, 1796, that the Indian delegates had not yet left the city as they planned to attend Ricketts' circus that evening." The paper thought "it must be highly entertaining to strangers, to see those aborigines express their surprise at the different performances exhibited at that place of entertainment."[104]

However, anyone who went to the circus expecting to see Indians react with awe and amazement was likely disappointed. Isaac Weld said that among the public exhibitions they saw in Philadelphia the Indians liked the performances of "horse riders and tumblers at the amphitheatre" and had the highest opinion of those people distinguished for their feats of activity. Even so, the performances "never drew forth from them, I observed, more than a smile, or a gentle laugh, followed by a remark in a low voice to their friend sitting next to them." Weld added that "at such a place as Philadelphia, notwithstanding their appearing so indifferent to every thing before them whilst strangers are present, yet, after having retired by themselves to an apartment for the night, they will frequently sit up for hours together. Laughing and talking of what they have seen in the course of the day."[105]

Like the Indian performers in the later Wild West shows, it is easy to see the chiefs in the city who staged dances in theaters and performed in equestrian feats in Ricketts's circus as commercially and shamefully exploited, simultaneously marginalized and exhibited in an alien environment. Like them, however, Indians onstage in the eighteenth century had multiple motives and experiences and made their own choices.[106] They presumably received some form of remuneration, and some may have enjoyed playing, and playing up, their part as Indians at the audience's expense. Chiefs in the city performed various roles in various spheres, and surely attached their own meanings to them. They recognized their audiences' assumptions and expectations, and in private they no doubt scoffed at their ignorance, gullibility, and pretensions. Yet when they acted out performances of "Indianness" before audiences, as when they combined Native dress with European clothing or smoked calumet pipes in government buildings, they also affirmed, and perhaps even flaunted, their Indigenous identity and tribal sovereignty in the centers of colonial power.

CHAPTER 8

Going Home

"BROTHERS," BENJAMIN FRANKLIN ADDRESSED CHOCTAW and Chickasaw chiefs as they departed Philadelphia in June, 1787, "You have a long Journey to take before you can see your beloved Country and your own Home. I pray the Great Spirit to preserve you & conduct you safely." To help them on their way, he wrote a note requiring all citizens of Pennsylvania who might encounter them on their travels "to treat them with justice, and protect them from Injuries, they being come from far distant & friendly Nations on public Business." The chiefs traveled by coach from Philadelphia to Fort Pitt at the expense of Congress, then they and their goods were shipped downriver to Chickasaw Bluffs on the Mississippi.[1] Even with such government assistance, however, homeward journeys were often no easier than outward journeys and could be just as dangerous. And once they were home, delegates sometimes viewed their visits very differently after memories of good words and generous gifts receded and the realities of the colonial relationship in their communities remained unchanged or worsened.

After sailing from Charleston on board the brig *Philadelphia,* Bloody Fellow, Nontuaka, and three other Cherokee leaders disembarked in Philadelphia on December 29, 1791.[2] During their stay in the city, in addition to attending the theater, they met with President Washington and requested increased compensation for lands they had ceded in a treaty with Governor William Blount the previous summer. "We came to Philadelphia with our eyes full of tears," Bloody Fellow told Henry Knox as they prepared to return home in February. "But since we have seen General Washington, and heard him speak through you, our tears are wiped away, and we rejoice in the prospect of our future welfare, under the protection of Congress." The Cherokees "were conveyed in a large stage coach drawn by four elegant horses," with several wagons hauling their baggage, provisions, and gifts from Congress to their nation.[3] They were generally well treated on their return travels, Knox informed Washington, "but sometimes alarmed by the folly and wickedness of the frontier people." Safely back in Cherokee country, Nontuaka reported on his trip at the National Council in June 1792 and urged his people to listen to the talks he and his fellow travelers had brought back. Having "been to Philadelphia to see the great beloved white man," Nontuaka declared, "my heart was made easy."[4] Unfortunately, the good feelings did not last long. After waiting six months for the redress the Cherokees had been promised, Bloody Fellow concluded, "Congress are Liars general Washington is a Liar & governour Blount is a Liar."[5]

Six years later Louis Philippe encountered Chickasaw chief George Colbert on his way home from Philadelphia, where he had sought in vain for help after suffering losses at the hands of the Creeks. Louis Philippe described Colbert as "a good fellow and very obliging," but Colbert told the future king of France that he was incensed at his treatment in Philadelphia, and had "told the officers discussing the problem that the United States consisted of *damned rascals.*" When they asked him if the Chickasaws had laws, he replied, "No . . . you don't need them except for villains and only villains like the Creeks and whites have them." Colbert headed home with few illusions about what the future held for the Chickasaws. "His glimpse of the whites' power had alarmed him, and his knowledge of the language, allowing him to overhear what was being said about the Indians, had only increased that fear," the French traveler wrote. "Certainly no effort is made to hide plans to strip the Indians of everything, and their eagerness to get on with it leads the whites often to paint the Indians in false colors."[6]

Returning delegates rarely received the warm welcomes at home that they sometimes experienced when they entered a city. And increasingly, as they traveled to and from a single national capital and dealt with a single-minded colonial power, they faced criticism, either from their own people or from other Indian nations, for what they did there, how they behaved when they returned, and what they became in later years.

Homeward journeys rarely passed without incidents and delays that incurred additional expense. A party of Iroquois returning from negotiations with the governor in Philadelphia in 1727 camped for four days and nights near the house of one Richard Thomas in Whiteland Township. His neighbors shared what they could with the Iroquois but were few and poor and could not supply all their needs, and the Indians killed one of Thomas's cows. Since the Indians had a letter of credit from the governor "to all persons to supply them with what they wanted," Thomas sought reimbursement for the loss of his cow, which he valued at £4.[7] Five Ojibwe, Odawa, and Potawatomi delegates returning from Philadelphia were delayed at Pittsburgh for a week in January 1799 because the river was impassable. They stayed with a Mrs. Mary Murphy, who provided them with board and lodging, oats and hay for their horses, brandy and spirits, breakfasts, dinners, and suppers, at a cost of $72.82. Their interpreter certified her bill, and Mrs. Murphy signed it by making her mark.[8]

Sometimes there were clashes with settlers, and delegates might be waylaid or even murdered on their way home. Governor Hamilton complained to Six Nations chiefs in 1749 about "mischiefs done by your People to Farmers & their Cattle in their Journeys to & from this City."[9] A letter from Charleston in January 1752, published in the press, claimed that eighty or ninety Cherokees who had recently left after making a treaty "attempted to ravish several Women, and were otherwise very insolent to the Inhabitants in our Back Settlements, on their Return Home, tho' they had made a strict League with us." According to the correspondent, they were ambushed by a Creek war party, who killed thirty-two of them.[10] In 1759, during the Anglo-Cherokee War, Governor Lyttelton provided a military escort to accompany Oconastota and other Cherokees on their journey home from Charleston but warned them their lives would be in danger if they deviated from the high road.[11] Charleston newspapers in June 1786 carried reports that the Choctaw delegates who had left the city "with the greatest satisfaction" after their talks with the governor and the presents they received "were attacked on their way home, and some of them killed."[12] There were reports of "premeditated mischief" planned against Cornplanter as the Seneca returned from Philadelphia in the fall of 1792.[13] And Joseph Brant, stopping for several days in New York City on his way home from Philadelphia the same year, apparently survived an aborted assassination attempt at his hotel on Broadway.[14]

Indian delegations from the South could return home by land or by sea. It was not an easy choice. Attakullakulla and the

Cherokee chiefs had sailed to New York on their mission to make peace with the Iroquois in 1768; the *New York Gazette* noted that they preferred "to return home by land than expose themselves again to the danger of the seas." Nevertheless, they embarked on the sloop *Sally* on Monday, April 11.[15] Having made their way to New York by land in 1790, Alexander McGillivray and his companions returned south by sea and then traveled overland to Creek country. The twenty Cherokees who visited Philadelphia in 1794 likewise set sail for home on Sunday morning, June 29. After eight days at sea, they disembarked at Charleston and headed home by land.[16] Concerned for their safety on the homeward leg of their journey, secretary of war Henry Knox called on General Andrew Pickens in Hopewell to help "prevent any catastrophe." Hearing that an attack was being planned, Pickens dispatched a company of militia to escort the delegates and their wagon of goods to the border of the Cherokee nation.[17]

The Shawnee leader Painted Pole or Red Pole had his baggage stolen as the delegation he and Blue Jacket had led to Philadelphia in the fall of 1796 was returning home. When the party reached Pittsburgh, Red Pole complained of a pain in his chest and head, which developed into pneumonia. Despite the best efforts of three American doctors, Red Pole died, to the profound grief of his companions. He was buried in the Trinity Church graveyard. A stone erected to his memory bore the inscription "Musquacanokan, or Red Pole, principal village chief of the Shawanoe Nation, Died at Pittsburgh the 28th January 1797, lamented by the United States." Blue Jacket and the other members of the delegation appreciated the treatment Red Pole received during his illness and were said to be "highly pleased at the attention & Respect paid to his funeral."[18]

Delegates often came home from the city loaded with gifts. Penobscots returning from Boston in 1736 took home £200 worth of gifts, including feathered hats to distinguish the chiefs who had accepted commissions from the governor. The governor intended these emblems of power to convey the Indians' subject status; the Indians wore them to reinforce their sovereignty in dealing with the English colonists who now lived on their land.[19] After mending fences with the British and selling land in the Susquehanna Valley, the 150 Iroquois people who attended the Albany Congress in 1754 went home with thirty wagonloads of presents, including 400 guns—a ratio, one historian points out, of two and a half guns for every man, woman, and child in the traveling party. "They had come to town to mend the broken Covenant Chain; they left looking like an NRA road show."[20] A few days after dining with Washington on

April 22, 1792, the Iroquois chiefs who had spent a month in the capital left for home laden with gifts from the government.[21] Bloody Fellow's Cherokee delegation that spring returned "loaded with Presents."[22] A large group of Chickasaws gathered in November 1794 to await Piominko's return with the goods he was bringing from Philadelphia.[23]

Bringing home and distributing large quantities of goods and gifts enhanced a chief's prestige but might also generate resentment, toward both those bearing the gifts and those who furnished them, especially if the gifts were obtained in exchange for ceding land. Creek chiefs who accompanied a multitribal delegation to Philadelphia in 1794 returned home with gifts, but secretary of war James McHenry allocated an additional $500 in gifts for others who had *not* made the trip, fearing that they might think that those who visited the seat of government got preferential treatment "and be inclined from that circumstance to follow the same course oftener than would be proper or convenient, or get discontented on the sight of presents, which they have not shared in."[24]

Occasionally delegates left the city with new people as well. A few fell in love on their travels. A story picked up by many newspapers reported that when Bloody Fellow's delegation departed Philadelphia for home, they were accompanied by a white girl "who had smitten the heart of one of the chiefs, during his residence in this city; and, it is said, has consented to become his wife." The girl in question, however, was probably Jane Dougherty, the daughter of a white trader in the Cherokee country, who had accompanied the delegation to Philadelphia and seems to have been already married to one of the group.[25] A matrimony notice announcing the marriage of "Sick quo in ne yonho, alias, John Walker, one of the chiefs of the Cherokee nation of Indians, to Miss Ann Jane Durant of this city" appeared in the Philadelphia press on January 7, 1797, and was picked up by newspapers from Georgia to Vermont.[26] Although we know little about them, romantic encounters clearly occurred when Indians were in town; in the nineteenth century at least two Indian delegates married white women while they were in Washington, and some Lakota performers in Buffalo Bill's Wild West shows returned home with wives after their European tours.[27]

After weeks and sometimes months in the city, followed by a difficult return journey, many delegates no doubt looked forward to getting home. But coming home sometimes initiated a new phase of adjustment. George Catlin's famous painting of Ah-jon-jon, an Assiniboine also known as the Light, who returned to the Upper Missouri from Washington, DC, in 1832, was meant as a cautionary moral tale of "an Indian Betrayed by Civilization." In the dual "before-and-after" portraits Catlin painted and the story he told, Ah-jon-jon came home cutting a comic figure in foppish dress, assuming airs, and holding forth about his experiences, only to be killed by one of his own people who dismissed him as a braggart and a liar. Having been immersed in a world he could not handle, it seemed, the naive and suddenly gentrified Indian had been corrupted morally, culturally, and politically, and met a tragic end back home.[28] Few homecomings from colonial cities were as tragic as that of Catlin's Ah-jon-jon. Still, reentry could be a difficult experience.

Long before Europeans appeared on the scene, Native leaders established and maintained relationships with other Indigenous peoples who lived far away and possessed exotic goods and powers. A leader's standing in his own community rested on his ability to deal with people who spoke different languages and practiced strange customs, to forge far-flung alliances, and to establish exchange routes that brought new goods into the community. Chiefs wore, displayed, and distributed "prestige goods"—perhaps copper, feathers, or marine shells—that demonstrated their success in cultivating connections with distant sources of power.[29]

Indian people who journeyed to places such as Philadelphia or Charleston, then, followed in a long tradition. They may not have accumulated the same exotic experiences and esoteric knowledge as transatlantic voyagers to foreign lands, but they frequently covered hundreds of miles and sometimes were away for months on end. Like their precontact forebears, delegates to American cities acquired knowledge of foreign peoples whose customs were strange if not barbaric, and they came home with enhanced diplomatic, spiritual, and economic influence that increased their status. They were recognized as having undergone a special experience and accorded respect for having blazed new trails. Their new connections, and what anthropologist Mary Helms called "the authority of distant knowledge," allowed them to position themselves as mediators between their communities and colonial capitals, between the familiar homeland and the wider outside world.[30] Bringing home tangible evidence of access to colonial wealth and power boosted one's standing in societies where leadership meant providing for followers. Leaders who had been to the city displayed peace medals, clothing, and other items as symbols of the experience, their authority, and their ability to represent their people in dealings with colonial governments or the United States.[31]

Travel to distant capitals, however, could be a two-edged sword. Returning travelers brought news and stories, goods and connections, but, like Ah-jon-jon, they also sometimes generated envy and distrust among those who had stayed home.[32] One of the Indians who had visited Paris in 1725 told Jean-Bernard Bossu that when he returned with stories of the opera, puppet shows, Versailles, and the Louvre, people accused him of telling tales. When he told them that there were more people in Paris than leaves on the trees of the forests, they responded that "since such a thing was impossible, the Europeans must have bewitched his eyes" and shown him the same people over and over again.[33] Although the story may have been exaggerated, Ostenaco reputedly said that he wanted to go to London because he believed his rival Attakullakulla owed all his influence to having visited King George, and Ostenaco wanted to see for himself if Attakullakulla "had not told them lies."[34] At the least, bragging about experiences and embellishing stories tested people's credulity and patience.

Indeed, delegates placed themselves in precarious and sometimes perilous positions when they returned to their community. Their receptions depended upon the purposes of their visit, their conduct in the city, and their behavior back at home. Those who made the journey for the well-being of their people would have enhanced their reputation. "I am come from afar, for the good of my women and children, for their present and future good," a Potawatomi chief named Como told Washington after making the long trek to Philadelphia with the Wabash and Illinois delegates in 1792.[35] Individuals who turned the journey into an opportunity for personal advancement fared less well. Those who used their visits for their own political purposes after they got home sometimes found that rivals challenged their claims or sought to emulate their experiences.

Some city-going chiefs may even have paid with their lives. Canasatego negotiated his last treaty in Philadelphia in 1749. Within a year he was dead, assassinated by poison. Whether he was killed for taking bribes in exchange for selling land or, as seems more likely, at the hands of a pro-French faction at Onondaga, his long association with the colonial government in Philadelphia proved costly.[36] Teedyuscung, another regular visitor to Philadelphia, fell afoul of intercolonial rivalry, as the Susquehanna Company settled colonists from Connecticut on lands claimed by Pennsylvania in the Wyoming

Valley. In April 1763 someone—likely agents of the Susquehanna Company—set fire to the Indian town of Wyoming, and Teedyuscung burned to death while asleep in his cabin.[37]

The visit to the capital of the new nation in 1790 was a significant event for the Creeks who made the journey. When they returned home and told what they had seen and done, one town commemorated the treaty by taking a new name: Nuyakv, pronounced "nu-yaw-kah," which is what the delegates heard when the residents of the city said "New Yorker."[38] The visit was perhaps not as momentous for Creek people as Americans thought it was, however; Creeks had been to London and Havana in the past.

The Treaty of New York may have been a personal coup for McGillivray, but it cost him dearly in Creek country. Rival chiefs said McGillivray did not show the treaty to the people when he returned home and that the nation did not hear of his cession of the Oconee lands until several years later. The mainly Upper Creek delegation who went to New York ceded mainly Lower Creek lands, and McGillivray made private deals, accepted bribes, and agreed to secret articles in the treaty. He had good reason to keep things quiet.[39] Although McGillivray presented himself as a national leader in his dealings with Spain, Britain, and the United States, many Creeks objected to his increasing authority and affiliation with colonial powers.[40] Louis Le Clerc de Milford, a Frenchman turned self-described Creek chief, said the other leaders were "greatly displeased" with the treaty and refused to ratify it.[41] McGillivray proudly showed visitors to his Little Talassee plantation the gifts Washington had given him—a set of gilt-bound books and a gold epaulette.[42] Despite this, when Spain made him a better offer— an annual stipend of $2,000—McGillivray signed a treaty at New Orleans with the Baron de Carondelet and renounced the Treaty of New York, giving up his American salary of $1,200 and returning to his Spanish alliance. He told Carondelet he never intended to be on good terms with the Americans, "a people I know to be the Natural & determined enemy of all the Indian Nations."[43]

After McGillivray died in 1793, Secretary Knox asked the U.S. agent among the Creeks to make arrangements to bring "about a dozen of the real chiefs" to Philadelphia to meet the president and Congress.[44] Superintendent of Indian affairs Benjamin Hawkins sought out those chiefs who had "been on a visit to New York, and seen much of the ways of the white people," as good prospects for promoting the government's "civilization program."[45] Visiting the American capital did not immediately ensure such an outcome, however. Both Bird Tail King (Tuskatchee Mico or Miccothlucco) and Hopothle or Hoboithle Mico (also known as the Talassee King) (see Plates 4 and 7) made the journey with McGillivray and shook hands with Washington in a pledge of perpetual friendship. Ten years later, Bird Tail King had a well-cultivated and fenced plantation, with hogs, cattle, horses, peach and apple trees, and grapevines, but, Hawkins complained, it took him a long time to "break through the old habits of the Indians."[46] McGillivray had denounced Hopothle Mico as an American pawn, easily bought, but Hopothle Mico denounced the Treaty of New York as a corrupt bargain, condemned recurrent land cessions, and opposed the United States government's "civilization program." An old man when the Creek War broke out in 1813, he died fighting the Georgians.[47]

As the United States government invited tribal leaders to Philadelphia to make alliances, undermine Native opposition, and promote American policies of "civilization," delegates who had been to the capital came under increasing suspicion in Indian country. Joseph Brant met with Knox several times when he went to Philadelphia in 1792, and he also met with Washington, a fellow Mason.[48] As it had with McGillivray, the government offered Brant bribes: a secret pension of $1,500, land for himself, and a reservation on the American side of the border for the Mohawks. Brant left Philadelphia in July, "apparently in the best dispositions," said Thomas Jefferson. Knox, Washington, and the press hoped he would be instrumental in bringing about a settlement with the Northwest confederacy. Brant was nonetheless not dazzled or deceived by the attention he received. He said he refused "several allurements of gain" the government offered him.[49] He assured the western tribes that he had not been bought by American dollars or fooled by Washington's smooth talk, and he warned them to stand united against the United States. The western Indians still suspected Brant had betrayed their interests and was serving the United States after his visit to Philadelphia. Hendrick Aupaumut claimed that Brant "felt guilty for going alone to Congress, contrary to what he recommended to those nations, that no individual nation or person should go to speak to the Big Knives."[50] Many of Brant's own people also looked askance at the lifestyle he adopted.

For his part, Brant called Aupaumut a "Yanky Indian."[51] Aupaumut was a Philadelphia regular and traveled west four times in the early 1790s in an effort to broker peace between the United States and the Indian confederacy. Timothy Pickering said Aupaumut "always manifested a steady attachment to the United States, and sustained a reputation entitling him to public confidence," but Aupaumut undertook the missions to reassert Mohican influence rather than simply to advance American interests. Although he trusted Washington, he had few illusions about white people who had cheated his ancestors out of their lands and who lied, stole, and killed Indians. He felt the western tribes were more likely to listen to a message delivered by "an Indian to whom they look upon as a true friend, who has never deceived or injured them."[52] Nevertheless, the taint of Philadelphia clung to Aupaumut.

Cornplanter built a good reputation among American officials and Quakers in Philadelphia. As early as his visit to Philadelphia in December 1790, Knox identified Cornplanter as "the fittest person to make use of to manage the six nations" and recommended that the government pay him a pension. By the time he left in the spring, Cornplanter could "be depended upon through all the changes of policy," Knox told Pickering. "He is our friend from the solid ties of interest, and we must rivet it by all ways and means in our power." There were allegations of bribery.[53] Many Senecas suspected that Cornplanter used his travels for his own ends and parlayed his connections with the federal government, the state of Pennsylvania, and the Quakers into private property and personal advancement, even as he agreed to the cession of Seneca lands.[54] In the spring of 1793, Senecas at Buffalo Creek took offense when he planned to return to Philadelphia without consulting them. "All persons who know the manner of proceeding among Indians will know that no person can act for the tribe in affairs of Importance unless specially authorized by a Solemn Council," Knox explained.[55]

When Cornplanter, Farmer's Brother, and Red Jacket carried an American peace offer to the Northwest confederacy in 1793, the Shawnees accused them of doing Washington's dirty work and trying to split the confederacy. The Seneca emissaries tried to argue that Washington was genuinely interested in peace. Red Pole and the Shawnees did not buy it and accused them of "always running to the Americans and telling them every thing."[56] In 1797, Cornplanter and Red Jacket signed the Treaty of Big Tree, ceding millions of acres of Seneca land. Red Jacket received a cash payment for his compliance. In later portraits, Red Jacket wore a peace medal Washington had given him during the visit to Philadelphia in 1792, evidently proud of it and his association with the first president. Many Senecas remembered him for the land cessions he made.[57]

Cornplanter traveled to Philadelphia again in 1797. The next year the first Quaker missionaries arrived among the Allegheny

Senecas and set up a demonstration farm to model the transition to an agricultural way of life. Cornplanter himself set an example of accommodation and entrepreneurial values. He had received grants of land from the government for his services, and he held one of those grants in fee simple, next to the reservation. When the Quakers built a sawmill there, near the location selected for their farm and mission school, Cornplanter treated it as his personal property and floated timbers from the mill downriver to be sold at Pittsburgh. When he demanded that the Allegheny Senecas let him move his sawmill to a better location on the reservation and still take the profits himself, a dispute ensued. Cornplanter ordered the whole band off his land; they moved upstream, deposed him as chief, and built their own sawmill. Cornplanter also built himself a new house. Opposition to Cornplanter and his policies of accommodation cost him political influence, and by the time he returned east again in 1802, to the nation's new capital at Washington, he was playing second fiddle to his half-brother, Handsome Lake, who told President Jefferson that Cornplanter was "cried down by the Sachems of Buffalo Creek."[58]

Little Turtle also deviated from the path and values expected of a Miami leader. As he passed through Pittsburgh on his way home from Philadelphia in March 1798, he was, according to press reports, "highly gratified with the reception he met with from the President of the United States, and the attention that has been paid him by every class of citizens."[59] He made return trips to the nation's capital and made himself a friend to the United States. Aided by William Wells, who became a U.S. Indian agent, Little Turtle urged his people to make the transition to a new way of life. He himself lived in a house the government built for him, received a government pension, wore American clothes, and ate American food. He also had a slave whom Jefferson had purchased for him. Little Turtle earned the esteem of his former American enemies, but many Miamis felt he had ceased to behave like a Miami chief, who traditionally did not live more lavishly than the people. According to territorial governor and future president William Henry Harrison, who had his own agenda and axes to grind, "nine tenths of that Tribe. . . utterly abhor both Wells and the Turtle."[60]

Little Turtle made his last trip to Washington in 1808–9. U.S. Indian agent John Johnston remembered him as "a man of great wit, humor, and vivacity, fond of the company of gentlemen, and delighted in good eating." Little Turtle died in 1812, said Johnston, "of a confirmed case of the gout, brought on by high living, and was buried with military honors by the troops of the United States."[61]

Interred with him as grave goods were corn and beans, red pigment, and a pipe tomahawk, as befitted a Miami chief, along with a sword, gun, and medal Washington had given him.[62]

After Jean Baptiste DuCoigne returned from the disastrous journey that left eight of his fellow delegates buried in Philadelphia, his interests began to appear immediate and personal rather than long-term and communal. DuCoigne continued to be a friend to the United States, in part to secure protection for his now tiny Kaskaskia tribe against more powerful neighbors. Like Little Turtle, he assisted land-grabbing William Henry Harrison in securing treaties, and in appreciation for his services he received a new house with a fenced-in field. Jefferson in 1804 believed "that every reasonable accommodation ought to be afforded the old Kaskaskias chief" and that DuCoigne should "be enabled to live decently, and in a due degree of independence." Harrison was ordered to furnish "suitable supplies for his family use, from time to time." Harrison agreed that DuCoigne was "a decent, sensible, gentlemanly man, by no means addicted to drink, and possessing a very strong inclination to live like a white man." In fact, Harrison added, "the prospect of being enabled to live comfortably, was the great motive with him for selling his lands." DuCoigne asked for coffee, sugar, and chocolate, as well as a ten-gallon keg of wine, "to shew, as he says[,] the other Indians how well he is treated by the United States, and how much like a gentleman he lives." Jefferson hoped DuCoigne's prosperity would encourage other Indians to emulate him in adopting American "civilization." Instead, DuCoigne alienated many of his own people by flaunting American goods and American connections. His long and proven friendship for the United States "gained him the hatred of all the other chiefs," Harrison said, and he recommended that the government take steps to provide for his safety as well as his material comfort. DuCoigne died in 1811. The local militia provided military honors at his funeral.[63]

Even Indian students, who had been literally schooled to promote American ways when they returned home, encountered and sometimes generated distrust. Farmer's Brother said he placed his grandson with the Quakers in Philadelphia "in the hopes that this youth, when he got learning, would be of great service to our nations, to inform us of the good customs and ways of the white people." Instead, when Farmer's Brother visited Philadelphia as part of a delegation two years later, he found his grandson in a tavern. Then he saw him gambling, taking dancing lessons, and visiting "a bad house, where were bad women." Such an education was no use to the Senecas, Farmer's Brother said, "for we know of no such things among us, of boys of such an age as he was, going into such company and following such bad ways." Instead of bringing home knowledge and skills that would help protect tribal lands, the grandson was more interested in accumulating private property. "Our hearts fell," said Farmer's Brother, "concluding that if we send more of our boys, and they should learn such bad ways as he had, that our land would be cut into small pieces, and our nation dispersed and ruined." Nevertheless, he resolved to try again and send the Quakers another grandson.[64] The Creek boy James Bailey, son of trader Richard Bailey and his Creek wife, was placed under the direction of the Quakers in Philadelphia. His older brother Richard was educated in Philadelphia by the government, but he "brought with him into the nation so much contempt for the Indian mode of life, that he has got himself into discredit with them."[65]

In the Scottish Highlands about this time, clan chiefs who spent increasing amounts of time in Edinburgh and London often developed lifestyles and connections that distanced them from their people.[66] Native American chiefs who traveled to American cities were not immune to similar pressures and temptations. Many of the hundreds of Indian delegates returned home changed men. By 1800, the federal government still hoped that they would bring about change among their own people, and that they would accomplish it by demonstrating their own individual progress in American ways. Such life changes often compromised rather than enhanced their reputation. Individual leaders who advanced themselves in American eyes often did so at the expense of their standing in their own communities. Tribal leaders who went to Washington, DC, might create a vital intermediary role for themselves, as generations of city-going chiefs had done before them. But if they agreed to land sales, they might earn an unsavory reputation as "treaty chiefs" or, worse, "whiskey chiefs." If they promoted U.S. programs and policies, they might be labeled "government chiefs" and ignored as puppets. Delegates who returned from the nation's capital found it increasingly difficult to shed the city. The power and policies of Washington followed them home.

Conclusion

I NDIAN PEOPLE INVITED AND ESCORTED into town, welcomed by the city fathers, and cheered by enthusiastic crowds; lodging in the finest hotels, wined and dined at formal dinners, and dropping by for breakfast in private homes; touring the city, seeing the sights, strolling in the park, sitting in church, and watching performances at the theater and circus; cared for by physicians, and, if they died, being carried to city burial grounds in funeral corteges of hundreds of people; traveling by stagecoach at government expense and staggering home under the weight of gifts. . . . Contrary to assumptions that Indians were nowhere to be seen in the cities of early America, and that they had retreated as Euro-American settlements advanced, it might seem that citizens could barely walk the streets without bumping into visiting tribal delegates who went about an endless round of social engagements, observing and participating in urban life.

These incidents were relatively few and far between, of course, fleeting moments in a long history more often typified by dispossession and racial violence. Yet it would be wrong to dismiss them as nothing more than aberrations, or to regard chiefs in the city as the naive dupes of colonial and federal officials who showed them a good time and then sent them home laden with presents and lies. Indigenous people participated in networks of power, knowledge, opportunity, mobility, and exchange before Europeans arrived, and they continued to participate in the extended networks that contact with newcomers created and necessitated.[1] Colonialism was a multipronged assault, and Native leaders dealt with colonial powers in multiple ways and in multiple places, including urban spaces, the very places where they are not supposed to have been. In changing times and circumstances, Attakullakulla led Cherokee war parties against the French and enjoyed attending the theater in London and New York and listening to spinet music in Williamsburg. Guyasuta fought against the British during the French and Indian War and in Pontiac's War; then he visited eastern cities dressed like a British army officer and apparently attended lectures on electricity; in the Revolution, he burned Hannahstown in western Pennsylvania; in 1790, he was back in Philadelphia. During the war for the Northwest Territory, Blue Jacket and Little Turtle destroyed an American army; during their visits to Philadelphia, they went to the museum, the theater, and the circus. Some Indians killed and scalped—or were killed and scalped by—colonists. Some Indian people—sometimes the same Indian people—also took afternoon tea and attended balls with colonists when they were in town.

Tribal delegates in Quebec, Montreal, Albany, Boston, New York, Philadelphia, and Charleston may have felt out of their element, but they were still powers in the land, with whom colonial authorities had to reckon and deal. The "chiefs now in this city" were not all Indigenous heroes waging unwavering resistance to settler colonialism. Nonetheless, they were on the front lines of contact, collision, and confluence with the Atlantic world. They made the city part of their geography, a space where they presented Indigenous views, pressed Indigenous agendas, leveraged Indigenous political influence, and confounded enduring stereotypes of savagery, even as they sometimes performed the roles that colonial officials and city crowds expected of them. Their visits, and the time they spent being wined, dined, and entertained, provided opportunities and occasions for Native strategy, leadership, and adaptation. They went not as supplicants and curiosities but to pursue their own goals and get what they wanted—allies, goods, access to resources, political leverage. If they may sometimes have been tourists, they were tourists with an agenda, and sometimes with an attitude. And if they may have performed prescribed roles, they performed them with purpose.

Tribal delegations kept coming after the new capital moved to Washington, DC.[2] As they had in the previous century, they stayed in hotels, went sightseeing, and passed the time as they waited to meet with government officials. The new capital was far from impressive in its early years. Public buildings were still under construction. The streets were unpaved and turned to mud when it rained. The city was built in a swamp and mosquitos plagued the residents. Hogs rooted through the trash in the streets. Nevertheless, despite its outward appearances, Washington was an imperial capital that could exercise tyrannical power in its dealings with Indigenous peoples.[3]

As secretary of war James McHenry laid out in a letter to Robert G. Harper, chair of the Ways and Means Committee, the protocols and policies for hosting delegations were well established by 1800:

> When Indians arrive at the seat of Government, a confidential person is appointed to procure lodgings for them; to superintend and inspect their conduct; to accompany them to places of entertainment; to procure for them the presents in clothing &c. which may be ordered; and to pay all accounts arising under his superintendence. Money is advanced to him, by warrant, for these purposes, and he settles his accounts in the usual way, by producing vouchers and receipts for the expenditures. Indians, also, occasionally receive actual money. This is paid for them by a warrant, drawn in their favor, expressive of its object, except in cases, and for particular services, which require a different course.

Times were changing, however, and with them the government's receptivity to Indian visitors. The defeat of the Northwest confederacy at Fallen Timbers in 1794, the Jay Treaty with Britain that same year, and the Treaty of Greenville and the Treaty of San Lorenzo with Spain in 1795 had secured the young republic's borders and altered the power dynamics. Responding to Harper's concerns about the expense of such visits, McHenry assured him that his goal was "to render less frequent the visits of Indians to the seat of Government, and to extend the influence of the United States within their nations, by the instrumentality of resident agents, and internal arrangements and measures, calculated to procure these ends."[4] Indian allies were less crucial to the United States, and expensive tribal delegations to the nation's capital were something to be tolerated rather than encouraged. Meanwhile, the government would extend its reach into Indian communities.

The federal government never again dealt with chiefs in the city from a position of weakness, and chiefs in the city never demanded attention as they had in the early 1790s. Tribal delegates to the nation's capital lacked the alternative diplomatic options their colonial predecessors had exploited when they visited various and often competing colonial capitals. They now confronted a nation whose existence and growth demanded their dispossession and subordination, a government that treated them as supplicants rather than state visitors, and an assumption that they were defeated peoples whose only hope for the future lay in selling land and adopting "civilization." Indian delegates made more treaties in Washington than in any other single place. As American expansion engulfed their homelands, they no longer negotiated the terms of their relationship with the colonial power; now they negotiated the terms of their survival.

Yet they kept showing up, with and without invitation.[5] Through the dark days of the nineteenth and twentieth centuries, tribal delegates traveled to Washington, DC, as they had once traveled to Albany, Philadelphia, or Charleston. They contested policy after policy, demanded change, and asserted their rights. They left their mark on the city in representations of Indianness on public buildings, bridges, and monuments, representations that the government appropriated as emblems of national identity and markers of American progress and Indian demise. They also made the imperial capital *their* capital. They established Native spaces and organizations, created an enduring Indigenous presence, and insisted that the United States government deal with them on a nation-to-nation basis.[6]

In September 2004 more than 20,000 Indigenous people from more than 500 Native nations and from throughout the Americas traveled to Washington, DC, for the long-awaited opening of the National Museum of the American Indian. On opening day, dressed in tribal regalia, they walked in a huge procession down the National Mall. Nothing like it had ever happened before on that scale. But though unprecedented in its size, the event had some very familiar aspects. Indian people in the capital for an occasion that was hoped to symbolize the beginning of a new era did many of the things chiefs in the city had done centuries before. They saw the sights, toured museums and art galleries, and went shopping. They dressed the part, performed their Indianness in public, and attracted crowds and media attention. Like Indian delegates who had made the cities of early America part of their world by their journeys, experiences, presences, performances, and deaths, they made a colonial capital the stage for a demonstration of Indigenous identity, survival, and sovereignty.

ABBREVIATIONS

ASPIA	*American State Papers: Documents, Legislative and Executive, of the Congress of the United States. Class II: Indian Affairs.* Walter Lowrie and Matthew St. Clair Clarke, eds. 2 vols. Washington, DC: Gales and Seaton, 1832–34.
Col. Recs. Penn.	*Colonial Records of Pennsylvania.* Samuel Hazard, ed. 16 vols. Harrisburg and Philadelphia: T. Fenn, 1838–1853. (Vols. 1–10: *Minutes of the Provincial Council of Pennsylvania.* Vols. 11–16: *Minutes of the Supreme Executive Council of Pennsylvania.*)
DHFFC	*Documentary History of the First Federal Congress, 1789–1791.* Linda Grant De Pauw et al., eds. 22 vols. to date. Baltimore: Johns Hopkins University Press, 1972–.
DRCHNY	*Documents Relating to the Colonial History of the State of New York.* Edmund B. O' Callaghan et al., eds. 15 vols. Albany: Weed, Parsons, 1853–57.
EAID	*Early American Indian Documents: Treaties and Laws, 1607–1789.* Alden T. Vaughan, gen. ed. 20 vols. Bethesda, MD: University Publications of America, 1979–2004.
JR	*The Jesuit Relations and Allied Documents: Travels and Explorations of the Jesuit Missionaries in New France, 1610–1791.* Reuben G. Thwaites, ed. 73 vols. Cleveland: Burrows Brothers, 1896–1901.
Penn. Archives	*Pennsylvania Archives.* 9 series, 138 volumes. Philadelphia and Harrisburg, 1852–1949.
PGW, Pres.	*The Papers of George Washington: Presidential Series.* Dorothy Twohig et al., eds. 19 vols. to date. Charlottesville: University of Virginia Press, 1987–.
PWD	Papers of the War Department, 1784–1800. Roy Rosenzweig Center for History and New Media, George Mason University. wardepartmentpapers.org.
WJP	*The Papers of Sir William Johnson.* James Sullivan et al., eds. 14 vols. Albany: University of the State of New York, 1921–65.

NOTES

INTRODUCTION

1. François Marbois, "Journey to the Oneidas, 1784," in *In Mohawk Country: Early Narratives About a Native People*, ed. Dean R. Snow, Charles T. Gehring, and William A. Starna (Syracuse: Syracuse University Press, 1996), 305–6.
2. John Hallam, "The Eighteenth-Century American Townscape and the Face of Colonialism," *Smithsonian Studies in American Art* 4 (Summer–Autumn 1990): 144–62; Jennifer Van Horn, *The Power of Objects in Eighteenth-Century British America* (Chapel Hill: University of North Carolina Press, 2017), ch. 1 (signaled progress at 58); Paul Musselwhite, *Urban Dreams, Rural Commonwealth: The Rise of Plantation Society in the Chesapeake* (Chicago: University of Chicago Press, 2019), 18.
3. Richard C. Wade, *The Urban Frontier: The Rise of Western Cities, 1790–1830* (Cambridge, MA: Harvard University Press, 1959).
4. Christine M. DeLucia, *Memory Lands: King Philip's War and the Place of Violence in the Northeast* (New Haven: Yale University Press, 2018), 85–86.
5. Coll Thrush, *Native Seattle: Histories from the Crossing-Over Place* (Seattle: University of Washington Press, 2007), 8.
6. Russel Thornton, Gary D. Sandefur, and Harold G. Grasmick, *The Urbanization of American Indians: A Critical Bibliography* (Bloomington: Indiana University Press, 1982); Joan Weibel-Orlando, *Indian Country, L.A.: Maintaining Ethnic Community in Complex Society* (Champaign: University of Illinois Press, 1993); Donald L. Fixico, *The Urban Indian Experience in America* (Albuquerque: University of New Mexico Press, 2000); Nicolas G. Rosenthal, *Reimagining Indian Country: Native American Migration and Identity in Twentieth-Century Los Angeles* (Chapel Hill: University of North Carolina Press, 2012); Thrush, *Native Seattle;* James B. LeGrand, *Indian Metropolis: Native Americans in Chicago, 1945–74* (Champaign: University of Illinois Press, 2005); Rosalyn R. Lapier and David R. Beck, *Native American Activism in Chicago, 1893–1934* (Lincoln: University of Nebraska Press, 2015); Cathleen D. Cahill, "Urban Indians, Native Networks, and the Creation of Modern Regional Identity in the American Southwest," *American Indian Culture and Research Journal* 42, no. 3 (2018): 71–92; Douglas K. Miller, *Indians on the Move: Native American Mobility and Urbanization in the Twentieth Century* (Chapel Hill: University of North Carolina Press, 2019).
7. Evelyn Peters and Chris Andersen, eds., *Indigenous in the City: Contemporary Identities and Cultural Innovation* (Vancouver: UBC Press, 2013), 1–5, 30, 195.
8. For example, Daniel H. Usner, *American Indians in Early New Orleans: From Calumet to Raquette* (Baton Rouge: Louisiana State University Press, 2018); Nathaniel F. Holly, "From Itsa'ti to Charlestown: The Urban Lives of Cherokees in Early America," Ph.D. dissertation, College of William and Mary, 2019; Dana Velasco Murillo, Mark Lentz, and Margarita R. Ochoa, eds., *City Indians in Spain's American Empire: Urban Indigenous Society in Colonial Mesoamerica and Andean South America, 1530–1810* (Brighton, UK: Sussex Academic Press, 2012).
9. *The Adams-Jefferson Letters: The Complete Correspondence Between Thomas Jefferson and Abigail and John Adams*, ed. Lester J. Cappon (Chapel Hill: University of North Carolina Press, 1987), 307. See Thomas A. Strohfeldt, "Warriors in Williamsburg: The Cherokee Presence in Virginia's Eighteenth Century Capital," *Journal of Cherokee Studies* 11 (1986): 4–18.

10. Quoted in Usner, *American Indians in Early New Orleans*, 34.
11. Dell Upton, *Another City: Urban Life and Urban Spaces in the New American Republic* (New Haven: Yale University Press, 2008), 22.
12. On the role of Indian delegations in the diplomacy that evolved in the early capital, see Stephanie L. Gamble, "Capital Negotiations: Native Diplomats in the American Capital, 1789–1837," Ph.D. diss., Johns Hopkins University, 2014.
13. Patrick Spero, *Frontier Country: The Politics of War in Early Pennsylvania* (Philadelphia: University of Pennsylvania Press, 2016), 159.
14. Lynette Russell, ed., *Colonial Frontiers: Indigenous-European Encounters in Settler Societies* (Manchester, UK: Manchester University Press, 2001), 1–15
15. Gilles Havard, *The Great Peace of Montreal of 1701: French-Native Diplomacy in the Seventeenth Century* (Montreal: McGill-Queens University Press, 2001), 111; Timothy J. Shannon, *Indians and Colonists at the Crossroads of Empire: The Albany Congress of 1754* (Ithaca: Cornell University Press, 2000), 139.
16. Jay Gitlin, Barbara Berglund, and Adam Arenson, eds., *Frontier Cities: Encounters at the Crossroads of Empire* (Philadelphia: University of Pennsylvania Press, 2012).
17. Leonard von Morzé, *Cities and the Circulation of Culture in the Atlantic World* (New York: Palgrave Macmillan, 2017); Jessica Choppin Rooney, "Introduction: Distinguishing Port Cities, 1500–1800," *Early American Studies* 15 (2017): 649–59.
18. For example, Bryan C. Rindfleisch, *George Galphin's Intimate Empire: The Creek Indians, Family, and Colonialism in Early America* (Tuscaloosa: University of Alabama Press, 2019).
19. Rob Harper, *Unsettling the West: Violence and State Building in the Ohio Valley* (Philadelphia: University of Pennsylvania Press, 2018), 34–35.
20. Jenny Hale Pulsipher, *Swindler Sachem: The American Indian Who Sold His Birthright, Dropped Out of Harvard, and Conned the King of England* (New Haven: Yale University Press, 2017).
21. Denise I. Bossy, "Spiritual Diplomacy, the Yamasees, and the Society for the Propagation of the Gospel: Reinterpreting Prince George's Eighteenth-Century Voyage to England," *Early American Studies* 12 (2014): 366–401.
22. Richard N. Ellis and Charlie R. Steen, eds., "An Indian Delegation in France," *Journal of the Illinois State Historical Society* 67 (1974): 385–405; Robert Michael Morrissey, *Empire by Collaboration: Indians, Colonists, and Governments in Colonial Illinois Country* (Philadelphia: University of Pennsylvania Press, 2015), 130–32.
23. Julie Ann Sweet, *Negotiating for Georgia: British-Creek Relations in the Trustee Era, 1733–1752* (Athens: University of Georgia Press, 2005), ch. 3; Sweet, "Will the Real Tomochichi Please Come Forward?," *American Indian Quarterly* 32 (2008): 141–77; Steven J. Peach, "Creek Indian Globetrotter: Tomochichi's Trans-Atlantic Quest for Traditional Power in the Colonial Southeast," *Ethnohistory* 60 (2013): 605–35; Nancy Shoemaker, "Wonder and Repulsion: North American Indians in Eighteenth-Century Europe," in *Europe Observed: Multiple Gazes in Early Modern Encounters*, ed. Kumkum Chatterjee and Clement Hawes (Lewisburg: Bucknell University Press, 2008), 173–97, Tomochico quote at 185; Holly, "From Itsa'ti to Charlestown," ch. 5.
24. *EAID* 5:253–60; *The Memoirs of Lieutenant Henry Timberlake*, ed. Duane H. King (Cherokee, NC: Museum of the Cherokee Indian, 2007), 55–72; John Oliphant, "The Cherokee Embassy to London, 1762," *Journal of Imperial and Commonwealth History* 27 (1999): 1–26; Alden T. Vaughan, *Transatlantic Encounters: American Indians in Britain, 1500–1776* (Cambridge: Cambridge University Press, 2006), 165–75; Stephanie Pratt, *American Indians in British Art, 1700–1840* (Norman: University of Oklahoma Press, 2004), 54–57 (verse at 55); Timothy J. Shannon, "'This Wretched Scene of British Curiosity and Savage Debauchery': Performing Indian Kingship in Eighteenth-Century Britain," in *Native Acts: Indian Performance, 1603–1832*, ed. Joshua David Bellin and Laura L. Mielke (Lincoln: University of Nebraska Press, 2011), 221–47.
25. Isabel Thompson Kelsay, *Joseph Brant, 1743–1807: Man of Two Worlds* (Syracuse: Syracuse University Press, 1984), 385.

26. Antoinette Burton, *At the Heart of Empire: Indians and the Colonial Encounter in Late-Victorian Britain* (Berkley: University of California Press, 1998), 1.

27. Christian F. Feest, ed., *Indians and Europe: An Interdisciplinary Collection of Essays* (Lincoln: University of Nebraska Press, 1999); Vaughan, *Transatlantic Encounters*; Kate Fullagar, *Savage Visit: New World People and Popular Imperial Culture in Britain, 1710–1795* (Berkeley: University of California Press, 2012); Jace Weaver, *The Red Atlantic: American Indigenes and the Making of the Modern World, 1000–1927* (Chapel Hill: University of North Carolina Press, 2014); Coll Thrush, *Indigenous London* (New Haven: Yale University Press, 2016); Nathaniel F. Holly, "Transatlantic Indians in the Early Modern Era," *History Compass* 14 (2016): 522–32; Cecilia Morgan, *Travellers Through Empire* (Montreal: McGill-Queen's University Press, 2017); Kate Fullagar, "Envoys of Interest: A Cherokee, a Ra'iatean, and the Eighteenth-Century British Empire," in *Facing Empire: Indigenous Experiences in a Revolutionary Age*, ed. Kate Fullagar and Michael A. McDonnell (Baltimore: Johns Hopkins University Press, 2018), 239–55; Kate Fullagar, *The Warrior, the Voyager, and the Artist: Three Lives in an Age of Empire* (New Haven: Yale University Press, 2020).

28. Katharine C. Turner, *Red Men Calling on the Great White Father* (Norman: University of Oklahoma Press, 1951); Herman J. Viola, *Diplomats in Buckskins: A History of Indian Delegations in Washington City* (Washington, DC: Smithsonian Institution Press, 1981; reprint, Bluffton, SC: Rivilo Books, 1995); C. Joseph Genetin-Pilewa, "The Indians' Capital City: Diplomatic Visits, Place, and Two-Worlds Discourse in Nineteenth-Century Washington, DC," in *Beyond Two Worlds: Critical Conversations on Language and Power in Native North America*, ed. James Joseph Buss and C. Joseph Genetin-Pilewa (Albany: SUNY Press, 2014), 117–35; Gamble, "Capital Negotiations: Native Diplomats in the American Capital."

29. Frederick E. Hoxie, "Exploring a Cultural Borderland: Native American Journeys of Discovery in the Early Twentieth Century," *Journal of American History* 79 (1992): 969–95, quote at 976.

30. Kate Fullagar and Michael A. McDonnell, "Introduction: Empire, Indigeneity, and Revolution," in *Facing Empire: Indigenous Experiences in a Revolutionary Age*, ed. Kate Fullagar and Michael A. McDonnell (Baltimore: Johns Hopkins University Press, 2018), 19–20.

31. Cary Miller, *Ogimaag: Anishinaabeg Leadership, 1760–1845* (Lincoln: University of Nebraska Press, 2010), 73–74.

32. David J. Norton, *Rebellious Younger Brother: Oneida Leadership and Diplomacy, 1750–1800* (DeKalb: Northern Illinois University Press, 2009), 8; William C. Reichel, ed., *Memorials of the Moravian Church* (Philadelphia: J. B. Lippincott, 1870), 1:83; *Penn. Archives*, 4th series, 1:826 ("Person of Consequence").

33. William A. Starna, "The Diplomatic Career of Canasatego," in *Friends and Enemies in Penn's Woods: Indians, Colonists, and the Racial Construction of Pennsylvania*, ed. William A. Pencak and Daniel K. Richter (University Park: Pennsylvania State University Press, 2004), 145; Susan Kalter, "Introduction," in *Benjamin Franklin, Pennsylvania, and the First Nations: The Treaties of 1736–62*, ed. Susan Kalter (Urbana: University of Illinois Press, 2006), 20.

34. *EAID* 13:241, 245 ("Mouth of the Nation"); *Col. Recs. Penn.* 8:124 ("not a Chief Man"), 736 (Shawnees).

35. Franklin B. Hough, ed., *Proceedings of the Commissioners of Indian Affairs, Appointed for the Extinguishment of Indian Titles in the State of New York* (Albany: Joel Munsell, 1861), 2:395–96. See also *EAID* 1: 175 for young Conestogas learning the ropes.

36. *JR* 6:243; Penn quoted in C. A. Weslager, *The Delaware Indians: A History* (New Brunswick, NJ: Rutgers University Press, 1972), 166; Cadwallader Colden, *The History of the Five Indian Nations of Canada* (New York: Allerton Book Co., 1902), 1:xxxiv; *The Journal of Nicholas Cresswell, 1774–1777* (New York: Dial Press, 1924), 117, 119.

37. Richard White, *The Roots of Dependency: Subsistence, Environment, and Social Change Among the Choctaws, Pawnees, and Navajos* (Lincoln: University of Nebraska Press, 1983), ch. 4; Dunbar Rowland, ed., *Mississippi Provincial Archives, 1763–1766: English Dominion* (Nashville: Brandon Printing Co., 1911), 1:229, 254.

38. *Penn. Archives*, 1st series, 3:68.

39. Alan Taylor, "Captain Hendrick Aupaumut: The Dilemmas of an Intercultural Broker," *Ethnohistory* 43 (1996): 431–57, Pickering quote at 436.

40. Papers of General Sir Frederick Haldimand, British Museum, Additional Mss., 21763: 99 (McLean quote); *The Correspondence of the Honourable Peter Russell with Allied Documents Relating to His Administration of Upper Canada*, ed. E. A. Cruikshank (Toronto: Ontario Historical Society, 1932–36), 1:160 ("able" and "artful"); Hough, *Proceedings of the Commissioners of Indian Affairs*, 2:465.

41. Archer Butler Hulbert, ed., *The Records of the Original Proceedings of the Ohio Company* (Marietta, OH: Marietta Historical Commission, 1917), 1:82.

42. Thomas S. Abler, *Cornplanter: Chief Warrior of the Allegany Senecas* (Syracuse: Syracuse University Press, 2007), 72–74 (visit to New York); Alan Taylor, *The Divided Ground: Indians, Settlers, and the Northern Borderland of the American Revolution* (New York: Alfred Knopf, 2005), 246–48.

43. Theda Perdue, *Cherokee Women: Gender and Culture Change, 1700–1835* (Lincoln: University of Nebraska Press, 1998); Gunlög Fur, *Nation of Women: Gender and Colonial Encounters Among the Delaware Indians* (Philadelphia: University of Pennsylvania Press, 2012); Alison Duncan Hirsch, "Indians, *Métis*, and Euro-American Women on Multiple Frontiers," in *Friends and Enemies in Penn's Woods: Indians, Colonists, and the Racial Construction of Pennsylvania*, ed. William A. Pencak and Daniel K. Richter (University Park: Pennsylvania State University Press, 2004), 63–84.

44. Witham Marshe, "Journal of the Treaty Held with the Six Nations," in *The Lancaster Treaty of 1744 with Related Documents*, ed. James H. Merrell (Boston: Bedford/St. Martin's, 2008), 120–21; Alison Duncan Hirsch, "'The Celebrated Madame Montour': 'Interpress' Across Early American Frontiers," *Explorations in Early American Culture* 4 (2000): 81–112.

45. *Memoirs of the Life of Catherine Phillips, to which are added some of her epistles* (London: J. Phillips & Son, 1797), 142.

46. Quoted in Taylor, "Captain Hendrick Aupaumut," 446.

47. *The Papers of George Washington: Retirement Series*, ed. W. W. Abbot et al. (Charlottesville: University Press of Virginia, 1998–99), 1:534.

48. Hough, *Proceedings of the Commissioners of Indian Affairs*, 2:331, 340.

49. Indians who went to Quebec in 1745 for an audience with the governor, left in exasperation after eight or ten days during which "no Notice was taken of them." *An Account of the Treaty held at the city of Albany in October 1745* (Philadelphia: B. Franklin, 1746), 18. Five Iroquois in Philadelphia in January 1759 were kept waiting for ten days because General John Forbes had "not yet condescended to see them"; *WJP* 10:91. It had less to do with condescension than with ill health. Forbes, who just months before had led the campaign against the French that captured Fort Duquesne at the Forks of the Ohio in what is today Pittsburgh, was dying, probably of stomach cancer.

50. Beverly McAnear, ed., "Personal Accounts of the Albany Congress of 1754," *Mississippi Valley Historical Review* 39 (1953): 735; *DRCHNY* 6:867–68.

51. *EAID* 14:23–36.

52. *ASPIA* 1:140–42; *PGW, Pres.*, 7:7–15; *Chainbreaker: The Revolutionary War Memoirs of Governor Blacksnake as Told to Benjamin Williams*, ed. Thomas A. Abler (Lincoln: University of Nebraska Press, 1989), 160–61, 176–77, 238–46.

53. Hoxie, "Exploring a Cultural Borderland"; Frederick E. Hoxie, "Ethnohistory for a Tribal World," *Ethnohistory* 44 (1997): 595–615.

54. I learned to appreciate the legibility of Brant's handwriting as a graduate student wading through the manuscript volumes of British Indian Department records in the Colonial Office records and the papers of Governor General Fredrick Haldimand of Quebec.

55. Viola, *Diplomats in Buckskins*, 11, 5; PWD.

56. *Jersey Chronicle*, May 23, 1794, 34, reprinted in *Federal Spy* (Springfield, MA), June 23, 1795, 2; *Hampshire Gazette*, July 8, 1792, 2.

57. Philp Freneau, *Tomo Cheeki, the Creek Indian in Philadelphia*, ed. Elisabeth Hermann (Frankfurt am Main: Peter Lang, 1987).

58. Charles J. Kappler, comp. and ed., *Indian Affairs: Laws and Treaties* (Washington, DC: Government Printing Office, 1904), 2:28.

59. Robert F. Berkhofer Jr., *The White Man's Indian: Images of the Indian from Columbus to the Present* (New York: Random House, 1978), esp. 72–80; Louis Armand de Lom d'Arce, Baron de Lahontan, *New Voyages to North-America: Containing an account of the several nations of that vast continent . . .* (London, 1703); Charles-Louis de Secondat, Baron de La Brède et de Montesquieu, *Persian Letters* (Paris, 1721).

60. Benjamin Franklin, *Two Tracts: Information to Those Who Would Remove to America, and Remarks Concerning the Savages of North America*, 2nd ed. (London: John Stockdale, 1784), 26–29.

61. For example, Wes Taukchiray, "American Indian References in the 'South-Carolina Gazette,'" *South Carolina Historical Magazine* 94 (1993): 185–92.

62. *The Collected Writings of Samson Occom, Mohegan*, ed. Joanna Brooks (New York: Oxford University Press, 2006), 99.

63. Franklin, *Two Tracts*, 25.

64. *Quebec to Carolina in 1785–1786: Being the Travel Diary and Observations of Robert Hunter, Jr., a Young Merchant of London*, ed. Louis B. Wright and Marion Tinling (San Marino, CA: Huntington Library, 1943), 37.

65. Kumkum Chatterjee and Clement Hawes, "Introduction," in *Europe Observed: Multiple Gazes in Early Modern Encounters*, ed. Kumkum Chatterjee and Clement Hawes (Lewisburg: Bucknell University Press, 2008), 2. Indigenous visitors were not alone in their reactions. People accustomed to a slower pace and unchanging daily routines in the countryside also were taken aback. Louis Sébastien Mercier, who wrote the best-selling twelve-volume *Tableau de Paris* in the 1780s, thought people were bound to question the glaring inequalities they saw in the cities—why did some ride in carriages while the rest went on foot?; Jeremy D. Popkin, *A New World Begins: The History of the French Revolution* (New York: Basic Books, 2019), 27.

66. James. H. Merrell, *Into the American Woods: Negotiators on the Pennsylvania Frontier* (New York: W. W. Norton, 1999), 67.

67. *Journal of a Tour in Unsettled Parts of North America in 1796 and 1797 by Francis Baily*, ed. Jack D. Holmes (Carbondale: Southern Illinois University Press, 1969), 54.

68. Fullagar, *The Warrior, the Voyager, and the Artist*, 102–5.

69. Cf. Rachel Sarah O'Toole, "Fitting In: Urban Indians, Migrants, and Muleteers in Colonial Peru," in *City Indians in Spain's American Empire*, ed. Dana Velasco Murillo, Mark Lentz, and Margarita R. Ochoa (Brighton, UK: Sussex Academic Press, 2012), 150, 154.

CHAPTER 1

1. *WJP* 6:30; *Peter Kalm's Travels in North America: The English Version of 1770*, ed. Adolph B. Benson (New York: Wilson-Erickson, 1937), 2:439.

2. Paul Musselwhite, "Annapolis Aflame: Richard Clarke's Conspiracy and the Imperial Urban Vision in Maryland, 1704–8," *William and Mary Quarterly* 71 (2014): 367.

3. Peter Nabokov and Robert Easton, *Native American Architecture* (New York: Oxford University Press, 1989), 12.

4. Jill E. Neitzel, ed., *Great Towns and Regional Polities in the Prehistoric American Southwest and Southeast* (Albuquerque: University of New Mexico Press, 1999) (Stephen Lekson quote at 20).

5. Bernal Díaz del Castillo, *The Discovery and Conquest of Mexico, 1517–1521* (New York: Farrar, Straus and Cudahy, 1956), 190; Susan Schroeder, "Whither Tenochtitlan? Chimalpahin and Mexico City, 1593–1631," in *City Indians in Spain's American Empire: Urban Indigenous Society in Colonial Mesoamerica and Andean South America, 1530–1810*, ed. Dana Velasco Murillo, Mark Lentz, and Margarita R. Ochoa (Brighton, UK: Sussex Academic Press, 2012), 67 (population figures).

6. Biloine Whiting Young and Melvin L. Fowler, *Cahokia: The Great American Metropolis* (Urbana: University of Illinois Press, 2000); Timothy R. Pauketat, *Cahokia: Ancient America's Great City on the Mississippi* (New York: Viking/Penguin, 2009).

7. Roger G. Kennedy, *Hidden Cities: The Discovery and Loss of Ancient North American Civilization* (New York: Penguin, 1994); George R. Milner, *The Mound Builders: Ancient Peoples of Eastern North America* (London: Thames and Hudson, 2004).

8. *The Voyages of Jacques Cartier*, ed. Ramsay Cook, (Toronto: University of Toronto Press, 1993), 59, 61.

9. Coll Thrush, "Urban Native Histories," in *The Oxford Handbook of American Indian History*, ed. Frederick E. Hoxie (New York: Oxford University Press, 2016), 555.

10. Marc Simmons, *The Last Conquistador: Juan de Oñate and the Settling of the Far Southwest* (Norman: University of Oklahoma Press, 1991), 162–63; Jesse Casana et al., "A Council Site at Etzanoa?: Multi-sensor Drone Survey at an Ancestral Wichita Settlement in Southeastern Kansas," *American Antiquity* 85 (Aug. 2020): 1–20.

11. *JR* 60:159; Robert Michael Morrissey, "The Power of the Ecotone: Bison, Slavery, and the Rise and Fall of the Grand Village of the Kaskaskia," *Journal of American History* 102 (2015): 667–92 ("walking distance" at 682); Morrissey, *Empire by Collaboration: Indians, Colonists, and Governments in Colonial Illinois Country* (Philadelphia: University of Pennsylvania Press, 2015), 52–56; Jacob F. Lee, *Masters of the Middle Waters: Indian Nations and Colonial Ambitions along the Mississippi* (Cambridge, MA: Harvard University Press, 2019), 13, 32, 56, 60.

12. Samuel Cole Williams, ed., *Adair's History of the American Indians* (1930; reprint, New York: Promontory Press, n.d.), 302, 355.

13. Joshua A. Piker, "'White & Clean' & Contested: Creek Towns and Trading Paths in the Aftermath of the Seven Years' War," in *American Encounters: Natives and Newcomers from European Contact to Indian Removal, 1500–1800*, 2nd ed., ed. Peter C. Mancall and James H. Merrell (New York: Routledge, 2007), 337–60; "world of towns" at 351; Joshua A. Piker, *Okfuskee, a Creek Indian Town in Colonial America* (Cambridge, MA: Harvard University Press, 2004), 6–9; Robbie Ethridge, *Creek Country: The Creek Indians and Their World* (Chapel Hill: University of North Carolina Press, 2003), 93–96. Naturalist William Bartram provided a list of Creek towns in the 1770s, many of which had square, well-ordered buildings and a council house. *William Bartram on the Southeastern Indians*, ed. Gregory A. Waselkov and Kathleen E. Holland Braund (Lincoln: University of Nebraska Press, 1995), 104–6, 108–9.

14. Nathaniel F. Holly, "From Itsa'ti to Charlestown: The Urban Lives of Cherokees in Early America," Ph.D. dissertation, College of William and Mary, 2019; Colin G. Calloway, "Chota: Cherokee Beloved Town in a World at War," in *The American Revolution in Indian Country* (Cambridge: Cambridge University Press, 1995), ch. 7; *The Memoirs of Lieutenant Henry Timberlake*, ed. Duane H. King (Cherokee, NC: Museum of the Cherokee Indian, 2007), 17 (townhouse); National Archives, UK, Colonial Office Records, C.O. 323/17: 233. Bartram listed forty-three Cherokee towns in the 1770s; *William Bartram on the Southeastern Indians*, 87–88.

15. "Enumeration of Indians Within the Northern Department," *DRCHNY* 7:582; *WJP* 10:878.

16. Susan Sleeper-Smith, *Indigenous Prosperity and American Conquest: Indian Women of the Ohio River Valley, 1690–1792* (Chapel Hill: University of North Carolina Press, 2018), Sabrevois quote and numbers at 57.

17. W. Raymond Wood and Thomas D. Thiessen, eds., *Early Fur Trade on the Northern Plains: Canadian Traders Among the Mandans and Hidatsas 1738–1818* (Norman: University of Oklahoma Press, 1985); Elizabeth A. Fenn, *Encounters at the Heart of the World: A History of the Mandan People* (New York: Hill and Wang, 2014), 24–26.

18. Thrush, "Urban Native Histories," 559.

19. *Journey to Pennsylvania by Gottlieb Mittelberger*, ed. and trans. Oscar Handlin and John Clive (Cambridge, MA: Harvard University Press, 1960), 37.

20. Sleeper-Smith, *Indigenous Prosperity and American Conquest;* Jessica Yirush Stern, *The Lives in Objects: Native Americans, British Colonists, and Cultures of Labor and Exchange in the Southeast* (Chapel Hill: University of North Carolina Press, 2017); Kathryn E. Holland

Braund, *Deerskins and Duffels: The Creek Indian Trade with Anglo-America, 1685–1815,* 2nd ed. (Lincoln: University of Nebraska Press, 2008), 121–25.

21. *Journals of the Military Expedition of Major General John Sullivan Against the Six Nations of Indians in 1779,* ed. Frederick Cook (Auburn, NY: Knapp, Peck, and Thomson, 1887), 26–27, 40, 48, 60, 71–72, 75, 88, 91, 94–95, 99, 111, 126–28, 142, 155, 162–63, 172, 175, 188, 231–32, 303; *Letters and Papers of Major General John Sullivan,* ed. Otis G. Hammond (Concord: New Hampshire Historical Society, 1939), 3:107–12, 129–32, 134.

22. Timothy Pickering Papers, Massachusetts Historical Society, reel 62: 157–74.

23. Stephen J. Hornsby, *British Atlantic, American Frontier: Spaces of Power in Early Modern British America* (Hanover, NH: University Press of New England, 2005), 180.

24. Evan Haefeli and Kevin Sweeney, *Captors and Captives: The 1704 French and Indian Raid on Deerfield* (Amherst: University of Massachusetts Press, 2003), 12–13; Margaret Bruchac, "Native Presence in Nonotuck and Northampton," in *A Place Called Paradise: Culture and Community in Northampton, Massachusetts, 1654–2004,* ed. Kerry Buckley (Northampton, MA: Historic Northampton, 2004), 18–38.

25. Gary B. Nash, *The Urban Crucible: The Northern Seaports and the Origins of the American Revolution* (Cambridge, MA: Harvard University Press, 1986), ix.

26. David Hamer, *New Towns in the New World: Images and Perceptions of the Nineteenth-Century Urban Frontier* (New York: Columbia University Press, 1990), 68. For example, William Cronon, *Nature's Metropolis: Chicago and the West* (New York: W. W. Norton, 1991).

27. Hornsby, *British Atlantic, American Frontier,* 185–87, 198–203.

28. Allen W. Trelease, *Indian Affairs in Colonial New York: The Seventeenth Century* (Ithaca: Cornell University Press, 1960), 178; *DRCHNY* 4:826 ("growingest").

29. Mark Peterson, *The City-State of Boston: The Rise and Fall of an Atlantic Power, 1630–1865* (Princeton, NJ: Princeton University Press, 2019), 19.

30. Newton D. Mereness, ed., *Travels in the American Colonies* (New York: Macmillan, 1916), 449.

31. *Journey to Pennsylvania by Gottlieb Mittelberger,* 26.

32. Nash, *Urban Crucible,* 1, 6–14, 32, 65–66, 99, 246; Carl Bridenbaugh, *Cities in the Wilderness: The First Century of Urban Life in America, 1625–1742* (New York: Ronald Press, 1938), chs. 5–8; Bridenbaugh, *Cities in Revolt: Urban Life in America, 1743–1776* (New York: Alfred A. Knopf, 1955), chs. 1, 3, 8 (population figures at 5, 216–17); Philadelphia figures from Billy G. Smith, ed., *Life in Early Philadelphia: Documents from the Revolutionary and Early National Periods* (University Park, PA: Pennsylvania State University Press, 1995), 10; Billy G. Smith, *The "Lower Sort": Philadelphia's Laboring People, 1750–1800* (Ithaca: Cornell University Press, 1990), 42–43.

33. Vaughn Scribner, *Inn Civility: Urban Taverns and Early American Society* (New York: New York University Press, 2019), 3–12.

34. Fernand Braudel, *The Structures of Everyday Life* (New York: Harper and Row, 1981), 479.

35. Dell Upton, *Another City: Urban Life and Urban Spaces in the New American Republic* (New Haven: Yale University Press, 2008), ch. 2.

36. Serena R. Zabin, *Dangerous Economies: Status and Commerce in Imperial New York* (Philadelphia: University of Philadelphia Press, 2009); Ellen Hartigan-O'Connor, *The Ties That Buy: Women and Commerce in Revolutionary America* (Philadelphia: University of Pennsylvania Press, 2009).

37. Bernard L. Herman, *Town House: Architecture and Material Life in the Early American City, 1780–1830* (Chapel Hill: University of North Carolina Press, 2005).

38. Christine M. DeLucia, *Memory Lands: King Philip's War and the Place of Violence in the Northeast* (New Haven: Yale University Press, 2018), 45.

39. *EAID* 11:7–8, 10–11, 23; also, John T. Juricek, *Colonial Georgia and the Creeks: Anglo-Indian Diplomacy on the Southern Frontier, 1733–1763* (Gainesville: University Press of Florida, 2010), 62; William Stephens, *A Journal of the Proceedings in Georgia* (London, 1742; reprint, Readex Microprint, 1966), 1:405–6, 2:199.

40. Pierre de Charlevoix, *Journal of a Voyage to North-America* (London: R. and J. Dodsley, 1761), 1:99–114, quotes at 104 and 111.

41. Benson, *Peter Kalm's Travels*, 2:427.

42. R. Cole Harris, ed., *Historical Atlas of Canada*, Vol. 1, *From the Beginning to 1800* (Toronto: University of Toronto Press, 1987), plate 50; Robert V. Wells, *The Population of the British Colonies in America Before 1776: A Survey of Census Data* (Princeton: Princeton University Press, 1975), 64.

43. Gilles Havard, *The Great Peace of 1701: French-Native Diplomacy in the Seventeenth Century* (Montreal: McGill-Queens University Press, 2001), 126–28; Alain Beaulieu and Roland Viau, *The Great Peace: Chronicle of a Diplomatic Saga* (Montreal: Éditions Libre Expression, 2001), 60, 66.

44. "Journal of Captain Phineas Stevens' Journey to Canada, 1752," in Mereness, *Travels in the American Colonies*, 322.

45. *John Long's Voyages and Travels in the Years 1768–1788*, ed. Milo Milton Quaife (Chicago: R. R. Donnely, 1922), 6 (Montreal), 9 (Caughnawaga); *DRCHNY* 6:582 ("a thousand souls"); Harris, *Historical Atlas of Canada*, 1: plate 47.

46. *The Memoir of John Durang, American Actor, 1785–1816*, ed. Alan S. Downer (Pittsburgh: University of Pittsburgh Press, 1966), 73.

47. Timothy J. Shannon, *Indians and Colonists at the Crossroads of Empire: The Albany Congress of 1754* (Ithaca: Cornell University Press, 2000), 115, 118, 120–26.

48. *Gentleman's Progress: The Itinerarium of Dr. Alexander Hamilton, 1744*, ed. Carl Bridenbaugh (Chapel Hill: University of North Carolina Press, 1948), 71–73; Benson, *Peter Kalm's Travels*, 1:332, 342 (dirty streets), 343 (wampum), 344 (reputation for love of money); "Journal of Warren Johnson, 1760–1761," in *In Mohawk Country: Early Narratives About a Native People*, ed. Dean R. Snow, Charles T. Gehring, and William A. Starna (Syracuse: Syracuse University Press, 1996), 253, 269; *WJP* 13:184. Lord Adam Gordon said the town was "dull and ill built," the streets "very dirty and crooked." Gordon, "Journal of an Officer who Travelled in America and the West Indies in 1764 and 1765," in Mereness, *Travels in the American Colonies*, 417.

49. Trelease, *Indian Affairs in Colonial New York*, ch. 8.

50. *DRCHNY* 3:393; 4:51 ("antient place"), 88; 5:441, 492, 671, 717; 7:15.

51. *EAID* 9:241; *Penn. Archives*, 4th series, 1:639.

52. Benson, *Peter Kalm's Travels*, 1:347.

53. Shannon, *Indians and Colonists at the Crossroads of Empire*, 127.

54. *Memoir of Lieut. Col. Tench Tilghman* (Albany: J. Munsell, 1876), 80–81.

55. Trelease, *Indian Affairs in Colonial New York*, 189; *DRCHNY* 13:551.

56. *ASPIA* 1:69.

57. *Col. Recs. Penn.* 2:46 (farewell); *Penn. Archives*, 1st series, 4:470; 4th series, 1:793 ("One People"); *EAID* 2:288. Indians from the Allegheny said they intended to make the trip in 1739 "to see our Brothers and warme o[u]r selves att the Fier kept for us their." *Penn. Archives*, 1st series, 1:551.

58. *Penn. Archives*, 4th series, 2:789–90, 956; *Col. Recs. Penn.* 7:476.

59. *Col. Recs. Penn.* 7:88–89; *EAID*, 3:21, 27; *Penn. Archives*, 1st series, 8:167, 176; 4th series, 2:593, 597; 3:292–93.

60. Bridenbaugh, *Cities in the Wilderness*, 175, 186, 254, 305–7; "Journal of Warren Johnson," 251–52, also in *WJP* 13:181–82.

61. *Penn. Archives*, 4th series, 2:144.

62. Bridenbaugh, *Gentleman's Progress*, 18, 21; Smith, *The "Lower Sort,"* 7, 34–35, 43, 206; *Journey to Pennsylvania by Gottlieb Mittelberger*, 36–37, 50–51; *Some Cursory Remarks Made by James Birket in His Voyage to North America, 1750–1751* (1916; reprint, Freeport, NY: Books for Libraries, 1971), 63, 69; Benson, *Peter Kalm's Travels*, 1:18–26, 33 (quote); "Journal of William Black, 1744," ed. R. Alonzo Brook, *Pennsylvania Magazine of History and Biography* 1 (1877): 405 ("best of its bigness"); Gordon, "Journal of an Officer," 410; Norman K. Risjord, *Jefferson's America, 1760–1815* (Madison, WI: Madison House Publishers, 1991), 3, 34; *Travels in the Colonies in 1773–1775, Described in the Letters of William Mylne*, ed. Ted Ruddock (Athens: University of Georgia Press, 1993), 73–74; Patrick McRobert, *Tour*

Through Part of the North Provinces of America (Edinburgh: Printed for the author, 1776), 41–42; "Journal of Josiah Quincy, Jr.," *Proceedings of the Massachusetts Historical Society,* 3rd ser., 49 (1915–16): 477.

63. American Philosophical Society, Robert Woodruff, Journal. 1785–1788, 54–55; *Life, Journals and Correspondence of Rev. Manasseh Cutler,* ed. William Parker Cutler and Julia Perkins Cutler (Cincinnati: Robert Clarke & Co., 1888), 1:284–85; *The New Democracy in America: Travels of Francisco de Miranda in the United States, 1783–84,* ed. John Z. Ezell, trans. Justin P. Wood (Norman: University of Oklahoma Press, 1963), 41–42; *Moreau de St. Méry's American Journey 1793–1798,* ed. and trans. Kenneth Roberts and Ana K. Roberts (Garden City, NY: Doubleday, 1947), 257–61; *Luigi Castiglioni's Viaggio: Travels in the United States of North America, 1785–87,* ed. and trans. Antonio Pace (Syracuse: Syracuse University Press, 1983), 225; J. P. Brissot de Warville, *New Travels in the United States of America, Performed in 1788* (London: J. S. Jordan, 1792; reprint, New York: Augustus M. Kelley, 1970), 243–46, 312–17.

64. Gary B. Nash, *First City: Philadelphia and the Forging of Historical Memory* (Philadelphia: University of Pennsylvania Press, 2002), 1; *The Stranger in America, 1793–1806 by Charles William Janson,* ed. Carl S. Driver (New York: Press of the Pioneers, 1935), 181–202.

65. *Penn. Archives,* 1st ser., 1:69; Jim Murphy, *An American Plague: The True and Terrifying Story of the Yellow Fever Epidemic of 1793* (New York: Clarion Books, 2003), 3, 6; Upton, *Another City,* 22. Murphy says 6,784 dwellings; Cutler said 10,000 houses, and Moreau 9,000. *Life, Journals and Correspondence of Rev. Manasseh Cutler,* 1:285; *Moreau de St. Méry's American Journey,* 257.

66. Kerby A. Miller, Arnold Schrier, Bruce D. Boling, and David N. Doyle, eds., *Irish Immigrants in the Land of Canaan: Letters and Memoirs from Colonial and Revolutionary America, 1675–1815* (New York: Oxford University Press, 2003), 7, 24, 253; Patrick Griffin, *The People with No Name: Ireland's Ulster Scots, America's Scots Irish, and the Creation of a British Atlantic World, 1689–1764* (Princeton: Princeton University Press, 2001), 90–97; R. J. Dickson, *Ulster Emigration to Colonial America 1718–1775* (London: Routledge and Kegan Paul, 1966), 32–33, 42–43, 55–56, 85–87; Michael Tepper, ed., *Emigrants to Pennsylvania, 1641–1819: A Consolidation of Passenger Lists from the Pennsylvania Magazine of History and Biography* (Baltimore: Genealogical Publishing Co., 1977); Maurice J. Bric, *Ireland, Philadelphia, and the Re-invention of America, 1760–1800* (Dublin: Four Courts Press, 2008), 31–45, 297–307.

67. Bridenbaugh, *Gentleman's Progress,* 20.

68. Benson, *Peter Kalm's Travels,* 32,

69. Smith, *Life in Early Philadelphia,* 223; Upton, *Another City,* 39.

70. Driver, *The Stranger in America,* 182–87.

71. Carole Shammas, "The Space Problem in Early United States Cities," *William and Mary Quarterly,* 3rd ser., 57, (2000): 511–12.

72. Smith, *The "Lower Sort,"* chs. 4 and 6.

73. Clare A. Lyons, *Sex Among the Rabble: An Intimate History of Gender and Power in the Age of Revolution, Philadelphia, 1730–1830* (Chapel Hill: University of North Carolina Press, 2006), 6–7.

74. Susan Branson, *These Fiery Frenchified Dames: Women and Political Culture in Early National Philadelphia* (Philadelphia: University of Pennsylvania Press, 2001).

75. Paul Musselwhite, "'This Infant Borough': The Corporate Political Identity of Eighteenth-Century Norfolk," *Early American Studies* 15 (2017): 801; Paul Musselwhite, *Urban Dreams, Rural Commonwealth: The Rise of Plantation Society in the Chesapeake* (Chicago: University of Chicago Press, 2019), 231.

76. Quoted in Richard Hofstadter, *America at 1750: A Social Portrait* (New York: Vintage, 1973), 157.

77. *A New Voyage to Carolina by John Lawson,* ed. Hugh Talmage Lefler (Chapel Hill: University of North Carolina Press, 1967), 8–10, 13.

78. Emma Hart, *Building Charleston: Town and Society in the Eighteenth-Century British Atlantic World* (Charlottesville: University of Virginia Press, 2010); cf. Kenneth E. Lewis, "The Metropolis and the Backcountry: The Making of a Colonial Landscape on the South Carolina Frontier," *Historical Archaeology* 33 (1999): 3–13.

79. H. Roy Merrins, ed., *The South Carolina Scene: Contemporary Views, 1697–1774* (Columbia: University of South Carolina Press, 1977), 34–36, 60–61. Deerskins data from Jace Weaver, *The Red Atlantic: American Indigenes and the Making of the Modern World, 1000–1927* (Chapel Hill: University of North Carolina Press, 2014), 270 and Kathryn E. Holland Braund, *Deerskins and Duffels: The Creek Indian Trade with Anglo-America, 1685–1815,* 2nd ed. (Lincoln: University of Nebraska Press, 2008), 96 (pack weights), 97–98. Nathaniel Holly recovers the presence of Indian burdeners and other workers in Charleston in "From Itsa'ti to Charlestown," ch. 3.

80. *EAID* 13:265.

81. *EAID* 13:103–6.

82. Merrins, *South Carolina Scene,* 32–33.

83. *A New Voyage to Carolina by John Lawson,* 8–9.

84. Merrins, *South Carolina Scene,* 180.

85. Gordon, "Journal of an Officer," 398; Pelatiah Webster in Merrins, *The South Carolina Scene,* 219–20.

86. David S. Shields, "Mean Streets, Mannered Streets: Charleston," *Common-Place* 3, no. 4 (July 2003).

87. Jennifer Van Horn, *The Power of Objects in Eighteenth-Century America* (Chapel Hill: University of North Carolina Press, 2017), 88–89.

88. George C. Rogers Jr., *Charleston in the Age of the Pinckneys* (Norman: University of Oklahoma Press, 1969), ch. 1.

89. "Journal of Josiah Quincy, Jr.," 456.

90. Hart, *Building Charleston,* 1.

91. Pelatiah Webster in 1765 said there were "5,000 whites and 20,000 blacks" in the city. Another visitor in 1774 reported "9 or 10,000 white inhabitants and about 30,000 black Negro slaves." Luigi Castiglioni gave a lower figure for the population of Charleston, 5,000 whites and 7,000 blacks, shortly after the Revolution. Merrins, *South Carolina Scene,* 219–20, 283; *Luigi Castiglioni's Viaggio,* 163.

92. Daniel H. Usner, *American Indians in Early New Orleans: From Calumet to Raquette* (Baton Rouge: Louisiana State University Press, 2018); Shannon Lee Dawdy, *Building the Devil's Empire: French Colonial New Orleans* (Chicago: University of Chicago Press, 2008) (Natchez at 79).

93. "Robertson's Report of Florida in 1763," in James W. Covington, ed., *The British Meet the Seminoles* (Gainesville: University of Florida Press, 1961), 5; Gordon, "Journal of an Officer," 394.

94. *Penn. Archives,* 1st series, 3:744–45; *EAID,* 3:721–22.

95. Daniel P. Barr, *A Colony Sprung from Hell: Pittsburgh and the Struggle for Authority on the Western Pennsylvania Frontier, 1744–1794* (Kent, OH: Kent State University Press, 2014); American Philosophical Society Library, Robert Woodruff, Journal, 1785–1788, 56; Richard C. Wade, *The Urban Frontier: The Rise of Western Cities, 1790–1830* (Cambridge, MA: Harvard University Press, 1959), 11 (census).

96. Catherine Cangany, *Frontier Seaport: Detroit's Transformation into an Atlantic Entrepôt* (Chicago: University of Chicago Press, 2014); Tiya Miles, *The Dawn of Detroit: A Chronicle of Slavery and Freedom in the City of the Straits* (New York: Free Press, 2017), 7–12; Brian Leigh Dunnigan, "Fortress Detroit, 1701–1826," in *The Sixty Years' War for the Great Lakes, 1754–1814,* ed. David Curtis Skaggs and Larry L. Nelson (East Lansing: Michigan State University Press, 2001), 167–85; Harris, *Historical Atlas of Canada,* 1: plate 41; Karen Marrero, "On the Edge of the West: The Roots and Routes of Detroit's Urban Eighteenth Century," in *Frontier Cities: Encounters at the Crossroads of Empire,* ed. Jay Gitlin,

Barbara Berglund, and Adam Arenson (Philadelphia: University of Pennsylvania Press, 2012), ch. 4.

97. On the French longlot settlement pattern in North America, see Carl J. Ekberg, *French Roots in the Illinois Country: The Mississippi Frontier in Colonial Times* (Urbana: University of Illinois Press, 1998), ch. 1.

98. "Enumeration of Indians within the Northern Department," *DRCHNY* 7:583 (150 Potawatomi warriors, 300 Odawa, 320 Ojibwe); "Bouquet Papers," *Collections of the Michigan Pioneer and Historical Society* 19 (1892): 48; "Croghan's Journal, 1765," in *Early Western Journals, 1748–1765*, ed. Reuben G. Thwaites (Lewisburg, PA: Wennawoods, 1998), 152–53.

99. Cangany, *Frontier Seaport*, ch. 2; population at 64.

100. Jay Gitlin, *The Bourgeois Frontier: French Towns, French Traders, and American Expansion* (New Haven: Yale University Press, 2010), ch. 1; 10, 17; Patricia Cleary, *The World, the Flesh, and the Devil: A History of Colonial St. Louis* (Columbia: University of Missouri Press, 2011), 42–43 (Missouris).

101. *Spain in the Mississippi Valley, 1765–1794: Translations of Materials from the Spanish Archives in the Bancroft Library, University of California, Berkeley*, trans and ed. Lawrence Kinnaird, Annual Report of the American Historical Association for the Year 1945 (Washington, D. C.: Government Printing Office, 1946–49), vol. 3, part 2: 160.

102. Herbert Eugene Bolton, ed., *Athanese De Mézières and the Louisiana-Texas Frontier, 1768–1780* (Cleveland: Arthur H. Clark, 1914), 2:223.

103. James Belich, *Replenishing the Earth: The Settler Revolution and the Rise of the Anglo-World, 1783–1939* (New York: Oxford University Press, 2009), 39.

CHAPTER 2

1. Helen Hornbeck Tanner, "The Land and Water Communication Systems of the Southeastern Indians," in *Powhatan's Mantle: Indians in the Colonial Southeast*, ed. Peter H. Wood, Gregory A. Waselkov, and M. Thomas Hatley (Lincoln: University of Nebraska Press, 1989), 6–20; Paul A. Wallace, *Indian Paths of Pennsylvania* (Harrisburg: Pennsylvania Historical and Museum Commission, 1965).

2. Philip Levy, *Fellow Travelers: Indians and Colonists Contesting the Early American Trail* (Gainesville: University Press of Florida, 2007), 37; James H. Merrell, *Into the American Woods: Negotiators on the Pennsylvania Frontier* (New York: W. W. Norton, 1999), ch. 3.

3. *Penn. Archives*, 4th series, 2:520, 939; 3:11, 362.

4. *Penn. Archives*, 4th series, 2:659, 956.

5. For example, in 1754, succeeding to the role of Half King, the Iroquois League's representative in the Ohio country, the Oneida chief Scarouady passed through Philadelphia on his way to Onondaga, the central council fire of the Six Nations. *Penn. Archives* 1st series, 2:114; 4th series, 2:314. When the British ransomed the niece of the Cherokee chief Attakullakulla from the Miamis, who had held her captive in the Illinois country, she canoed down the Mississippi, then sailed around the Florida peninsula and up the Atlantic to Charleston; from there she traveled overland by trading paths back to the Cherokee towns. Christina Snyder, *Slavery in Indian Country: The Changing Face of Captivity in Early America* (Cambridge, MA: Harvard University Press, 2010), 194; H. Roy Merrins, ed., *The South Carolina Scene: Contemporary Views, 1697–1774* (Columbia: University of South Carolina Press, 1977), 242.

6. Richmond P. Bond, *Queen Anne's American Kings* (Oxford: The Clarendon Press, 1952), 40–41.

7. Daniel H. Usner, *American Indians in Early New Orleans: From Calumet to Raquette* (Baton Rouge: Louisiana State Press, 2018), 8–9, 19; Richard N. Ellis and Charlie R. Steen, eds., "An Indian Delegation in France," *Journal of the Illinois State Historical Society* 67 (1974): 385–405.

8. Kate Fullagar, *The Warrior, the Voyager, and the Artist: Three Lives in an Age of Empire* (New Haven: Yale University Press, 2020), 102–5.

9. Isabel Thompson Kelsay, *Joseph Brant, 1743–1807: Man of Two Worlds* (Syracuse: Syracuse University Press, 1984), 160, 175, 181.

10. C. A. Weslager, *The Delaware Indians: A History* (New Brunswick, NJ: Rutgers University Press, 1972), 197–202.

11. *EAID* 1: ch. 9; Walking Purchase deed at 457–59; *Penn. Archives*, 1st series, 1:541-43; 3rd series, 1:86–87; Charles Thomson, *An Enquiry into the Causes of the Alienation of the Delaware and Shawnee Indians from the British Interest* (London: J. Wilkie, 1759; reprint, Philadelphia: J. Campbell, 1867), 33–35.

12. *EAID* 1:415; *Col. Recs. Penn.* 4:54. The Delawares did, however, offer condolences for the recent death of Governor Patrick Gordon.

13. Jay Gitlin, *The Bourgeois Frontier: French Towns, French Traders, and American Expansion* (New Haven: Yale University Press, 2010), 18.

14. H. Frank Eshelman, *Annals of the Susquehannocks and Other Indian Tribes of Pennsylvania, 1500–1763* (1908; reprint, Lewisburg, PA: Wennawoods, 2000), 139.

15. Michael Witgen, *An Infinity of Nations: How the Native New World Shaped America* (Philadelphia: University of Pennsylvania Press, 2012), 244–46, 251–60; Pekka Hämäläinen, *Lakota America: A New History of Indigenous Power* (New Haven: Yale University Press, 2019), 11–12; Gary Clayton Anderson, *Kinsmen of Another Kind: Dakota-White Relations in the Upper Mississippi Valley, 1650–1862* (Lincoln: University of Nebraska Press, 1984), 35; *DRCHNY* 9:609 (twenty-two arrows).

16. Hämäläinen, *Lakota America*, 74–75, 83: Gwen Westerman and Bruce White, *Mni Sota Makoce: The Land of the Dakota* (Minneapolis: Minnesota Historical Press, 2012), 65; Brett Rushforth, *Bonds of Alliance: Indigenous and Atlantic Slaveries in New France* (Chapel Hill: University of North Carolina Press, 2010), 193 ("halfway across the world").

17. Paul L. Stevens, "Wabasha Visits Governor Carleton, 1776: New Light on a Legendary Episode of Dakota-British Diplomacy on the Great Lake Frontier," *Michigan Historical Review* 16 (Spring 1990): 21–48; Correspondence and Papers of Governor General Sir Frederick Haldimand, British Museum, London, Additional Manuscripts, 21757:289 ("uncommon abilities"), 332; 21771:108–9 ("prince").

18. William L. McDowell Jr., ed., *Documents Relating to Indian Affairs 1750–1754* (Columbia: South Carolina Department of Archives and History, 1958), 517 (500 miles); *EAID* 5:115; Thomas A. Strohfeldt, "Warriors in Williamsburg: The Cherokee Presence in Virginia's Eighteenth Century Capital," *Journal of Cherokee Studies* 11 (1986): 7.

19. William L. McDowell Jr., ed., *Journals of the Commissioners of the Indian Trade, 1710–1718* (Columbia: South Carolina Department of Archives and History, 1955), 168; *EAID* 14:39.

20. *EAID* 14:151–52.

21. Greg O'Brien, *Choctaws in a Revolutionary Age, 1750–1830* (Lincoln: University of Nebraska Press, 2002), ch. 4 ("great civility" at 66); Greg O'Brien, "The Conqueror Meets the Unconquered: Negotiating Cultural Boundaries on the Post-Revolutionary Southern Frontier," *Journal of Southern History* 67 (2001): 50, 67; William P. Palmer, ed., *Calendar of Virginia State Papers* (Richmond: Virginia State Library, 1875–93), 4:268; *Charlestown Evening Gazette*, Feb. 18, 20–21, 24–25, 27, Mar. 1–4, 6–8, 10, 13–14, 16–18, 1786; Mary Sarah Bilder, "Without Doors: Native Nations and the Convention," unpublished ms.

22. *Penn. Archives*, 1st series, 2:133.

23. Mary W. Helms, *Ulysses' Sail: An Ethnographic Odyssey of Power, Knowledge, and Geographical Distance* (Princeton, NJ: Princeton University Press, 1988), 80–94; O'Brien, "The Conqueror Meets the Unconquered," 51.

24. Quoted in Merrell, *Into the American Woods*, 130.

25. Merrell, *Into the American Woods*, 146.

26. Levy, *Fellow Travelers*, 65.

27. *Penn. Archives*, 1st series, 2:634 ("good mind to Scalp"), 777; 4th series, 2:338, 344–45, 709.

28. *Penn. Archives*, 1st series, 3:405, 554–55, 692; 4th series, 2:807–8.

29. *Penn. Archives*, 4th series, 2:790.

30. *EAID* 18:221; Louise Phelps Kellogg, ed., *Frontier Advance on the Upper Ohio, 1778–1779* (Madison: Wisconsin State Historical Society, 1916), 306–7, 384–85, 465.

31. Knox to Kirkland, Mar. 7, 1792; Kirkland to Knox, Mar. 10, 1792, PWD.

32. *Penn. Archives*, 4th series, 3:221–22, 239-40, 321, 328-29.

33. *Penn. Archives*, 1st series, 3:278–79.

34. *Penn. Archives*, 1st series, 12:300.

35. Thomas S. Abler, *Cornplanter: Chief Warrior of the Allegany Senecas* (Syracuse: Syracuse University Pres, 2007), 73, 158, 185; *Chainbreaker: The Revolutionary War Memoirs of Governor Blacksnake*, ed. Thomas S. Abler (Lincoln: University of Nebraska Press, 1989), 160, 174–76. Francisco de Miranda traveled the same route by "a coach which leaves periodically almost every day of the week and in which the passengers enjoy the advantage of promptitude in traveling and the cheapness and convenience of taking their baggage with them." *The New Democracy in America: Travels of Francisco de Miranda in the United States, 1783–84*, ed. John Z. Ezell, trans. Justin P. Wood (Norman: University of Oklahoma Press, 1963), 69. The coach left from the Indian Queen Hotel and could make it to New York in one day. *Federal Gazette and Philadelphia Daily Advertiser,* June 14, 1794, 4. Before the Revolution the New York–Philadelphia stage ran three mornings a week in the summer months and cost 20s. Patrick McRobert, *Tour Through Part of the North Provinces of America* (Edinburgh: Printed for the author, 1776), 56.

36. Thomas W. Cowger and Mitch Caver, *Piominko, Chickasaw Leader* (Ada, OK: Chickasaw Press, 2017), 66–67; *New York Morning Post,* Nov. 13, 1789, 2; *PGW, Pres.* 4:262; 5:214–15.

37. For example: Captn. John Woods acct. for Expences &c. for the Indians, Settled Jan. 6, 1788; Knox to Kirkland, Mar. 7, 1792; Kirkland to Knox, Mar. 10, 1792; Knox to Isaac Craig, May 8, 1793; Timothy Pickering to William Blount, Jan 20, 1796; Isreal Chapin Jr., Estimate of Expenses of Sundry Mohawks, Feb. 1, 1796; Craig to Samuel Hodgdon, Oct. 24, 1796 (?); Peter Hagner to James McHenry, Mar. 15, 1798; William Simmons to McHenry, Mar. 20, 1798, all in PWD.

38. *Penn. Archives*, 4th series, 1:377; 2:790.

39. *Penn. Archives*, 4th series, 3:134.

40. *EAID* 4:266; 13:173. Similarly, Teedyuscung swept clean the meeting room of the Pennsylvania State House with a metaphorical wing; *EAID* 2:401, 3:343.

41. Addison quote in Joseph Roach, *Cities of the Dead: Circum-Atlantic Performance* (New York: Columbia University Press, 1996), 15–16.

42. *Gentleman's Progress: The Itinerarium of Dr. Alexander Hamilton, 1744,* ed. Carl Bridenbaugh (Chapel Hill: University of North Carolina Press, 1948), 112. On the Iroquois delegates to the conference, see *Pennsylvania Gazette,* July 19, Aug. 14, 1744.

43. Patrick Spero, *Frontier Rebels: The Fight for Independence in the American West, 1765–1776* (New York: W. W. Norton, 2018), 34; American Philosophical Society Library, Robert Woodruff, Journal, 1785–1788, 56 ("largest inland Town").

44. Witham Marshe, "Journal of the Treaty Held with the Six Nations," in *The Lancaster Treaty of 1744 with Related Documents,* ed. James H. Merrell (Boston: Bedford/St. Martin's, 2008), 110.

45. *Massachusetts Mercury,* May 3, 1793, 1, reprinted in *The Diary or Loudon's Register,* New York, May 10, 1793, 2, and *Massachusetts Spy,* May 16, 1793, 4.

46. *Federal Gazette,* Apr. 12, 1792, 3; *Henry Wansey and His American Journal, 1794,* ed. David John Jeremy (Philadelphia: American Philosophical Society, 1970), 116–17.

47. Peter Silver, *Our Savage Neighbors: How Indian War Transformed Early America* (New York: W. W. Norton, 2008), 98, 135, 159–60.

48. Louise Phelps Kellogg, ed., *Early Narratives of the Northwest, 1634–1699* (New York: Scribner's Sons, 1917), 240, 242.

49. Benjamin Franklin, *Two Tracts: Information to Those Who Would Remove to America, and Remarks Concerning the Savages of North America,* 2nd ed. (London: John Stockdale, 1784), 33–34.

50. John Heckewelder, *History, Manners, and Customs of the Indian Nations Who Once Inhabited Pennsylvania and the Neighboring States* (Philadelphia: Historical Society of Pennsylvania, 1876; reprint, New York: New York Times and Arno Press, 1971), 189–90.

51. Peter Charles Hoffer, *Sensory Worlds in Early America* (Baltimore: Johns Hopkins University Press, 2003); Martin Jay, "In the Realm of the Senses: An Introduction," *American Historical Review* 116 (Apr. 2011): 307–15 (quote at 307); Sophia Rosenfeld, "On Being Heard: A Case for Paying Attention to the Historical Ear," *American Historical Review* 116 (Apr. 2011): 316–334; Mark S. R. Jenner, "Follow Your Nose? Smell, Smelling, and Their Histories," *American Historical Review* 116 (Apr. 2011): 335–51; Richard Cullen Rath, *How Early America Sounded* (Ithaca: Cornell University Press, 2003). The senses act as filters between the outside world and the mind, and do so according to culture and experience. Things may look, sound, and smell the same to everyone, but, as Emily Cockayne asks, "what made eyes water, ears ache, noses wrinkle, fingers withdraw and mouths close?" Emily Cockayne, *Hubbub: Filth, Noise, and Stench in England, 1600–1770* (New Haven: Yale University Press, 2007), quote at 21.

52. *The Collected Writings of Samson Occom, Mohegan,* ed. Joanna Brooks (New York: Oxford University Press, 2006), 266–67.

53. Diaries of John Adams, Massachusetts Historical Society, diary # 2: Monday, March 18 [i.e., 19?], 1759.

54. *Penn. Archives,* 1st series, 1:69.

55. Chrestien Le Clercq, *New Relation of Gaspesia, with the Customs and Relation of the Gaspesian Indians,* ed. and trans. William F. Ganong (Toronto: Champlain Society, 1910), 311.

56. *The Works of John Adams,* ed. Charles Francis Adams (Boston: Little, Brown, 1850), 2:353 (diary entry, Aug. 23, 1774).

57. Patrick Campbell, in Charles M. Johnston, ed., *The Valley of the Six Nations: A Collections of Documents on the Indian Lands of the Grand River* (Toronto: Champlain Society, 1964), 61.

58. *WJP* 13:202.

59. *Citizen Soldier: The Revolutionary War Journal of Joseph Bloomfield,* ed. Mark E. Lender and James Kirby Martin (Newark: New Jersey Historical Society, 1992), 91.

60. Timothy J. Shannon, *Indians and Colonists at the Crossroads of Empire: The Albany Congress of 1754* (Ithaca: Cornell University Press, 2000), 138–39; Beverly McAnear, ed., "Personal Accounts of the Albany Congress of 1754," *Mississippi Valley Historical Review* 39 (1953): 742 ("speak Indian"); *DRCHNY* 6:867–68 ("large ears"). An Indian named Tom Wileman who came to Albany with several "French Indians" the following year was considered "very fit to get Intelligence for them" because he spoke both Dutch and English; *Penn. Archives,* 1st series, 2:350.

61. *Penn. Archives,* 1st series, 2:724; 3:397.

62. *Penn. Archives,* 1st series, 3:107 (Denny); 319 (Croghan).

63. *Penn. Archives,* 1st series, 3:236; 4th series, 2:845–46 (unprecedented); *DRCHNY* 7:289–94; James H. Merrell, "'I Desire All That I Have Said May Be Taken Down Aright': Revisiting Teedyuscung's 1756 Treaty Council Speeches," *William and Mary Quarterly,* 3rd series, 63 (2004): 777–826.

64. *DRCHNY* 9:609.

65. Céline Carayon, *Eloquence Embodied: Nonverbal Communication Among French and Indigenous Peoples in the Americas* (Chapel Hill: University of North Carolina Press, 2019), 150–51; *Col. Recs. Penn.* 1:586.

66. Bond, *Queen Anne's American Kings,* 29.

67. Rena Vassar, ed., "Some Short Remarks on the Indian Trade in the Charikees and in Management Thereof Since the Year 1717," *Ethnohistory* 8 (1961): 417.

68. Edward Wheelock, ed., *Penhallow's Indian Wars: A Facsimile Reprint of the First Edition, Printed in Boston in 1726* (Freeport, NY: Books for Libraries Press, 1971), 98; *Boston Gazette,* Sept. 9, 1723, 2.

69. Excerpt from the *Virginia Gazette* in McDowell, ed., *Documents Relating to Indian Affairs 1750–1754*: 151, 154; *EAID* 5:113–14, 121; Strohfeldt, "Warriors in Williamsburg," 4, 8; "Diary of John Blair," *William and Mary Quarterly,* 1st series, 8 (July 1899), 1–17, quotes at 9–11.

70. *Virginia Gazette,* Nov. 17, 1752, 2; Strohfeldt, "Warriors in Williamsburg," 9.

71. David H. Corkran, *The Cherokee Frontier: Conflict and Survival, 1740–62* (Norman: University of Oklahoma Press, 1962), 67; *EAID* 5:258 ("caressed and courted").

72. *Col. Recs. Penn.* 2:565–66; 2:603.

73. *Penn. Archives,* 1st series, 1:233–34.

74. Merrell, *Into the American Woods,* 167.

75. *Col. Recs. Penn.* 3:572.

76. *EAID* 1:431.

77. *Col. Recs. Penn.* 4:79; *Penn. Archives,* 4th series, 1:521, 842 (Thomas quote).

78. Eric Hinderaker, *The Two Hendricks: Unraveling a Mohawk Mystery* (Cambridge, MA: Harvard University Press, 2010), 252–53; *Penn. Archives,* 4th series, 2:716 (Albany); *Col. Recs. Penn.* 6:243.

79. *WJP* 8:615–16; *Col. Recs. Penn.* 10:55.

80. *Penn. Archives,* 1st series, 3:286.

81. *Penn. Archives,* 1st series, 3:456–57, 461. On occasion, Teedyuscung tried to set the time and place, as well as the agenda, for meetings in Philadelphia. In March 1762, he asked Sir William Johnson to come to the city and told the governor, "Turn your face to the Road that comes from Philadelphia, & in fourteen days you shall see your Brother coming in to look at you Work." Johnson put him off and persuaded him to meet at Easton, a more convenient and less expensive location about seventy miles north of Philadelphia. *Penn. Archives,* 1st series, 4:75, 77, 78, 81.

82. *DRCHNY* 4:876 (Robert Livingston told the Board of Trade).

83. Tracy Neal Leavelle, *The Catholic Calumet: Colonial Conversion in French and Indian North America* (Philadelphia: University of Pennsylvania Press, 2012), 1–2; Robert Michael Morrissey, *Empire by Collaboration: Indians, Colonists, and Governments in Colonial Illinois Country* (Philadelphia: University of Pennsylvania Press, 2015), 136–38; Usner, *American Indians in Early New Orleans,* 17–18.

84. *At a Conference Held at Deerfield in the County of Hampshire, the Twenty Seventh Day of August, 1735* (Boston, 1735), Newberry Library, Chicago (https://archive.org/details/Ayer_154_M4_M4_1735), 2.

85. Shannon, *Indians and Colonists at the Crossroads of Empire,* 129.

86. *Col. Recs. Penn.* 7:216–17.

87. Serena R. Zabin, *Dangerous Economies: Status and Commerce in Imperial New York* (Philadelphia: University of Philadelphia Press, 2009); Ellen Hartigan-O'Connor, *The Ties That Buy: Women and Commerce in Revolutionary America* (Philadelphia: University of Pennsylvania Press, 2009).

88. *Col. Recs. Penn.* 4:86.

89. *Penn. Archives,* 4th series, 1:795, 815–16; William A Starna, "The Diplomatic Career of Canasatego," in *Friends and Enemies in Penn's Woods: Indians, Colonists, and the Racial Construction of Pennsylvania,* ed. William A. Pencak and Daniel K. Richter (University Park: Pennsylvania State University Press, 2004), 146 (famine).

90. *Col. Recs. Penn.* 8:701–2; *Penn. Archives,* 4th series, 3:135–36.

91. *EAID* 13:161, 252; William L. McDowell Jr., ed., *Documents Relating to Indian Affairs 1754–1765* (Columbia: South Carolina Department of Archives and History, 1970), 557.

92. *EAID* 2:202; Paul A. Wallace, *Conrad Weiser, 1697–1760: Friend of Colonist and Mohawk* (Philadelphia: University of Pennsylvania Press, 1945), 279–85; *New-York Weekly Journal,* Aug. 17, 1749, 3; *Boston Gazette,* Aug. 29, 1749, 1.

93. *Col. Recs. Penn.* 6:344 (Scarouady); Reuben G. Thwaites, ed., *Early Western Journals, 1748–1765* (Lewisburg, PA: Wennawoods, 1998), 209 (Shamokin Daniel).

94. *Col. Recs. Penn.* 15: 229; Captn. John Woods acct. for Expences &c. for the Indians, Settled Jan. 6, 1788, PWD.

95. Merrins, *The South Carolina Scene,* 220.

96. *South Carolina Gazette,* May 27–June 3, 1732, in *EAID* 13:149; *New England Weekly Journal,* July 31, 1732: 1–2.

97. *South Carolina Gazette,* July 16, 1737, 3; *EAID* 13:163–65.

98. Hennig Cohen, *The South Carolina Gazette, 1732–1775* (Columbia: University of South Carolina Press, 1953), 92, 96, 107–20; George C. Rogers Jr., *Charleston in the Age of the Pinckneys* (Norman: University of Oklahoma Press, 1969), 110.

99. Joshua Piker, *Okfuskee: A Creek Town in Colonial America* (Cambridge, MA: Harvard University Press, 2004), 27–37, 48–56, 107.

100. Claudio Saunt, *A New Order of Things: Property, Power, and the Transformation of the Creek Indians, 1733–1816* (Cambridge: Cambridge University Press, 1999), 11, 14–17.

101. *EAID* 2:251; John T. Juricek, *Colonial Georgia and the Creeks: Anglo-Indian Diplomacy on the Southern Frontier, 1733–1763* (Gainesville: University Press of Florida, 2010), 213; John Walton Caughey, *McGillivray of the Creeks* (Norman: University of Oklahoma Press, 1938), 6; Robbie Etheridge, "Creeks and Americans in the Age of Washington," in *George Washington's South*, ed. Tamara Harvey and Greg O'Brien (Gainesville: University Press of Florida, 2004), 278–79.

102. Juricek, *Colonial Georgia and the Creeks*, 218–19; Edward J. Cashin, *Henry Ellis and the Transformation of British North America* (Athens: University of Georgia Press, 1997), 88–89.

103. *EAID* 14:44; *South Carolina Gazette*, Feb. 20, 1758, 2.

104. *South Carolina Gazette*, Aug. 26, 1774, 10.

105. Claudio Saunt, *West of the Revolution: An Uncommon History of 1776* (New York: W. W. Norton, 2014), 188–203.

106. Caughey, *McGillivray of the Creeks*, 65, 72.

107. Caughey, *McGillivray of the Creeks*, 13–17, 62; Saunt, *A New Order of Things*, esp. ch. 3.

108. Walter Lowrie and Matthew St. Clair Clarke, eds., *American State Papers: Foreign Relations* (Washington, DC: Gales and Seaton, 1832), 1:278–79; Caughey, *McGillivray of the Creeks*, 25, 75–76; Saunt, *New Order of Things*, 78.

109. William S. Coker and Thomas D. Watson, *Indian Traders of the Southeastern Spanish Borderlands: Panton, Leslie and Company and John Forbes and Company, 1783–1847* (Pensacola: University of West Florida Press, 1986); Saunt, *New Order of Things*, 75–79; Kathryn E. Holland Braund, *Deerskins and Duffels: The Creek Indian Trade with Anglo-America, 1685–1815*, 2nd edn. (Lincoln: University of Nebraska Press, 2009), ch. 9.

110. *PGW, Pres.* 3:124; 4:475, 530; Henry Knox Papers, Massachusetts Historical Society, reel 53: 164, p. 10.

111. Caughey, *McGillivray of the Creeks*, 261–63; *PGW, Pres.* 3:134 (Knox). On debates about Indian nationhood in the early Republic, see Gregory Ablavsky, "Species of Sovereignty: Native Nationhood, the United States, and International Law, 1783–1795," *Journal of American History* 106 (Dec. 2019): 591–613.

112. Carolyn Thomas Foreman, "Alexander McGillivray, Emperor of the Creeks," *Chronicles of Oklahoma* 7 (Mar. 1929): 114; William Marinus Willett, *A Narrative of the Military Actions of Colonel Marinus Willett, Taken Chiefly from His Own Manuscript* (New York: G. & C. & H. Carvill, 1831), 110.

113. *The Diaries of George Washington*, ed. Donald Jackson and Dorothy Twohig (Charlottesville: University Press of Virginia, 1976–79), 6:85; *Penn. Archives*, 11:711.

114. *The Federal Gazette and Philadelphia Daily Advertiser*, July 14, 1790, 2; *Journals of the Council of State of Virginia*, 5:198–99; *Narrative of the Military Actions of Colonel Marinus Willett*, 111–12.

115. *Pennsylvania Journal*, July 21, 1790, 3; *The City Gazette* (Charleston), Aug. 17, 1790, 2; *The Federal Gazette and Philadelphia Daily Advertiser*, July 19, 1790, 2; *Pennsylvania Gazette* (Philadelphia), July 21, 1790; *Pennsylvania Journal and the Weekly Advertiser* (Philadelphia), July 21, 1790; *Penn Archives*, 4th series, 4:103 (formal welcome).

116. *Narrative of the Military Actions of Colonel Marinus Willett*, 112.

117. Caughey, *McGillivray of the Creeks*, 279.

118. *Narrative of the Military Actions of Colonel Marinus Willett*, 112–13; *The Federal Gazette and Philadelphia Daily Advertiser*, July 23, 1790, 3; Aug. 6, 1790, 2; *New York Daily Gazette*, July 21, 1790, 489; July 22, 1790, 695; July 27, 1790, 71; *Columbian Centinel*, July 31, 1790, 166; *Carlisle Gazette*, Aug. 8, 1790, 2; *The Pennsylvania Packet and Daily Advertiser*, July 29, 1790, 2.

119. *New-York Journal,* July 30, 1790, 3.
120. Simon P. Newman, *Parades and the Politics of the Street: Festive Culture in the Early American Republic* (Philadelphia: University of Pennsylvania Press, 1997).
121. J. Leitch Wright Jr., *William Augustus Bowles, Director General of the Creek Nation* (Athens: University of Georgia Press, 1967), 47–55, 73–78; National Archives, UK, Foreign Office Records, F.O. 4/8:410–12; 9:5–17, 69–74, 81–82; 11:181–82, 208; 14:295–300; 24:423–49; Colonial Office Records, C.O. 42/68: 279–304; *ASPIA* 1:246–51, 255; *The* (London) *Times,* Mar. 17, 1791, 3, col. 2 (dined with Spanish ambassador).
122. Charles A. Weeks, *Paths to a Middle Ground: The Diplomacy of Natchez, Boukfouka, Nogales and San Fernando de las Barrancas, 1791–1795* (Tuscaloosa: University of Alabama Press, 2005); Usner, *American Indians in Early New Orleans,* 36–37.
123. *Moreau de St. Méry's American Journey, 1793–1798,* ed. and trans. Kenneth Roberts and Anna K. Roberts (Garden City, NY: Doubleday, 1947), 276.
124. The Papers of Samuel Kirkland, Dartmouth College, Rauner Library, MS-867; Diary, May 1790–Feb. 17, 1791, 33–38; *The Journals of Samuel Kirkland,* ed. Walter Pilkington (Clinton, NY: Hamilton College, 1980), 208–9.
125. *Penn. Archives,* 4th series, 4:160, 166.
126. Colin G. Calloway, *The Victory with No Name: The Native American Defeat of the First American Army* (New York: Oxford University Press, 2015).
127. *ASPIA* 1:203; Clarence E. Carter, ed., *The Territorial Papers of the United States,* Vol. 4, *The Territory South of the River Ohio, 1790–1796* (Washington, DC: Government Printing Office, 1934), 111, 116; Stan W. Hoig, *The Cherokees and Their Chiefs in the Wake of Empire* (Lafayetteville: University of Arkansas Press, 1998), 75.
128. *ASPIA* 1:245.
129. *ASPIA* 1:226, 228–29, 245, 249.
130. Timothy Pickering Papers, Massachusetts Historical Society, reel 61: 307 ("all convenient speed"); *The Papers of Alexander Hamilton Digital Edition,* ed. Harold C. Syrett (Charlottesville: University of Virginia Press, Rotunda, 2011), 11:373.
131. *Independent Gazetteer* (Philadelphia), March 17, 1792, 3; *Pennsylvania Journal,* Mar. 21, 1792, 3.
132. *ASPIA* 1:229; Alan Taylor, *The Divided Ground: Indians, Settlers, and the Northern Borderland of the American Revolution* (New York: Alfred Knopf, 2006), 271 (quoting Kirkland to Knox, Jan. 5, 1791); *The Diary of Elizabeth Drinker,* ed. Elaine Forman Crane et al. (Boston: Northeastern University Press, 1991), 1:477; *Boston Gazette,* Apr. 16, 1792, 1; *Daily Advertiser* (New York), Mar. 17, 1792, 2; *Middlesex* (Connecticut) *Gazette,* Mar. 24, 1792, 3; *Spooner's Vermont Journal,* Apr. 3, 1792, 2; *Hampshire Gazette,* Apr. 4, 1792, 3; *Salem Gazette,* Apr. 3, 1792, 2.
133. *Claypoole's Daily Advertiser,* Mar. 27, 1792, 2; *General Advertiser,* Mar. 28, 1792, 2.
134. "We hear there are just published and to be sold by William Young, at the southwest corner of Chestnut and Second Streets, price 1-8 of a dollar: Minutes of Debates in Council on the banks of the Ottawa river, commonly called the Miamia of the Lake; said to be held there in November last, by several Indian Nations, after defeating the army of the United States." *Daily Advertiser,* Mar. 17, 1792, 2.
135. Kelsay, *Joseph Brant,* 459–63; Taylor, *Divided Ground,* 253–65, 275; William L. Stone, *Life of Joseph Brant–Thayendanegea* (New York: George Dearborn & Co., 1838), 2:319–26; *ASPIA* 1:228; *PGW, Pres.* 9:588–89; 10:310–12, 491.
136. *Albany Gazette,* June 14, 1792, 2; Kelsay, *Joseph Brant,* 465–68 ("jaunt" at 465).
137. John Stagg to Samuel Hodgdon, Feb. 13, 1793, PWD.
138. Henry Knox asked William Blount "to persuade the principal Chiefs of the Cherokees to repair to this place," and Blount sent a message to Hanging Maw, a principal chief of the Overhill Cherokees, that President Washington desired to shake them by the hands in Philadelphia; "he will direct that you shall be comfortably accommodated on your way, and farther, upon your arrival here, he flatters himself, that, by being face to face, the remembrance of all former injuries will be done away, and that we may establish a

firm and lasting peace and friendship." Carter, *Territorial Papers of the United States,* 4:279; *ASPIA* 1:431.

139. *The American Minerva,* June 9, 1794, 3. Englishman Henry Wansey was in town that summer and saw the delegates. He intended to make their acquaintance, tell them he was a subject of King George, smoke the calumet with them and procure a belt of wampum, but he was so shocked to hear that one of them boasted of having shed human blood enough to swim in "that I never wished to see them any more." Instead he resorted to talking about the evils of drink among Indians. *Henry Wansey and His American Journal,* 116–17.

140. *The Daily Advertiser* (New York), July 16, 1794, 2; (Charleston) *City Gazette and Daily Advertiser,* Aug. 4, 1794, 3; Aug. 8, 1794, 3.

141. *PGW, Pres.* 19:333; Dorothy Twohig, ed., *The Journal of the Proceedings of the President, 1793–1797* (Charlottesville: University of Virginia Press, 1981), 312.

142. Cowger and Caver, *Piominko,* 96–101.

143. Timothy Pickering Papers, 35:208.

144. Pickering to Blount, Jan. 20, 1796, PWD.

145. *ASPIA* 2:579; John Sugden, *Blue Jacket: Warrior of the Shawnees* (Lincoln: University of Nebraska Press, 2000), 213; "Letters of Colonel John Francis Hamtramck," *Collections of the Michigan Pioneer Historical Society* 34 (1904): 739 (quote).

146. *Anthony Wayne, A Name in Arms: The Wayne-Knox-Pickering-McHenry Correspondence,* ed. Richard C. Knopf (Pittsburgh: University of Pittsburgh Press, 1960), 532; William Heath, *William Wells and the Struggle for the Old Northwest* (Norman: University of Oklahoma Press, 2015), 237.

147. Sugden, *Blue Jacket,* 214–15.

148. Kelsay, *Joseph Brant,* 576–77.

149. Little Turtle was the celebrity, but the Wyandot chief Tarhe, or the Crane, also merited attention. Secretary of War McHenry ordered "a sorrel horse for the Wyandot Chief (Crane) now in this city." McHenry and Hodgdon to John Harris, Jan. 25, 1798, PWD.

150. *Mirror* (Concord, NH), Mar. 13, 1798, 3–4.

151. *Courier of New Hampshire,* Dec. 15, 1798, 2. In New York, according to the press, they were astonished and indignant to discover that French emissaries had represented Americans "to be weak and unwarlike and to live in small huts like themselves."

152. James Wilkinson had apparently promised him an annual stipend. Secretary McHenry questioned the wisdom of such a move, as no individual chief had been given a stipend before and Wolf's Friend was from a faction not yet friendly to the United States; he recommended giving an equal gift to the chiefs of each faction. A Seneca chief who was in the city at the same time was looking to collect on gifts that had been promised to that nation. James McHenry to John Adams, Jan. 27, 1799, PWD.

CHAPTER 3

1. Daniel Ingram, *Indians and British Outposts in Eighteenth-Century America* (Gainesville: University Press of Florida, 2012).

2. George Harwood Phillips, "Indians in Los Angeles, 1781–1875: Economic Integration, Social Disintegration," *Pacific Historical Review* 49 (1980): 427–51.

3. Dana Velesco Murillo, *Urban Indians in a Silver City: Zacatecas, Mexico, 1546–1810* (Stanford: Stanford University Press, 2016); Laurent Corbeil, *The Motions Beneath: Indigenous Migrations of the Urban Frontier of New Spain* (Tucson: University of Arizona Press, 2018); J. H. Elliott, *Empires of the Atlantic World: Britain and Spain in America 1492–1830* (New Haven: Yale University Press, 2006), 94 (Potosí population). More broadly, Dana Velasco Murillo, Mark Lentz, and Margarita R. Ochoa, eds., *City Indians in Spain's American Empire: Urban Indigenous Society in Colonial Mesoamerica and Andean South America, 1530–1810* (Eastbourne, UK: Sussex Academic Press, 2012).

4. Nan Wolverton, "'A Precarious Living': Basket Making and Related Crafts Among New England Indians," in *Reinterpreting New England Indians and the Colonial Experience,* ed.

Colin G. Calloway and Neal Salisbury (Boston: Colonial Society of Massachusetts, 2003), 341–68. See also Sarah H. Hill, *Weaving New Worlds: Southeastern Cherokee Women and Their Basketry* (Chapel Hill: University of North Carolina Press, 1997), 55–60.

5. Daniel H. Usner Jr., "American Indians in Colonial New Orleans," in *Powhatan's Mantle: Indians in the Colonial Southeast*, ed. Peter H. Wood, Gregory A. Waselkov, and M. Thomas Hatley (Lincoln: University of Nebraska Press, 1989), 104.

6. Alden T. Vaughan and Deborah A. Rosen, eds., *New England and Middle Atlantic Laws*, in *EAID* 17 ("knock at the dore" at 89); Daniel Gookin, *Historical Collections of the Indians in New England* (1792; reprint, n.p.: Towtaid, 1970), 60–62.

7. *EAID* 17:509.

8. Susannah Shaw Romney, *New Netherland Connections: Intimate Networks and Atlantic Ties in Seventeenth-Century America* (Chapel Hill: University of North Carolina Press, 2014), 169–71.

9. Allen W. Trelease, *Indian Affairs in Colonial New York: The Seventeenth Century* (Ithaca: Cornell University Press, 1960), 219.

10. Thomas E. Burke Jr., *Mohawk Frontier: The Dutch Community of Schenectady, New York, 1661–1710*, 2nd ed. (Albany: State University of New York Press, 2009), 145.

11. *DRCHNY* 3:261, 473, 476, 510.

12. *DRCHNY* 5:65, 587.

13. *DRCHNY* 1:182.

14. Vaughan and Rosen, *New England and Middle Atlantic Laws*, 499–500. On baking for the Native American market, see Romney, *New Netherland Connections*, 155–57 ("contraband cookies" at 157).

15. Quoted in Burke, *Mohawk Frontier*, 142.

16. *WJP* 4:84, 147–48.

17. Burke, *Mohawk Frontier*, ch. 4, quote at 145–46.

18. Daniel K. Richter, *The Ordeal of the Longhouse: The Peoples of the Iroquois League in the Era of European Colonization* (Chapel Hill: University of North Carolina Press, 1992), 168.

19. *Gentleman's Progress: The Itinerarium of Dr. Alexander Hamilton, 1744*, ed. Carl Bridenbaugh (Chapel Hill: University of North Carolina Press, 1948), 65.

20. William L. McDowell Jr., ed., *Colonial Records of South Carolina: Documents Relating to Indian Affairs, 1750–1754* (Columbia: South Carolina Department of Archives and History, 1958), 92.

21. *The Papers of Benjamin Franklin*, ed. Leonard W. Labaree (New Haven: Yale University Press, 1959–), 5:122: *Col. Recs. Penn.* 6: 276 (Hendrick quote), 280–81.

22. Julian Ursyn Niemcewicz, *Under Their Vine and Fig Tree: Travels Through America in 1797–1799, 1805 with Some Further Account of Life in New Jersey*, ed. and trans. Metchie J. E. Budka (Elizabeth, NJ: Grassman, 1965), 187.

23. Gabriela Ramos, "'*Mi Tierra*': Indigenous Migrants and Their Hometowns in the Colonial Andes," in *City Indians in Spain's American Empire: Urban Indigenous Society in Colonial Mesoamerica and Andean South America, 1530–1810*, ed. Dana Velasco Murillo, Mark Lentz, and Margarita R. Ochoa (Eastbourne, UK: Sussex Academic Press, 2012), 136.

24. *JR* 6:237; 7:265; 9:107; 10:33; 11:11, 17, 49, 81; 12:39–57, 111–13, 255 ("filled with little Huron girls"); 13:9; 14:127, 231; 19:39–57; 22:183–99; 24: 119-21; 25:225–45.

25. *JR* 16:29, 33; 18:169; 19:9–25, 39–57; 20:239 ("all sick persons"); 22:183–99; 49:199.

26. *DRCHNY* 9:687; Richter, *Ordeal of the Longhouse*, 197.

27. Gilles Havard, *The Great Peace of Montreal of 1701: French-Native Diplomacy in the Seventeenth Century* (Montreal: McGill-Queens University Press, 2001), 127; Alain Beaulieu and Roland Viau, *The Great Peace: Chronicle of a Diplomatic Saga* (Montreal: Éditions Libre Expression, 2001), 60, 66; Brett Rushforth, "Insinuating Empire: Indians, Smugglers, and the Imperial Geography of Eighteenth-Century Montreal," in *Frontier Cities: Encounters at the Crossroads of Empire*, ed. Jay Gitlin, Barbara Berglund, and Adam Arenson, eds. (Philadelphia: University of Pennsylvania Press, 2012), ch. 3; Brett Rushforth, *Bonds of*

Alliance: Indigenous and Atlantic Slaveries in New France (Chapel Hill: University of North Carolina Press, 2010) ("Mohawk women" at 309; "did belong" at 310).

28. Rushforth, *Bonds of Alliance,* 178 (13 or 14 percent), ch. 6.

29. Pekka Hämäläinen, *Lakota America: A New History of Indigenous Power* (New Haven: Yale University Press, 2019), 74–75; Rushforth, *Bonds of Alliance,* 193–96.

30. Christine M. DeLucia, *Memory Lands: King Philip's War and the Place of Violence in the Northeast* (New Haven: Yale University Press, 2018), 45.

31. Margaret Ellen Newell, *Brethren by Nature: New England Indians, Colonists, and the Origins of American Slavery* (Ithaca: Cornell University Press, 2015), 54–57, 66–67 (Winthrop), 86 ("garb of servants").

32. *EAID* 17:89, 101.

33. Benjamin Trumbull, *A Complete History of Connecticut, Civil and Eecclesiastical, from the Emigration of its First Planters from England* (Hartford: Hudson and Goodwin, 1797), 1:349; on pre-war ties between Indians and English, see James D. Drake, *King Philip's War: Civil War in New England, 1675–1676* (Amherst: University of Massachusetts Press, 1999), ch. 2.

34. *EAID* 17:126, 149, 279, 282, 403. Boston did not officially lift the ban until 2005! DeLucia, *Memory Lands,* 32 (citing *The Boston Globe,* May 20, 2005), 48–49.

35. Lisa Brooks, *Our Beloved Kin: A New History of King Philip's War* (New Haven: Yale University Press, 2018), 223–34; DeLucia, *Memory Lands,* ch. 1, esp. 49–51 ("memoryscape").

36. *DRCHNY* 3:253; Brooks, *Our Beloved Kin,* 176, 226, 310–12.

37. Brooks, *Our Beloved Kin,* 330–33, 335–38; DeLucia, *Memory Lands,* 53.

38. *EAID* 17:47; Daniel Gookin, "A Memorandum of Indian Children Put Forth into Service to the English, August 10, 1676," in *The Sovereignty and Goodness of God by Mary Rowlandson with Related Documents,* ed. Neal Salisbury, 2nd ed. (Boston: Bedford Books, 2018), 155–58; DeLucia, *Memory Lands,* 55–57.

39. Cf. Paul Charney, "'Much Too Worthy . . .': Indians in Seventeenth-Century Lima," in *City Indians in Spain's American Empire: Urban Indigenous Society in Colonial Mesoamerica and Andean South America, 1530–1810,* ed. Dana Velasco Murillo, Mark Lentz, and Margarita R. Ochoa (Eastbourne, UK: Sussex Academic Press, 2012), 91–92, and Ramos, "'Mi Tierra': Indigenous Migrants and Their Hometowns," 140.

40. *DRCHNY* 4:343.

41. *New England Courant,* Jan. 11, 1725, 2.

42. *Boston Gazette,* Sept. 5, 1726, 2; *Boston News-Letter,* Sept. 8, 1726, 2, Sept. 15, 2.

43. *EAID* 17:176–78, 326, 452, 455; Newell, *Brethren by Nature,* 203–5; Jared Hardesty, *Unfreedom: Slavery and Dependence in Eighteenth-Century Boston* (New York: New York University Press, 2016), 63–64, 92–93, 97–98. New England curbed and then ended the importation of "Carolina Indians," especially when the Yamasee War in 1715 threatened to generate a flood of disruptive Indian captives.

44. *Abstract and Index of the Records of the Inferior Court of Pleas (Suffolk County Court) Held at Boston 1680–1698* (Boston: Historical Records Society, 1940), 147.

45. *Abstract and Index of the Records of the Inferior Court of Pleas,* 135.

46. *Abstract and Index of the Records of the Inferior Court of Pleas,* 109, 112, 119, 127–28, 131–32.

47. *Boston Gazette,* July 8–15, 1728, 2.

48. *Boston News-Letter,* Sept. 19–26, 1728, 2; March 2–9, 1732, 2; Sept. 7–14, 1732, 2; *New-England Weekly Journal,* Aug. 30, 1731, 2.

49. *Boston News-Letter,* Sept. 19–26, 1728, 2.

50. "The Journal of Madam Knight," in *Journeys in New Worlds: Early American Women's Narratives,* ed. William L. Andrews (Madison: University of Wisconsin Press, 1990), 105.

51. DeLucia, *Memory Lands,* 67–68.

52. Daniel R. Mandell, *Behind the Frontier: Indians in Eighteenth-Century Eastern Massachusetts* (Lincoln: University of Nebraska Press, 1996), 161–63, 177–78 (quote and Atttucks), 199 (Hawley quote).

53. *Luigi Castiglioni's Viaggio: Travels in the United States of North America, 1785–87,* ed. and trans. Antonio Pace (Syracuse: Syracuse University Press, 1983), 20.

54. Quoted in Colin G. Calloway, "Introduction: Surviving the Dark Ages," in *After King Philip's War: Presence and Persistence in Indian New England,* ed. Colin G. Calloway (Hanover, NH: University Press of New England, 1997), 8.

55. Ruth Wallis Herndon and Ella Wilcox Sekatau, "The Right to a Name: The Narragansett People and Rhode Island Officials in the Revolutionary Era," in *After King Philip's War: Presence and Persistence in Indian New England,* ed. Colin G. Calloway (Hanover, NH: University Press of New England, 1997), 114–43; Ruth Wallis Herndon, "Racialization and Feminization of Poverty in Early America: Indian Women as 'the Poor of the Town' in Eighteenth-Century Rhode Island," in *Empire and Others: British Encounters with Indigenous Peoples, 1600–1850,* ed. Martin Daunten and Rick Halpern (Philadelphia: University of Pennsylvania Press, 1999), 186–203, quote at 187.

56. Sharon V. Salinger, *Taverns and Drinking in Early America* (Baltimore: Johns Hopkins University Press, 2002), 235–36, citing Robert Love Diary, Apr. 5 and Apr. 22, 1766, Massachusetts Historical Society. Robert Love was a "warner" between 1765 and 1774; Cornelia H. Dayton and Sharon V. Salinger, *Robert Love's Warnings: Searching for Strangers in Colonial Boston* (Philadelphia: University of Pennsylvania Press, 2014).

57. Cf. Murillo, Lentz, and Ochoa, eds., *City Indians in Spain's American Empire,* 33, 99, 128, 159, 161, 229.

58. *Columbian Gazetteer,* Jan. 6, 1794, 3.

59. Thomas L. Doughton, "Unseen Neighbors: Native Americans of Central Massachusetts, a People Who Had 'Vanished," in *After King Philip's War: Presence and Persistence in Indian New England,* ed. Colin G. Calloway (Hanover, NH: University Press of New England, 1997), 209.

60. *Col. Recs. Penn.* 2:183.

61. John F. Watson, ed. and comp., *Annals of Philadelphia, and Pennsylvania, in the Olden Time* (Philadelphia: Edwin S. Stuart, 1884), 2:163; Horace Mather Lippincott, *Early Philadelphia: Its People, Life and Progress* (Philadelphia: J. B. Lippincott, 1917), 35.

62. *Journey to Pennsylvania by Gottlieb Mittelberger,* ed. and trans. Oscar Handlin and John Clive (Cambridge, MA: Harvard University Press, 1960), 63.

63. *The Diary of Hannah Callender Sansom: Sense and Sensibility in the Age of the American Revolution,* ed. Susan E. Klepp and Karin Wulf (Ithaca: Cornell University Press, 2010), 174.

64. Dawn G. Marsh, *A Lenape Among the Quakers: The Life of Hannah Freeman* (Lincoln: University of Nebraska Press, 2014), 28–29, 162.

65. George C. Rogers Jr., *Charleston in the Age of the Pinckneys* (Norman: University of Oklahoma Press, 1969), 8; Joshua A. Piker, "'White & Clean' & Contested: Creek Towns and Trading Paths in the Aftermath of the Seven Years' War," in *American Encounters: Natives and Newcomers from European Contact to Indian Removal, 1500–1800,* ed. Peter C. Mancall and James H. Merrell, 2nd ed. (New York: Routledge, 2007), 337–60; William L. McDowell Jr., ed. *Journals of the Commissioners of the Indian Trade* (Columbia: South Carolina Department of Archives and History, 1955, 1992), 126–28, 132, 149–56, 201; Wilma A. Dunaway, *Women, Work, and Family in the Antebellum Appalachian South* (Cambridge: Cambridge University Press, 2008), 57, 197; Sarah H. Hill, *Weaving New Worlds: Southeastern Cherokee Women and Their Basketry* (Chapel Hill: University of North Carolina Press, 1997), 55–60; Samuel Cole Williams, ed., *Adair's History of the American Indians* (1930 reprint, New York: Promontory Press, n.d.), 456. For a full treatment of Indian presence and participation in the city's life and economy, see Nathaniel F. Holly, "From Itsa'ti to Charlestown: The Urban Lives of Cherokees in Early America," Ph.D. dissertation, College of William and Mary, 2019.

66. *EAID* 13:89 (1693 complaint); McDowell, *Journals of the Commissioners of the Indian Trade,* 49, 160–61, 186, 232–33.

67. McDowell, *Journals of the Commissioners of the Indian Trade,* 12, 125–28, 131. For a fuller discussion of this episode, see Nathaniel Holly, "'The Indian Woman Peggy': Mobility, Marriage, and Power in an Early American City," *Early Modern Women* 14 (Fall 2019): 85–94.

68. UK National Archives, Colonial Office Records, C.O. 5/1328: 28–29; *Penn. Archives,* 4th series, 2:204–06, 214–16, 220; Ian K. Steele, "Shawnee Origins of Their Seven Years' War,"

Ethnohistory 53 (2006): 657–58; McDowell, *Documents Relating to Indian Affairs, 1750–1754*, 421–29 (interrogation of the prisoners), 432–33, 442–46; Holly, "From Itsa'ti to Charlestown," 360–73.

69. Holly, "From Itsa'ti to Charlestown," ch. 7; *EAID* 14:178–81; Christina Snyder, *Slavery in Indian Country: The Changing Face of Captivity in Early America* (Cambridge, MA: Harvard University Press, 2010), 90 (sailors).

70. Patricia Cleary, *The World, the Flesh, and the Devil: A History of Colonial St. Louis* (Columbia: University of Missouri Press, 2011), 117.

71. Daniel H. Usner Jr., "Colonial Projects and Frontier Practices: The First Century of New Orleans History," in *Frontier Cities: Encounters at the Crossroads of Empire*, ed. Jay Gitlin, Barbara Berglund, and Adam Arenson, eds. (Philadelphia: University of Pennsylvania Press, 2012), 27–45, quote at 35.

72. Daniel H. Usner Jr., *Indians, Settlers, and Slaves in a Frontier Exchange Economy: The Lower Mississippi Valley Before 1783* (Chapel Hill: University of North Carolina Press, 1992); Elizabeth N. Ellis, "The Many Ties of the Petites Nations: Relationships, Power, and Diplomacy in the Lower Mississippi Valley, 1685–1785," Ph.D. dissertation, University of North Carolina–Chapel Hill, 2015, ch. 3.

73. Daniel H. Usner, *American Indians in Early New Orleans: From Calumet to Raquette* (Baton Rouge: Louisiana State University Press, 2018), 38–39.

74. Usner, "American Indians in Colonial New Orleans," 121.

75. Usner, *American Indians in Early New Orleans;* Usner, "American Indians in Colonial New Orleans," 114–16; *Thirty Thousand Miles with John Heckewelder or Travels Among the Indians of Pennsylvania, New York and Ohio in the 18th Century*, ed. Paul A. W. Wallace (1958; reprint, Lewisburg, PA: Wennawoods, 1998), 75–76; Daniel H. Usner Jr., *American Indians in the Lower Mississippi Valley: Social and Economic Histories* (Lincoln: University of Nebraska Press, 1998), 69, 111, 115 (food market).

76. Usner, *American Indians in Early New Orleans*, 27, 49–56; Fortescue Cuming, *Sketches of a Tour Through the Western Country*, in *Early Western Travels, 1748–1846*, ed. Reuben G. Thwaites (Cleveland: Arthur H. Clark, 1907), 4:365–66; Usner, "Colonial Projects and Frontier Practices," 37.

77. *Thirty Thousand Miles with John Heckewelder*, 290–91; Gregory Ablavsky, *Federal Ground: Governing Property and Violence in the First U.S. Territories* (New York: Oxford University Press, 2021), 61–63.

78. Isaac Weld Jr., *Travels Through the States of North America, and the Provinces of Upper and Lower Canada, During the Years 1795, 1796, and 1797*, 2nd ed. (London: John Stockdale, 1799), 2:187; *Correspondence of Lieut. Governor John Graves Simcoe*, ed. E. A. Cruikshank (Toronto: Ontario Historical Society, 1923–31), 4:247.

79. Elizabeth Simcoe, *Mrs. Simcoe's Diary*, ed. Mary Quayle Innis (Toronto: Macmillan Company of Canada, 1965), 72.

80. Margaret Connell Szasz, *Indian Education in the American Colonies, 1607–1783* (Albuquerque: University of New Mexico Press, 1988), 67–75; Shannon Lee Dawdy, *Building the Devil's Empire: French Colonial New Orleans* (Chicago: University of Chicago Press, 2008), 58–59; Jenny Hale Pulsipher, *Swindler Sachem: The American Indian Who Sold His Birthright, Dropped Out of Harvard, and Conned the King of England* (New Haven: Yale University Press, 2017), 71–84.

81. Benjamin Franklin, *Two Tracts: Information to Those Who Would Remove to America, and Remarks Concerning the Savages of North America*, 2nd ed. (London: John Stockdale, 1784), 26–29. Canasatego's briefer response is in Julian P. Boyd and Carl Van Doren, eds., *Indian Treaties Printed by Benjamin Franklin, 1736–1762* (Philadelphia: Historical Society of Pennsylvania, 1938), 76, and *EAID* 2:107.

82. *EAID* 2:469; 3:39, 56; *Penn. Archives*, 1st series, 2: 318.

83. *EAID* 5:223, 225.

84. James H. Merrell, *Into the American Woods: Negotiators on the Pennsylvania Frontier* (New York: W. W. Norton, 1999), 73; *Col. Recs. Penn.* 8:756, 770; *Penn. Archives*, 4th series, 3: 174; *EAID* 3:654.

85. Varnum Lansing Collins, "Indian Wards at Princeton," *Princeton University Bulletin* 13 (1902): 101–6; C. A. Weslager, *The Delaware Indians: A History* (New Brunswick, NJ: Rutgers University Press, 1972), 309–11; Worthington C. Ford et al., eds., *Journals of the Continental Congress, 1774–1789*, (Washington, DC: Government Printing Office, 1904–37), 21:842–43; 28:411(Congressional committee), 468; Papers of Henry Knox, Massachusetts Historical Society, reel 26: 129 (Congress funds in 1790); *PGW, Pres.* 2:433–35; 3:152, 403–4 (White Eyes complaints); 4:215.

86. *PGW, Pres.* 3:466, 573; 7:257.

87. John Walton Caughey, *McGillivray of the Creeks* (Norman: University of Oklahoma Press, 1938), 283; William Knox to Henry Knox, July 14, 1790, PWD.

88. Stephanie L. Gamble, "Capital Negotiations: Native Diplomats in the American Capital, 1789–1837," Ph.D. diss. Johns Hopkins University, 2014, 130; *The Collected Works of Benjamin Hawkins, 1796–1810*, ed. Thomas Foster (Tuscaloosa: University of Alabama Press, 2003), 99–100, 126–27, 168.

89. *ASPIA* 1:144; [Letter of Cornplanter to the Philadelphia Quakers and their reply], *Bulletin of Friends Historical Association* 26 (Autumn 1936): 86–87; Dawn Peterson, *Indians in the Family: Adoption and the Politics of Antebellum Expansion* (Cambridge, MA: Harvard University Press, 2017), 44, 49–50.

90. Timothy Pickering Papers, Massachusetts Historical Society, reel 59: 219–22; *PGW, Pres.* 19:151; Expenses of Henry Abeel, Seneca Indian, Feb. [?], 1796, PWD.

91. Kari Elizabeth Rose Thompson, "Inconsistent Friends: Philadelphia Friends and the Development of Native American Missions in the Long Eighteenth Century," Ph.D. dissertation, University of Iowa, 2013, 133–35, 158–70; Peterson, *Indians in the Family*, 44, 62, 64–66; William Simmons to Timothy Pickering, Jan. 16, 1796; Simmons to James McHenry, Jan. 26, 1799, Certification of payments, Jan. 26, 1799, Jan. 12, 1801, all PWD.

92. *DRCHNY* 4:176.

93. Colin G. Calloway, *New Worlds for All: Indians, Europeans, and the Remaking of Early America*, 2nd ed. (Baltimore: Johns Hopkins University Press, 2013), 185.

94. *Penn. Archives*, 1st series, 2:244–45; *Col. Recs. Penn.* 6:276, 278–79.

95. Peter Silver, *Our Savage Neighbors: How Indian War Transformed Early America* (New York: W. W. Norton, 2008), 131; "Fragments of a Journal Kept by Samuel Foulke, of Bucks County," *Pennsylvania Magazine of History and Biography* 5 (1881): 67 ("Contagion"); *Thirty Thousand Miles with John Heckewelder*, 71.

96. *Thirty Thousand Miles with John Heckewelder*, 75–76.

97. On the Paxton Boys massacre, see Kevin Kenny, *Peaceable Kingdom Lost: The Paxton Boys and the Destruction of William Penn's Holy Experiment* (New York: Oxford University Press, 2009), chs. 13–18; Merrell, *Into the American Woods*, 285–88; Jane T. Merritt, *At the Crossroads: Indians and Empires on a Mid-Atlantic Frontier, 1700–1763* (Chapel Hill: University of North Carolina Press, 2003), 283–94; Silver, *Our Savage Neighbors*, 174–90; *Col. Recs. Penn.* 9:89, 92–95, 100–110; *Penn. Archives*, 1st series, 4: 147–49, 151–55, 160–62; 4th series, 3:256–76; John R. Dunbar, ed., *The Paxton Papers* (The Hague: Martinus Nijhoff, 1957).

98. "Diary of the Indian Gemeinlein on Pilgrimage, 1764," Bethlehem Digital History Project, Moravian Indian Diaries, http://bdhp.moravian.edu/community_records/christianindians/diaires/amboy/1764amboy.html; *Thirty Thousand Miles with John Heckewelder*, 78; *Col. Recs. Penn.* 9:110–13, 121–22.

99. "Diary of the Indian Gemeinlein"; *Thirty Thousand Miles with John Heckewelder*, 80; *Col. Recs. Penn.* 9:122–38.

100. "Diary of the Indian Gemeine in the Barracks in Philadelphia," Bethlehem Digital History Project, Moravian Indian Diaries, http://bdhp.moravian.edu/community_records/christianindians/diaires/barracks/1764/translation64.html; *Thirty Thousand Miles with John Heckewelder*, 81.

101. Usner, "American Indians in Colonial New Orleans," 122; Usner, *American Indians in Early New Orleans*, 42.
102. On urban homeland, see DeLucia, *Memory Lands*, 32.

CHAPTER 4

1. *Col. Recs. Penn.* 3:426.
2. *Col. Recs. Penn.* 3:459, 463, 507 (accounts).
3. *Col. Recs. Penn.* 4:341–42. See also *Penn. Archives*, 1st series, 1:394, 551.
4. Pekka Hämäläinen, *Lakota America: A New History of Indigenous Power* (New Haven: Yale University Press, 2019), 13; Gary Clayton Anderson, *Kinsmen of Another Kind: Dakota-White Relations in the Upper Mississippi Valley, 1650–1862* (Lincoln: University of Nebraska Press, 1984), 35.
5. Gilles Havard, *The Great Peace of Montreal of 1701: French-Native Diplomacy in the Seventeenth Century* (Montreal: McGill-Queens University Press, 2001), 130–35; Alain Beaulieu and Roland Viau, *The Great Peace: Chronicle of a Diplomatic Saga* (Montreal: Éditions Libre Expression, 2001), 71, 99.
6. *EAID* 20:380–81.
7. John Duffy, *Epidemics in Colonial America* (Baton Rouge: Louisiana State University Press, 1953), 32–33, 35–36, 46, 51–54, 57, 59–60, 65–66, 128, 131–33; Carl Bridenbaugh, *Cities in the Wilderness: The First Century of Urban Life in America, 1625–1742* (New York: Ronald Press, 1938), 86–87, 240–41, 399–400, 402; Bridenbaugh, *Cities in Revolt: Urban Life in America, 1743–1776* (New York: Alfred A. Knopf, 1955), 327–28; Gary B. Nash, *The Urban Crucible: The Northern Seaports and the Origins of the American Revolution* (Cambridge, MA: Harvard University Press, 1986), 66, 113–14.
8. *An Account of the Treaty held at the city of Albany in October 1745* (Philadelphia: B. Franklin, 1746), 3.
9. Quoted in Paul A. Wallace, *Conrad Weiser, 1697–1760: Friend of Colonist and Mohawk* (Philadelphia: University of Pennsylvania Press, 1945), 238.
10. Billy G. Smith, ed., *Life in Early Philadelphia: Documents from the Revolutionary and Early National Periods* (University Park: Pennsylvania State University Press, 1995), 11.
11. Billy G. Smith, *The "Lower Sort": Philadelphia's Laboring People, 1750–1800* (Ithaca: Cornell University Press, 1990), 30–31, 51, 165.
12. Duffy, *Epidemics in Colonial America*, 34–35, 78, 83, 87, 100, 127, 134–35; *EAID* 1:422; Smith, *"Lower Sort,"* 47–48, 51.
13. *Penn. Archives*, 1st series, 1:769.
14. *Penn. Archives*, 4th series, 2:308.
15. *Col. Recs. Penn.* 5:478; *EAID* 2:244; 5:111.
16. William L. McDowell Jr., ed., *Colonial Records of South Carolina: Documents Relating to Indian Affairs, 1750–1754* (Columbia: South Carolina Department of Archives and History, 1958), 107 ("very fatal"); William L. McDowell Jr., ed., *Colonial Records of South Carolina: Documents Relating to Indian Affairs, 1754–1765* (Columbia: South Carolina Department of Archives and History, 1970), 9 (mosquitos gone), 13, 46 (best warriors), 49, 68, 128 ("good Talk"), 134 ("often lost People"), 141 (put off until fall), 191 (Creek fear), 453 ("Wee lost"); *EAID* 13:103–6 (Creeks and Cherokees there in 1721), 217, 241 (Cherokee chiefs at Nov. 1751 treaty), 276 (99 Creeks), 293–95 (Saluda meeting). See Nathaniel F. Holly, "From Itsa'ti to Charlestown: The Urban Lives of Cherokees in Early America," Ph.D. dissertation, College of William and Mary, 2019, 341–52, for Cherokee sickness in Charleston and the treatments they received.
17. Jennifer Van Horn, *The Power of Objects in Eighteenth-Century British America* (Chapel Hill: University of North Carolina Press, 2017), 184–85.
18. *EAID* 16:284–86; Duffy, *Epidemics in Colonial America*, 34, 36, 38, 82–83, 94–95; Bridenbaugh, *Cities in the Wilderness*, 87–88, 240, 399–400; Bridenbaugh, *Cities in Revolt*, 129–30; *The Papers of Henry Bouquet*, ed. S. K. Stevens, Donald H. Kent, and Autumn L. Leonard (Harrisburg: Pennsylvania Historical and Museum Commission, 1972–1994), 1:124;

Suzanne Krebsbach, "The Great Charlestown Smallpox Epidemic of 1760," *South Carolina Historical Magazine,* 97 (Jan. 1996): 30–37.

19. H. Roy Merrins, ed., *The South Carolina Scene: Contemporary Views, 1697–1774* (Columbia: University of South Carolina Press, 1977), 230.

20. *Col. Recs. Penn.* 4:81–82; *EAID* 1:422.

21. *WJP* 2:438, 440; *EAID* 3:18, 49, 56; Wallace, *Conrad Weiser,* 432.

22. *DRCHNY* 7:102.

23. *Col. Recs. Penn.* 6:589; *Penn. Archives,* 4th series, 2:22, 24–25, 35–37 (1747 visit), 729–34 ("sincere friend" at 733).

24. *Penn. Archives,* 1st series, 2:684–85; Wallace, *Conrad Weiser,* 441–43.

25. *EAID* 3:103; *Col. Recs. Penn.* 7:199.

26. *Col. Recs. Penn.* 7:309–10.

27. *EAID* 3:160–61, 170, 178, 189 n. 88; *Penn. Archives,* 4th series, 2:753; James H. Merrell, *Into the American Woods: Negotiators on the Pennsylvania Frontier* (New York: W. W. Norton, 1999), 238–42; Samuel Parrish, *Some Chapters in the History of the Friendly Association for Regaining and Preserving Peace with the Indians by Pacific Measures* (Philadelphia: Friends Historical Association, 1877), 61 (dying request); *WJP* 9:566.

28. *Penn. Archives,* 4th series, 2:789; *Col. Recs. Penn.* 7:476, 479, 498–99, 513, 517.

29. *Penn. Archives,* 4th series, 3:127.

30. *The Papers of Thomas Jefferson Digital Edition,* ed. James P. McClure and J. Jefferson Looney (Charlottesville: University of Virginia Press, Rotunda, 2008–2020), *Main Series,* 1:8.

31. *Penn. Archives,* 1st series, 7:292.

32. Paul Kelton, *Cherokee Medicine, Colonial Germs: An Indigenous Nation's Fight Against Smallpox, 1518–1824* (Norman: University of Oklahoma Press, 2015), 163–64.

33. *WJP* 13:390.

34. David J. Norton, *Rebellious Younger Brother: Oneida Leadership and Diplomacy, 1750–1800* (DeKalb: Northern Illinois University Press, 2009), 32–33, 136, 171; *Col. Recs. Penn.* 9:775–76; *WJP* 7:117, 1121; 8:46 ("forward fellow"), 160, 202, 247–48, 260–61, 405–8; 9:944; 10:443 (in Boston); 12:890; 13:189 (seasick); *Boston Evening Post,* Oct. 28, 1771, 2; *Penn. Archives,* 1st series, 4:440 (condolence ceremony).

35. *DRCHNY* 8:290–91.

36. John Walton Caughey, *McGillivray of the Creeks* (1938; reprint, Columbia: University of South Carolina Press, 2007), 277; "New Letters of Abigail Adams, 1788–1801," ed. Stewart Mitchell, *Proceedings of the American Antiquarian Society* 55 (1947): 168–69.

37. *PGW, Pres.* 10:317; *Gazette of the United States,* Mar. 24, 1792; *Independent Gazetteer,* Mar. 24, 1792, 3; *Pennsylvania Journal,* Mar. 28, 1792, 3; *Pennsylvania Gazette,* Mar. 28, 1792, 3; *New Hampshire Gazette,* Apr. 11, 1792, 2; *Dunlap's American Daily Advertiser,* Mar. 21, 1792, 3; Mar. 26, 3; Mar. 27, 3; *Claypoole's Daily Advertiser,* Mar. 22, 1792, 3; Mar. 27, 3; *Connecticut Journal,* Apr. 4, 1792, 3; *Boston Gazette,* Apr. 9, 1792, 2; *Massachusetts Spy,* Apr. 12, 1792, 3.

38. *Extracts from the Diary of Jacob Hiltzheimer, of Philadelphia, 1765–1798,* ed. Jacob Cox Parsons (Philadelphia: Wm. F. Fell, 1893), 174.

39. *The Diary of Elizabeth Drinker,* ed. Elaine Foreman Crane et al. (Boston: Northeastern University Press, 1991), 1:478; 2:1244 ("sight daily to be seen").

40. *Claypoole's Daily Advertiser,* Mar. 28, 1792, 3.

41. *ASPIA* 1:231; *PGW, Pres.* 10:316.

42. Reply of Headmen of Five Nations to Pickering, Apr. [?], 1792, PWD.

43. *National Gazette,* Apr. 23, 1792; *Claypoole's Daily Advertiser,* Mar. 27, 1792, 2 (Keondawania, "head warrior"); Apr. 24, 1792, 3; *Independent Gazetteer and Agricultural Repository,* Apr. 28, 1793, 3.

44. *Albany Register,* Aug. 12, 1793, 1.

45. William N. Fenton, *The Great Law and the Longhouse: A Political History of the Iroquois Confederacy* (Norman: University of Oklahoma Press, 1988), 566.

46. *Anthony Wayne, a Name in Arms: The Wayne-Knox-Pickering-McHenry Correspondence,* ed. Richard C. Knopf (Pittsburgh: University of Pittsburgh Press, 1960), 302–5; Anthony

Wayne to Knox, Jan. 25, 1794, and Wayne to Chiefs of the Six Nations, Mar. 26, 1794, PWD; William N. Fenton, "A Further Note on Iroquois Suicide," *Ethnohistory* 33 (1986): 453–54.

47. *Thirty Thousand Miles with John Heckewelder, or Travels Among the Indians of Pennsylvania, New York & Ohio in the 18th Century*, ed. Paul A. Wallace (1958; reprint, Lewisburg, PA: Wennawoods, 1998), 258–93.

48. *ASPIA* 1:240, 320.

49. *Thirty Thousand Miles with John Heckewelder*, 284; *PGW, Pres.* 11:368–70. On DuCoigne's earlier visit, see *The Papers of Thomas Jefferson Digital Edition*, ed. James P. McClure and J. Jefferson Looney (Charlottesville: University of Virginia Press, Rotunda, 2008–2020) *Main Series*, 6:43, 60–64n; 24:806. Robert M. Owens, "Jean Baptiste DuCoigne, the Kaskaskias, and the Limits of Thomas Jefferson's Friendship," *Journal of Illinois History* 5 (Summer 2002): 112–15.

50. *Thirty Thousand Miles with John Heckewelder*, 288; "Minutes of a Conference with the Illinois and Wabash Indians," *Papers of Thomas Jefferson Digital Edition, Main Series*, 25:112–18; *PGW, Pres.* 15:7n; *Massachusetts Spy*, Jan 24, 1793, 3 (inoculated: *The New-Jersey Journal*, Jan 16, 1793, 2; *Pittsburgh Gazette*, Jan.19, 1793, 3).

51. Dorothy Twohig, ed., *The Journal of the Proceedings of the President, 1793–1797* (Charlottesville: University of Virginia Press, 1981), 40, 42–43; *PGW, Pres.* 12:79–80, 82–90; *Papers of Thomas Jefferson Digital Edition, Main Series*, 25:112–18.

52. *Private Affairs of George Washington: From the Records and Accounts of Tobias Lear, Esquire, His Secretary*, ed. Stephen Decatur (Boston: Houghton Mifflin, 1933), 325.

53. Christ Church Philadelphia Archives, Burial Account Books, St. Peter's Burial Account Book, 1789–93; https://christchurchphila.pastperfectonline.com/archive/1E4DA900-8B59-4D97-99A6-042513961954; Charles R. Hildeburn, ed., *The Inscriptions of St. Peter's Church Yard, Philadelphia, Copied and Arranged by the Rev. William White Bronson* (Camden: Sinnickson Chew, Printer, 1879), 518. I am grateful to Richard Groves of Philadelphia for bringing this information to my attention.

54. *PGW, Pres.* 12:551–53; Twohig, *Journal of the Proceedings of the President*, 45 (pipes to War Office).

55. *PGW, Pres.* 12:137–39; 15:6–7 (Knox quote); *ASPIA* 1:338, 470 (Knox quote); Twohig, *Journal of the Proceedings of the President*, 44.

56. Duffy, *Epidemics in Colonial America*, ch. 4.

57. Julia P. Mansfield, "The Disease of Commerce: Yellow Fever in the Atlantic World, 1793–1805," Ph.D. dissertation, Stanford University, 2017; Jim Murphy, *An American Plague: The True and Terrifying Story of the Yellow Fever Epidemic of 1793* (New York: Clarion Books, 2003); J. H. Powell, *Bring Out Your Dead: The Great Plague of Yellow Fever in Philadelphia in 1793* (1949; reprint, Philadelphia: University of Pennsylvania Press, 1993); Smith, *Life in Early Philadelphia*, 14, 226–27: Stephen Fried, "Yellow Fever Stalks the Founders," *American Heritage* 65, no. 2 (Spring 2020).

58. *Papers of Thomas Jefferson Digital Edition, Main Series*, 27:7.

59. Clarence E. Carter, ed., *The Territorial Papers of the United States*, Vol. 4, *The Territory South of the River Ohio, 1790–1796* (Washington, DC: Government Printing Office, 1934), 305, 307; *ASPIA* 1:458.

60. Mansfield, "Disease of Commerce."

61. "Journal of Warren Johnson, 1760–1761," in *In Mohawk Country: Early Narratives About a Native People*, ed. Dean R. Snow, Charles T. Gehring, and William A. Starna (Syracuse: Syracuse University Press, 1996), 251; *WJP* 13:182.

62. Céline Carayon, *Eloquence Embodied: Nonverbal Communication Among French and Indigenous Peoples in the Americas* (Chapel Hill: University of North Carolina Press, 2019), 154–55; Kathleen M. Brown, *Foul Bodies: Cleanliness in Early America* (New Haven: Yale University Press, 2009), 156–57.

63. *JR* 44:297.

64. *DRCHNY* 4:714.

65. Samuel Cole Williams, ed., *Adair's History of the American Indians* (1930; reprint, New York: Promontory Press, n.d.), 126; Brown, *Foul Bodies*, 203–4.

66. Brown, *Foul Bodies*, 10, 196–97.

67. American Philosophical Society, Benjamin Rush, Memorable Facts, Events, Opinions, 1789–1791, 122.

68. *Penn. Archives*, 4th series, 4:394–98, 405–12.

69. *JR* 20:239.

70. Williams, *Adair's History of the American Indians*, 247 (arm), 295 (smallpox).

71. Virgil J. Vogel, *American Indian Medicine* (Norman: University of Oklahoma Press, 1970).

72. *The Voyages of Jacques Cartier*, ed. Ramsay Cook (Toronto: University of Toronto Press, 1993), 76–80.

73. *A New Voyage to Carolina by John Lawson*, ed. Hugh Talmage Lefler (Chapel Hill: University of North Carolina Press, 1967), 17–18 (quote), 26 (quote), 134, 226.

74. Rev. John Heckewelder, *History, Manners, and Customs of the Indian Nations Who Once Inhabited Pennsylvania and the Neighboring States* (Philadelphia: Historical Society of Pennsylvania, 1876), 228; *Thirty Thousand Miles with John Heckewelder*, 121.

75. Dawn G. Marsh, *A Lenape Among the Quakers: The Life of Hannah Freeman* (Lincoln: University of Nebraska Press, 2014), 94–95.

76. Kelton, *Cherokee Medicine, Colonial Germs*, ch. 2.

77. William Heath, *Blacksnake's Path: The True Adventures of William Wells* (Westminster, MD: Heritage Books, 2008), 238.

78. *The Autobiography of Benjamin Rush*, ed. George W. Corner (Princeton: Princeton University Press, 1948), 240–41; C. F. Volney, *View of the Climate and Soil of the United States of America* (London: J. Johnson, 1804), 401; Harvey Carter, *The Life and Times of Little Turtle* (Urbana: University of Illinois Press, 1987), 4–6; William Heath, *William Wells and the Struggle for the Old Northwest* (Norman: University of Oklahoma Press, 2015), 246–47.

79. John Adams to James Wilkinson, Feb. 4, 1798, Founders Online.

80. American Philosophical Society, Benjamin Rush, Commonplace Book, 1792–1813, 127.

81. In November 1799, for example, Henry Knox gave instructions to conduct Indians from Philadelphia and deliver presents to the families of those who died in the city. Abner Prior to William Simons, Nov. 20, 1799, PWD.

82. *Papers of Thomas Jefferson Digital Edition, Main Series*, 36:274–90; Kelton, *Cherokee Medicine, Colonial Germs*, 176; *Alexandria Times*, May 28, 1802, 3; *Republican Gazette*, June 8, 1802, 4.

83. Herman J. Viola, *Diplomats in Buckskins: A History of Indian Delegations in Washington City* (1981; reprint, Bluffton, SC: Rivilo Books, 1995), ch. 9.

PICTURING CHIEFS IN THE CITY

1. Thomas L. McKenney and James Hall, *History of the Indian Tribes of North America; with biographical sketches and anecdotes of the principal chiefs: embellished with one hundred and twenty portraits, from the Indian gallery in the Department of War, at Washington*, 3 vols. (Philadelphia: E. C. Biddle, 1836–44); Herman J. Viola, *Diplomats in Buckskins: A History of Indian Delegations in Washington City* (1981; reprint, Bluffton, SC: Rivilo Books, 1995), 174–88, quote at 176.

2. Stephanie Pratt, *American Indians in British Art, 1700–1840* (Norman: University of Oklahoma Press, 2005); Beth Fowkes Tobin, *Picturing Imperial Power: Colonial Subjects in British Imperial Painting* (Durham, NC: Duke University Press, 1999), ch. 2; Richard H. Saunders and Ellen G. Miles, *American Colonial Portraits, 1700–1776* (Washington, DC: Smithsonian Institution Press, 1987), 23; *DRCHNY* 5:270 (Nicholson).

3. Jennifer Van Horn, *The Power of Objects in Eighteenth-Century British America* (Chapel Hill: University of North Carolina Press, 2017), ch. 2.

4. William J. Buck, "Lappawinzo and Tishcohan, Chiefs of the Lenni Lenape," *Pennsylvania Magazine of History and Biography* 7 (1883): 215–18; Francis Jennings, *The Ambiguous Iroquois Empire: The Covenant Chain Confederation of Indian Tribes with English Colonies from Its Beginnings to the Lancaster Treaty of 1744* (New York: W. W. Norton, 1984), 336 (flattering);

Roland Edward Fleischer, "Gustavus Hesselius," Ph.D. dissertation, Johns Hopkins University, 1964, 59–65, 73–83; Roland E. Fleischer, *Gustavus Hesselius: Face Painter to the Middle Colonies* (Trenton: New Jersey State Museum, 1987), 36–37, 60–63; Saunders and Miles, *American Colonial Portraits,* 22 ("does Justice"), 153–55.

5. Eric Hinderaker, *The Two Hendricks: Unraveling a Mohawk Mystery* (Cambridge, MA: Harvard University Press, 2010), 6, 253, 331 n. 98.

6. *The Autobiography of Colonel John Trumbull, Patriot-Artist, 1765–1843,* ed. Theodore Sizer (New Haven: Yale University Press, 1953), 166–167; Virginia Pounds Brown and Linda McNair Cohen, *Drawing by Stealth: John Trumbull and the Creek Indians* (Montgomery, AL: NewSouth Books, 2016).

7. *The Memoirs of Lt. Henry Timberlake,* ed. Duane H. King (Cherokee, NC: Museum of the Cherokee Indian Press, 2007), 55.

8. Kate Fullagar, *The Warrior, the Voyager, and the Artist: Three Lives in an Age of Empire* (New Haven: Yale University Press, 2020), ch. 3.

9. Elizabeth Hutchinson, "'The Dress of His Nation': Romney's Portrait of Joseph Brant," *Winterthur Portfolio* 45 (Summer/Autumn 2011): 221.

10. *General Advertiser,* Mar. 28, 1792, 2; Thomas S. Abler, "Governor Blacksnake as a Young Man? Speculations on the Identity of Trumbull's 'The Young Sachem,'" *Ethnohistory* 34 (1987): 329–51.

11. William H. Truettner, *Painting Indians and Building Empires in North America, 1710–1840* (Berkeley: University of California Press, 2010), 57.

12. Hutchinson, "'The Dress of His Nation,'" 209–27 (quotes at 209 and 225); Tobin, *Picturing Imperial Power,* 99–100 (Rigaud portrait).

13. Truettner, *Painting Indians and Building Empires in North America,* 56.

CHAPTER 5

1. *EAID* 3:357; *Col. Recs. Penn.* 7:51.

2. William C. Reichel, ed., *Memorials of the Moravian Church* (Philadelphia: J. B. Lippincott, 1870), 1:342–48.

3. *EAID* 3:746.

4. Gilles Havard, *The Great Peace of Montreal of 1701: French-Native Diplomacy in the Seventeenth Century* (Montreal: McGill-Queens University Press, 2001); Alain Beaulieu and Roland Viau, *The Great Peace: Chronicle of a Diplomatic Saga* (Montreal: Éditions Libre Expression, 2001), 66.

5. Allan W. Trelease, *Indian Affairs in Colonial New York: The Seventeenth Century* (Ithaca: Cornell University Press, 1960), 221; A. J. F. Van Laer, ed. and trans., *Minutes of the Court of Albany, Rensselaerswyck and Schenectady* (Albany: University of the State of New York Press, 1926–32), 1:280, 303 ("old sachems"), 306; 2: 105–6, 244–45 (quote), 257 (200 Mohawks); 3:340–41, 462, 498–99; *EAID* 9:34–36, 142–45 (sheds); *DRCHNY* 5:701.

6. Beverly McAnear, ed., "Personal Accounts of the Albany Congress of 1754," *Mississippi Valley Historical Review* 39 (1939): 733.

7. Witham Marshe, "Journal of the Treaty Held with the Six Nations," in *The Lancaster Treaty of 1744 with Related Documents,* ed. James H. Merrell (Boston: Bedford/St. Martin's, 2008), 110.

8. *EAID* 20:275.

9. *EAID* 20:489–90.

10. *EAID* 20:425.

11. Paul A. Wallace, *Conrad Weiser, 1697–1760: Friend of Colonist and Mohawk* (Philadelphia: University of Pennsylvania Press, 1945), 68–69.

12. *EAID* 2:33.

13. *Col. Recs. Penn.* 4:581–83; *Penn. Archives,* 4th series, 1:795; *EAID* 2:47–48.

14. John F. Watson, ed. and comp., *Annals of Philadelphia, and Pennsylvania, in the Olden Time.* 3 vols. (Philadelphia: Edwin S. Stuart, 1884), 2:163.

15. Philip Padelford, ed., *Colonial Panorama, 1775: Dr. Robert Honyman's Journal for March and April* (San Marino, CA: Huntington Library, 1939), 16; *Col. Recs. Penn.* 10:238; *Penn. Archives,* 1st series, 4:615.

16. *Penn. Archives,* 1st series, 7:362, 364.

17. *EAID* 13:119; William L. McDowell Jr., ed., *Documents Relating to Indian Affairs 1750–1754* (Columbia: South Carolina Department of Archives and History, 1958), 210–11.

18. *The Adams-Jefferson Letters: The Complete Correspondence Between Thomas Jefferson and Abigail and John Adams,* ed. Lester J. Cappon (Chapel Hill: University of North Carolina Press, 1987), 307.

19. Watson, *Annals of Philadelphia,* 2:171.

20. Richard L. Bushman, *The Refinement of America: Persons, Houses, Cities* (New York: Alfred A. Knopf, 1992), 162–63; Bernard L. Herman, *Town House: Architecture and Material Life in the Early American City, 1780–1830* (Chapel Hill: University of North Carolina Press, 2005), 253; *The New Democracy in America: Travels of Francisco de Miranda in the United States, 1783–84,* ed. John Z. Ezell, trans. Justin P. Wood (Norman: University of Oklahoma Press, 1963), 41; American Philosophical Society Library, Robert Woodruff, Journal, 1785–1788, 20.

21. *Penn. Archives,* 1st series, 12:321.

22. *Col. Recs. Penn.* 16:512–13, 457; *Penn. Archives,* 4th series, 4:109–11.

23. *Col. Recs. Penn.* 16:501–6, 510–11; *Penn. Archives,* 1st series, 11:741; 4th series, 4:112.

24. Kirkland to Knox, Mar. 10, 1792, PWD.

25. Herman, *Town House,* 253–54; *The Papers of Alexander Hamilton Digital Edition,* ed. Harold C. Syrett (Charlottesville: University of Virginia Press, Rotunda, 2011), 11:377.

26. Peter Thompson, *Rum Punch and Revolution: Taverngoing and Public Life in Eighteenth-Century Philadelphia* (Philadelphia: University of Pennsylvania Press, 1999), 59, 188, 190.

27. *Henry Wansey and His American Journal, 1794,* ed. David John Jeremy (Philadelphia: American Philosophical Society, 1970), 104; Bushman, *Refinement of America,* 164.

28. Jeremy, *Henry Wansey and His American Journal,* 116–17.

29. Herman J. Viola, *Diplomats in Buckskins: A History of Indian Delegations in Washington City* (1981; reprint, Bluffton, SC: Rivilo Books, 1995), 120–33.

30. John Sugden, *Blue Jacket: Warrior of the Shawnees* (Lincoln: University of Nebraska Press, 2000), 54.

31. E.g., *EAID* 3:35.

32. Francis Jennings, *The Ambiguous Iroquois Empire: The Covenant Chain Confederation of Indian Tribes with English Colonies from Its Beginnings to the Lancaster Treaty of 1744* (New York: W. W. Norton, 1984), 336.

33. M. A. LaCombe, *Political Gastronomy: Food and Authority in the English Atlantic World* (Philadelphia: University of Pennsylvania Press, 2012): Herman, *Town House,* 73; Merrell, *Lancaster Treaty of 1744,* 71–72, 122–24. Witham Marshe said that he and the other secretaries at the treaty "carved the meat for them, served them with cider and wine, mixed with water, and regulated the economy of the two tables. The chiefs seemed prodigiously pleased with their feast, for they fed lustily, drank heartily, and were very greasy before they finished their dinner, for, bye the bye, they made no use of their forks."

34. Anthony F. C. Wallace, *King of the Delawares: Teedyuscung, 1700–1763* (1949; Syracuse: Syracuse University Press, 1990), 183.

35. Martha A. Zierden and Elizabeth J. Reitz, "Animal Use and the Urban Landscape in Colonial Charleston, South Carolina, USA," *International Journal of Historical Archaeology* 13 (September 2009): 327–65; H. Roy Merrins, ed., *The South Carolina Scene: Contemporary Views, 1697–1774* (Columbia: University of South Carolina Press, 1977), 284.

36. Arthur Orrmont, *Diplomat in Warpaint: Chief Alexander McGillivray of the Creeks* (London: Abelard-Schuman, 1968), 147.

37. *The Federal Gazette and Philadelphia Daily Advertiser,* July 23, 1790, 3; Aug. 6, 1790, 2; *New York Daily Gazette,* July 21, 1790, 489; July 22, 1790, 695; July 27, 1790, 71; *Carlisle Gazette,* Aug. 8, 1790, 2; *The Pennsylvania Packet and Daily Advertiser,* July 29, 1790, 2; *The Daily Advertiser* (New York), Aug. 4, 1790, 2.

38. *DHFFC* 22:1131, 1165; "New Letters of Abigail Adams, 1788–1801," ed. Stewart Mitchell, *Proceedings of the American Antiquarian Society* 55 (1947): 168–69.
39. *DHFFC* 20:2417–19.
40. *DHFFC* 20:2379.
41. *ASPIA* 2:476.
42. Cary Carson, *Face Value: The Consumer Revolution and the Colonizing of America* (Charlottesville: University of Virginia Press, 2017), quote at 8; Serena R. Zabin, *Dangerous Economies: Status and Commerce in Imperial New York* (Philadelphia: University of Philadelphia Press, 2009); Bushman, *Refinement of America*; David Jaffee, *A New Nation of Goods: The Material Culture of Early America* (Philadelphia: University of Pennsylvania Press, 2010); Lois Green Carr and Lorena S. Walsh, "Changing Lifestyles and Consumer Behavior in the Colonial Chesapeake," in *Of Consuming Interests: The Style of Life in the Eighteenth Century,* ed. Cary Carson, Ronald Hoffman, and Peter J. Albert (Charlottesville: University Press of Virginia, 19904), 59–166.
43. Ferdinand M. Bayard, *Travels of a Frenchman in Maryland and Virginia with a Description of Philadelphia and Baltimore in 1791,* ed. and trans. Ben C. McCary (Ann Arbor, MI: Edwards Brothers, 1950), 130.
44. *Peter Kalm's Travels in North America: The English Version of 1770,* ed. Adolph B. Benson (New York: Wilson-Erickson, 1937), 1:190–91; *WJP* 2:576, 587, 603, 618; 3:23; 6:182; 13:647–65 (inventory); Reichel, *Memorials of the Moravian Church,* 234–35.
45. Timothy Pickering Papers, Massachusetts Historical Society, reel 62: 157–74.
46. Catherine Cangany, *Frontier Seaport: Detroit's Transformation into an Atlantic Entrepôt* (Chicago: University of Chicago Press, 2014), 42–43 (Weld quote at 43), 57–61 (dining ware, tea, etc.), 63–64 (Indian department).
47. Knox to Kirkland, Apr. 21, 1792, PWD.
48. Patrick Campbell, *Travels in the Interior Inhabited Parts of North America in the Years 1791 and 1792,* ed. H. H. Langton (Toronto: Champlain Society, 1937), 164–70; see also Isaac Weld Jr., *Travels Through the States of North America, and the Provinces of Upper and Lower Canada, During the Years 1795, 1796, and 1797,* 2nd ed. (London: John Stockdale, 1799), 2:279–80.
49. *The Travel Journals of Henrietta Marchant Liston: North America and Lower Canada, 1796–1800,* ed. Louise V. North (Lanham, MD: Lexington Books, 2014), 91.
50. Isabel Thompson Kelsay, *Joseph Brant, 1743–1807: Man of Two Worlds* (Syracuse: Syracuse University Press, 1984), 576–77.
51. John to Abigail Adams, Dec. 4, 1796, in *The Adams Papers: Adams Family Correspondence,* ed. C. James Taylor et al. (digital ed.), 11:430 (http://rotunda.upress.virginia.edu/); William Heath, *William Wells and the Struggle for the Old Northwest* (Norman: University of Oklahoma Press, 2015), 239–40; Sugden, *Blue Jacket,* 54.
52. *EAID* 3:9; *Col. Recs. Penn.* 7:52.
53. *Extracts from the Diary of Jacob Hiltzheimer, of Philadelphia, 1765–1798,* ed. Jacob Cox Parsons (Philadelphia: Wm. F. Fell, 1893), 164.
54. *Extracts from the Diary of Jacob Hiltzheimer,* 174.
55. Bayard, *Travels of a Frenchman in Maryland and Virginia,* 105–7, 115. Bayard misidentified or misremembered Cornplanter (Planteur de maïs) as a Delaware.
56. *General Advertiser,* June 27, 1794, 3.
57. *Col. Recs. Penn.* 9:255 (first nation); *EAID* 3:28, 31; Wallace, *King of the Delawares,* 66; Samuel Parrish, *Some Chapters in the History of the Friendly Association for Regaining and Preserving Peace with the Indians by Pacific Measures* (Philadelphia: Friends Historical Association, 1877), 12; *The Diary of Hannah Callender Sansom: Sense and Sensibility in the Age of the American Revolution,* ed. Susan E. Klepp and Karin Wulf (Ithaca: Cornell University Press, 2010), 31, 45.
58. Jane T. Merritt, *At the Crossroads: Indians and Empires on a Mid-Atlantic Frontier, 1700–1763* (Chapel Hill: University of North Carolina Press, 2003), 225–30; *WJP* 3:773; Peter Silver, *Our Savage Neighbors: How Indian War Transformed Early America* (New York, 2008), 209 (Paxton propaganda).

59. Kari Elizabeth Rose Thompson, "Inconsistent Friends: Philadelphia Quakers and the Development of Indian Missions in the Long Eighteenth Century," Ph.D. dissertation, University of Iowa, 2013, 117.

60. *The Diary of Elizabeth Drinker,* ed. Elaine Forman Crane et al. (Boston: Northeastern University Press, 1991), 1:480. The other guests were Isaac Zane and his daughter Sally, John Parrish, Wlliam Savery, and Ben Wilson. Savery and Parrish attended an abortive treaty with the Northwestern Indians the next year as observers with a five-man Quaker delegation, and the Treaty of Canandaigua in fall 1794.

61. *Diary of Elizabeth Drinker,* 2:1022–24, daughter at 1024 n; Thompson, "Inconsistent Friends," 162–63.

62. Heath, *William Wells and the Struggle for the Old Northwest,* 254–55; Kate Haulman, *The Politics of Fashion in Eighteenth-Century America* (Chapel Hill: University of North Carolina Press), 221; Susan Branson, *These Fiery Frenchified Dames: Women and Political Culture in Early National Philadelphia* (Philadelphia: University of Pennsylvania Press, 2001), 134–42.

63. McHenry to Wells, Dec. 24, 1801, Indiana Historical Society, Northwest Territory Collection, MO367, box 3, folder 5, no. 30.

64. *Jeffersonian America: Notes on the United States of America, Collected in the Years 1805–6–7 and 11–12 by Sir Augustus John Foster Bart,* ed. Richard B. Davis (San Marino, CA: Huntington Library, 1954), 43.

65. W. J. Rorabaugh, *The Alcoholic Republic: An American Tradition* (New York: Oxford University Press, 1979), 7–10; Sharon V. Salinger, *Taverns and Drinking in Early America* (Baltimore: Johns Hopkins University Press, 2002), 1–4.

66. Carl Bridenbaugh, *Cities in Revolt: Urban Life in America, 1743–1776* (New York: Alfred A. Knopf, 1955), 156–62; Rorabaugh, *Alcoholic Republic,* chs. 1–2; Bushman, *Refinement of America,* 161 (100 in 1744); Thompson, *Rum Punch and Revolution,* 2 (Paris and Rotterdam), 59 (Indian Queen and Indian King), 82 (Mohawk King); Salinger, *Taverns and Drinking,* 50, 54–55, 184–88 (Penn's concern at 184); Vaughn Scribner, *Inn Civility: Urban Taverns and Early American Civil Society* (New York: New York University Press, 2019), 14 (Boston and New York figures); *Col. Recs. Penn.* 5:428-30.

67. Salinger, *Taverns and Drinking,* 226–27, 232–33 (Hell Town); Carson, *Face Value,* 22–24 (cockfighting etc.); Scribner, *Inn Civility,* 14, 38 (camel and leopard). In 1788 New York passed a law imposing fines or imprisonment on tavern keepers who allowed cockfighting, gambling, billiard tables, or shuffleboards in their houses. Thomas E. V. Smith, *The City of New York in the Year of Washington's Inauguration, 1789* (New York: Anson D. F. Randolph, 1889), 120.

68. "You know that of a long time we very much dislike the appearance of Rhum in this Town," chiefs from Onoquaga told Sir William Johnson in 1770; *WJP* 7:348.

69. *Col. Recs. Penn.* 2:603–4; *Penn. Archives,* 4th series, 1: 330-32; C. A. Weslager, *The Delaware Indians: A History* (New Brunswick, NJ: Rutgers University Press, 1972), 197–202 ("bender" at 202).

70. *Col. Recs. Penn.* 3:403–4; *EAID,* 1:159–60, 178, 332–33.

71. *WJP* 12:915.

72. Peter C. Mancall, *Deadly Medicine: Indians and Alcohol in Early America* (Ithaca: Cornell University Press, 1995).

73. Scribner, *Inn Civility,* 15, 25–26, 90, 97–98, 208 n. 40.

74. *DRCHNY* 12:318.

75. Trelease, *Indian Affairs in Colonial New York,* 189; *Journal of Jasper Danckaerts, 1679–1680,* ed. Bartlett Burleigh James and J. Franklin Jameson (New York: Scribner's Sons, 1913), 79.

76. Salinger, *Taverns and Drinking,* 23, 28–29.

77. Trelease, *Indian Affairs in Colonial New York,* 190; *DRCHNY* 13:551–52.

78. *DRCHNY* 3:479.

79. Havard, *The Great Peace of Montreal,* 128; Beaulieu and Viau, *The Great Peace,* 68–69.

80. Pierre de Charlevoix, *Journal of a Voyage to North-America* (London: R. and J. Dodsley, 1761), 1:219; Jan Grabowski, "French Criminal Justice and Indians in Montreal, 1670–1760," *Ethnohistory* 43 (1996): 405–29.

81. Scribner, *Inn Civility*, 14–16.

82. Thompson, *Rum Punch and Revolution*, 75 (Indians and slaves excluded).

83. *Col. Recs. Penn.* 1:373.

84. Salinger, *Taverns and Drinking*, 36; *Col. Recs. Penn.* 2:603–4; 4:86–87 (quote); 5:397; *Penn. Archives*, 1st series, 3:437, 519–20 (quote).

85. *Penn. Archives*, 1st series, 2:389.

86. Salinger, *Taverns and Drinking*, 237–39.

87. *Col. Recs. Penn.* 7:87.

88. *EAID* 3:106–7, 109, 126, 185n (Gascoon); *Penn. Archives*, 1st series, 2:724–25; *Col. Recs. Penn.* 7:694; Reichel, *Memorials of the Moravian Church*, 265, 275 (Elisabeth); Wallace, *King of the Delawares*, 212 (drunk at State House).

89. *EAID* 3:541–42.

90. William L. McDowell Jr., ed., *Colonial Records of South Carolina: Documents Relating to Indian Affairs, 1750–1754* (Columbia: South Carolina Department of Archives and History, 1958), 229–30.

91. Salinger, *Taverns and Drinking*, 196–99; Scribner, *Inn Civility*, 14 (400 taverns).

92. Salinger, *Taverns and Drinking*, 37.

93. E. B. O'Callaghan et al., eds., *The Documentary History of the State of New York* (Albany: State Printer, 1849–1858), 2:91–92.

94. Timothy J. Shannon, *Indians and Colonists at the Crossroads of Empire: The Albany Congress of 1754* (Ithaca: Cornell University Press, 2000), 130; McAnear, "Personal Accounts of the Albany Congress of 1754," 743 ("Face of Day").

95. *EAID* 20:410, 425–26, 428, 431–32, 456, 649, 651.

96. Merrell, *Lancaster Treaty of 1744*, 44, 71–72, 122–24.

97. *DRCHNY* 8:609–10 (church and Cartwright's Tavern); Franklin B. Hough, ed., *Proceedings of the Commissioners of Indian Affairs, Appointed for the Extinguishment of Indian Titles in the State of New York* (Albany: Joel Munsell, 1861), 2:266–313.

98. Bayard, *Travels of a Frenchman in Maryland and Virginia*, 123–24.

99. *Col. Recs. Penn.* 2:604.

100. *New-Hampshire Gazette*, Apr. 18, 1792, 3.

101. Peter Hagner to James McHenry, Mar. 15, 1798; William Simmons to James McHenry, Mar. 20, 1798, PWD.

102. *EAID* 1:431; *Col. Recs. Penn.* 4:93–94, and see 6:140–41, 146, 150, 161, 218–19; *Penn. Archives*, 1st series, 2:211–12.

103. *Thirty Thousand Miles with John Heckewelder, or Travels Among the Indians of Pennsylvania, New York & Ohio in the 18th Century*, ed. Paul A. Wallace (1958; reprint, Lewisburg, PA: Wennawoods, 1998), 113.

104. Louis Philippe, *Diary of My Travels in America*, trans. Stephen Becker (New York: Delaware Press, 1977), 90.

105. *Gazette of the United States*, Apr. 4, 1792, 1.

CHAPTER 6

1. *PGW, Pres.* 10:141; Pickering to Knox, Aug. 10, 1791, Timothy Pickering Papers, Massachusetts Historical Society, 60:115–16.

2. Herman J. Viola, *Diplomats in Buckskins: A History of Indian Delegations in Washington City* (1981; reprint, Bluffton, SC: Rivilo Books, 1995).

3. Isaac Weld Jr., *Travels Through the States of North America, and the Provinces of Upper and Lower Canada, During the Years 1795, 1796, and 1797*, 2nd ed. (London: John Stockdale, 1799), 2:261–62.

4. Richard L. Bushman, *The Refinement of America: Persons, Houses, Cities* (New York: Alfred A. Knopf, 1992), xi, 110–27.

5. Chrestien Le Clercq, *New Relation of Gaspesia, with the Customs and Relation of the Gaspesian Indians*, ed. and trans. William F. Ganong (Toronto: Champlain Society, 1910), 103–4.

6. *Journey to Pennsylvania by Gottlieb Mittelberger*, ed. and trans. Oscar Handlin and John Clive (Cambridge, MA: Harvard University Press, 1960), 36–37 (beauty of city), 65 (Indian critique).

7. Jessica Chopin Rooney, "Introduction: Street and Global Perspectives on the City," *Eighteenth-Century Studies* 50 (2017): 14–53.

8. For example, *Travels in the Confederation (1783–1784), from the German of Johann David Schoepf*, ed. and trans. Alfred J. Morrison (Philadelphia: William J. Campbell, 1911), 60.

9. *The Diary of Elizabeth Drinker*, ed. Elaine Forman Crane et al. (Boston: Northeastern University Press, 1991), 2:1067, and citing John C. Lowber, *Ordinances of the Corporation of the City of Philadelphia* (Philadelphia: Moses Thomas, 1812), 145, 147.

10. Quoted in Dell Upton, *Another City: Urban Life and Urban Spaces in the New American Republic* (New Haven: Yale University Press, 2008), 42–43.

11. Weld, *Travels Through the States of North America*, 2:261–62.

12. Paul A. Wallace, *Conrad Weiser, 1697–1760: Friend of Colonist and Mohawk* (Philadelphia: University of Pennsylvania Press, 1945), 71; citing Historical Society of Philadelphia, Penn MSS, Accounts, Large Folio, 1:53.

13. Billy G. Smith, *The "Lower Sort": Philadelphia's Laboring People, 1750–1800* (Ithaca: Cornell University Press, 1990), 78; William Heath, *William Wells and the Struggle for the Old Northwest* (Norman: University of Oklahoma Press, 2015), 238–39.

14. Bushman, *Refinement of America*, 157, 162, 165.

15. *Journey to Pennsylvania by Gottlieb Mittelberger*, 50–51; *Some Cursory Remarks Made by James Birket in his Voyage to North America, 1750–1751* (1916; reprint, Freeport, NY: Books for Libraries, 1971), 69.

16. *Life, Journals and Correspondence of Rev. Manasseh Cutler*, ed. William Parker Cutler and Julia Perkins Cutler (Cincinnati: Robert Clarke, 1888), 1:271–72.

17. Clare A. Lyons, *Sex Among the Rabble: An Intimate History of Gender and Power in the Age of Revolution, Philadelphia, 1730–1830* (Chapel Hill: University of North Carolina Press, 2006).

18. "Journal of William Black, 1744," ed. R. Alonzo Brook, *Pennsylvania Magazine of History and Biography* 1 (1877): 416.

19. J. P. Brissot de Warville, *New Travels in the United States of America, Performed in 1788* (1792; reprint, New York: Augustus M. Kelley, 1970), 202; Lyons, *Sex Among the Rabble* (Brazilian visitor quoted at 192); Clare A. Lyons, "Mapping an Atlantic Sexual Culture: Homoeroticism in Eighteenth-Century Philadelphia," *William and Mary Quarterly* 60 (2003): 119–54.

20. Examples of advertisements for venereal cures: *Pennsylvania Gazette*, Jan. 31, 1749, 4; Sept. 5, 1765, 1; Sept 12, 1765, 8; Sept. 19, 1765, 5. *Moreau de St. Méry's American Journey 1793–1798*, ed. and trans. Kenneth Roberts and Ana K. Roberts (Garden City, NY: Doubleday, 1947), 177–78. An old colleague and fellow refugee offered him "a stock of certain small contrivances—ingenious things said to have been suggested by the stork," he wrote, and "I did not want to deprive my business of a profitable item." Although "they were primarily intended for the use of French colonials, they were in great demand among Americans, in spite of the false shame so prevalent among the latter."

21. *Moreau de St. Méry's American Journey*, 146 (streets), 148 (population), 156 (prostitutes). A Scottish visitor on the eve of the Revolution had witnessed similar scenes; Patrick McRobert, *Tour Through Part of the Northern Provinces of America, Being a Series of Letters Wrote on the Spot, in the Years 1774 & 1775* (Edinburgh: Printed for the author, 1776), 10, 12.

22. Viola, *Diplomats in Buckskins*, 155.

23. On Peale's Museum at the time: *The Stranger in America, 1793–1806 by Charles William Janson*, ed. Carl S. Driver (New York: Press of the Pioneers, 1935), 197–200. *The Selected Papers of Charles Willson Peale and His Family*, ed. Lillian B. Miller et al. (New Haven: Yale University Press, 1983), 2:160–62. The account of this "Remarkable Occurrence" (and quote) appeared in multiple newspapers, including the *Philadelphia Gazette and Universal Daily*, Dec. 6, 1796, 2; *Register of the Times*, Dec. 9, 1796, 2; *Massachusetts Mercury*, Dec. 12,

1796, 2; *New Jersey Journal,* Dec. 14, 1796, 2; *Connecticut Gazette,* Dec. 15, 1796, 2; *Boston Gazette,* Dec. 19, 1796, 3; *Minerva,* Dec. 20, 1796, 3; *The United States Chronicle,* Dec. 22, 1796, 3; 1796; *Providence Gazette,* Dec. 24, 1796, 3; *Dartmouth Centinel* (Hanover, NH), Dec. 26, 1796, 3; *Amherst Village Messenger,* Dec. 27, 1796, 205; *Litchfield Monitor,* Dec. 28, 1796, 1; Heath, *William Wells and the Struggle for the Old Northwest,* 243–44.

24. *Claypoole's Daily Advertiser,* Aug. 12, 1797, 3; *Selected Papers of Charles Willson Peale,* 2:765.

25. Heath, *William Wells and the Struggle for the Old Northwest,* 251–52.

26. *Pennsylvania Journal,* Nov. 11, 1772, 3; *New York Gazette,* Nov. 17, 1772, 3; *Connecticut Gazette,* Nov. 20, 1772, 2–3; *Virginia Gazette,* Dec. 3, 1772, 2.

27. Jean-Pierre Blanchard, *Journal of my forty-fifth ascension, being the first performed in America, on the Ninth of January, 1793* (1793; reprint, Tarrytown, NY: William Abbatt, 1918); *The Papers of Thomas Jefferson Digital Edition,* ed. James P. McClure and J. Jefferson Looney (Charlottesville: University of Virginia Press, Rotunda, 2008–2020), Main Series, 24:806; *Delaware Gazette,* Jan. 5, 1793, 3; *Federal Gazette and Daily Advertiser,* Jan. 9, 1793, 3; *The New-Jersey Journal,* Jan. 16, 1793, 2; *Pittsburgh Gazette,* Jan. 19, 1793, 3; *The Weekly Register,* Norwich, CT; Jan. 22, 1793, 1 ("gratified'); *Massachusetts Spy,* Jan. 24, 1793, 3; *PGW, Pres.* 11:602.

28. Quoted in Nancy Shoemaker, "Wonder and Repulsion: North American Indians in Eighteenth-Century Europe," in *Europe Observed: Multiple Gazes in Early Modern Encounters,* ed. Kumkum Chatterjee and Clement Hawes (Lewisburg, PA: Bucknell University Press, 2008), 181. An Ojibwe named Maungwaudus who traveled with George Catlin to London in the 1830s said: "Like musketoes in America in the summer season, so are the people in this city, in their numbers and biting one another to get a living." On the face of it, this was the noble savage exposing the corruptions of Europe; in fact, Maungwaudus was a former Methodist minister, George Henry, who used his Indian name to organize a troupe of Ojibwes, and gave traveling exhibitions of Indian customs and demonstrations in scalping. "By all accounts a slick operator," the former preacher was accustomed to giving non-Indian audiences what they wanted. Christopher Mulveg, "Among the Sag-a-noshes: Ojibwa and Iowa Indians with George Catlin in Europe, 1843–1848," in *Indians and Europe: An Interdisciplinary Collection of Essays,* ed. Christian F. Feest (Lincoln: University of Nebraska Press, 1999), 264–72; Brian W. Dippie, *Catlin and His Contemporaries: The Politics of Patronage* (Lincoln: University of Nebraska Press, 1990), 107–9.

29. Billy G. Smith, ed., *Life in Early Philadelphia: Documents from the Revolutionary and Early National Periods* (University Park: Pennsylvania State University Press, 1995), 10; Smith, *The "Lower Sort,"* 42–43; Dell Upton, *Another City: Urban Life and Urban Spaces in the New American Republic* (New Haven: Yale University Press, 2008), 20 (1790 census figures).

30. C. F. Volney, *View of the Climate and Soil of the United States of America: to which are added some accounts of Florida, the French Colony on the Scioto, certain Canadian Colonies, and the Savages or Natives* (London: J. Johnson, 1804), 408–9.

31. Volney, *View of the Climate and Soil of the United States of America,* 422–24.

32. Volney, *View of the Climate and Soil of the United States of America,* 430–34. In March 1798, Jefferson sent the English agriculturalist William Strickland some seeds, including those from what he called the "Wabash melon," a plant native to "the country of the Miamis." He likely acquired the seeds from Little Turtle. *Papers of Thomas Jefferson, Main Series,* 36:274n.

33. Quoted in Shoemaker, "Wonder and Repulsion," 185.

34. John Heckewelder, *History, Manners, and Customs of the Indian Nations Who Once Inhabited Pennsylvania and the Neighboring States* (1876; reprint, New York: New York Times and Arno Press, 1971), 189.

35. J. Franklin Jameson, ed., *Narratives of Early Pennsylvania, West New Jersey and Delaware, 1630–1707* (New York: Charles Scribner's Sons, 1912), 233.

36. *JR* 2:73; Benjamin Franklin, *Two Tracts: Information to Those Who Would Remove to America, and Remarks Concerning the Savages of North America,* 2nd ed. (London: John Stockdale, 1784), 25–26; *William Bartram on the Southeastern Indians,* ed. Gregory A. Waselkov and Kathleen E. Holland Braund (Lincoln: University of Nebraska Press, 1995), 116–17.

37. A. J. F. Van Laer, ed. and trans., *Minutes of the Court of Albany, Rensselaerswyck and Schenectady* (Albany: University of the State of New York Press, 1926–32), 1:327–28.
38. *WJP* 4:118.
39. *WJP* 12:337. In 1767 two Ojibwe prisoners were sent from Detroit to be "conducted from Post to Post till they shall reach Albany."
40. Daniel Gookin, *Historical Collections of the Indians in New England*, Collections of the Massachusetts Historical Society (1792; reprint, n.p.: Towtaid, 1970), 38–39. The Mohawks were suspected of malicious designs against the English, who essentially let them go with a warning.
41. *WJP* 10:962.
42. *WJP* 10:410–11.
43. *EAID* 14:353.
44. The United States had similar responses to Lakota justice in the late nineteenth century; Sidney L. Harring, *Crow Dog's Case: American Indian Sovereignty, Tribal Law, and United States Law in the Nineteenth Century* (Cambridge: Cambridge University Press, 1994).
45. *Penn. Archives*, 4th series, 1:387, 450.
46. *EAID* 13:256; William L. McDowell Jr., ed., *Colonial Records of South Carolina: Documents Relating to Indian Affairs, 1750–1754* (Columbia: South Carolina Department of Archives and History, 1958), 208–12, 274–80. For an excellent treatment of the affair, see Joshua Piker, *The Four Deaths of Acorn Whistler: Telling Stories in Colonial America* (Cambridge, MA: Harvard University Press, 2013).
47. *EAID* 13:259.
48. *Penn. Archives*, 4th series, 3:104, 143.
49. Jan Grabowski, "French Criminal Justice and Indians in Montreal, 1670–1760," *Ethnohistory* 43 (1996): 405–29.
50. *EAID* 13:327–28 (Catawba case); *WJP* 9:622, 642, 685–876, 769; *DRCHNY* 7:250, 253.
51. John Smolenski, "The Death of Sawantaeny and the Problem of Justice on the Frontier," in *Friends and Enemies in Penn's Woods: Indians, Colonists, and the Racial Construction of Pennsylvania*, ed. William A. Pencak and Daniel K. Richter (University Park: Pennsylvania State University Press, 2004), 104–28.
52. Michael Meranze, *Laboratories of Virtue: Punishment, Revolution, and Authority in Philadelphia, 1760–1835* (Chapel Hill: University of North Carolina Press, 1996), 45–48; John F. Watson, ed. and comp., *Annals of Philadelphia, and Pennsylvania, in the Olden Time* (Philadelphia: Edwin S. Stuart, 1884), 1:309, 361. In 1743 an African American brought to the whipping post "took out his knife and cut his throat before the crowd" rather than suffer the punishment.
53. "Travel Diary of the little Indian Gemeine—1764," Jan. 23, Moravian Indians—Travel Diary, http://bdhp.moravian.edu/community_records/christianindians/diaires/travel/1764travel.html.
54. *DRCHNY* 4:364–65, 428, 453–54.
55. *Pennsylvania Packet and Daily Advertiser*, Nov. 24, 1785, 2.
56. *WJP* 8:1146.
57. *WJP* 8:1139 ("Most Dismal"), 1179 ("sober Lad"); Meranze, *Laboratories of Virtue*, 21–22; Samson Occom, *A Sermon Preached at the Execution of Moses Paul, An Indian, Who Was Executed at New Haven, on the 2d of September 1772, for the Murder of Mr. Moses Cook, Late of Waterbury, on the 7th of December 1771. Preached at the Desire of Said Paul* (New London: T. Greene, [1772]).
58. Meranze, *Laboratories of Virtue*, 150–57; John H. Alexander, *Render Them Submissive: Responses to Poverty in Philadelphia, 1760–1800* (Amherst: University of Massachusetts Press, 1980); *Travels in the Confederation 1783–1784, from the German of Johann David Schoepf*, 70–72.
59. Brissot de Warville, *New Travels in the United States of America*, 201–2, 206.
60. *Life, Journals and Correspondence of Rev. Manasseh Cutler*, 1:279–81.
61. Brissot de Warville, *New Travels in the United States of America*, 212–13. Moreau de St. Méry's *American Journey*, 355–56, also described the city's hospitals and asylums.

62. Watson, *Annals of Philadelphia*, 1:360–61; Negley K. Teeters, *The Cradle of the Penitentiary: The Walnut Street Jail at Philadelphia, 1773–1835* (Philadelphia: Temple University Press, 1955); Meranze, *Laboratories of Virtue*, 183, 224–25.

63. Louis P. Masur, *Rites of Execution: Capital Punishment and the Transformation of American Culture, 1776–1865* (New York: Oxford University Press, 1989).

64. Meranze, *Laboratories of Virtue*, esp. 21, 167–69.

65. Julian Ursyn Niemcewicz, *Under Their Vine and Fig Tree: Travels Through America in 1797–1799, 1805 with Some Further Account of Life in New Jersey*, ed. and trans. Metchie J. E. Budka (Elizabeth, NJ: Grassman, 1965), 33–34.

66. Kathryn E. Holland Braund, "The Creek Indians, Blacks, and Slavery," *Journal of Southern History* 57 (1991): 601–36; Christina Snyder, *Slavery in Indian Country: The Changing Face of Indian Captivity* (Cambridge, MA: Harvard University Press, 2010); Robert Michael Morrissey, *Empire by Collaboration: Indians, Colonists, and Governments in Colonial Illinois Country* (Philadelphia: University of Pennsylvania Press, 2015).

67. *WJP* 4:95; *DRCHNY* 7:577; Claudio Saunt, "'The English Has Now a Mind to Make Slaves of Them All': Creeks, Seminoles, and the Problem of Slavery," *American Indian Quarterly* 22 (1998): 157–80.

68. Kenneth Morgan, "Slave Sales in Colonial Charleston," *English Historical Review* 133 (1998): 905–27.

69. Vaughn Scribner, *Inn Civility: Urban Taverns and Early American Civil Society* (New York: New York University Press, 2019), 37.

70. McRobert, *Tour Through Part of the Northern Provinces of America*, 12.

71. Shannon Lee Dawdy, *Building the Devil's Empire: French Colonial New Orleans* (Chicago: University of Chicago Press, 2008), 193, 202.

72. Jennifer Van Horn, *The Power of Objects in Eighteenth-Century British America* (Chapel Hill: University of North Carolina Press, 2017), 188–89; "Journal of a French Traveler in the Colonies, 1765," *American Historical Review* 26 (July 1921): 745; J. Hector St. John de Crèvecoeur, *Letters from an American Farmer* (London: J. M. Dent, 1971), 172–73.

73. "Journal of Josiah Quincy, Jr.," *Proceedings of the Massachusetts Historical Society*, 3rd ser., 49 (1915–16): 457.

74. *EAID* 3:99; Anthony F. C. Wallace, *King of the Delawares: Teedyuscung, 1700–1763* (1949; Syracuse: Syracuse University Press, 1990), 40; William C. Reichel, ed., *Memorials of the Moravian Church* (Philadelphia: J. B. Lippincott, 1870), 1:219–20.

75. *JR* 68:209–11; Tracy Neal Leavelle, *The Catholic Calumet: Colonial Conversion in French and Indian North America* (Philadelphia: University of Pennsylvania Press, 2012), 1–2, 13, 97, 125, 187.

76. *Gentleman's Progress: The Itinerarium of Dr. Alexander Hamilton, 1744*, ed. Carl Bridenbaugh (Chapel Hill: University of North Carolina Press, 1948), 110.

77. Pierre de Charlevoix, *Journal of a Voyage to North-America* (London: R. and J. Dodsley, 1761), 1:117 (Lorette); *A Tour of Four Great Rivers: The Hudson, Mohawk, Susquehanna and Delaware in 1769, Being the Journal of Richard Smith*, ed. Francis Whiting Halsey (New York: Scribner, 1906), 64–68, 87 (Oquaga); *The Journal of Nicholas Cresswell, 1774–1777* (New York: Dial, 1924), 106 (Wal-hack-tap-poke or Schonbrunn); *Col. Recs. Penn.* 9:612 (Fort Augusta); *Diary of David McClure, 1748–1820*, ed. Franklin B. Dexter (New York: Knickerbocker Press, 1899), 50–52 (Moravian Delawares on the Muskingum); Reuben G. Thwaites and Louse P. Kellogg, eds., *The Revolution on the Upper Ohio, 1775–1777* (Madison: Wisconsin Historical Society, 1908), 64 (Thomas Walker on Moravian Indian services); Charles M. Johnston, ed., *The Valley of the Six Nations: A Collection of Documents on the Indian Lands of the Grand River* (Toronto: Champlain Society, 1964), 60 (Patrick Campbell at Grand River "never saw more decorum or attention paid in any church in all my life").

78. *Peter Kalm's Travels in North America: The English Version of 1770*, ed. Adolph B. Benson (New York: Wilson-Erickson, 1937), 1:20–24.

79. Eric Hinderaker, *The Two Hendricks: Unraveling a Mohawk Mystery* (Cambridge, MA: Harvard University Press, 2010), 15–16, 40–41.

80. William B. Hart, *"For the Good of their Souls": Performing Christianity in 18th-Century Mohawk Country* (Amherst: University of Massachusetts Press, 2020).

81. *DRCHNY* 4:692–93; Hart, "*For the Good of Their Souls*," 57–59.

82. *DRCHNY* 4:730, 7344.

83. *DRCHNY* 5:317, 349, 351, 358, 468, 509.

84. *WJP* 6:464; 7:666–68.

85. Beverly McAnear, ed., "Personal Accounts of the Albany Congress of 1754," *Mississippi Valley Historical Review* 39 (1939): 736.

86. *Memoir of Lieut. Col. Tench Tilghman* (Albany: J. Munsell, 1876), 95–97.

87. *Citizen-Soldier: The Revolutionary War Diary of Joseph Bloomfield*, ed. Mark E. Lender and James Kirby Martin (Newark: New Jersey Historical Society, 1982), 90–91.

88. Thomas E. V. Smith, *The City of New York in the Year of Washington's Inauguration, 1789* (New York: Anson D. F. Randolph, 1889), 125.

89. *Pennsylvania Journal*, July 21, 1790, 3; *The City Gazette* (Charleston), Aug. 17, 1790, 2.

90. Bushman, *Refinement of America*, 174 (1725 and ornate), illustration at 173; Van Horn, *Power of Objects*, 59 (1727–54 and rivaling London churches).

91. Bushman, *Refinement of America*, 180.

92. "Journal of William Black," quote at 411.

93. Franklin, *Two Tracts*, 35–39.

94. *Col. Recs. Penn.* 6: 280-81 (Kahnawakes); *DRCHNY* 6:294. Hendrick was angered by having to go to Albany in 1745, at a time of sickness in the city, to see the commissioner of Indian affairs, rather than the commissioner traveling to see him.

95. H. Frank Eshelman, *Annals of the Susquehannocks and Other Indian Tribes of Pennsylvania, 1500–1763* (1908; Lewisburg, PA: Wennawoods, 2000), 206.

96. *Diary of David McClure*, 80–81.

97. "Address by Red Jacket, Oct. 2, 1800," in "Letters of the Reverend Elkanah Holmes from Fort Niagara in 1800," *Publications of the Buffalo Historical Society* 6 (1903): 200; *The Collected Speeches of Sagoyewatha, or Red Jacket*, ed. Granville Ganter (Syracuse: Syracuse University Press, 2006), 105. It was a theme Red Jacket would reiterate: Peter Nabokov, *Native American Testimony: A Chronicle of Indian-White Relations from Prophecy to the Present, 1492–1900* (New York: Penguin, 1992), 58.

98. Samuel Cole Williams, ed., *Adair's History of the American Indians* (1930; reprint, New York: Promontory Press, n.d.), 460, 463.

CHAPTER 7

1. Timothy J. Shannon, "'This Wretched Scene of British Curiosity and Savage Debauchery': Performing Indian Kingship in Eighteenth-Century Britain," in *Native Acts: Indian Performance, 1603–1832*, ed. Joshua David Bellin and Laura L. Mielke (Lincoln: University of Nebraska Press, 2011), 221–47; Kate Flint, *The Transatlantic Indian 1776–1930* (Princeton: Princeton University Press, 2009), 60.

2. Céline Carayon, *Eloquence Embodied: Nonverbal Communication Among French and Indigenous Peoples in the Americas* (Chapel Hill: University of North Carolina Press, 2019).

3. *Jean-Bernard Bossu's Travels in the Interior of North America 1751–1762*, ed. and trans. Seymour Feiler (Norman: University of Oklahoma Press, 1962), 84.

4. Kate Haulman, *The Politics of Fashion in Eighteenth-Century America* (Chapel Hill: University of North Carolina Press, 2011); Linda Baumgarten, *What Clothes Reveal: The Language of Clothing in Colonial and Federal America* (Williamsburg, VA, and New Haven: Colonial Williamsburg Foundation in association with Yale University Press, 2011); Richard L. Bushman, *The Refinement of America: Persons, Houses, Cities* (New York: Alfred A. Knopf, 1992), xii; Emma Hart, *Building Charleston: Town and Society in the Eighteenth-Century British Atlantic World* (Charlottesville: University of Virginia Press, 2010), 11, 132–33.

5. Julian Ursyn Niemcewicz, *Under Their Vine and Fig Tree: Travels Through America in 1797–1799, 1805 with Some Further Account of Life in New Jersey*, ed. and trans. Metchie J. E. Budka (Elizabeth, NJ: Grassman, 1965), 38.

6. Baumgarten, *What Clothes Reveal*, ch. 4, esp. 106.

7. Fell quoted in Haulman, *The Politics of Fashion in Eighteenth-Century America*, 177.

8. *Some Cursory Remarks Made by James Birket in His Voyage to North America, 1750–1751* (1916; reprint, Freeport, NY: Books for Libraries, 1971), 21.

9. Bushman, *Refinement of America*, 197; *Adams Family Correspondence*, ed. L. H. Butterfield et al. (Cambridge, MA: Harvard University Press, 1963), 1:3.44–47.

10. *Journey to Pennsylvania by Gottlieb Mittelberger*, ed. and trans. Oscar Handlin and John Clive (Cambridge, MA: Harvard University Press, 1960), 65.

11. Sarah E. M. Scher and Billie J. A. Follensbee, eds., *Dressing the Part: Power, Dress, Gender, and Representation in the Pre-Columbian Americas* (Gainesville: University Press of Florida, 2017).

12. Susan Sleeper-Smith, *Indigenous Prosperity and American Conquest: Indian Women of the Ohio River Valley, 1690–1792* (Chapel Hill: University of North Carolina Press, 2018), 165–202.

13. Caroline Wigginton, "In a Red Petticoat: Coosaponaskeesa's Performance of Creek Sovereignty in Colonial Georgia," in *Native Acts: Indian Performance, 1603–1832*, ed. Joshua David Bellin and Laura L. Mielke (Lincoln: University of Nebraska Press, 2011), 169–73.

14. *Gentleman's Progress: The Itinerarium of Dr. Alexander Hamilton, 1744*, ed. Carl Bridenbaugh (Chapel Hill: University of North Carolina Press, 1948), 98.

15. Claudio Saunt, "Taking Account of Property: Social Stratification Among the Creek Indians in the Early Nineteenth Century," *William and Mary Quarterly* 24 (2000), 733–60, Emistisego quote at 759; *William Bartram on the Southeastern Indians*, ed. Gregory A. Waselkov and Kathleen E. Holland Braund (Lincoln: University of Nebraska Press, 1995), 147; Dorothy Downs, "British Influences on Creek and Seminole Men's Clothing, 1733–1858," *American Anthropologist* 33 (June 1980): 46–65; Downs, *Art of the Florida Seminole and Miccosukee Indians* (Gainesville: University Press of Florida, 1995), chs. 1–2.

16. *WJP* 3:161; *EAID* 13:170–71.

17. Baumgarten, *What Clothes Reveal*.

18. Timothy J. Shannon, "Dressing for Success on the Mohawk Frontier: Hendrick, William Johnson, and the Indian Fashion," *William and Mary Quarterly* 53 (1996): 13–42; Elizabeth Hutchinson, "'The Dress of His Nation': Romney's Portrait of Joseph Brant," *Winterthur Portfolio* 45 (Summer/Autumn 2011): 209 ("performed identity"); Beth Fowkes Tobin, "Cultural Cross-Dressing in British American Portraits of British Officers and Mohawk Warriors," in *Picturing Imperial Power: Colonial Subjects in British Imperial Painting* (Durham, NC: Duke University Press, 1999), ch. 3; Janet Catherine Berlo, "Men of the Middle Ground: The Visual Culture of Native-White Diplomacy in Eighteenth-Century North America," in *American Adversaries: West and Copley in a Transatlantic World*, ed. Emily Ballew Neff and Kailyn H. Weber (Houston: Museum of Fine Arts, 2013), 104–15.

19. *JR* 52:225–27.

20. Carayon, *Eloquence Embodied*, 358–64; Gilles Havard, *The Great Peace of Montreal of 1701: French-Native Diplomacy in the Seventeenth Century* (Montreal: McGill-Queen's University Press, 2001), 138–39.

21. *JR* 44:295.

22. *Gentleman's Progress: The Itinerarium of Dr. Alexander Hamilton, 1744*, 112 (Hendrick in Boston), 141 (French Mohawks); Shannon, "Dressing for Success on the Mohawk Frontier."

23. Anthony F. C. Wallace, *Teedyuscung, King of the Delawares, 1700–1763* (1949; reprint, Syracuse: Syracuse University Press, 1990), 1, 105; C. A. Weslager, *The Delaware Indians: A History* (New Brunswick, NJ: Rutgers University Press, 1972), 234; *Penn. Archives*, 1st series, 3:717 ("List of Necessaries"); William C. Reichel, ed., *Memorials of the Moravian Church* (Philadelphia: J. B. Lippincott, 1870), 1:355.

24. *Penn. Archives*, 1st series, 3:293; Wallace, *Teedyuscung*, 162.

25. *Diary of David McClure, 1748–1820*, ed. Franklin B. Dexter (New York: Knickerbocker Press, 1899), 42.

26. Richard Smith, *A Tour of Four Great Rivers: The Hudson, Mohawk, Susquehanna and Delaware in 1769*, ed. Francis W. Halsey (Port Washington, N.Y.: Ira J. Friedman, 1964), 84 (blue broadcloth); Tobin, *Picturing Imperial Power*, 15–16, 99; Hutchinson, "'The Dress of His Nation,'" 209–28.

27. C. F. Volney, *View of the Climate and Soil of the United States of America* (London: J. Johnson, 1804), 405, 426.
28. *The Federal Gazette and Philadelphia Daily Advertiser,* July 23, 1790, 3; Aug. 6, 1790, 2; *New York Daily Gazette,* July 21, 1790, 489; July 22, 1790, 695; July 27, 1790, 71; *Carlisle Gazette,* Aug. 8, 1790, 2; *The Pennsylvania Packet, and Daily Advertiser,* July 29, 1790, 2; *The Daily Advertiser* (New York), Aug. 4, 1790, 2.
29. *DHFFC* 20:2412–17.
30. Thomas E. V. Smith, *The City of New York in the Year of Washington's Inauguration, 1789* (New York: Anson D. F. Randolph, 1889), 95–99.
31. *Luigi Castiglioni's Viaggio: Travels in the United States of North America, 1785–87,* ed. and trans. Antonio Pace (Syracuse: Syracuse University Press, 1983), 96.
32. J. P. Brissot de Warville, *New Travels in the United States of America, Performed in 1788* (1792; reprint, New York: Augustus M. Kelley, 1970), 156–57.
33. *Life, Journals and Correspondence of Rev. Manasseh Cutler,* ed. William Parker Cutler and Julia Perkins Cutler (Cincinnati: Robert Clarke, 1888), 1:231.
34. The phrase "savage refinement" was actually used by the Sioux author Charles Eastman, but it accurately reflects expectations and attitudes here.
35. Philip H. Round, "Performing Indian Publics: Two Native Views of Indian Diplomacy to the Western Nations in 1792," in *Native Acts: Indian Performance, 1603–1832,* ed. Joshua David Bellin and Laura L. Mielke (Lincoln: University of Nebraska Press, 2011), 249–80.
36. Sandra M. Gustafson, *Eloquence Is Power: Oratory and Performance in Early America* (Chapel Hill: University of North Carolina Press, 2000), 115–16.
37. Isabel Thompson Kelsay, *Joseph Brant, 1743–1807: Man of Two Worlds* (Syracuse: Syracuse University Press, 1984), 385.
38. Jennifer Van Horn, *The Power of Objects in Eighteenth-Century British America* (Chapel Hill: University of North Carolina Press, 2017), 256–63; William Nelson, ed., *Documents Relating to the Colonial History of the State of New Jersey* (Newark: Archives of the State of New Jersey, 1880–1949), 19:488.
39. *DHFFC,* 22:1149–53; *New York Daily Gazette,* July 22, 1790, 695; Philip J. Deloria, *Playing Indian* (New Haven: Yale University Press, 1998), 54–56; Carol Smith-Rosenberg, *This Violent Empire: The Birth of an American National Identity* (Chapel Hill: University of North Carolina Press, 2010), 191–206.
40. Homi K. Bhaba, *The Location of Culture* (London: Routledge, 1994), 86.
41. *Pennsylvania Packet,* Apr. 20, 1786, 2; *Pennsylvania Evening Herald,* Apr. 22, 1786, 3; *New York Packet,* Apr. 24, 1786, 3; *Daily Advertiser,* Apr. 25, 1786, 2; *Maryland Journal,* Apr. 25, 1786, 2; *Continental Journal and Weekly Advertiser,* May 4, 1786, 3.
42. Deloria, *Playing Indian,* 45–46; Roger D. Abrahams, "White Indians in Penn's City: The Loyal Sons of St. Tammany," in *Riot and Revelry in Early America,* ed. William Pencak, Matthew Dennis, and Simon P. Newman (University Park: Pennsylvania State Press, 2002), 179–204.
43. *New York Packet,* Feb. 16, 1790, 3.
44. *The Daily Advertiser* (New York), Aug. 4, 1790, 2; *New-York Morning Post,* Aug. 5, 1790, 2; *New York Packet,* Aug. 5, 1790, p. 2-3; *Federal Gazette,* Aug. 6, 1790, 2–3; *The Daily Advertiser* (New York), Aug. 4, 1790, 2.
45. *New-York Journal and Patriotic Register,* Mar. 2, 1793, 3.
46. Colin G. Calloway, *White People, Indians, and Highlanders: Tribal Societies and Colonial Encounters in Scotland and America* (New York: Oxford University Press, 2008); J. Russell Snapp, *John Stuart and the Struggle for Empire on the Southern Frontier* (Baton Rouge: Louisiana State University Press, 1996), 87.
47. *New-York Journal,* Aug. 17, 1790, 3; "Extract from the *Pennsylvania Packet and Daily Advertiser,* August 18, 1790," in John Walton Caughey, *McGillivray of the Creeks* (1938; reprint, Columbus: University of South Carolina Press, 2007), 279.
48. Shannon, " 'This Wretched Scene of British Curiosity and Savage Debauchery,' " 241.

49. Daniel H. Usner, *American Indians in Early New Orleans: From Calumet to Raquette* (Baton Rouge: Louisiana State University Press, 2018), xiii–xiv. Deloria, *Playing Indian,* examines the phenomenon among non-Indians, but does not explore instances of Indians playing Indian. By the late nineteenth century, Indians who traveled beyond their home communities found that it "was never enough that they *were* Indians, they always had to *be* them as well," and conform to preconceptions and stereotypes; Peter Nabokov, *How The World Moves: The Odyssey of an American Indian Family* (New York: Viking, 2015), 290.

50. Thomas A. Strohfeldt, "Warriors in Williamsburg: The Cherokee Presence in Virginia's Eighteenth Century Capital," *Journal of Cherokee Studies* 11 (1986): 17.

51. *General Advertiser,* Mar. 28, 1792, 2; *Claypoole's Daily Advertiser,* Mar. 29, 1792, 2; *Federal Gazette and Philadelphia Daily Advertiser,* Mar. 30, 1792, 3.

52. John Quincy Adams to Abigail Adams, July 12, 1794, Founders Online ("assisted in smoking"); *Memoirs of John Quincy Adams: Comprising Portions of His Diary, from 1795–1848,* ed. Charles Francis Adams (Philadelphia: J. B. Lippincott, 1874), 34–35 ("ridiculous"); Thomas W. Cowger and Mitch Caver, *Piominko, Chickasaw Leader* (Ada, OK: Chickasaw Press, 2017), 96–101.

53. Dunbar Rowland and A. G. Sanders, comp., trans., and ed., *Mississippi Provincial Archives: French Dominion, 1729–1748,* 2nd edn., rev. and ed. Patricia Kay Galloway (Baton Rouge: Louisiana State University Press 1984), 147, 218; James R. Atkinson, *Splendid Land, Splendid People: The Chickasaw Indians to Removal* (Tuscaloosa: University of Alabama Press, 2004), 34, 71, 97, 262n; Patricia Galloway, "'So Many Little Republics': British Negotiations with the Choctaw Confederacy, 1765," *Ethnohistory* 41 (1995): 520, 535 n. 43; Charles A. Weeks, *Paths to a Middle Ground: The Diplomacy of Natchez, Boukfouka, Nogales, and San Fernando de las Barrancas, 1791–1795* (Tuscaloosa: University of Alabama Press, 2005), 35–36, 211, 218; *EAID* 4:266 (Williamsburg).

54. Joshua David Bellin and Laura L. Mielke, eds., *Native Acts: Indian Performance, 1603–1832* (Lincoln: University of Nebraska Press, 2011).

55. Cecilia Morgan, "Performing for 'Imperial Eyes': Bernice Loft and Ethel Brant Monture, Ontario, 1930s–60s," in *Contact Zones: Aboriginal and Settler Women in Canada's Colonial Past,* ed. Katie Pickles and Myra Rutherdale (Vancouver: UBC Press, 2005), 67–89.

56. Laura L. Mielke, "Introduction," in *Native Acts: Indian Performance, 1603–1832,* ed. Joshua David Bellin and Laura L. Mielke (Lincoln: University of Nebraska Press, 2011), 5.

57. *PGW, Pres.* 3: 143 (Knox); *New York Morning Post,* June 18, 1787, 2 (Baltimore quote); *Pennsylvania Mercury and Universal Advertiser,* June 15, 1787, p. 3; *Georgia State Gazette,* Sept. 8, 1787, p. 2 (Washington and Convention members). I am grateful to Mary Sarah Bilder for sharing "Without Doors: Native Nations and the Convention," her essay-in-progress on the Indians who were in Philadelphia when the Constitutional Convention was meeting.

58. *PGW, Pres.* 10:142–43; Timothy Pickering Papers, Massachusetts Historical Society, reel 62: 11; *The Papers of Alexander Hamilton Digital Edition,* ed. Harold C. Syrett (Charlottesville: University of Virginia Press, Rotunda, 2011), 11:375–77.

59. Richmond P. Bond, *Queen Anne's American Kings* (Oxford: Clarendon Press, 1952), 3–4; Eric Hinderaker, "The 'Four Indian Kings' and the Imaginative Construction of the first British Empire," *William and Mary Quarterly* 53 (1996): 498–500.

60. Usner, *American Indians in Early New Orleans,* 83.

61. Heather S. Nathans, *Early American Theatre from the Revolution to Thomas Jefferson: Into the Hands of the People* (Cambridge: Cambridge University Press, 2003), 17–18, 63–64; *Penn. Archives,* 1st series, 3:656–57 ("powerful Engine").

62. Quoted in Nancy Shoemaker, "Wonder and Repulsion: North American Indians in Eighteenth-Century Europe," in *Europe Observed: Multiple Gazes in Early Modern Encounters,* ed. Kumkum Chatterjee and Clement Hawes (Lewisburg: Bucknell University Press, 2008), 179.

63. Alden T. Vaughan, *Transatlantic Encounters: American Indians in Britain, 1500–1776* (Cambridge: Cambridge University Press, 2006), 143.

64. *Virginia Gazette,* Nov. 17, 1752, 2; Strohfeldt, "Warriors in Williamsburg," 9; Miles P. Grier, "Staging the Cherokee *Othello*: An Imperial Economy of Indian Watching," *William and Mary Quarterly* 73 (2016): 73–106.

65. Smith, *The City of New York in the Year of Washington's Inauguration,* 166.

66. *Pennsylvania Gazette,* Dec. 24, 1767; *Boston Post-Boy and Advertiser,* Dec. 28, 1767, 2; *New-York Journal,* Dec. 17, 1767, 3; *New York Gazette,* Dec. 7–14, 1767, 1, Dec. 17, 1767, 3.

67. Eugene H. Jones, *Native Americans as Shown on the Stage, 1753–1916* (Metuchen, NJ: Scarecrow Press, 1988), 10–12.

68. *WJP* 12:339–40, 456–58; *DRCHNY* 8:38–53.

69. George C. D. Odell, *Annals of the New York Stage* (New York: Columbia University Press, 1927–49), 1:131 (advertisement); *Providence Gazette, and Country Journal,* Apr. 9, 1768, 3; *Pennsylvania Journal,* Apr. 14, 1768, 3.

70. *Penn. Archives,* 1st series, 10:141–43; Nathans, *Early American Theatre;* Michael Meranze, *Laboratories of Virtue: Punishment, Revolution, and Authority in Philadelphia, 1760–1835* (Chapel Hill: University of North Carolina Press, 1996), 160–67 ("urban entertainment" at 160).

71. Susan Branson, *These Fiery Frenchified Dames: Women and Political Culture in Early National Philadelphia* (Philadelphia: University of Pennsylvania Press, 2001), ch. 3.

72. *Luigi Castiglioni's Viaggio,* 95.

73. *New York Packet,* Mar. 6, 1786, 3; *New York Daily Advertiser,* Mar. 8, 1786, 3, Mar. 9, 2; Odell, *Annals of the New York Stage,* 1:243.

74. Odell, *Annals of the New York Stage,* 1:289–90.

75. *New York Daily Gazette,* July 22, 1790, 695; *City Gazette* (Charleston reprinting from Philadelphia), Aug. 17, 1790, 2; *Philadelphia Gazette and Universal Daily Advertiser,* June 20, 1794, 3.

76. *The Federal Gazette and Philadelphia Daily Advertiser,* July 19, 1790, 2.

77. *Albany Gazette,* Aug. 30, 1790, 2.

78. *Dunlap's American Daily Advertiser,* Jan. 4, 1792, 1.

79. *Salem Gazette,* July 7, 1792, 2.

80. In August 1793, Governor Blount, from Philadelphia, sent a message to Hanging Maw that President Washington desired to shake their hands in Philadelphia in the fall and strongly urged him and other chiefs to undertake the journey; "He will direct that you shall be comfortably accommodated on your way, and farther, upon your arrival here, he flatters himself, that, by being face to face, the remembrance of all former injuries will be done away, and that we may establish a firm and lasting peace and friendship." *ASPIA* 1:431.

81. *Philadelphia Gazette,* June 20, 1794, 3.

82. Newspapers announced that the Indians "will be present at Messrs. Warren and Sons' Benefit this evening at the New Theatre." *Gazette of the United States,* July 3, 1795, 3; see also July 13; *Federal Intelligencer, and Baltimore Daily Gazette,* July 9, 1795, 2.

83. John F. Watson, ed. and comp., *Annals of Philadelphia, and Pennsylvania, in the Olden Time* (Philadelphia: Edwin S. Stuart, 1884), 1:473 (New Theater); *Moreau de St. Méry's American Journey 1793–1798,* ed. and trans. Kenneth Roberts and Ana K. Roberts (Garden City, NY: Doubleday, 1947), 345–46.

84. Nathans, *Early American Theatre,* 93–94.

85. *Moreau de St. Méry's American Journey,* 348.

86. James S. Moy, "Entertainments at John B. Ricketts's Circus, 1793–1800," *Educational Theatre Journal* 30 (1978): 186–202.

87. Odell, *Annals of the New York Stage,* 1:396.

88. *The Daily Advertiser,* Mar. 7, 1795, 3.

89. *The Daily Advertiser,* Mar. 13, 1795, 3.

90. Odell, *Annals of the New York Stage,* 1:419.

91. Nathans, *Early American Theatre,* 102–5; *The Memoir of John Durang, American Actor 1785–1816,* ed. Alan S. Downer (Pittsburgh: University of Pittsburgh Press, 1966), 43, 95.

92. *Gazette of the United States,* Dec. 30, 1795, 3.

93. *Aurora General Advertiser* (Philadelphia), Jan. 2, 1796, 2.

94. *Memoir of John Durang*, 47.

95. *Aurora General Advertiser*, Mar. 10, 1796, 2.

96. *Aurora General Advertiser*, Dec. 13, 1796, 2.

97. Rev. Eleazar Williams, *Life of Te-ho-ra-gwa-ne-gen, Alias Thomas Williams, a Chief of the Caughnawaga Tribe of Indians in Canada* (Albany: J. Munsell, 1859); *At a Treaty held at the city of New-York, with the nations or tribes of Indians denominating themselves "the Seven Nations of Canada"* (New York: 1796?); Charles J. Kappler, comp., *Indian Affairs: Laws and Treaties*, Vol. 2, *Treaties* (Washington, DC: Government Printing Office, 1904), 45–46; *PGW, Pres.* 19:431; Geoffrey E. Buerger, "Eleazar Williams: Elitism and Multiple Identity on Two Frontiers," in *Being and Becoming Indian: Biographical Studies of North American Frontiers*, ed. James A. Clifton (Chicago: Dorsey Press, 1989), 112–36; Michael Leroy Oberg, *Professional Indian: The American Odyssey of Eleazer Williams* (Philadelphia: University of Pennsylvania Press, 2015).

98. *Memoir of John Durang*, 70–73 (Kahanawake), 87 (Lorette).

99. *Memoir of John Durang*, 79–80.

100. *Claypoole's American Daily Advertiser*, Jan. 10, 1798, 2.

101. Niemcewicz, *Under Their Vine and Fig Tree*, 45.

102. *Aurora General Advertiser*, Dec. 14, 1799, 3.

103. L. G. Moses, *Wild West Shows and the Images of American Indians, 1883–1933* (Albuquerque: University of New Mexico Press, 1996).

104. *Claypoole's American Daily Advertiser*, Jan. 19, 1796, 3.

105. Isaac Weld Jr., *Travels Through the States of North America, and the Provinces of Upper and Lower Canada, During the Years 1795, 1796, and 1797*, 2nd ed. (London: John Stockdale, 1799), 2:263–64, 266.

106. Moses, *Wild West Shows and the Images of American Indians*.

CHAPTER 8

1. *Spain in the Mississippi Valley, 1765-1794: Translations of Materials from the Spanish Archives in the Bancroft Library, University of California, Berkeley*, trans. and ed. Lawrence Kinnaird, Annual Report of the American Historical Association for the Year 1945 (Washington, DC: Government Printing Office, 1946-49), vol. 3, part 2: 229, 236-37.

2. *ASPIA* 1:203, 245; *New Hampshire Gazette*, Jan. 18, 1792, 2; Feb. 4, 1792, 3; *General Advertiser* (Philadelphia), Dec. 31, 1791, 3; *New York Journal and Patriotic Register*, Dec. 31, 1791, 415.

3. *ASPIA* 1:206; *Litchfield Monitor*, Mar. 28, 1792.

4. Clarence E. Carter, ed., *The Territorial Papers of the United States*, Vol. 4, *The Territory South of the River Ohio, 1790–1796* (Washington, DC: Government Printing Office, 1934), 148, 150; *ASPIA* 1:271.

5. *PGW, Pres.* 14:150.

6. Louis Philippe, *Diary of My Travels in America*, trans. Stephen Becker (New York: Delaware Press, 1977), 97.

7. *Penn. Archives*, 1st series, 1:205–6.

8. Account of Mary Murphy for Boarding Indian Chiefs, Jan. 17, 1799, PWD.

9. *Penn. Archives*, 4th series, 2: 119.

10. *New York Gazette*, Mar. 30, 1752, 21.

11. *EAID* 14:116.

12. *Charleston Evening Gazette*, June 5, 1786, 3.

13. Wayne to Knox, Oct. 19, 1772, PWD.

14. William L. Stone, *Life of Joseph Brant-Thayendanegea* (New York: Alexander Blake, 1838), 2:330.

15. *New-York Gazette*, Apr. 4, 1768, 4; *Providence Gazette, and Country Journal*, Apr. 9, 1768, 3; *Pennsylvania Journal*, Apr. 14, 1768, 3.

16. On board the brig *Fame* piloted by Captain Hunt. *Gazette of the United States*, July 1, 1794, 3; *South Carolina State Gazette*, Aug. 8, 1794, 3.

17. Stephanie L. Gamble, "Capital Negotiations: Native Diplomats in the American Capital, 1789–1837," Ph.D. dissertation, Johns Hopkins University, 2014, 97–98; Knox to Pickens, June 27, 1794, and Pickens to Knox, Sept. 6, 1794, PWD.

18. William Heath, *William Wells and the Struggle for the Old Northwest* (Norman: University of Oklahoma Press, 2015), 245; *Claypoole's Daily Advertiser,* Aug. 12, 1797, 3; Isaac Craig to James McHenry, Mar. 2, 1797, PWD ("inexpressible grief" and "Respect").

19. Ian Saxine, *Properties of Empire: Indians, Colonists, and Land Speculators on the New England Frontier* (New York: New York University Press, 2019), 141–42.

20. Timothy J. Shannon, *Iroquois Diplomacy on the Early American Frontier* (New York: Penguin, 2008), 142.

21. *PGW, Pres.* 10:310, 316–17.

22. Carter, *Territorial Papers of the United States,* 4:135.

23. *ASPIA* 2:539.

24. Gamble, "Capital Negotiations," 183.

25. *Pennsylvania Journal,* Feb. 29, 1792, 3; *General Advertiser,* Feb. 29, 1792, 3; *Weekly Museum,* Mar. 3, 1792, 3; *Farmer's Journal* (Danbury, CT), Mar. 12, 1792, 3; *New Hampshire Gazette,* March 21, 1792, 2; Stan W. Hoig, *The Cherokees and Their Chiefs in the Wake of Empire* (Fayetteville: University of Arkansas Press, 1998), 75.

26. *Claypoole's Daily Advertiser,* Jan.7, 1797, 2; *Philadelphia Minerva,* Jan. 7, 1797, 3; *Daily Advertiser,* Jan. 11, 1797, 3; *Weekly Museum,* Jan. 14, 1797, 3; *Newport Mercury,* Jan. 17, 1797, 2; *Massachusetts Mercury,* Jan. 17, 1797, 3; *Columbian Museum and Savannah Advertiser,* Jan. 24, 1797, 4; *Federal Galaxy* (Brattleboro, VT), Jan. 27, 1797, 3. A Creek delegation left Alexander Durant—a son of Alexander McGillivray's oldest sister, Sophie, who had eleven children—in the city the year before to be educated by the Quakers. The coincidence of surnames is intriguing, but there is no record that Sophie had a daughter named Ann Jane. I am grateful for guidance on this question from Kathleen DuVal, Robbie Ethridge, Claudio Saunt, Paul Vickers, and Gregory Waselkov. John Walker participated in a treaty delegation to Washington, DC, in 1816; Hoig, *The Cherokees and Their Chiefs,* 119.

27. Herman J. Viola, *Diplomats in Buckskins: A History of Indian Delegations in Washington City* (1981; reprint, Bluffton, SC: Rivilo Books, 1995), 145; Sam A. Maddra, *Hostiles? The Lakota Ghost Dance and Buffalo Bill's Wild West* (Norman: University of Oklahoma Press, 2006), 142–44; Colin G. Calloway, *First Peoples: A Documentary Survey of American Indian History,* 6th ed. (Boston: Bedford/St. Martin's, 2019), 680.

28. John C. Ewers, "When the Light Shone in Washington," in *Indian Life on the Upper Missouri* (Norman: University of Oklahoma Press, 1968), 75–90.

29. Daniel K. Richter, *Before the Revolution: America's Ancient Pasts* (Cambridge, MA: Harvard University Press, 2011), 28–29.

30. Mary W. Helms, *Ulysses' Sail: An Ethnographic Odyssey of Power, Knowledge, and Geographical Distance* (Princeton, NJ: Princeton University Press, 1988); Steven J. Peach, "Creek Indian Globetrotter: Tomochichi's Trans-Atlantic Quest for Traditional Power in the Colonial Southeast," *Ethnohistory* 60 (2013): 605–35; Sami Lakomäki, "Globalizing Indigenous Histories: Comparison, Connectedness, and New Contexts for Native American History," in *Twenty-First Century Perspectives on Indigenous Studies: Native North America in (Trans) Motion,* ed. Birgit Däwes, Karsten Fitz, and Sabine N. Meyer (New York: Routledge, 2015), 187–203 (heirs to tradition at 197); Greg O'Brien, "The Conqueror Meets the Unconquered: Negotiating Cultural Boundaries on the Post-Revolutionary Southern Frontier," *Journal of Southern History* 67 (2001): 67–68; Philp Levy, *Fellow Travelers: Indians and Colonists Contesting the Early American Trail* (Gainesville: University Press of Florida, 2007), 6–8.

31. Northern Arapaho chiefs who returned to Wyoming from Washington in the nineteenth century displayed peace medals, clothing, and other gifts they had received as symbols of their authority and their ability to represent their people in dealings with the United States government. Loretta Fowler, *Arapahoe Politics, 1851–1978: Symbols in Crises of Authority* (Lincoln: University of Nebraska Press, 1982), 79.

32. Helms, *Ulysses' Sail*, 66, 82.

33. *Jean-Bernard Bossu's Travels in the Interior of North America 1751–1762*, ed. and trans. Seymour Feiler (Norman: University of Oklahoma Press, 1962), 83–84.

34. *EAID* 5:258 (quote); Alden T. Vaughan, *Transatlantic Encounters: American Indians in Britain, 1500–1776* (Cambridge: Cambridge University Press, 2006), 247; cf. Kate Fullagar, *The Warrior, the Voyager, and the Artist: Three Lives in an Age of Empire* (New Haven: Yale University Press, 2020), 79.

35. *The Papers of Thomas Jefferson Digital Edition*, ed. James P. McClure and J. Jefferson Looney (Charlottesville: University of Virginia Press, Rotunda, 2008–2020), *Main Series* , 25:115.

36. *Col. Recs. Penn.* 5:467, 474, 480, 486; *EAID* 2:241, 245; William A. Starna, "The Diplomatic Career of Canasatego," in *Friends and Enemies in Penn's Woods: Indians, Colonists, and the Racial Construction of Pennsylvania*, ed. William A. Pencak and Daniel K. Richter (University Park: Pennsylvania State University Press, 2004), 160–65.

37. Colin G. Calloway, *The Scratch of a Pen: 1763 and the Transformation of North America* (New York: Oxford University Press, 2006), 54–55.

38. *The Collected Works of Benjamin Hawkins, 1796–1810*, ed. Thomas Foster (Tuscaloosa: University of Alabama Press, 2003), 45s; Susan Shown Harjo, ed., *Nation to Nation: Treaties Between the United States and American Indian Nations* (Washington, DC: Smithsonian Books, 2014), 139.

39. *ASPIA* 2:602, 605–6.

40. Claudio Saunt, *A New Order of Things: Property, Power, and the Transformation of the Creek Indians, 1733–1816* (Cambridge: Cambridge University Press, 1999), 68.

41. Louis LeClerc Milford, *Memoir, or A Cursory Glance at My Different Travels & My Sojourn in the Creek Nation*, ed. John Francis McDermott, trans. Geraldine De Courcy (Chicago: R. R. Donnelley & Sons, 1956), 100.

42. John Pope, *A Tour Through the Southern and Western Territories of the United States of North America* (Richmond: John Dixon, 1792), 47, 51.

43. Kinnaird, *Spain in the Mississippi Valley, 1765– 1794*, pt. 3: 22, 57–58; John Walton Caughey, *McGillivray of the Creeks* (Norman: University of Oklahoma Press, 1938), 332, 337.

44. *ASPIA* 1:366–67. For sketches of the leading Creek chiefs at this time, see Kevin Kokomoor, *Of One Mind and of One Government: The Rise and Fall of the Creek Nation in the Early Republic* (Lincoln: University of Nebraska Press, 2018), 184–92.

45. *Collected Works of Benjamin Hawkins*, 60s, 70–71.

46. *Collected Works of Benjamin Hawkins*, 60s.

47. Caughey, *McGillivray of the Creeks*, 103, 139; *Collected Works of Benjamin Hawkins*, 27s; Saunt, *New Order of Things*, 215, 220, 265; J. Leitch Wright Jr., *Creeks and Seminoles: Destruction and Regeneration of the Muscolgulge People* (Lincoln: University of Nebraska Press, 1986), 118, 150, 175.

48. *ASPIA* 1:236–37; *The Correspondence of Lieut. Governor John Graves Simcoe, with Allied Documents Relating to His Administration of the Government of Upper Canada*, ed. Ernest A. Cruikshank (Toronto: Ontario Historical Society, 1923–31), 5:18–19. On Brant as a Mason, see Joy Porter, *Native American Freemasonry: Associationalism and Performance in America* (Lincoln: University of Nebraska Press, 2011), 194–206.

49. Isabel Thompson Kelsay, *Joseph Brant, 1743–1807: Man of Two Worlds* (Syracuse: Syracuse University Press, 1984), 470–74; *Papers of Thomas Jefferson, Main Series*, 24:133 ("best dispositions"); Stone, *Life of Joseph Brant-Thayendanegea*, 2:328–29 ("allurements of gain").

50. *Correspondence of Lieut. Governor John Graves Simcoe*, 1:243; 2:59; "A Narrative of an Embassy to the Western Indians from the Original Manuscript of Hendrick Aupaumut," ed. B. H. Coates, *Memoirs of the Historical Society of Pennsylvania* 2 (1827), pt. 1: 118.

51. *Correspondence of Lieut. Governor John Graves Simcoe*, 5:34.

52. "A Narrative of an Embassy to the Western Indians," 70 (Pickering), 76, 78, 128; Alan Taylor, "Captain Hendrick Aupaumut: The Dilemmas of an Intercultural Broker," *Ethnohistory*

43 (1996): 431–57; Rachel Wheeler, "Hendrick Aupaumut: Christian-Mahican Prophet," *Journal of the Early Republic* 25 (2005): 187–220; Richard White, *The Middle Ground: Indians, Empires and Republics in the Great Lakes Region, 1650–1815* (Cambridge: Cambridge University Press, 1991), 458–59.

53. *PGW, Pres.* 7:121–27; Timothy Pickering Papers, Massachusetts Historical Society, Boston, reel 61: 232.

54. Thomas S. Abler, *Cornplanter: Chief Warrior of the Allegany Senecas* (Syracuse: Syracuse University Pres, 2007), 151–52, 193–97.

55. Knox to Isaac Craig, Mar. 9, 1793, Knox to Wayne, Mar. 7, 1793, PWD.

56. *Correspondence of Lieut. Governor John Graves Simcoe*, 1:224.

57. Christopher Densmore, *Red Jacket: Iroquois Diplomat and Orator* (Syracuse: Syracuse University Press, 1999), 37–38; Laurence M. Hauptman, *The Tonawanda Senecas' Heroic Battle Against Removal* (Albany: State University of New York Press, 2011), 5–6, 13.

58. Abler, *Cornplanter*, 137–53 ("cried down" at 147); Kari Elizabeth Rose Thompson, "Inconsistent Friends: Philadelphia Friends and the Development of Native American Missions in the Long Eighteenth Century," Ph.D. dissertation, University of Iowa, 2013, 170–90.

59. *Commercial Advertiser*, New York, Mar. 26?, 1798, 3 (notice is March 27).

60. *The Papers of Alexander Hamilton Digital Edition*, ed. Harold C. Syrett (Charlottesville: University of Virginia Press, Rotunda, 2011), 23:79 (house); Logan Esarey, ed., *Governors' Messages and Letters* (Indianapolis: Indiana Historical Commission, 1922), 1:76–77, 164.

61. John Johnston, *Recollections of Sixty Years on the Ohio Frontier* (1915; reprint, Van Buren, OH: Eastern Frontier/R. E. Davis, 2001), 19–20.

62. Donald H. Gaff, "Three Men from Three Rivers: Navigating between Native and American Identity in the Old Northwest Territory," in *The Boundaries Between Us: Natives and Newcomers Along the Frontiers of the Old Northwest Territory, 1750–1850*, ed. Daniel P. Barr (Kent, OH: Kent State University Press, 2006), 149.

63. Robert M. Owens, "Jean Baptiste DuCoigne, the Kaskaskias, and the Limits of Thomas Jefferson's Friendship," *Journal of Illinois History* 5 (Summer 2002): 121–33; Esarey, *Governors' Messages and Letters*, 1:100, 115.

64. Dawn Peterson, *Indians in the Family: Adoption and the Politics of Antebellum Expansion* (Cambridge, MA: Harvard University Press, 2017), 74–75; "Address by Farmer's Brother, October 21, 1800," in "Letters of the Reverend Elkanah Holmes from Fort Niagara in 1800," *Publications of the Buffalo Historical Society* 6 (1903): 201–2; *The Collected Speeches of Sagoyewatha, or Red Jacket*, ed. Granville Ganter (Syracuse: Syracuse University Press, 2006), 105.

65. *Collected Works of Benjamin Hawkins*, 31s, 99–100.

66. Colin G. Calloway, *White People, Indians, and Highlanders: Tribal Peoples and Colonial Encounters in Scotland and America* (New York: Oxford University Press, 2008), 176–88.

CONCLUSION

1. Jane Carey and Jane Lydon, eds., *Indigenous Networks: Mobility, Connections and Exchange* (New York: Routledge, 2014).

2. For example: New York, January 25, 1801: "On Saturday evening arrived in town on their way to Washington, five Indian chiefs, viz. Red Jacket, and three others of the Seneca nation, and Saucoresa, of the Tuscarora tribe, accompanied by Mr. Jasper Parrish, their interpreter." *Federal Gazette and Baltimore Daily Advertiser*, Jan. 30, 1801, 3.

3. D. W. Meinig, *The Shaping of America: A Geographical Perspective on 500 Years of History*, Volume 1, *Atlantic America, 1492–1800* (New Haven: Yale University Press, 1986), 370.

4. *ASPIA* 2:644–45.

5. Herman J. Viola, *Diplomats in Buckskins: A History of Indian Delegations in Washington City* (1981; reprint, Bluffton, SC: Rivilo Books, 1995), ch. 3.

6. Viola, *Diplomats in Buckskins;* C. Joseph Genetin-Pilawa, "The Indians' Capital City: Diplomatic Visits, Place, and Two-Worlds Discourse in Nineteenth-Century

Washington, D.C.," in *Beyond Two Worlds: Critical Conversations in Language and Power in Native North America*, ed. James Joseph Buss and C. Joseph Genetin-Pilawa (Albany: SUNY Press, 2014), 117–35; Joseph Genetin-Pilawa, *The Indians' Capital City* (Chapel Hill: University of North Carolina Press, forthcoming); Cécile R. Ganteaume, *Officially Indian: Symbols That Define the United States* (Washington, DC: National Museum of the American Indian/Smithsonian Institution, 2017).

INDEX

For the benefit of digital users, indexed terms that span two pages (e.g., 52–53) may, on occasion, appear on only one of those pages.

Page numbers ending with "f" indicate a figure. Page numbers starting with "PG" refer to the portrait gallery.